News on the American Dream
A History of the Portuguese Press
in the United States

News on the American Dream

A History of the Portuguese Press
in the United States

Alberto Pena Rodríguez

Translated by Serena Rivera with Gloria de Sá

Foreword by Frank F. Sousa

Tagus Press. UMass Dartmouth. Dartmouth, Massachusetts

*Tagus Press is the publishing arm of the
Center for Portuguese Studies and Culture at
the University of Massachusetts Dartmouth.*
Center Director: Victor K. Mendes

Portuguese in the Americas 27
Tagus Press at the University of Massachusetts Dartmouth
© 2020 Alberto Pena Rodríguez

Executive Editor: Mario Pereira
Series Editors: Christopher Larkosh & Gloria de Sá
Copyedited by William Nelles, Diana Simões,
Sonia P. Pacheco, and Eli Evans
Cover Design: Frank Gutbrod
Designed and typeset by Inês Sena

The acknowledgements were translated by Gloria de Sá
and the conclusion was translated by Asher A. Pereira.

For all inquiries, please contact:
Center for Portuguese Studies and Culture/Tagus Press
University of Massachusetts Dartmouth
285 Old Westport Road
North Dartmouth MA 02747–2300
(508) 999-8255, fax (508) 999-9272
https://www.umassd.edu/portuguese-studies-center/

ISBN: 978-1-933227-89-4
Library of Congress Control Number: 2020931189

For my wife, Estela,
and my children, Lina and Denís,
my great sources of inspiration

Contents

List of Illustrations

1. Cover of *A Liberdade*. Copy of July 7, 1934. Portuguese-American Digital Newspaper Collection, Ferreira-Mendes Portuguese-American Archives, Claire T. Carney Library Archives and Special Collections, University of Massachusetts Dartmouth.

2. Portrait of Manuel das Neves Xavier, editor of *A Civilização* (Boston and New Bedford, Massachusetts). Ferreira-Mendes Portuguese-American Archives, Claire T. Carney Library Archives and Special Collections, University of Massachusetts Dartmouth.

3. Cover of *O Arauto*. Copy of September 4, 1909. Portuguese-American Digital Newspaper Collection, Ferreira-Mendes Portuguese-American Archives, Claire T. Carney Library Archives and Special Collections, University of Massachusetts Dartmouth.

4. Cover of *A California Alegre*. Copy of December 21, 1937. Portuguese-American Digital Newspaper Collection, Ferreira-Mendes Portuguese-American Archives, Claire T. Carney Library Archives and Special Collections, University of Massachusetts Dartmouth.

5. Cover of *Portugal na California*. Copy of September 1935. Portuguese-American Digital Newspaper Collection, Ferreira-Mendes Portuguese-American Archives, Claire T. Carney Library Archives and Special Collections, University of Massachusetts Dartmouth.

6. Cover of *O Jornal de Noticias* (Erie, Pennsylvania). Copy of June 26, 1880. Biblioteca Pública e Arquivo Regional de Ponta Delgada.

7. Cover of *A Voz Portugueza* (San Francisco, California). Copy of June 29, 1887. Portuguese-American Digital Newspaper Collection, Ferreira-Mendes Portuguese-American Archives, Claire T. Carney Library Archives and Special Collections, University of Massachusetts Dartmouth.

8. Cover of *A União Portugueza* (San Francisco, California). Copy of February 23, 1893. Portuguese-American Digital Newspaper Collection, Ferreira-Mendes Portuguese-American Archives, Claire T. Carney Library Archives and Special Collections, University of Massachusetts Dartmouth.

9. Cover of *O Popular* (Honolulu, Oahu, Hawaii). Copy of October 5, 1911. Portuguese-American Digital Newspaper Collection, Ferreira-Mendes Portuguese-American Archives, Claire T. Carney Library Archives and Special Collections, University of Massachusetts Dartmouth.

10. Cover of *O Luso Hawaiiano* (Honolulu, Hawaii). Copy of December 13, 1890. Portuguese-American Digital Newspaper Collection, Ferreira-Mendes Portuguese-American Archives, Claire T. Carney Library Archives and Special Collections, University of Massachusetts Dartmouth.

11. Cover of *Alvorada* (New Bedford, Massachusetts). Copy of February 12, 1919. Portuguese-American Digital Newspaper Collection, Ferreira-Mendes Portuguese-American Archives, Claire T. Carney Library Archives and Special Collections, University of Massachusetts Dartmouth.

12. Portrait of Affonso Gil Mendes Ferreira, editor of *O Heraldo Portuguez* (Taunton, Massachusetts). Ferreira-Mendes Portuguese-American Archives, Ferreira-Mendes Papers. Claire T. Carney Library Archives and Special Collections, University of Massachusetts Dartmouth.

13. Cover of *O Colonial*. Copy of April 3, 1931. Portuguese-American Digital Newspaper Collection, Ferreira-Mendes Portuguese-American Archives, Claire T. Carney Library Archives and Special Collections, University of Massachusetts Dartmouth.

14. Cover of *O Heraldo Portuguez* (Taunton, Massachusetts). Copy of May 1, 1931. Portuguese-American Digital Newspaper Collection, Ferreira-Mendes Portuguese-American Archives, Claire T. Carney Library Archives and Special Collections, University of Massachusetts Dartmouth.

15. Cover of *O Lavrador Português* (Hanford, California). Copy of August 22, 1914. Portuguese-American Digital Newspaper Collection, Ferreira-Mendes Portuguese-American Archives, Claire T. Carney Library Archives and Special Collections, University of Massachusetts Dartmouth.

16. Cover of *A Colonia Portuguesa*. Copy of March 25, 1924. Portuguese-American Digital Newspaper Collection, Ferreira-Mendes Portuguese-American Archives, Claire T. Carney Library Archives and Special Collections, University of Massachusetts Dartmouth.

17. Cover of *O Portugal*. Copy of October 5, 1933. Portuguese-American Digital Newspaper Collection, Ferreira-Mendes Portuguese-American Archives, Claire T. Carney Library Archives and Special Collections, University of Massachusetts Dartmouth.

18. Cover of *Diario de Noticias* (New Bedford, Massachusetts). Copy of November 28, 1947. Portuguese-American Digital Newspaper Collection, Ferreira-Mendes Portuguese-American Archives, Claire T. Carney Library Archives and Special Collections, University of Massachusetts Dartmouth.

19. Portrait of João Rodrigues Rocha. Ferreira-Mendes Portuguese-American Archives, Rocha Papers. Claire T. Carney Library Archives and Special Collections, University of Massachusetts Dartmouth.

20. Photo-news from the *Diario de Noticias,* "O Natal dos empregados do Diario de Noticias" [Diario de Noticias employees at Christmas]. Copy of December 27, 1950. Portuguese-American Digital Newspaper Collection, Ferreira-Mendes Portuguese-American Archives, Claire T. Carney Library Archives and Special Collections, University of Massachusetts Dartmouth.

List of Tables

Foreword to Alberto Pena Rodríguez's
News on the American Dream: A History of the Portuguese Press in the United States

The saying "Journalism is the first draft of history," often attributed to Philip L. Graham, the late publisher and co-owner of the *Washington Post*, captures the important role played by the press in general and the ethnic press in particular. The ethnic press in America—newspapers and magazines written mostly by and for members of groups whose identity is informed by a shared history, geography, language, and religion—is, as Alberto Pena Rodríguez shows us in *News on the American Dream: A History of the Portuguese Press in the United States*, an essential source for understanding the world-view, dreams, objectives, and interests of immigrant groups.

As ethnic communities evolve and adapt to their new surroundings, ethnic newspapers have historically played the dual role of providing information from their country of origin as well as the immigrant community itself—information rarely available in the mainstream media—while also interpreting the adopted society for the immigrant who is not fluent in English. In conveying features of American life that are different from those of the old country, the ethnic press thus offers a guide to the new world through news stories or occasional in-depth articles and implicitly through advertisements of American (and Ethnic-American) products and services. The different sections of a newspaper thereby provide something of an education in the American experience (and American Dream) for immigrants curious about their new land and society. The press also promotes group pride, defending the good name of the country of origin and that of the immigrant community itself. The press helps immigrants to navigate their new society *and* provides alternative perspectives, sometimes at odds with how they are portrayed in the mainstream, dominant society.

In these respects, Alberto Pena Rodríguez's *News on the American Dream: A History of the Portuguese Press in the United States*, the first book-length, comprehensive history of the Portuguese-American press, makes a major contribution to our understanding of how the press has conveyed and at the same time has had a direct impact on the Portuguese-American experience from the nineteenth century to the present. This meticulously researched monograph is based on 167 Portuguese-American newspapers and magazine titles published across the United States since 1877. Gathering a wealth of information, the volume discusses the Portuguese ethnic press from its formative years, when newspapers were often a one- to two-person operation and quite amateurish, into the period of full maturity, and culminating with the contemporary papers. Great effort and care has gone into uncovering and providing dates, places, duration, and frequency of publication, as well as the location in different libraries of the relatively limited number of extant newspapers. Scholars will be indebted to Pena Rodríguez's research for years to come, and *News on the American Dream* will surely become a standard reference in the field.

News on the American Dream builds upon ground-breaking bibliographical work in essays like Leo Pap's "The Portuguese Press" (1987), the first survey of Portuguese-American newspapers; Edgar C. Knowlton's "The Portuguese Press in Hawaii" (1960); and Geoffrey L. Gomes's "The Portuguese Language Press in California, 1888-1928." Among other sources for Pena Rodríguez's study are two books by Eduardo de Carvalho, consul of Portugal in Boston in the mid-1920s, namely, *A Língua Portuguesa nos Estados Unidos* (1925) and *Os Portugueses na Nova Inglaterra* (1931), that refer to and quote from several Portuguese papers in New England from that period, some no longer extant. Pena Rodríguez's *News on the American Dream*, along with these studies, helps fill lacunae in seminal studies on the Portuguese in the U.S., like Pap's *Portuguese-American Speech* (1949) and *The Portuguese-Americans* (1981) and Francis M. Rodgers' "Portuguese" in the *Harvard Encyclopedia of American Ethnic Groups* (1981), volumes that contributed significantly to the social history of Portuguese immigration but that left out reference to the press or mentioned it only in passing. *News on the American Dream* ensures that the Portuguese-American press can no longer be ignored.

News on the American Dream further highlights personalities whose work in newspapers, as publishers or editors, formed Portuguese-American public opinion and had a profound impact on the more than 140 years of the Portuguese press in this country. The work of these figures, both men and women, contributed to the development of a sense of belonging, cohesion, and identity within a Portuguese America comprised of isolated "islands," i.e., separate Portuguese communities on the East Coast, West Coast, and Hawaii. The work of this distinguished group of Portuguese Americans helped immigrants connect to their homeland and to each other in different states, while providing relief from the drudgery of factory work and the isolation of fishing and farm life. Ultimately, these newspapers reflect competing allegiances for the immigrant working to reconcile a sense of Portugueseness with gratitude to a new country that had afforded new opportunities in the present and the future.

The development of a sense of a broad and coastal Portuguese America was promoted, wittingly or unwittingly, by many of the newspapers that published news from communities dispersed throughout the country. This was particularly the case for papers with national ambitions, like *O Jornal de Noticias* (1877-1884), in Erie, PA, a city not usually associated with Portuguese immigration. The advertisements published in this paper, copies of which are located in the Biblioteca Pública e Arquivo Regional de Ponta Delgada (Azores), are particularly revealing as they convey a sense of early Portuguese America through advertisements of Portuguese-named and owned hotels in cities like Boston (Maritimo Hotel), and, less expectedly, San Luís Obispo, CA (Luzitano Hotel), as well as announcements from immigrants hoping to locate relatives and friends in different cities and states. Pena Rodríguez's work helps recover this history and the histories of other communities, like the one in Oakland, CA, that barely registers in Portuguese-American collective memory today, but that a hundred years ago was perhaps the most vibrant Portuguese community in California, with the first "national" church in California (Saint Joseph's, razed in the 1960s) and 16 newspapers, a number exceeded only by New Bedford, MA. Pena Rodríguez's book is unrivalled in the kind of detail and information that it provides.

Pena Rodríguez also deals at length with three newspapers that he terms "paradigmatic," namely, the *Diario de Noticias* (1919-1973), the only daily ever published for any substantial length of time (and available online at the UMass Dartmouth Ferreira-Mendes Portuguese-American Archives), and the three major (weekly) Portuguese papers today: *Luso-Americano* (1928-) and the *Portuguese Times* (1971-). The only long-term bilingual newspaper ever published, *O Jornal*, founded in 1975 but published in Portuguese and English since 1990, could reasonably be added to this list. (This may be the only Portuguese paper ever owned by a major American media company). *News on the American Dream* also helps save from oblivion individuals like Carlos Almeida, the former long-time secretary general of the União Portuguesa do Estado da Califórnia (UPEC), who had the foresight and dedication to collect and preserve newspapers that otherwise would not be available for reading and study today. Pena Rodríguez likewise acknowledges institutions, such as the Bancroft Library at UC Berkeley, the Library of Congress, and the Ferreira-Mendes Portuguese-American Archives at UMass Dartmouth, whose preservation and conservation of Portuguese-American newspapers made this book possible and whose collections will undoubtedly form the basis of future studies.

Building on the work of Pena Rodríguez and others, future researchers will be able to study how the press was the voice and reflection *of* and active contributor *to* the social, intellectual, artistic, and literary pursuits of Portuguese Americans. In a new world where the immigrant felt alien, newspapers in their mother tongue—a fundamental marker of ethnic identity—allowed immigrants to feel a sense of belonging to their local community and also to the larger, wider, imagined Portuguese America, in part by publishing news from across the U.S. through columns written by numerous correspondents. This process of connecting immigrants was particularly relevant before mass media and contemporary digital media and social networks, when the written word, printed in newspapers, was the primary means of communication within a region and across a nation. Future studies may also reveal the public role of the Portuguese press in connecting these communities to the established social, political, and economic powers in the cities and regions where the immigrants settled. Other research could expand on what Pena Rodríguez has written here and investigate in closer detail the influence of the clergy (Catholic, but also Protestant) in the Portuguese press, particularly in the formative years.

The reaction in Portuguese-American newspapers to perceived derogatory articles in the mainstream press or in other publications, such as Donald Taft's *Two Portuguese Communities in New England* (1923), has already produced a recent essay by the Portuguese anthropologist Cristiana Bastos on the racialization of the Portuguese in New England and should allow for additional studies. Yet other avenues for research could be the role of the Portuguese in industrial strikes, the role of consuls of Portugal and the Portuguese government, particularly during the Salazar regime, as well as the relationship between the Portuguese-American press and the creation of the Estado Novo, a topic on which Pena Rodríguez will soon publish. More recently, how did the Portuguese ethnic press cover the notorious Big Dan's incident in New Bedford, and was its perspective markedly different from the negative portrayal of the community in national mainstream newspapers? One thing is certain: the Portuguese newspapers catalogued by Pena Rodríguez will allow, through the analysis of content, an understanding of the many histories of Portuguese America. Moreover, this book will facilitate the participation of the Portuguese in the ongoing conversation on ethnic media. The increased awareness that Pena Rodríguez's study raises about the Portuguese press in America will hopefully lead to more gifts of materials to archives, including the business papers of some of the newspapers, allowing scholars to study challenges related to circulation, advertising, and formatting, and even the mechanical production of the Portuguese press in America.

In the meantime, what might be the future of the Portuguese-American press? We can go back to the future, as it were, and consider the fate of the Portuguese press in Hawaii, which disappeared due to a particular immigration history (related to time-specific contract labor) and tightened immigration restrictions in the early twentieth century. In 1930 the editor and future owner of *Diario de Noticias*, João Rocha, anticipated the decline and end of Portuguese-American journalism, due to the restrictive immigrations laws passed in the 1920s, as Pena Rodríguez points out. Of course, foretelling the future is always risky and Rocha was proven wrong, as the Azorean Refugee Act of 1958 and 1960 and the Immigration and Naturalization Act of 1965 brought a wave of better-educated Portuguese immigrants to these shores. Nonetheless, the precipitous decline of Portuguese immigration that began in 1983 has reduced the total number of Portuguese print newspapers to four, though some online publications are having limited success, including the *Portuguese-American Journal* and *Feel Portugal*.

Even if there were a resurgence in immigration, who is to say that the press, at least the printed version, could compete with the new technologies and survive? Indeed, one could argue that other technologies, namely radio and television, had a profound and deleterious impact on the Portuguese press. Pena Rodríguez makes reference to the importance of the relationship between the Portuguese-American press and radio and television, though he could not pursue it at length as the topic falls out of the scope of this study. But perhaps Pena Rodríguez, who is a prolific scholar of media and communications studies, or other scholars will take up the challenge of writing a book on the history of these media, and analyze, for example, how the advent of radio programming in the early 1930s, which first took advantage of print media to promote itself, eventually syphoned readers away from newspapers, not unexpectedly, in a community whose literacy rates were relatively low and that had not cultivated the habit of reading newspapers in the country of origin. What is the place of Portuguese-American radio in American broadcasting? How did it function as a unifying force, as newspaper had done before and continues to do up to the present? How did the much higher financial demands in order to gain access to ownership, as compared to print media, affect this media in the Portuguese community? Ownership of full-time Portuguese radio stations and the professionalization of radio did occur, and the medium is still thriving in Massachusetts and California. More narrowly, what was the impact of extraordinary, bigger-than-life radio personalities like Ferreira Mendes in New England and Joaquim Esteves in California in the Golden Age of individual Portuguese radio programs?

Portuguese-American television is another media area that would merit its own study, similar to the one that newspapers receive here. As an example, one could mention The Portuguese Channel of New Bedford and its limited but relevant impact in Massachusetts and Rhode Island, as it produced and still produces some ethnically and locally relevant content. Of equal or greater interest may be RTPi (Portuguese Public Television International), which was added in the mid-1990s to cable in cities across Portuguese America with appreciable Portuguese populations. This development changed the Portuguese media landscape in the U.S. and helped maintain cultural and linguistic bonds to the country of origin. On the other hand, it may have contributed to the alienation of the immigrant from U.S. society and its political process. Compared to the ethnic press or ethnic radio, RTPi did not include significant local news *by* Portuguese-Americans and coverage *of* the Portuguese community. In other words, has RTPi contributed significantly to the ongoing process of self-definition of Portuguese America, given that the programming is neither local nor tied to the immigrant experience in any significant way, since the immigrants are simply considered an extension of Portugal? Might RTPi have retarded the process of assimilation by disseminating information that was not directly useful to the circumstance of the Portuguese in America? (The production of ethnically relevant content, *in loco*, was unfortunately not economically viable, as the attempt and failure to launch a studio at UMass Dartmouth in the late 1990s and early 2000s suggests.)

Another area of future research, building upon *News on the American Dream*, could be the study of the content of the magazines listed by Pena Rodríguez. These might have been less parochial and provincial, as they were published monthly. We know that they were more carefully edited, with longer, more in-depth articles, and included creative aspects of the community, while promoting leading figures from different professions and walks of life. Less focused on daily life, they combated social and historical erasure, just as the newspapers did, while contributing to the development of the sense of a distinct Portuguese-American identity. Some, like the *Boletim da UPEC*, published poetry by the most important immigrant poet to date, Alfred Lewis. Yet another avenue of study could be coverage dedicated to things Portuguese-American in the mainstream press, including by Portuguese-American reporters. For example, in the late 1930s and early 1940s *The Sun* in Lowell, MA, had a Portuguese reporter, Armando Santos, who was also a radio announcer on a local radio station. More recently, the New Bedford *Standard Times* and Fall River *Herald News* had Portuguese reporters. Did this lead to a different or more sympathetic coverage of the community?

The possible disappearance of the Portuguese press might reflect a wider sobering reality: a vital, living, separate, and powerfully unique experience will be ending through acculturation, assimilation, as is the usual order of things in the immigrant experience. Nonetheless, future generations will still have access to the history of that experience, contributions to the multicultural, multi-ethnic American experience through the newspapers that have been saved from destruction and made readily and widely available online. As a first draft of history, the press will endure in archives and contribute valuably to the work of future scholars. Ultimately, the extant newspapers studied by Pena Rodríguez—and other newspapers that may be located and preserved in a labor of love inspired in part by this book—will enable present and future generations to explore, celebrate, and understand the society and culture of Portuguese America.

Frank F. Sousa
University of Massachusetts Lowell

.

Acknowledgments

I would like to express my gratitude to all the individuals and organizations that have contributed to this work. First and foremost, my thanks go to the institutions that provided the financial support for my investigation at the different archives and research centers in the United States and Portugal: the Luso-American Development Foundation (FLAD), the Calouste Gulbenkian Foundation, and Spain's Ministry of Education. A very special thanks goes to the Center for Portuguese Studies and Culture at the University of Massachusetts Dartmouth, which provided me with the opportunity to carry out this research while teaching in the PhD program in Luso-Afro-Brazilian Studies and Theory as the Hélio & Amélia Pedroso/Luso-American Foundation Endowed Chair Professor in Portuguese Studies. It was a great honor for me.

In addition to the University of Massachusetts Dartmouth, three other American universities supported the project. At various periods in 2012 and 2013, I had the opportunity to work as a visiting scholar at Harvard University, the University of California Berkeley, and Brown University. These universities provided necessary institutional support to help advance my project. I am also grateful for the opportunities to deliver lectures at the Minda de Gunzburg Center for European Studies at Harvard, the Institute of European Studies at Berkeley, and the Department of Foreign Languages and the Center for Portuguese Studies and Culture at UMass Dartmouth.

At each of these institutions, there were people who have been key in making this book possible. First, I want to recognize Prof. Mário Mesquita, who inspired me, motivated me, and without whose support nothing would have happened. I also thank Miguel Vaz for his friendship and support during my trips to the United States. I am also grateful to the former president of

FLAD, Prof. Vasco Rato, and former executive administrator, Michael Baum, for kindly sponsoring my projects on Portuguese-American communities.

Both Prof. Frank Sousa, current director of the Saab Center for Portuguese Studies at the University of Massachusetts Lowell and former director of the Center for Portuguese Studies and Culture at UMass Dartmouth, and Prof. Onésimo T. Almeida of the Department of Portuguese & Brazilian Studies at Brown University were crucial in the development of the project. Whatever is best about this book also belongs to them. Prof. Luis Fernández Cifuentes treated me with great generosity at Harvard, where I also had the cordial help of Prof. José Manuel Martínez Sierra, director of the Real Colegio Complutense at Harvard, who provided me with an ideal space to read, think, and write during my stay in Cambridge. The same was true of Prof. Deolinda Adão who welcomed me kindly at UC Berkeley's Portuguese Studies Program. At the Universidad Nacional de Educación a Distancia (UNED), I am indebted to Prof. Hipólito de la Torre Gómez, who was essential to my reaching a new milestone in my academic career as a result of this study.

I would also like to acknowledge the important contribution of the Ferreira-Mendes Portuguese-American Archives and its director, Prof. Maria Gloria de Sá, whose encouragement, caring, and academic contributions have been fundamental. I am also grateful to Carlos Almeida for his hospitality and help while I was doing research at the Freitas Library in San Leandro, CA, where I was cordially received by its director, Tim Borges, and all his staff. There were many other people who made academic suggestions, responded to my requests for information or reviewed my texts, such as Professors Donald Warrin and Fernando M. Silva of UC Berkeley; Jose C. Moya of Columbia University; Jorge Pedro Sousa of Fernando Pessoa University; George Monteiro of Brown University; Geoffrey Gomes of Chabot College; Ron Fortier of UMass Dartmouth; Lusa Ponte of the University of the Azores; and Diana G. Simões of UMass Lowell. I would also like to express my gratitude to Manuel Adelino Ferreira, former director of the *Portuguese Times*, who carefully reviewed the manuscript for mistakes, and Ms. Otília Ferreira, who kindly met with me one afternoon to discuss her father, the popular radio journalist Affonso Gil Mendes Ferreira, who is mentioned in the book.

I also want to thank all the librarians, employees, journalists, and editors who helped me in the search for documentation and data collection:

Sonia Pacheco and Judith Farrar at the Ferreira-Mendes Portuguese-American Archives; Margaret Mutter at Brown's John D. Rockefeller Jr. Library; Timothy Engels at Brown's John Hay Library; Shirey Lynn at Harvard's Widener Library; Andrea Kupski-Keane and Katherine Killough at Harvard's Department of Romance Languages and Literatures; Melisa Costa at the Center for Portuguese Studies and Culture; Mark Procknik at the New Bedford Whaling Museum Research Library and Archives; Fatima Alves at the Arquivo Histórico Diplomático of Lisbon; Ana Fernandes and Odete Martins at the Arquivos Nacionais da Torre do Tombo in Lisbon; the vice-consul of Portugal in Providence Leonel R. Teixeira; Armanda Silva at Brown's Department of Portuguese & Brazilian Studies; and all the anonymous people who assisted me at the National Library of Portugal. I would also like to acknowledge the support provided by the current and former directors of the Center for Portuguese Studies and Culture at UMass Dartmouth, Professors Victor K. Mendes and João Paraskeva, as well as the former directors of Tagus Press, Professors Christopher Larkosh and Tim Walker, for all the efforts made in the process of editing the manuscript. I wish, as well, to show my gratitude to Mário Pereira, Executive Editor of Tagus Press, for his professionalism and kindness. During my stay at UMass Darmtouth I shared very pleasant moments with Professors Dário Borim, Michael Baum, Tim Walker, Gláucia Silva, Victor K. Mendes, Anna Klobucka, Christopher Larkosh, Isabel F. Rodrigues, Carlos Benavides, Noémia DeMelo, Blanca Rodríguez Miravet, Rick Hogan and Daniela Melo. Last but not least, and for different reasons, I also want to show my appreciation to Judit and Jeffrey Correia, Francisco Resendes, Leo Schick, Rosana and Rick Sasse, Carmelo Rosa, Teresa Burnay, Leonor Roquette, Paula Vicente and Fabián Aradas.

To all, my heartfelt thanks.

*The Portuguese press is the soul of the community!
It announces our festivals, defends the interests of our
compatriots, promotes our organizations, publishes news
from our homeland, rekindles our patriotism, explores
local issues, and communicates to the various Portuguese
settlements the sad news of those who drew their last breath
of life in this country, away from the land of their birth...
Research the history of Portuguese language newspapers
in this country, and you shall find that their publication
is an odyssey of sacrifices, sorrows and disappointments,
immolated on the altar of the Motherland and the
Portuguese language...*[1]

Introduction

Objective

The present study aims to shed light on the newspapers published by and for
Portuguese immigrants and their descendants in the United States, as well
as publications that were founded or published by individuals who may not
have been of Portuguese origin but that were intended for a Lusophone audience of which the Portuguese always constituted the majority.

Before going any further, some concepts should be clarified. In the
context of this study, the term "Portuguese American" refers to persons of
Portuguese origin living in the United States. This includes immigrants and
persons born in the United States who trace their origins to continental Portugal, Madeira, or the Azores. Most Portuguese Americans are of Azorean
origin. The term "Lusophone" refers to Portuguese-speaking groups, including Portuguese, Brazilians, Cabo Verdeans, and the natives of other countries

that were former Portuguese colonies. Until the last decade of the twentieth century, when immigration from Brazil increased, the number of non-Portuguese Lusophones living in the U.S. was negligible. The only exception was Cabo Verdeans, who immigrated to America as Portuguese citizens until 1975, when Cabo Verde became independent from Portugal.

The Portuguese-American press is of extraordinary importance for understanding the history of the Portuguese diaspora in the United States. The publication of the first Portuguese-American newspaper in Erie, Pennsylvania, in 1877 marked the beginning of a new era in Portuguese-American history. From then on Portugal became news in America and Portuguese Americans became producers of information, creating their own means of social communication, and public self-representation. Narrated throughout these publications are thousands of diverse histories of immigration and settlement within the United States that reveal a set of personal and collective dreams regarding the experience of the Portuguese in the United States. Many of these publications were ephemeral, and many are forever lost. Nevertheless, the collections in the Ferreira-Mendes Portuguese-American Archives at the University of Massachusetts Dartmouth and in the Freitas Library of the Portuguese Fraternal Society of America in San Leandro, California, have preserved enough examples to provide the foundation for this study.[2] Together, these collections provide sufficient material for an overview of the social, linguistic, cultural, and economic characteristics of the Portuguese in the United States; what they thought about themselves and their role as immigrants in the United States; how they saw Portugal and its governments; how they kept their traditions alive through cultural events; and how they related to other ethnic groups and to the dominant local culture. In particular, these publications provide us with an opportunity to understand how the Portuguese built their own "American Dream," a concept that encompasses the material prosperity obtained through a system that provides equal opportunity for everyone, regardless of parentage and national origin, allows for success based on the hard work of the individual, and promotes the attainment of self-fulfillment through a life lived in freedom.[3]

In addition, each newspaper was an important agent of social change and played a relevant political role within the community. The Portuguese-language press never had greater freedom than in its American incarnations. While the government of the United States did occasionally exercise control or censorship over the media (e.g., during the Second World War), the Portuguese-American press went largely unnoticed by the authorities. Since the content was in Portuguese, it was considered of marginal interest to the nation at large and usually subjected to less rigorous control than the press published in English. But within the Portuguese-American community, the influence of some of the newspapers was enormous. They were instruments for promoting businesses, ideas, activities, and institutions; campaigning for or against various projects in the community; and creating and guiding opinion on all matters of concern or interest to Portuguese Americans.

As noted by João P. Brum, one of the more prominent publishers of the Portuguese community in California, newspaper publishing was a difficult and uncertain business venture: "to produce newspapers was the business of poets, idealists, those unable to catch a cat by its tail."[4] But for many, the financial risks of publishing were outweighed by the potential benefits: publishing a newspaper could provide power, give visibility in the community, grant prestige and, if managed reasonably well, provide enough profit to live on. This explains why many immigrants of limited means and inadequate preparation decided to publish newspapers, often from their own homes. In the beginning, most of these intrepid editors were typographers with little knowledge of journalistic practices and with limited writing skills. Some met with little success, but others succeeded in achieving their "American Dream" through their roles in the Portuguese-American press. This was the case for more than a dozen Portuguese immigrants who founded multiple periodicals. Some of the most notable figures who fit this profile are António Maria Vicente, Arthur Vieira Ávila, João Rodrigues Rocha, Pedro Laureano Claudino da Silveira, and João P. Brum, whose stories will be explored here.

The development of the Portuguese-American press is directly related to the Portuguese migratory movement itself. The appearance and disappearance of titles founded by Portuguese individuals depended not only on the arrival of new immigrants, but also on the economic and social changes that forced many members of the Portuguese community to migrate between states or cities.[5] Portuguese migration within the United States explains why some newspapers changed location or even titles several times throughout their existence.[6]

Ethnic newspapers, traditionally overlooked as historical resources and notorious for the degree of difficulty they present for scholars who try to locate them (now much ameliorated by digitization projects), have come to constitute important sources for historians in areas such as politics and economics. Newspapers are essential to those trying to become familiar with the culture of a community and the way it represents itself.[7] It should also be noted that the press has always been an important political agent.[8] In modern history, there are many events that can only be properly explained by calling attention to the role that newspapers (and the media in general) have played at defining moments.[9] The version of reality portrayed in the media can change reality.[10] In this sense, the *media* has become an agent of historical change. History is an ongoing process of change in which various political, social, economic, and cultural elements influence the human narratives that are essential for creating and understanding the identity symbols of a society.[11] Journalistic representations of reality in history model and mold cultural perception and engage closely with the idiosyncrasies of the people represented.[12] In the past century, the proliferation of the media and the exponential increase in the production of news stories made the media into agents of "metahistorical" change that acted on all levels and even had the power to influence some historical processes.[13]

This is indeed what happened in the Portuguese community in the United States. Their own journalistic production not only formed part of their historical account, but also contributed to the construction of Portuguese-American social identity. Its ideology and symbology are directly related to the editorial discourse of the newspapers established in the cities that became cultural havens for Portuguese immigrants, making Portuguese-American newspapers a valuable key for decoding the public discourse of the group.[14] The Portuguese press was also useful in developing strategies to promote and defend the group's interests; stimulate social cohesion, political consensus, and cultural convergence; and support the establishment of all sorts of associations. Collaboration among Portuguese immigrants did not just function through the establishment of institutions that promoted such common projects as charitable, educational, and social insurance initiatives. It was largely through journalistic discourse that the group managed to create a public opinion in its own voice, separate from English-language public discourse.[15] Thanks to the strength of their press, Portuguese Americans were able to create a unique sense of belonging to a new society by promoting their own cultural values and projecting an image that made them more visible. In so doing, they were able to affirm their political, commercial, and sociocultural position within the complex ethnic diversity of North American society, particularly in the states of Massachusetts and California, where the Portuguese risked being assimilated into the groups that preceded them.[16] Moreover, the media facilitated cooperation among the various Portuguese-American settlement communities, allowing the development of strategies designed to create cohesive social movements and community projects that strengthened the group's position within the American social fabric.

At the individual level, one of the main motivating factors for reading the Portuguese-American press was to remain connected to one's origins through news about Portugal and the Portuguese-American community. In part, what readers looked for in these publications was simply that most essential identifying and cultural of signs: the language. Although there was a high rate of illiteracy among Portuguese immigrants, especially among those who immigrated in the late nineteenth century and the first third of the twentieth century, it is likely that the urge to maintain contact with Portuguese culture stimulated the acquisition of reading skills among them.[17]

In addition, these newspapers played an important role in the economic development of the Portuguese-American community. They offered a perfect medium for merchants and other businesses to promote their products and services among the fellow countrymen who were their main customers. Advertisements for supermarkets, clothing stores, shoe stores, inns, funeral homes, bakeries, and hairdressers, among other businesses and companies owned by the Portuguese, attracted Portuguese customers by appealing to the trust that was provided by belonging to the same culture, speaking the same language, and sharing the same immigrant status in the United States. The appeal to patriotism was also a constant among the advertisers in Portuguese-American newspapers. And, of course, the immigrant press provided a platform from which politicians could directly address Portuguese speakers in their campaigns.

These newspapers are likewise valuable for documenting daily occurrences in places with large Portuguese populations.[18] Through these sources, one can better understand the level of social integration experienced by immigrants in different territorial and historical contexts; assess their ability to adapt to the dominant English-language sociocultural environment; identify the principal public leaders of the Portuguese-American community; discover which Portuguese businesses and companies were relevant; find trends in public opinion about American, Portuguese, and international politics; determine the most widely used symbols of identity; and learn how the use of the Portuguese language evolved. Each Portuguese-American newspaper is, in this sense, an exceptional source of information.

This work analyzes all known periodicals aimed at Portuguese immigrants and their descendants, regardless of the subject, content, longevity, business strategy or language. Institutional bulletins circulated exclusively to their members, with content confined to their institutional activities, are not included in this study. These types of publications, which engaged in an administrative rather than an informative discourse, were not exclusively addressed to the Portuguese-American community and were not produced in accordance with journalistic methods. There is one exception, however: the *Boletim da U.P.E.C.*, whose extensive duration—from 1898 to 2009—and wide diffusion in California make it too important to overlook. Unreliable and incomplete data preclude an exhaustive account of the history of the Portuguese-American press, but within these limitations this study aims to be as comprehensive as possible, covering a collection of 167 Portuguese-American newspapers and magazines (see Appendix A).

Review of the Literature

This study is not intended to be a history of the Portuguese diaspora in the United States.[19] Instead, it aims to provide a historical study of Portuguese-American newspapers by adopting an interdisciplinary approach that complements the characterization of the group provided by other studies. This book aims to offer a different, though not entirely new, window into the social behavior of Portuguese Americans through the analysis of their print media.[20]

An extensive bibliography on the history of Portuguese emigration to the United States exists and has contributed numerous ideas and data to this project, including those that help us to generate a map of the most important centers of Portuguese settlement in the United States. Historically, these centers have been concentrated in Massachusetts, California, Rhode Island, New Jersey, New York, Connecticut, and Hawaii, though the population is spread in some degree throughout all states.[21] Within certain cities, the number and proportion of persons of Portuguese origin have been particularly high, providing the critical mass necessary for the development of a variety of ethnic institutions. Paradigmatic among these is New Bedford, Massachusetts, whose initial immigration history is related to the whaling and textile industries and whose population of Portuguese descent exceeded 33% of its 95,000 inhabitants in 2010.[22] Taking into account the territorial distribution and concentration of persons of Portuguese origin has been essential in the development of this project because there is a direct relationship between the size of the community and its newspaper production. Predictably, more newspapers were founded in localities with higher immigrant populations, and New Bedford has been the city with the largest number of Portuguese-American newspapers, with a total of thirty-eight titles.

Despite the visibility and impact of this journalism in the Portuguese-American community since the late nineteenth century, there have been very few academic monographs on the subject. The pioneering work in this field dates from 1960, when Edgar C. Knowlton published his short article "The Portuguese Language Press of Hawaii," which discusses to the newspapers edited by Portuguese immigrants in Hawaii during the late nineteenth and early twentieth century.[23] Knowlton's article provides a list of Portuguese newspapers published in the Hawaiian archipelago, discusses the main features of their contents, and offers biographical information for some of the editors. In 1983, Geoffrey L. Gomes presented his master's thesis "The Portuguese Language Press in California, from 1880 to 1928" at California State University at Hayward (eventually published in 1995).[24] This study was of particular relevance because it gave the topic of Portuguese newspapers in the United States the kind of importance needed to make it of interest to subsequent researchers. Gomes's study provides an interesting tour of the Portuguese press in California by examining the views of its major newspapers on American politics during the period from 1880, when Manoel Stone founded the first newspaper in California, *A Voz Portugueza*, until 1928. Gomes offers an extensive analysis of editorials related to the political issues of that time, during which more than twenty Portuguese-American newspapers were published in California.

In 1987, Leo Pap, another pioneer, published a chapter on Portuguese newspapers in a book on the ethnic press in the United States.[25] Here, Pap offers a general overview of the historical development of the Portuguese-American press, confirming the extraordinary influence of newspapers among Portuguese immigrants, and provides useful data on newspapers published in several other states, including Hawaii. Rui Antunes Correia (2004 and 2009) also addressed this aspect of Portuguese immigration in his study of the role played by New Bedford's *Diario de Noticias* within the Portuguese-American community in the 1930s, using documentary and oral sources to elaborate on the newspaper's ideological stances and its influence as the newspaper of reference within the Portuguese community.[26]

In addition to these four pioneering studies, there have also been a number of recent articles that address the issue.[27] Directly or indirectly, the topic of Portuguese-American newspapers is also discussed in books and articles related to Portuguese immigration to the United States. A case in point was Eduardo de Carvalho, a consul of Portugal in Boston in the 1920s, who criticized the lack of professionalism in what he defined as Portuguese "colonial journalism." According to Carvalho's observations, Portuguese-American newspapers were not published according to journalistic criteria, but were rather subject to improvisation driven by a pressing need to secure advertisements.[28]

Within the general literature about the ethnic press in the United States, there is only one chapter on the Portuguese-American press, the already-cited work by Pap, published in a volume edited by Sally M. Miller, which lists twenty-seven different groups with their own language media.[29] The ethnic press in the United States is, therefore, a phenomenon that embraces an extensive ethnic and cultural spectrum.[30] Other authors who have addressed specific aspects of the history of the ethnic press in the United States include William L. Joyce (1976),[31] Jan Kowalick (1978),[32] Lauren Kessler (1984),[33] H. M. Lai (1987),[34] Sandra L. Jones Ireland (1990),[35] Melissa A. Jonhson (2000),[36] K. Viswanath and Pamela Arora (2000),[37] and Leara D. Rhodes (2010).[38]

Research Methodology and Sources

The documentary basis for this study rests on a broad collection of periodical publications from which I have attempted to construct a coherent historical narrative.[39] My intention in compiling this list has been to be as exhaustive as possible, so the rule of thumb in the development of the list used in this analysis has been to include almost all publications whose existence could be verified. This is not to say that this research covers *all* of the Portuguese-American titles ever published. Given that many of them no longer exist, and that in many cases the evidence about them derives from unreliable, secondary or indirect sources, many publications mentioned in various sources have been left out of this study.[40] Nevertheless, the list put together for this study does include periodicals whose existence has not been verified by direct physical examination either because no extant copies exist or, if they do, they could not be found. Their inclusion was based on information from indirect sources, mainly journalistic, usually from news stories that reported their founding. In doing this, it is assumed that newspaper reports are sufficiently reliable historical sources for this purpose, though they sometimes contain errors that must be addressed.

Newsletters of various fraternal, cultural or business organizations were also excluded from this study since their contents tend to be specific to the organization they represent. The only exception is the *Boletim da U.P.E.C*, the newsletter of the Portuguese Union of the State of California, whose extensive and interesting history deserves mention. However, some of them will be occasionally mentioned as examples of this particular genre. In this group are publications such as the *Bulletin of the Associated Milk Producers* (edited by Mário Bettencourt da Câmara, San Francisco, California, 1920-1923?), the *Boletim Oficial do Montepio Operário* (Fall River, Massachusetts), the *Boletim Anual da Fundação Beneficiente Faialense* (Massachusetts), the *Boletim da SPRSI*

(Official Organization of the Portuguese Society of Queen Saint Isabel, California), and the *Boletim da IDES* (Official Organization of the Fraternity of the Holy Ghost, California).

In addition to the difficulties associated with establishing the existence of particular newspapers, there were also significant obstacles in developing comprehensive and rigorous profiles for those included in this study. A major cause of these difficulties is the fact that many titles were so ephemeral that there are no extant copies, and their brief trajectory has become unclear. But even those that were more enduring often presented challenges. Many had offices in different cities (some appearing in as many as five locations), and many even changed states. Frequently owners and editors also changed, resulting in changes to the title, format, and other aspects of the paper. Moreover, many periodicals had an irregular and intermittent production history. Finally, sources sometimes provide contradictory clues about newspapers of which no copies are preserved. In some cases, conflicting data from up to three different sources on the same newspaper was found, showing discrepancies related to the period and frequency of the newspapers' publication.

There are many ways to create categories and establish methodological guidelines in the study of periodicals. Some approaches follow standards and guidelines that prioritize taxonomic categories, especially those related to physical appearance. In this case, such factors as the size of each specimen, its exact measurements, type of paper and printing, typographical quality, content distribution, and column layout must be described in detail to produce an accurate physical description of the newspaper. Other methods are oriented more toward the content of the newspapers. Different categories are established depending on the type of article (editorial, news, advice column, feature, etc.) and assessed quantitatively or qualitatively. If the object of study relates to a specific topic, the space devoted to it may be calculated and the number of items related to the matter counted. Thematic classifications can also be made to take into account multiple variables, including geographical, historical, and political groupings. However, there is no ideal methodology. The best method is to apply reasonable and consistent, if admittedly *ad hoc*, standards.

This study offers a general overview of the material, typically including a description of some physical elements, such as formatting and average number of pages, specification and description of the type of content, a time-frame of the origin and demise of each newspaper, publication frequency, and identification of the primary agents responsible for founding, editing, and writing them. The methodology also takes note of the primary language of the publication, the location of its headquarters, and its main areas of dissemination and distribution. Additionally, it takes into account subtitles, advertisements, and promotional slogans, noting salient ideological biases when appropriate, and supplying bibliographical information for the archives or other sources where the data can be examined or verified.

No system of categorization is always ideal, but this method was chosen for the development of the overall list for three main reasons: 1) it is consistent with the type of study to be carried out, primarily because of its interdisciplinary nature; 2) it is appropriate to its critical dimension (in order to better understand the dynamics of operation of each newspaper and its integration into the social and cultural context) as well as its practical side (defining essential characteristics); and 3) it manages to combine a large number of categories that allow for an understanding of each newspaper in a more complete form, encompassing both the physical aspects of each newspaper as well as its content. This approach aims to provide a reliable understanding of the object of study, especially with regard to its historical significance within the Portuguese-American community.

In developing this project, two basic parameters were used for the breakdown of the newspapers. The first took into account distribution by state in order to understand the overall geographical distribution of the Portuguese ethnic press. The second, which aimed at outlining the development of this press over time, involved a listing in chronological order by states and cities. The research also attempts to identify the origins of the founders, editors, and owners of the newspapers. Whenever possible, I reproduce some representative content from each publication during its initial stages and samples of its most historically significant headlines as a means of understanding their editorial line as well as other aspects of interest, such as their linguistic and idiomatic registers. Apart from a few exceptions, such as the magazine *Portugal Today*, published in New York in the late 1950s, and the newspaper *Portuguese Heritage Journal*, published in Florida in the 1990s, all of the periodicals use Portuguese as their only or main language, though the use of English has been increasing over time as the number of readers born in the United States increases. Fall River's *O Jornal*, for example, is currently almost completely bilingual.

Primary sources used include documents from the archival collections of the Historical Diplomatic Archives and the National Archives in Lisbon; the Embassy of Portugal in Washington, D.C.; and the consulates of Portugal in Boston, New York, New Bedford, Fall River, San Francisco, and Providence. Although they may present a biased image of the community, due to certain political interests, and their numeric data is not entirely reliable, since it is based on voluntary registration, diplomatic and consular records have been particularly useful, for they can contain discontinued copies of newspapers not listed in any other archive, as well as special reports on the Portuguese-American press that provide key details. Consulting these documents has been particularly slow due to bureaucratic restrictions, especially since a large portion of the documents, including material from the 1930s, has yet to be processed by the Commission for the Selection of Declassification of the Ministry of Foreign Affairs of Portugal. But, above all, the analysis relies on resources from institutions within the United States, especially the Ferreira-Mendes Portuguese-American Archives at the University of Massachusetts Dartmouth and the Freitas Library of the Portuguese Fraternal Society of America in San Leandro, CA, the two collections with the largest number of newspapers published by the Portuguese in North America. This study also relied on numerous other institutions with copies or collections of Portuguese newspapers, including the Boston Public Library, the Kendall l. Research Library at the New Bedford Whaling Museum, the Harvard College Library, the Bancroft Library at the University of California Berkeley, the John Hay Library at Brown University, as well as the digital archives of several academic institutions.

In the case of secondary sources, the research has focused on six areas: the history of the Portuguese press in general; the phenomenon of Portuguese migration to the United States; the broader history of the ethnic press in North America; Portuguese-American identity and culture; studies regarding press, language, and communication in the Portuguese diaspora; and works published by Portuguese-American journalists or Portuguese intellectuals living in the United States.

In compiling a bibliography, the following libraries were essential: the Rockefeller Library at Brown University, the Widener Library at Harvard University, the Claire T. Carney Library at the University of Massachusetts Dartmouth, the Freitas Library, the Bancroft Library at the University of California Berkeley, the National Library of Portugal, and the General Library of the University of Coimbra.

Structure and Content of the Study

The work has been divided into five chapters. The first chapter establishes the context of the research in its two primary dimensions: the histories of the ethnic press and of Portuguese immigration to the United States. The second chapter provides a quantitative, chronological, and geographical overview of the Portuguese-American press in the United States. In addition, it examines the characteristics of its journalistic production, including thematic symbology, types of content, and the nature of its relationships with diplomatic representatives of the Portuguese government. This chapter also provides brief biographical profiles of pioneering editors. The third and fourth chapters are historical journeys through the newspaper titles published in different decades and regions, from the beginning of their publication to the present. The fifth chapter is a study of four paradigmatic cases: the *Diario de Noticias* of New Bedford, the *Jornal Português* of Oakland, the *Luso-Americano* of Newark, and the *Portuguese Times* of New Bedford. The study concludes that the Portuguese press in the United States has historically played a symbolic role as a fundamental cultural instrument in the diaspora and has been a platform for disseminating public instruction among immigrants, fostering social cohesion, political consensus, and associative projects. The Portuguese-American community managed to create a public opinion with its own voice, independent from and sometimes in conflict with the dominant mainstream discourse in English.

There are certainly other valid approaches, methodologies, and topics of interest that might have been pursued here, but this project has been guided mainly by the attempt to construct a kind of scholarly chronicle of the pursuit of the "American Dream" by means of the Portuguese-American press.

Chapter 1

Immigration and the Ethnic Press in the United States

The Value and Historical Significance of Ethnic Journalistic Production

The main source for quantitative data on the historical evolution of newspapers produced by immigrant communities remains Robert E. Park's *The Immigrant Press and Its Control* (1922). Park's statistics track the ethnic press through the period of its greatest expansion, during the stage of mass immigration from Europe between 1890 and 1920. During this period, over twenty-two million people immigrated to the United States, mainly through the ports of New York and San Francisco.[1] According to *N.W. Ayer and Son's American Newspaper Annual and Directory*, by the mid-1910s there were more than 1,300 foreign language newspapers in the United States, published in some thirty different languages (see Table 1).[2] These newspapers had an estimated total circulation of 2.6 million copies.[3] Although these sources do not provide information on the Portuguese press, during the 1910s there were 18 newspapers published in Portuguese (see Table 9).

Leara D. Rhodes distinguishes three major phases in the production of the ethnic press, each directly related to migratory cycles to the United States.[4] The first great wave begins in the colonial period and extends until 1865. About 10 million immigrants settled in the United States during this period. They came mainly from England, Ireland, Germany, France, Scandinavia, the Netherlands, and China. According to Ulf Jonas Bjork, 300 foreign language publications were registered during this phase, mostly in French and German.[5]

Table 1. Evolution of the Foreign Language Press in the U.S. (1886–1975)

Year	Number of Newspapers
1886	796
1900	1163
1917	1323
1920	1052
1930	1037
1960	698
1975	960

Source: Sally M. Miller, ed., *The Ethnic Press in the United States. A Historical Analysis and Handbook* (New York-Westport, Connecticut-London: Greenwood Press, 1987), 13. See also, Leara D. Rhodes (2010): 13-14.

Between 1865 and 1890, a new phase begins with a comparable number of immigrants. The end of the American Civil War and European wars, and the momentum from the Industrial Revolution, along with the beginning of the railway era, encouraged the movement of workers. The myth of the West, the search for free farmland, and the Gold Rush were important additional stimuli. Moreover, members of various religious groups, such as the Mennonites, Baptists, and German Quakers, decided to emigrate to the United States when some European states passed discriminatory laws against them. During the third phase, which would last from 1900 until 1930, a steady increase in the number of newspapers created by immigrant communities would continue until migratory restrictions imposed with the Emergency Immigration Act of 1921 and the Immigration Act of 1924 reduced the rate of growth of the immigrant press. As a result, the number of newspapers dropped from 1,323 in 1917 to 1,037 in 1930 (see Table 1). This downward trajectory accelerated during the following decades, a period marked by low immigration, and did not increase until the 1970s, after the Immigration and Nationality Act of 1965 eliminated the national origins quota system. Overall, as indicated in Table 1, from a total of 796 in 1886, the number of foreign-language newspapers rose steadily until the end of the First World War. Following this peak, it entered a period of decline that lasted until the early 1970s. Its most productive period was between 1884 and 1920, when 3,444 newspapers were founded. The majority of these had an ephemeral existence, which is one of the defining characteristics of this type of press. On average, for every 100 newspapers founded, 93 ceased operation.[6]

Despite the short lifespan of most of its newspapers, the ethnic press was not a marginal phenomenon with a low level of impact in the United States. Rather, it played a major role in the public relations and political strategies of several organizations and institutions during different historical periods and involved major political figures. As evidence of this, Rhodes mentions the experience of three extraordinary figures in American history who were also important to the history of the American ethnic press: Abraham Lincoln, Joseph Pulitzer, and Carlo Barsotti.

In his efforts to win the White House in 1859, Lincoln paid $400 to Theodore Canisius for the German ethnic newspaper *Illinois Staatsanzeiger* in Springfield, IL. According to Rhodes, this strategy helped secure him the German-American vote. After the election, Canisius reassumed control of his newspaper and was named Consul of the United States in Vienna.[7]

Joseph Pulitzer was an immigrant born in Budapest, Hungary, who came to the United States in 1864 to fight for the Union in the Civil War. When the conflict ended, he worked as a reporter for the German-American newspaper *Westliche Post*, based in St. Louis, MO. In 1874, Pulitzer acquired the *Staats-Zeitung* in the same city, and subsequently the *St. Louis Dispatch*, which he merged with the *Westliche Post*. In 1887, he founded the *Evening World* in New York City, where he became a spokesperson for the Democratic Party. He had fierce competition from the *New York Morning Journal*, led by William Randolph Hearst, whose sensationalist bent made him one of the founders of "yellow journalism." Upon his death, Pulitzer left part of his fortune to the Columbia University School of Journalism, which, in 1917, created the prestigious awards that bear his name.[8]

In 1880, in New York, Carlo Barsotti founded *Il Progresso Italo Americano*, an Italian-language newspaper, which became the foreign language newspaper with the largest circulation in the city. Barsotti used its pages to publicize the contributions of Italians to the progress of the United States and garner political influence. Largely due to his reporting, several memorials were erected in the city in honor of Italian figures, such as Giuseppe Garibaldi, Dante Alighieri, and Giovanni da Verrazzano.[9] Among many other examples of the influence of the ethnic press in American political life, one could mention Benjamin Franklin, who, in 1732, published a Philadelphia newspaper aimed at German immigrants.[10]

According to Jerzy Zubrzycki, the contents of newspapers created by the immigrant communities established in the United States tend to share a number of common themes, such as "news of the country of settlement, world news, home-country news, group life and interests, [and] editorial features."[11] However, there are notable variations, with language itself being a key factor, as each language provides a unique filter for the interpretation of the same reality.[12] The cultural structure of the immigrant community also influences what and how facts are reported. The unique characteristics of each society, which are based on the cultural traditions and ideological structure of its identity imaginary, likewise influence and condition information discourse.[13] The type of publication, the public, and the intentions of individual editors with respect to the subject at hand also influence the construction of the journalistic narrative.[14] The world view of each individual newspaper, within its own community, is distinctive. Its version of reality—of its own reality within the American universe—can offer a unique perspective for the understanding of social dynamics outside the dominant local culture,[15] and show the level of public influence within its particular political and socioeconomic context.[16]

For many immigrants, newspapers became a fundamental connection between their community of residence, their country of origin, and the United States. One of the primary functions of the ethnic press was to educate immigrants in their roles as American citizens, while providing information about their countries of origin and promoting political causes. As time went on, they would adapt to the changing needs of the community. For example, as immigrants formed new families in the United States, the number of potential readers who had been schooled in English increased, and this prompted many ethnic newspapers to begin including content in two languages.

Despite the need to connect with Portuguese-American readers who spoke only English, some Portuguese newspapers were reluctant to use the local language because it went against their commitment to the protection and dissemination of Portuguese. The *Diario de Noticias* of New Bedford, for example, publicly disapproved of the introduction of systematic contributions in English. An editorial published on November 25, 1932, rejected the use of English as an official language of "community" newspapers. While it was understood that children of Portuguese immigrants born on American soil wanted readings in English, the paper argued that, "in order to educate, in the American sense, the children of the Portuguese or any other community, the pages of these newspapers should not be Americanized. Leave that to the Americans." [17] The *Diario* adamantly opposed the "infiltration" of English in the Portuguese press, despite being in favor of creating specific sections in this language for the second generation:

> We have no doubt in affirming, in principle, our disagreement with this practice. Either there is a need for a community press or there is not. If there is, and if it is this press that fights for and defends the native tongue as an instrument of ethnic cohesion, then bilingualism destroys this instrument... Neither for sentimental nor for practical reasons is the use of both languages by the ethnic press defensible. . . We are not at all opposed to the introduction of American sections aimed at the new generations that do not know our language. We believe that it would be very useful to dedicate these sections to educational materials that would make them proud of their heritage. [18]

The ethnic press attempted to find a market niche that complemented that of the local American press by publishing news that the American press did not offer, particularly stories related to the countries of origin, immigration and naturalization policies, and news about what was happening within the ethnic community itself. [19] In addition to providing information that targeted the concerns and needs of immigrants, the ethnic press promoted the cultural and spiritual identification needed for immigrants to integrate into their new environment.

For those involved in its creation, the ethnic press was a means of survival, but also an opportunity for professional growth. According to Robert E.

Park,[20] the majority of ethnic newspapers were founded by individuals of some means, often associated with ownership of financial institutions or travel agencies, as was the case with the owner of *Alvorada* and *Diario de Noticias*, Guilherme Machado Luiz. There were others, however, who had to rely on the support of associative, fraternal, political or religious organizations in order to succeed. For this reason, some of the newspapers were financed by religious congregations or by priests who took on roles that went beyond their spiritual duties.[21] Among these was Father Joseph (José) Cacella, founder and editor of *O Portugal* and *A Luta*, based in New York City.[22] Eduardo de Carvalho, Consul of Portugal in Boston between 1922 and 1925,[23] recognized the power and influence of the Catholic press in the community, but complained bitterly about the failure of these publications to cooperate in the promotion of new patriotic ideals that emerged as a result of the establishment of the Portuguese Republic on October 5, 1910:

> If every priest left his granite tower of exclusivity and put the exceptional influence that he still enjoys at the great service of the country, erasing the perhaps understandable and legitimate bitterness and hatred, . . . the Portuguese community would, in fact, be an extension of Portugal in New England and not, as it still is today, a transitional state—increasingly shorter and more precarious—between Portugal and America. Thus, the Catholic press, far from helping with the achievement of that common goal, is the biggest obstacle to its realization—to the detriment of the Church itself.[24]

The commercial success of the non-English ethnic press depended heavily on the residential characteristics of its intended readership. Finding readers was relatively easy in urban areas, when immigrants were heavily concentrated in ethnic neighborhoods. But when the group was geographically dispersed or the numbers were low, the costs of promotion and distribution increased dramatically. For this reason, many periodical publications were ephemeral or had irregular periodicity, as illustrated in a report sent by Victor Verdades de Faria, Consul General of Portugal in New York, to his ambassador in Washington on August 20, 1935:

As for the press, New York has seen many weeklies appear and disappear. At least five have ceased operations in a period of seven years; they were never able to attain the economic stability needed to survive. All the publishers have been individuals full of good intentions but lacking in the complex skills that the job demands.[25]

As explained by Rhodes, poverty and low levels of literacy among immigrants added to the difficult mission of the ethnic press:

Ethnic newspapers began with high hopes for the editors and publishers, who had a vision and wanted to share it with their people. Some editors thought it was their duty to educate their country's people on issues and ideas. These editors soon discovered that the early immigrants were concerned more about local issues, especially those that would affect them and their ability to get ahead. Others were too tired, too poor, too battered to take seriously the issues spouted in the various ethnic newspapers.[26]

As the foregoing paragraphs demonstrate, publishing a newspaper under these circumstances required much ambition and fortitude. To succeed in the ethnic newspaper business, one needed a great capacity to dream and to believe that it was possible to attain the "American Dream" through ethnic journalism.

The Press and the Origins of the Portuguese Presence in the United States

The arrival of the Portuguese in North American territory can be traced back to the Spanish colonization of the continent, when soldiers and sailors of Portuguese origin participated in expeditions in the service of Spain.[27] Notable among them was the sailor João Rodrigues Cabrilho (Juan Rodríguez Cabrillo, in Spanish), who, on September 28, 1542, became the first European navigator to reach the coast of California, as part of a maritime expedition originating in Mexico.[28] This episode is particularly important because it has become one of the historic facts most frequently used by the Portuguese-American press to claim a role for the Portuguese in the discovery and colonization of North

America. This was especially true in California, where various publications and organizations took up the task of telling Cabrilho's story. One of the most salient was an association composed of Cabrillo Civic Clubs from several cities that, between 1937 and 1938, published a magazine entitled *Cabrillo Commentator*.[29] In 1942, the most influential and long-lived newspaper of the Portuguese-American press in California, the *Jornal Português*, published more than fifty commemorative pages dedicated to the "Four Hundredth Anniversary of the Discovery of California by João Rodrigues Cabrilho."[30] Among the many texts dedicated to Cabrilho, there is a poem by the popular priest and poet Guilherme Silveira da Glória, editor of *O Amigo dos Cathólicos* and of *A Liberdade*, that began as follows:

> California is pretty, California is beautiful!
> Of North America, the most brilliant star.
> Land of promise, terrestrial paradise,
> Dream of nature, angelic smile!
> Shrouded in mists for centuries,
> Waiting for a celestial, divine light,
> To guide Captain Cabrilho to its shores,
> And upon her shed a dazzling brilliance![31]

For Joaquim Rodrigues da Silva Leite, editor of *Portugália* and the *Cabrillo Commentator* and literary editor of *A Revista Portuguêsa*, "it is difficult to find another name in history that contains within itself as many expressions of the most beautiful qualities of the Portuguese race as that of Cabrilho."[32]

There is evidence that another Portuguese navigator of Azorean origin, João Corte Real, explored the regions of Labrador and Newfoundland in the beginning of the sixteenth century. Although there is no information on whether he came ashore in the territory now belonging to the United States, it is believed that he was shipwrecked somewhere along the American East Coast. The discovery of Dighton Rock in Berkley, Massachusetts, on which American researcher Edmund Delabarre believed he had found inscriptions relating to the Portuguese navigator, one of them being the date 1511, sparked a long and controversial debate that was widely discussed in the Portuguese-American media.[33] If Delabarre's findings were correct, then they would provide evidence that the East Coast was explored by a Portuguese.[34] Coverage of this issue by the Portuguese-American press raised interest in the history of the Portuguese in the United States and was fundamental in the founding and promotion of the museum that the State of Massachusetts created to house the rock, a replica of which is kept in the Museu da Marinha in Lisbon.

There were other legendary episodes in the history of the colonization of North America that the Portuguese-American press has used to forge an identity for the Portuguese ethnic community in the United States. Among those, special attention was paid to the life of Peter Francisco, a heroic soldier in the American War of Independence, referred to as "The Giant of the Revolution" by the literature of the time. Although George Monteiro's research questions the Portuguese origin of this historical leader and the mythological discourse around his figure,[35] some people believe that Peter Francisco was born on the island of Terceira, Azores, on June 23, 1760, and that at the age of five, he was abandoned at the wharf in City Point, Virginia, by the captain of a Portuguese ship heading to Brazil.[36] The young boy was adopted by a local judge who thought that he had established his origin and name, Pedro Francisco, and tried to contact his parents by letter but never received a reply. In 1777, at the age of 16, Peter Francisco joined the Continental Army in the war against Great Britain. Peter's bravery earned him public recognition from George Washington, who highlighted Peter as a hero among heroes by noting that "Without him, we would have lost two crucial battles, perhaps the war, and with it our freedom."[37] Based on this portrayal he has become one of the most popular military figures of the American Revolution and part of the patriotic mythology of the United States.[38] There is even a Society of Descendants of Peter Francisco, which has managed to build his complete family tree.[39]

The Portuguese-American press played an important role in asserting the Portuguese origin of Peter Francisco, which had been excluded from many of the official American accounts.[40] In 1926, Vasco de Sousa Jardim, a Portuguese journalist living in Fall River, Massachusetts, and Augusto Furtado, a priest from Somerset, Massachusetts, in collaboration with the magazine *American Legion*, organized a campaign to raise awareness about the origin of Peter Francisco among Portuguese immigrants.[41] Years later, Attorney

Edmund Dinis of New Bedford and the Portuguese Continental Union of Boston created an award, "The Peter Francisco Medal," to recognize people who distinguished themselves in the promotion of Portugal and its culture. Among the recipients were John F. Kennedy (President of the United States), Basil Brewer (owner of the *Standard Times*, New Bedford), Joseph Martin (Speaker of the House of Representatives during the presidencies of Harry S. Truman and Dwight D. Eisenhower), John dos Passos (writer of Portuguese descent), João R. Rocha (director and owner of *Diario de Noticias*), and Aníbal Branco (editor of *O Independente*).

In Newark, NJ, the newspaper *Luso-Americano* and the Portuguese-American Scholarship Foundation developed a successful campaign to name the urban triangle between Ferry Street, Edison Place, and Railroad Avenue, where many Portuguese reside, as Peter Francisco Park. The project was completed in 1976 with the unveiling of an obelisk in honor of the Portuguese-American hero in his eponymous square.[42] In 1953, the governor of Massachusetts, Christian A. Herter, designated March 15 as Peter Francisco Day and on March 12, 1954, Arthur R. Harriman, the mayor of New Bedford, made an official proclamation (published in the Portuguese press) ordering that the Portuguese flag be raised alongside the American flag at City Hall in honor of Peter Francisco and the Portuguese-American community.[43]

Portuguese Immigration and the Establishment of the Portuguese-American Community

Throughout the late nineteenth century and the first decades of the twentieth century, Brazil and the United States were the preferred destinations for Portuguese emigration, with Brazil receiving the lion's share. Between 1880 and 1959, according to the Brazilian Institute of Geography and Statistics, 1,529,851 Portuguese entered Brazil, while during roughly the same period (1870 to 1950) 258,892 settled in the United States.[44] In the first case, knowledge of the language, common culture, social networks, and symbols of the colonial past were crucial in attracting emigration from Portugal. Still, cultural differences between Portugal and the United States notwithstanding, during this period other factors made North America an attractive destination. Top among these were the opportunities that the United States offered as a new "promised land" and the recruitment of Azorean crewmembers for the American whaling industry.[45]

According to the Observatory of Portuguese Emigration, the flow of emigration from Portugal to the United States can be divided into five historical periods. The first took place during the latter part of the eighteenth century, from the Azores to New England; the second occurred in the second half of the nineteenth century, also from the Azores, with California as the main destination; the third happened at the turn of the twentieth century, and involved primarily the movement of families from Madeira to Hawaii; the fourth took place in the first decades of the twentieth century, when more than 147,000 Portuguese entered the United States; and the fifth and last was the great wave that occurred between 1960 and 1980, and comprised around 175,000 migrants.[46] Since then, as shown in Figure 1, which is based on data from the *Yearbook of Immigration Statistics 2012*, [47] there has been a considerable decline in migratory flows. The decline is a result of the adoption of restrictive policies by the United States and the entrance of Portugal into the European Union in 1986, which encouraged greater migration within Europe.

By the second half of the twentieth century, Canada also began to attract significant numbers of Portuguese immigrants, as did Venezuela and Argentina, principally after the Second World War.[48] Marcelo J. Borges's *Chains of Gold: Portuguese Migration to Argentina in Transatlantic Perspective* provides a detailed demographic and socioeconomic analysis of the characteristics of Portuguese immigrants to Argentina, who originated mainly from the Algarve and Beira Alta regions. The arrival of these immigrants extended from the time of Spanish colonization to the first half of the twentieth century.[49] In fact, as Jose C. Moya has shown, the Portuguese at one point were Argentina's second largest group of immigrants, after the Spaniards, who themselves came mainly from Galicia,[50] an Atlantic region that borders Portugal.[51]

Currently, the United States is, along with Brazil, France, and Switzerland, one of the countries with the largest number of Portuguese immigrants, although in the case of the two European countries the history of Portuguese emigration is much more recent. According to data from 2017, there are around 600,000 natives of Portugal residing in France; over 220,000 in Switzerland, nearly 170,000 in Brazil, and close to 148,000 in the United States.[52]

Figure 1 Portuguese Immigrants Entering the United States by Decade

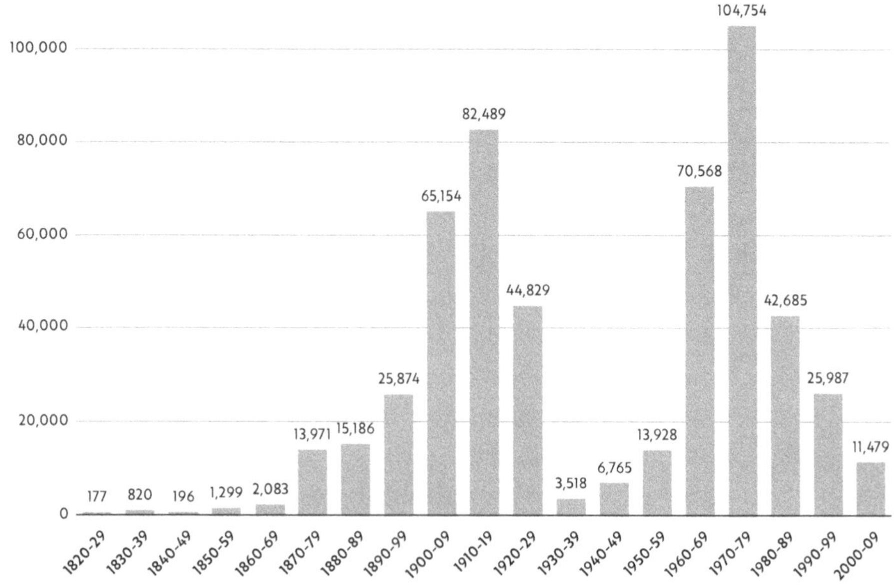

Source: Based on Data from the *Yearbook of Immigration Statistics 2012*

In this country, most Portuguese immigrants and their descendants are concentrated within a handful of regions and states. According to data from the United States Census Bureau, around 37% of immigrants born in Portugal live in the New England Region, mainly in Massachusetts. Another 37% reside in the Mid-Atlantic Region, mostly in New Jersey and New York. Of the remainder, 15% are established in the Pacific Region, primarily in California and Hawaii.[53] It should also be noted that about 60% of the Portuguese-American population lives in Massachusetts and California, though their presence extends, albeit in a reduced way, to all states, with a total population of about 1.5 million people.[54]

According to Leo Pap,[55] the first Portuguese communities in America date to 1640, when Jewish groups of Portuguese origin settled in New Amsterdam (now New York). Subsequently, contact between the American and Portuguese whaling industries led to the arrival of an increasing number of Azoreans in the mid-nineteenth century, as documented by Donald Warrin[56] and by

David Bertão.[57] This flow of immigrants increased in subsequent decades, reaching its height between 1900 and 1920, a period that includes more than half of the total number of immigrants arriving between 1870 and 1930.[58]

The development of the textile industry in New Bedford, Fall River, and other mill towns in the states of Massachusetts and Rhode Island was the major attraction for this mass migration, which, though composed primarily of Azoreans, also included significant numbers of people from mainland Portugal and Madeira. The general causes of this exodus were the general lack of economic resources, including farmland, and, especially in the case of the Azores, overpopulation.[59] Shipping companies also played a role, as some tried to increase their business by advertising tickets to the United States in local European newspapers.[60] Their advertisements promised comforts and conveniences, including the possibility of reaching the West Coast by rail from port cities along the Eastern seaboard.[61]

From 1850 onwards, Portuguese immigrants began to arrive in California, settling in San Francisco and in the southern areas of the state, where there was intense agricultural activity.[62] In these areas, they established agricultural enterprises, including produce, livestock, and dairy farms, which would become quite successful. During the last quarter of the twentieth century, these businesses came to control about half of the milk production in California and, to this day, are still part of the social fabric of the Portuguese-American community of California.[63] Many others gravitated toward the fishing industry, working on ships that had their mooring along the California and New England coasts, especially in New Bedford, which has historically been the fishing port of reference in Massachusetts.[64]

Between 1880 and 1900, a large contingent of Portuguese immigrants from the Azores and Madeira arrived in Hawaii, some in whaling ships and others attracted by campaigns recruiting Europeans to work on the sugar plantations.[65] On May 5, 1882, the governments of Hawaii and Portugal signed the *Provisional Convention Between Portugal and the Hawaiian Islands*, which established a legal framework for economic and commercial exchanges between the two countries, protecting and encouraging the arrival of new Portuguese workers.[66] The majority of them established residence in Honolulu, on the main island, in the neighborhoods of Punchbowl and Kaka'ako. Other groups settled in various parts of Kauai and the Kona district on the island of Hawaii. Gradually, the Portuguese were integrated into the local community, opening small business and farms and introducing butter, sweet bread (now called "Hawaiian bread") and the ukulele to the islands. [67] Harsh working conditions and feelings of isolation in the Hawaiian plantations led some Portuguese to found newspapers in order to defend their interests and strengthen their sense of community.[68]

As indicated in Figure I, the 1930s saw the lowest number of Portuguese immigrants enter the United States since the 1860s, when 2,083 immigrants arrived. In 1920, when American authorities prepared a census of the ethnic origins of its mainland population, 105,000 whites of foreign birth reported Portuguese as their mother tongue. By 1940, according to Pap, that number had decreased to 84,000. Although it is estimated that about a quarter of the nearly 250,000 Portuguese immigrants (the majority Azoreans) that settled in the United States between 1870 and 1921 returned to Portugal at some point, the decline was mostly the result of the immigration quota laws passed in the 1920s, which reduced the number of visas allotted to Portugal to 440 per year[69] and caused a forty-year hiatus in Portuguese immigration. Because of this interruption of the migratory flow, the 1930s are an especially interesting decade as it offers a portrait of the Portuguese community almost halfway through its migratory trajectory, between the two decades during which the largest number of immigrants arrived—the 1910s and the 1970s, with 82,489 and 104,754, respectively (Figure I).

Data from the Portuguese Embassy in the United States shows that in 1930 the Portuguese-American community consisted of 376,893 people, with approximately 150,000 of them residing in Massachusetts and Rhode Island, 20,000 in the New York City area, and 100,000 in California. The breakdown of the report is as follows: Portuguese immigrants, 118,242; children of immigrants, 159,863; grandchildren of immigrants, 45,000; newcomers, 26,000; and residents of Hawaii, 27,588.[70]

A similar report prepared by the consul of Portugal in San Francisco stated that there were 36,029 natives of Portugal living in California, of whom 22,695 originated in continental Portugal, 12,700 in the Azores, and 134 in Madeira.[71] In the case of Hawaii, the figure was 13,870, with 7,165 living in Honolulu. These data can be compared to the figures provided by Luís da Câmara Pina of the Institute of Military Studies in Lisbon in his *Dever de Portugal para com as Comunidades Lusíadas da América do Norte* (1945).[72] Based on data from the Ministry of Foreign Affairs and from the National Institute of Statistics of Portugal, he estimated that in 1930 the Portuguese-American community totaled approximately 465,000 individuals, when counting three generations: Portuguese immigrants, their children, and their grandchildren.[73] Pina's work was officially presented before the single-party congress of the Estado Novo regime, the National Union.[74] His objective was to document the social and economic value of the Portuguese community in the United States. "The associative life of the Portuguese in America is intense and profitable," Pina points out in his report.[75] He highlights the existence of 140 recreational associations in New England, along with mutual aid societies, with $5.5 million in capital in 1939, and total profits of $600,000.[76] In California, he went on to inform the congress, much of the economic activity of the Portuguese was concentrated in milk production. In 1937, according to his data, about 450,000 of the 1,128,208 cows in the state of California belonged to the Portuguese, with a total market value of $30,237,500.[77] Pina depicts the economic success of the Portuguese-American community as a collective triumph:

> This is a mass of people, a group, that is advancing, that is, improving. We are not talking about outstanding individual successes, of this one or that one making it big in the American scene. This is a story about the honest and orderly life of half a million Portuguese who are not enslaved by money, and who, perhaps unknowingly, provide a magnificent example of human dignity... They are gainfully employed in a wide variety of occupations. They hold positions in administration, public services, and even in politics. They run businesses and lead industries. In short, they have attained a measure of prosperity that grants them a safe and carefree middle-class status.[78]

Although the Portuguese community had always shown the capacity for economic success and, compared to Portugal, might be doing well, its overall economic situation in the 1930s was difficult, owing to the financial crisis that then afflicted the United States.[79] In New Bedford, for example, the closing of textile mills in the late 1920s had forced thousands to return to Portugal or move to other parts of North America.[80] António Ferro, a Portuguese intellectual who visited New England and California in 1927 and later became director of the Office of National Propaganda of the Estado Novo regime,[81] noted the difficulties faced by Portuguese-Americans at the time. In an article published in Oakland's *A Colonia Portuguesa* on December 17, 1927, he attributes the problem to the excessive number of cotton mills and competition from new textiles in the international market. However, what Ferro laments most is the "crisis of the community," caused by the new immigration restrictions:

> The Portuguese of New England don't give up nor do they let themselves be defeated by the economic crisis. Some head to California, others to Newark, others choose a new way of life. They find employment in radio equipment factories, in automobile factories, in Boston shoe factories... In America, there is a solution for every crisis. But the worst crisis is the crisis of the community itself, the immigration law that so drastically reduced our immigration quota... The Portuguese community, all communities, especially those of Latin origin, are doomed to disappear. Only the future will tell whether the United States will not also suffer because of this unjust decision.[82]

As predicted by Ferro, following the passage of the National Origins Act of 1924, immigration flows were severely curtailed. In April 1935, the *Diario de Noticias*, citing official American statistics, stated that the arrival of new immigrants in the New Bedford area had been "insignificant." But it added that there had been no great exodus of immigrants to their countries of origin and that the Portuguese were still the largest ethnic group there. According to the article, the city had a total of 112,000 inhabitants (108,000 white and 4,000 black), with the white population being made up of 25,000 Americans, 26,000 Portuguese, 22,000 French Canadians, 17,000 English, 8,000 Poles, and 8,000 from other backgrounds.[83]

During the Depression, the press was affected by a decline in the number of readers and a significant increase in the price of paper. Some print media were forced to downsize in order to reduce costs, while others had to close altogether.[84] In Massachusetts, for example, of the twenty-three Portuguese newspapers founded in the 1920s, only six survived into the next decade. In the state of California, however, the number of new titles increased from five to eleven, possibly because the economic situation was more favorable for many of the Portuguese there, especially those working in agriculture. According to the consul of Portugal in San Francisco,

> Given that most of the Portuguese work in agriculture, their life is, therefore, a simple and abundant country life. In California, the Portuguese farmer has distinguished himself by his expertise in cultivating the land, his hard work and his frugality. He can get three crops out of the same land that an American can get only one. He is not wasteful, but he does not deprive himself of the necessities of life. He takes advantage of the means at his disposal and lives in clean comfort just like any American farmer. Moreover, his recognized qualities of adaptability and self-esteem ensure that his standard of living is not lower than that of other races.[85]

Based on the report, agricultural workers in California in the 1930s made about $50 a month, with room and board, dairy workers $150, cashiers and clerks between $90 and $175, seamen $45, river fishermen $120, laborers three to five dollars a day, and dockworkers 80 cents per hour.

Although job opportunities on the East Coast were not as good as in California, average salary ranges were similar. According to the consul of Portugal in New Bedford, in 1934 a Portuguese immigrant could earn, on average, $15 a week in the cotton textile industry. Most lived in rental houses and paid an average of three dollars a week in rent, which included running water, gas, and, in most cases, coal or oil heat. Regarding their physical appearance and dress, the Portuguese diplomat pointed out that, "Hygienic conditions are good. As far as clothing, both women and men dress normally; suits and dresses have the same cut and appearance as those of the wealthier classes, with the only difference being the quality of the fabric."[86]

As reported by Xara Brazil Rodrigues, consul of Portugal in Boston, in 1934, according to the records of the consulates in New England, 80% of those registered were operators and workers in the textile factories, workshops, or agriculture, "in conformity with their limited education."[87] Further evidence that the majority of Portuguese immigrants were factory or unskilled workers is given in Table 2, which is based on data from the Portuguese consulate in Boston.

Table 2. Occupational Distribution of the Portuguese in Massachusetts (1934)

	Boston	New Bedford	Fall River	Providence	Total
Factory Workers	203	605	428	625	1,861
Laborers	409	202	41	260	912
Merchants	1	5	7	10	23
Industrialists	53	-	10	37	100
Property Owners	5	-	21	29	55
Professionals	3	6	2	2	13
Mariners	73	26	8	17	124
Housewives	18	156	42	131	347
Other	15	-	2	-	17
Total	780	1000	561	1,111	3,452

Source: Consulate of Portugal in Boston. Diplomatic Historical Archive of Lisbon.[88]

In 1934, according to this source, 1,861 of the 3,452 individuals registered, or over 50 percent, were factory workers. Conversely, the number of merchants and industrialists was relatively small. At this time, the Portuguese community's main commercial and industrial establishments in New England were found in New Bedford and Fall River due to the higher concentration of Portuguese immigrants in these cities.

In 1935, according to consular records, there were 7,504 Portuguese immigrants residing in New York and 4,566 in New Jersey. The Consul General of Portugal in New York, whose jurisdiction contained twenty-five American states, drew an interesting anthropological profile of Portuguese immigrants in the area:

With regard to living conditions and clothing, we could repeat what was stated in our report of 1929. That is to say, that they do not differ significantly from other groups, Southern European or otherwise. There are examples of clean, airy, Portuguese homes, with comforts unknown to many members of the higher classes in Portugal. It is above all among the Portuguese with family in the two states that we describe in more detail, and among those born in the U.S., that this is the case. One should not, however, fail to point out that the opposite is also true among many who live in less favorable conditions, either as a result of the spirit of forced savings that leads them to put away as much as they can in order to return to the homeland, or because of the lack of habits of comfort and hygiene. It is not uncommon to see a group of three or four individuals sharing the same room, living under conditions of unhealthy overcrowding and lack of privacy. With regard to apparel, the Portuguese always wear decent clothes and shoes. As for food, unless he is unemployed, in which case the inns ("Casas de Bordo" as they are called by distortion of the English "boarding-house") usually extend them credit, the immigrant is well fed. There are no Portuguese businesses in the area close to the General Consulate. There are, however, some establishments managed by Portuguese and Luso-Americans, especially restaurants, guesthouses, grocery stores, delicatessens, coal shops, florists, dairies and fish markets.[89]

As the foregoing paragraphs indicate, after an initial period of massive immigration at the beginning of the twentieth century, which was followed by immigration restrictions and an economic crisis, the Portuguese community had consolidated its presence in the United States, both on the East and the West Coast. Portuguese immigrants and their descendants became part of the social and economic structure of the country, while maintaining their own social and cultural identity, which were promoted and protected by a variety of clubs and associations. Documents from the Portuguese Embassy in Washington, stored in the Diplomatic Historical Archive of Lisbon, include dozens of reports about the organizations created by the Portuguese immigrants in the United States. An in-depth analysis of them would require a separate study, but their propagandistic role in favor of the preservation of the Portuguese language and culture was significant. An example of this, from outside Massachusetts and California, where there were dozens of such associations and clubs, was the Club Social Português de Yonkers in New York, which had close to one hundred members in January 1934. As indicated in its bylaws, language was one of the essential marks of Portuguese identity and, therefore, central to the club's mission, which was:

> To bring together persons of Portuguese birth and those of Portuguese origin, making them a strong, respected, and prestigious community, using Portuguese as the official language, while respecting the constituted powers of Our Dear Homeland and those of the country in which we live.[90]

During the historic visit of Cardinal Manuel Gonçalves Cerejeira to New England in September 1936, the consul of Portugal in Boston, Euclides da Costa Goulart, lamented publicly "the fact that the community had stopped growing for lack of new blood coming from the homeland to reinvigorate it."[91] However, in that same year, 120,000 individuals born in the United States acknowledged Portuguese as their mother tongue. This, suggested Leo Pap, means that, if we include the parents, between 120,000 and approximately 200,000 people residing in the United States (excluding those of Cabo Verdean origin and those residing in Hawaii) used Portuguese as their daily language.[92] This explains why, on the whole, the founding of newspapers in the 1930s (27) went on at about the same rate as in the previous decade (34). Nevertheless, in the 1940s only three new newspapers emerged, and this trend would continue until the 1960s. But, despite the economic crisis and the immigration restrictions in the 1930s and 1940s, the Portuguese were becoming economically and socially integrated while maintaining their ethnic culture.

Between 1880 and 1930, the Portuguese-American community founded 100 newspapers, almost two-thirds of the 167 titles considered in this study (see Appendix A). The abundance of newspapers at this time is paralleled by the number of fraternal and other ethnic organizations. On November 10, 1933, the Office of National Propaganda (SPN) solicited from the embassy in Washington a complete list of the "societies, associations or clubs of any kind" created by the Portuguese in the United States, with data regarding their political tendencies and the characteristics of their members. According to that report, in 1934 there were eighty-six clubs, six newspapers, nineteen parishes, three schools, one library, and thirty-eight mutual aid societies, charitable organizations, religious, work-related or other types of associations. In New England alone, around 15,000 Portuguese and their descendants were members of an institution related to the community.[93] In this region, the Portuguese could read *O Popular, Diario de Noticias, O Colonial, O Independente, Novidades,* and *A Voz da Colonia.* Between New York and New Jersey, there were fifteen institutions affiliated with the community and two newspapers, *O Portugal* and *A Tribuna.*[94] California was home to eleven associations, almost all fraternal organizations, as well as six clubs and six newspapers: *A União Portuguesa, A Liberdade, Jornal Português, O Portugal, O Progresso,* and *O Clarim.* In Hawaii, there were only three institutions, all charities, with no newspaper in circulation by this point in time, due to the closure of the last newspaper published in the archipelago, *O Facho,* in 1927.[95]

Changes in American immigration policy in the 1950s and 1960s encouraged a new wave of Portuguese immigration. First, the eruptions of the Capelinhos volcano on the island of Faial, which occurred between September 27, 1957, and October 24, 1958, led to the passage of the Azorean Refugee Act of 1958, which allowed for the entrance of thousands of immigrants from the Azores, outside of the Portuguese national quota.[96] Then in 1965, the Immigration and Nationality Act abolished the quota system, precipitating another increase in Portuguese immigration. In 1967, as a result of these developments, Portugal was the country with the fourth highest number of immigrants entering the United States.[97] In 1990, according to a brief from the United States Census Bureau, 429,860 individuals spoke Portuguese at home.[98]

This new wave of immigration gave a boost to the publishing of Portuguese-American newspapers, which had decreased between 1940 and 1960 (with only five newspapers founded) as a result of a lack of new readers. The high point for newspaper production occurred in the 1970s, with fifteen new titles, the majority published in New England. The increase in readership supported not only the several papers created in the 1970s, such as the *Portuguese Times* (founded in Newark and then moved to New Bedford) and

A Tribuna Portuguesa (founded in 1979 in San José, but now published out of Modesto), but also older ones like the historic *Luso-Americano* (created in 1928 in Newark and reestablished there in 1939) and the *Diario de Noticias* (established in New Bedford in 1919 as *A Alvorada*). In 1973, however, with the death of its owner and director, João Rodrigues Rocha, the *Diario de Noticias*, the flagship of the Portuguese-American press on the East Coast, ceased publication. In the last two decades of the twentieth century (1980-1999), a total of eleven new newspapers were founded, but as the flow of immigrants dwindled, so did the growth of the Portuguese ethnic press with only three new papers founded since 2000.

Language, Journalism, and "Consular Regionalism"

Rates of illiteracy are an important factor to keep in mind when attempting to understand the history of Portuguese Americans.[99] The official reports of American immigration studied by Pap indicate that almost 70% of Portuguese immigrants above the age of fourteen who arrived between 1899 and 1910 were illiterate, including Guilherme Machado Luiz, who would found the illustrious *Diario de Noticias*. This statistic placed the Portuguese at the bottom of the literacy scale and was largely a reflection of the situation in Portugal, which had the highest rate of illiteracy in Europe.[100] According to Pap, after the fall of the monarchy and the inauguration of the Republic in 1910, the percentage of illiterate adults dropped to 50% between 1911 and 1917. With the implementation of a mandatory literacy test for immigrants in the United States in 1917 and the improvement of schooling in Portugal, however, the rates of illiteracy among Portuguese immigrants in the United States declined. The rate was further reduced in 1929 when the Portuguese government prohibited the emigration of illiterate persons. Nevertheless, illiteracy clearly represented a problem for the ethnic press, which was also affected by the general tendency of immigrants to adopt English for increased economic opportunity as well as social status.[101]

The topic of the use of the native language by immigrants is a complex one, and a full analysis would have to take into account not only their usage of English and Portuguese, but also the dialects in use among continental and Azorean immigrants, as well as the frequent use of anglicisms that resulted from adapting to a new linguistic context.[102] Reading the Portuguese-American press reveals a language full of neologisms and linguistic traces from English, as well as grammatical mistakes, particularly during the first wave of mass immigration, when editors and publishers had limited access to education.[103]

Technical problems in the printing of newspapers also contributed to the existence of errors. In 1915 *O Lavrador Português* apologized to its readers because the American print-shop they used to put out the newspaper did not have the "ç" symbol.[104] The absence of the cedilla could alter the meaning of certain words, sometimes to humorous effect, such as when the Californian weekly *Jornal Português* reported that Germany had given some "caca" planes to Portugal.[105] Typographical errors, however, were not the only problems that plagued the Portuguese-American press, as pointed out by the New Bedford newspaper *A Era Nova*, in an editorial of January 12, 1924:

> If the Portuguese press in North America were the one and only standard by which the value of the community was assessed, we would be forced to confess, with painful honesty, this community to be the most decadent and backward amongst all those that contribute to the greatness and progress of this powerful nation. With rare and laudable exceptions, the Portuguese newspapers are made up of a badly translated and poorly joined patchwork, in a language that clearly shows it was written by hands that Providence intended more for repairing shoes than for wielding a pen. The beautiful language of Camões and Vieira suffers such mistreatment in these torture chambers, that it looks more repugnantly fistulous than the Leper of Aosta.[106]

In his *A Língua Portuguesa nos Estados Unidos* (based on a consular report and published in 1925), Consul Eduardo de Carvalho argues that the systematic modification of words and the frequent use of Americanisms in the Portuguese spoken by immigrants could make it a distinct dialect. According to Carvalho, this dialect has four main features:

English terms and Americanisms applied to things and objects that the immigrant was unfamiliar with in Portugal; Portuguese terms employed to mean something different from what the original means; English phrases and American idioms translated literally into Portuguese; and the use of English syntax.[107]

Carvalho states that the press plays a paramount role in the development and dissemination of this "neo-language" created by the Portuguese-American community, which could be summed up in the term "portinglês."[108] According to Carvalho, the lack of preparation and professional expertise on the part of the editors in translating from English and in writing in Portuguese contributed to the creation of this new vocabulary. The following cases are taken from Carvalho's catalog of examples: "cometer suicídio" instead of "suicidar-se" for "to commit suicide;" "escola alta" instead of "liceu" for "high school;" "dar um pári" instead of "dar uma festa" for "to give a party;" "Aramesverdes" for "Adamsville;" "Betefete" for "New Bedford;" "Canérica" or "Canériquete" for "Connecticut;" "Mãe-e-filha" for "Mansfield;" "Ai dou nou" instead of "não sei" for "I don't know;" "Não se boda" instead of "não se incomode" for "don't bother;" and "andateca" instead of "casa funerária" for "undertaker."[109]

Moreover, Portuguese immigrants, in their desire to achieve integration and, probably, to avoid stigmatization, seem to have adapted their own names into English at a higher rate than other ethnicities: John for João, Mary for Maria, Tony for António, Perry for Pereira, etc. The *Diario de Noticias* saw this as a lack of appreciation of the values of Portuguese culture.[110] Aware of the problems that the Portuguese language in the United States faced, *A Alvorada* argued in an editorial of December 6, 1926, that there were only two means of preserving the Portuguese language—newspapers and churches:

> We should never forget that our priests also play an important and inescapable role in keeping the love of the language alive. If it weren't for the newspaper and the pulpit, the use of the Portuguese language would have almost disappeared in America. Hence, it is necessary that all reinforce this message and give this issue their utmost attention and commitment in order to prevent the problem from getting worse.[111]

After his diplomatic mission in Boston, Carvalho took stock of his experience in New England and of the situation of the Portuguese community in the United States in a series of epistolary texts, inspired by articles originally published between 1926 and 1927 in *O Colonial*, that were later published in a book entitled *Os Portugueses na Nova Inglaterra* (1931). To some extent, Carvalho may have been trying to settle accounts with the community, which had been critical of the Portuguese consular missions in the United States for their lack of professionalism. The press often felt empowered to tell consuls how to act. As noted by the *Alvorada Diária* on August 26, 1921,

> Everywhere a consul should be fair, just, and tolerant. In America a consul should be all this and more, *energetic, efficient,* and *helpful.* When a Portuguese individual needs any service in a public office in America, he is accustomed to being served at that moment. 'Come back later' or 'come back tomorrow' are sentences that he is no longer accustomed to hearing.[112]

According to Carvalho, the complaints gave rise to what he called "consular regionalism," which he described in the following way:

> So, we are many thousands of Azoreans and we have no Azorean consul? Each regional immigrant community should have its own representative! We are tired of being exploited and bossed around by boys from the Mainland![113]

For Carvalho, irresponsible and unsound journalism should be challenged: "Whenever a newspaper is created for profit and not for the dissemination of ideas, it frequently devolves into an inventor or an exploiter of scandals."[114]

The lack of professional expertise and ethical rigor within journalism caused many confrontations between editors and public officials.[115] The *Jornal Português* of California, for example, was sued on two occasions in the 1970s by the honorary consul of Portugal in Los Angeles for publishing false statements regarding his financial situation, and by the secretary-treasurer of the Portuguese Union of the State of California, who had been wrongly accused of having collaborated with PIDE, the political police of the Portuguese dictatorship.[116] In a 1945 article entitled "Portuguese Newspapers Sued" the *Jornal Português* itself reported all the complaints filed against Portuguese-American newspapers in California, including *A Voz Portugueza*, *A União Portuguesa*, *O Arauto*, and *A Liberdade*.[117]

One of the lawsuits with serious repercussions was filed in 1929 by the consul of Portugal in Providence, Abílio de Oliveira Águas, against the *Diario de Noticias* of New Bedford. Águas sought $50,000 in compensation from the newspaper for alleged defamation in a series of articles that attacked him personally.[118] Águas, who had been dismissed from his position for complaining publicly about the deplorable conditions under which Cabo Verdean immigrants travelled to the United States in boats belonging to a shipping company sponsored by the dictatorship, was the subject of an oppositional campaign by the *Diario*, which justified and applauded the decision of Lisbon's government. "We are not surprised by the news since the behavior of this particular official has long warranted his resignation, despite the bloated importance of his proclaimed patriotism, with which he, on many occasions, tried to win the good graces of those poor in spirit,"[119] stated the newspaper, which went on to add that "The community must certainly still remember what the Portuguese-American press reported about the acts of bad faith and petulance used by Abílio O. Águas in order to get appointed as consul of Portugal in Providence."[120] Although there were demonstrations in support of Águas, demanding his reinstatement, the newspaper attributed this support to his political maneuvers and manipulation of the community.[121] The *Diario de Noticias* referred to the demonstrations as "bluff" and to those who supported the diplomat as a "gang," describing them as a "half dozen individuals of dubious character," and attacking the ex-consul without hesitation:

> The dignity and courage displayed by Mr. Águas in exaggerating the importance of all that takes place around him are indeed remarkable. In his vanity and pretentiousness, Mr. Águas imagined himself momentarily elevated to the summit of high diplomacy. The consular chancery of Providence already seemed to him an embassy that would soon be transferred to Washington. But since all that is nothing more than boastfulness and petulance ends up in ridicule, Mr. Águas was no exception.

Soon the community came to realize that all of the alleged patriotism of the manager of the consular office was nothing more than a scheme to achieve certain ends.[122]

The *Diario de Noticias* justified its animosity toward the diplomat by focusing on his inappropriate public behavior on several occasions. They accused him of having "petulantly" had himself photographed in the port of Providence with 250 boxes of relief aid that the Portuguese of New England had gathered to send to the victims of the earthquake that occurred on August 31, 1926, in Faial, Azores; of promoting a Portuguese business association from which he attacked the "entire consular body" of New England; and of claiming for himself the role of "leader" of the Portuguese-American community.[123] João Rodrigues Rocha, nicknamed "O Rochinha" by other journalists, was one of Águas's main detractors in the *Diario de Noticias*. Rocha penned several articles that questioned his loyalty and commitment to the Portuguese community during the election campaign of October 1929, in which the former consul was an adviser to the Democratic incumbent candidate to the Rhode Island Senate, Peter G. Gerry.[124] In order to thwart the work of his compatriot, Rocha asked the public to vote for the Republican candidate, Jesse H. Metcalf, whom he considered more suitable for defending Portuguese-American interests.[125] Águas sent a letter of protest to the newspaper, which Rocha then included in a response article in which he predicted a resounding victory for the Republican Party, and added that Rocha's accusations against the former consul had been documented. In his letter to the editor, Águas sought to protect the interests of the Democratic candidate from the negative consequences of the attacks on his own personal prestige:

> Your newspaper has persistently attacked me in a way that I choose not to characterize. For better or for worse, I have chosen to remain silent, allowing you to prove in the courts the accusations you have made against me, and allowing the members of the community, where we all are known, to judge for themselves. Were it not for the fact that, in order to target me, you are now starting to attack third parties, I would have remained in that state of muteness typical of those who have a clear

conscience. But since you are now attacking members of the American society, before whom I always tried to make the Portuguese appear dignified and deserving of respect, I feel compelled to speak up and send my protest against the attacks directed at former Senator Peter Goelet Gerry simply because this gentleman has chosen to distinguish me with his friendship.[126]

Rivalries of this type and others that pitted groups or organizations against each other were frequently exploited by newspapers in order to increase their audience. The freedom of the press and the editorial policies of newspaper owners, who struggled to gain a large enough audience in order to subsist, directly or indirectly encouraged these types of dynamics. There was hardly any controversial public issue in the community that was not promptly debated in the Portuguese-American press. However, this situation was not exclusive to the Portuguese-American press; it had been common, historically, among newspapers of other ethnic communities.[127] According to Rhodes, "business or not, the ethnic press transferred the home country rivalries and political disputes to the United States."[128]

Carvalho's report argues that the community was defenseless against newspapers that could attack individuals and institutions without any intervention from the local authorities, who paid little attention to these issues due to their lack of knowledge of the language and of the issues that were uniquely relevant to foreigners. For Carvalho, the only solution for the victims of these defamatory articles, some of which were a product of "vulgar delirium" or journalistic "sadism," was to translate the articles into English and deliver them to the court:

But the majority of the victims would rather be abused than contribute to letting other groups know what the Portuguese, or some of those who call themselves Portuguese, are like. It's like a fight behind closed doors. Nobody calls the police. In the interest of the Motherland, Community and Justice, the author of the article inveighs against the government, the consuls, an association, an initiative, an effort, a colleague who gets a good order or a half-page ad, an individual who committed the crime of becoming rich, admired or otherwise distinguished himself. Never during the periods in which the violent Portuguese press was the most violent did it reach the extremes reached by the pamphleteers of the community, who sometimes appear to suffer from a vulgar delirium, sadism, impropriety.[129]

The harsh accusations of the Portuguese diplomat did not sit well with the Portuguese-American press, but on this occasion, they eschewed controversy. The newspapers of New England responded through an editorial published in the *Diario de Noticias* that accepted the criticism elegantly, calling for unity against division:

> Without much encouragement, the Portuguese have done a lot in this country. They need someone to guide them, not divide them. They need a cohesion campaign that makes them feel the power of their national soul, enabling them to realize all sorts of wonders. That is the feeling responsible for the so-called miraculous enterprising spirit of the Portuguese when outside of their own country. In terms of numbers, we have enough Portuguese to achieve anything—for all kinds of institutions, for all kinds of initiatives. Let's not underestimate these. Let's instead emphasize their moral and material importance and make them the institutions of all Portuguese. Let's call on all of our people to participate in the campaign of our own development and prestige. Let's not fight each other. There is enough room for all projects to come to fruition. Let's openly discuss our problems. Nobody wants mysteries or chiefs. The first cannot be understood and the second cannot be tolerated. Let's recognize the good intentions of everyone, which does not mean that we will blindly accept everything that is presented to us as dogma.[130]

Carvalho, who would later become consul of Portugal in Porto Alegre, Brazil, after passing through Boston, also published *Pregar no Deserto* (1929), in which he called attention to the need to create an international Lusophone lobby that would take advantage of the networks of Portuguese immigrant communities.[131] With a patriotic discourse that sought to bring together all

Portuguese under a common sentiment in defense of the interests of Portugal, Carvalho showed that the major Portuguese communities in Massachusetts, California, New York, and New Jersey, were not just connected to each other, but also to similar communities throughout the world. In his view, isolation was one of the greatest weaknesses of the Portuguese-American community. While acknowledging his lack of objectivity, he argued that his criticisms were intended as an honest contribution to the common cause on behalf of the Portuguese-American community:

> These letters are a work of propaganda and a work of propaganda was never a work of rigorous accuracy and criticism. Honest propaganda does not go outside the Truth, but it has to go outside the narrow confines that facts and men get accustomed to. What our compatriots of the old Boston Consulate are, what they are worth, what they do and what they can do, the excellence of the institutions that they created, the level of improvement that they reached, and the role that they play relative to Portugal and the U.S. would be the topic of a deep and well-thought-out study that I do not have the capacity to write.[132]

Chapter 2

The Dimensions of
the Portuguese Press
in the United States

Quantitative, Chronological,
and Geographical Characteristics

A quantitative, chronological, and geographic approach facilitates an understanding of the extent, sizes, types, and categories of the newspapers published by the immigrant groups that have arrived in the United States. These groups, including Germans, Irish, Italians, French, Chinese, Hispanics, and others, have consistently created their own media as instruments of social cohesion, mutual aid, and as a means of promoting their projects within the same socio-cultural imaginary. Within this context, use of the vernacular language was of crucial importance in order to create a public opinion with its own voice that could resist the dominant mainstream discourse in English and that could make their own ethnic group more visible, while affirming their own cultural traditions and customs.

The journalistic discourse used by ethnic newspapers almost always attempted to strengthen identity and defend common interests, while also maintaining an emotional bond with the country of origin. The German community, for example, the largest in the United States (with about 50 million people, including immigrants and their descendants), founded several hundred journalistic titles, some of which have played an important role in American history. The Portuguese-American community, with around 1.2 million people,[1] has also been active in American ethnic journalism, especially during periods of higher immigration. The following aspects are perhaps the most characteristic of the Portuguese-American press: 1) it is a press created by persons of Portuguese origin, with a few exceptions from Brazil and Cabo Verde; 2) the majority of the founders and editors come from one particular region of Portugal—the Azores; 3) despite having a special interest in information concerning Azorean issues, it is a press that displays universal coverage with news related to Africa, Asia, America, Oceania, and, of course, Europe; 4) the concentration of Portuguese immigrants in Massachusetts, California, and Hawaii gave the press broad territorial distribution with its strongest influence on the two coasts.

In 1933, Alexandre Alberto Sousa Pinto of Portugal's Department of Public Education[2] solicited from the owner of the *Diario de Noticias*, Guilherme Machado Luiz, a report on the Portuguese press in North America.[3] Joaquim Borges de Menezes, a native of Terceira who had been the director of several Portuguese media outlets in Massachusetts and California and was, therefore, familiar with the Portuguese journalistic activities on both coasts of the United States, collaborated in the preparation of the document. The report, which was published in full on August 4, 1933, in the *Diario de Noticias,* gives a brief history of the periodicals produced by Portuguese immigrants in American territory[4] and provides valuable information for understanding the impact of the Portuguese-American press, especially at the beginning of this period when newspapers in Portuguese were experiencing difficulties surviving in the United States:

> [Publishing a Portuguese-language newspaper] is a superb, heroic stubbornness. Everything conspires toward its annihilation: the lack of any incentive from the distant homeland to encourage these initiatives; the hostility of the environment in which it takes place, always intent on the task of assimilating newcomers; the rampant illiteracy among the members of the community.[5]

The report emphasizes the sacrifices made by newspaper editors, who worked without any government support under unfavorable circumstances.

This would explain, in part, why the majority of the newspapers founded by Portuguese immigrants had brief lifespans, especially after the restrictions on Portuguese immigration and the financial difficulties of the Great Depression:

> The Portuguese-American community is currently going through an extremely difficult time in the aftermath of the terrible economic crisis that shook up this country and added another dark page to the painful, black tragedy of Portuguese journalistic activity. But the economic crisis itself only made worse a situation that was always precarious, always tempestuous—a seascape where ships were always running aground, falling apart, sinking. Never in the history of the Portuguese community in the U.S. has there been a single journalistic enterprise that was able to accumulate enough resources to keep it going. Their stability and survival is measured by the personal sacrifices of those who attempt them, those who start them. Lacking their own printshops and being written by amateurs and dilettanti, in order to cut expenses, both dailies and lesser publications fall into the maelstrom. These are the conditions under which most of our community newspapers operate.[6]

Several key characteristics were taken into account in order to carry out the quantitative study of Portuguese newspapers in the U.S. The first was geographical distribution, which was subdivided into two categories—states and cities.

As indicated in Table 3, there were ten states with newspapers created by the Portuguese-American community. Since newspaper production was directly related to the arrival and concentration of Portuguese immigrants in different states and cities at particular historical periods, most newspapers were found on the East Coast, especially New England, with Massachusetts and Rhode Island accounting for almost half (75) of the total publications, while California and Hawaii accounted for over one third (61). According to Table 3, the city that gave origin to the highest number of Portuguese-American newspapers was New Bedford, home to at least 38 newspapers. Oakland, CA, and Newark, NJ, had the second and third most, with 16 and 15 titles, respectively.

Table 3. Ranking of Portuguese-American Newspapers by State and City

STATE			CITY		
Ranking	Name	Number	Ranking	Name	Number
1	Massachusetts	68	1	New Bedford, MA	38
2	California	49	2	Oakland, CA	16
3	New Jersey	16	3	Newark, NJ	15
4	Hawaii	12	4	Fall River, MA	12
5	New York	11	5	New York, NY	11
6	Rhode Island	7	6	Honolulu, HI	9
7	Pennsylvania	1	7	San Francisco, CA	7
8	Connecticut	1	8	Cambridge, MA	7
9	Florida	1	9	Boston, MA	5
10	Virginia	1	10	Providence, RI	4
TOTAL		167	TOTAL		124 (of 167)

Source: Calculated by the autor.

As the states with the largest Portuguese populations, Massachusetts and California published the most titles, followed by New Jersey, Hawaii, and New York, although, as can be seen in Table 9 in Appendix B, Hawaii's production was concentrated in the three decades between 1880 and 1910, and that of New York and New Jersey did not start until around 1920 when Portuguese migration to these states experienced a substantial increase.

As can be seen in Table 9 in Appendix B, almost all of the Portuguese newspapers published in the U.S. between 1877 and 1920 were found in Massachusetts, California and Hawaii, with the exception of *O Luso-Brazileiro*, were founded in New York in 1918. With immigration to Hawaii almost coming to an end after the second decade of the twentieth century, no more titles founded in that state. However, on the U.S. mainland, the 1920s and 1930s saw a proliferation of new titles (61). Over one fourth of those (16) were created in states where there had been none (i.e., New Jersey, Rhode Island, and Connecticut) or nearly none (i.e., New York) prior to 1920, but the vast majority were founded in the two states with the largest Portuguese populations—Massachusetts and California. Curiously, though restrictions on Portuguese immigration began to be imposed in 1921, the almost 45,000 immigrants that arrived during that decade (Figure 1) and the influx from previous years provided a sufficient audience to support a number of journalistic projects. In Massachusetts alone, 23 newspapers were founded in the 1920s, most in the city of New Bedford.

After 1940, however, the number of new titles declined significantly. Between 1940 and 1970, a period with nearly no immigration from Portugal, only ten new titles were founded, half of them in New York and New Jersey. By the 1970s, however, with the last wave of Portuguese immigration, 15 new publications were created, with New Jersey accounting for the largest number of these (six). After the 1970s, journalistic production began to dwindle in keeping with declining immigration flows. It is believed that only three significant titles have been founded since 2000.

Table 9 in Appendix B also shows that between 1880 and 1900 eleven titles were created in Massachusetts. This figure parallels that of California, which had twelve newspapers during the same period. Between 1900 and 1930, sixteen titles were created in California, but in the 1920s, in contrast to Massachusetts, only five newspapers were founded. California experienced the highest growth in its history in the 1930s, with eleven new titles. Something similar occurred in New York and New Jersey in the 1930s when nine titles were founded there. This may have been due to the arrival of Portuguese immigrants from other states, such as Massachusetts, where industries which had traditionally employed a large percentage of those immigrants were severely affected by labor strikes and the Great Depression. In subsequent decades, the Portuguese community of California did not reach the same figures for newspaper publications as in the previous years. According to the data, for twenty years, between 1940 and 1960, there were no new Portuguese-American publications in California, and from 1960 until today, there have only been ten new titles.

The reduced number of new immigrants that followed the national origins quota laws of the 1920s and the Great Depression resulted in a decline in journalistic output in the period between 1940 and 1970. An upturn occurs only in the 1970s (with fifteen publications in total) when the second great wave of migration, which began with the departure of Azorean refugees fleeing the volcanic eruptions on the island of Faial toward the end of 1957, brought close to 105,000 Portuguese to the U.S. (Figure 1). During this time, other states such as New Jersey and Rhode Island began to gain prominence, with eleven titles appearing between 1960 and 1980. In the same period, Massachusetts had five new titles, but from 1980 until the present only one new title has been created, the ephemeral artisanal magazine, *Luzonet Magazine* (2002).

As can be seen in Table 9 in Appendix B, the most productive states were those on the Atlantic coast with 107 publications in total. California and Hawaii, the two great centers of the Pacific, had a total of 61 newspapers. Massachusetts and Rhode Island, with their long-standing history of Portuguese immigration and large number of settlers, had the highest number of titles in New England, but New York and New Jersey also experienced a period of significant production during the 1930s. In Connecticut, on the other hand, there is evidence of one newspaper, *O Trabalho* (Danbury, 1939), which lasted one year. Florida and Virginia also had one publication each—the *Portuguese Heritage Journal* (Coral Gables, 1991), which lasted three years, and the magazine *ComunidadesUSA*, which emerged in Manassas, Virginia, in 2006.

When looking at the development of the Portuguese-American press by state, two cases deserve mention—Pennsylvania and Hawaii. Although the presence of Portuguese in Pennsylvania has been a constant throughout the years,[7] journalistic output has been largely symbolic, with evidence of the existence of only one newspaper, *O Jornal de Noticias* (1877), which emerged in Erie in the nineteenth century. This state, however, has the distinction of being the home of the first Portuguese-American newspaper in U.S. history. But the case that perhaps excites the most curiosity is that of Hawaii, where twelve newspapers were founded, with the majority of them (7) beginning in the 1890s, following the arrival of large numbers of immigrants who were recruited to work in the sugarcane plantations.

While in Hawaii and California the Portuguese worked primarily in agriculture, elsewhere they were concentrated mainly in the manufacturing sectors of urban areas. In the case of Massachusetts, the city of New Bedford is the main reference point, as more than half (38) of newspapers founded statewide (68) have been based in this city. The other three top cities for most newspaper titles are Fall River (12), Cambridge (7), and Boston (5), though there were editions in Taunton (2), Fairhaven (2), Lowell (1), and Lynn (1). This demonstrates the extraordinary importance New Bedford had in the history of Portuguese immigration, especially during the first great wave at the beginning of the twentieth century. Rhode Island also had multiple cities with newspapers: Providence (3), Bristol (2), Pawtucket (1), and East Providence (1), but newspaper production was also concentrated in New Jersey (16) and New York. In New Jersey, 15 out of the 16 were located in Newark, with the other one in Kearny, and in the state of New York, all eleven titles were based in New York City.

The Portuguese population in California, in contrast to that of the East Coast, is characterized by greater geographic dispersion and rural residence, as a result of its involvement in farming and ranching. But even in California, most newspapers were established in urban areas, such as the San Francisco Bay Area, with Oakland (16), San Francisco (7), and Hayward (5) being the most prominent. San José (4) and San Leandro (4) were also important centers of newspaper activity, but titles were also established in Sacramento (2), Tulare (2), Alameda (1), Tracy (1), Fresno (1), Pleasanton (1), Newark (1), Lemoore (1), and Newman (1). In Hawaii, even though the Portuguese population was involved in agriculture, newspaper production was concentrated in the capital city of Honolulu (6) and in the town of Hilo (3), located on the Big Island.

Circulation, Contents, and Other Elements of Journalistic Production

It is important to know the circulation figures for each newspaper. Although circulation figures do not correspond to the number of readers, since one newspaper can be read by multiple readers, it is useful in estimating the impact of the publication. In the case of the Portuguese-American press, circulation depended on four key factors: 1) the readership that each newspaper was able to create through its professional strategies and commercial policies; 2) the number of potential readers in a particular target area; 3) the price of paper, which could make the marginal cost of each copy so expensive that the printing of additional copies would be unprofitable unless the volume of advertisement grew; and 4) printing technology, as some printing presses did not have the technical capacity to print more than a certain number of copies. Newspapers that wanted to increase circulation in order to boost profits had to invest in their printing facilities. This was the case with New Bedford's *A Alvorada*. After the influx of Portuguese during the 1910s, its owner, Guilherme Machado Luiz, decided to renovate their printing press in August 1922 in order to increase circulation. This forced Luiz to suspend publication for fifteen days,[8] but, ultimately, the investment paid off. With a large contingent of newcomers who wanted to be informed about what was happening in their homelands, especially in the Azores, where the majority came from, sales took off. The success of *A Alvorada* motivated Guilherme Machado Luiz to start a more ambitious newspaper project in 1927—the *Diario de Noticias*. This extraordinary newspaper would become one of the newspapers with the highest circulation figures in the history of the Portuguese-American press, sometimes surpassing 15,000 copies, a figure that was higher than the readership for some contemporary newspapers in Portugal.

A *Colonia Portuguesa* of Oakland, CA, provides another case of technological upgrading for the sake of increasing circulation. After incorporating, the newspaper decided to take a quantum leap by inaugurating a new facility with modern machinery and equipment, which cost them $60,000.[9] On December 16, 1927, the newspaper published a promotional report in English about its modern printing facilities and the changes it had made to improve the paper. The title was "Portuguese Newspaper Enjoys Record Year." According to the report, *A Colonia Portuguesa* considered its new equipment the best among ethnic newspapers in the United States:

> The "Portuguese Colony," the largest foreign language newspaper in California has just finished the greatest year in its history. Gain after gain in circulation and advertising has placed the "Colony" in a commanding position in California newspaperdom. The "Portuguese Colony" is the mouthpiece of more than 200,000 Portuguese in the state of California. Its circulation is greater than all other Portuguese newspapers in

the State. An investment of more than $60,000 in machinery and equipment, in addition to many thousands of dollars' worth of other assets, makes the "Colony" plant the finest equipped of its kind in America. The Portuguese Colony Inc. has never failed to pay a stock dividend, and all departments have been consistent moneymakers.[10]

Whether or not the claims of *A Colonia Portuguesa* are accurate is a question that is difficult to answer. Data about the circulation and impact of this type of press are difficult to obtain, for it requires the cobbling together of different sources that do not always yield a very complete or consistent picture.

What is known about the circulation of some historical newspapers comes largely from annual directories designed to guide advertisers in choosing the most appropriate newspapers for marketing their products or services. Some of them, such as the H.W. Kastor & Sons *Newspaper and Magazine Directory* and the Geo P. Rowell & Co. *American Newspaper Directory*, included Portuguese newspaper titles and allow us to glimpse the circulation figures of these publications. Thanks to these directories, we know, for instance, that in 1906 *O Correio Portuguez* of New Bedford had a circulation of 2,500,[11] and that in the same city *O Independente* printed 2,706 copies.[12] In San Francisco, *O Progresso Californiense* claimed a print run of 2,300 in 1887,[13] and *A União Portuguesa*, 4,000.[14] Nelson Chesman & Co's *Newspaper Rate Book 1899: Including a Catalogue of Newspapers and Periodicals in the United States and Canada* credits Oakland's *O Arauto* with a circulation of 5,000 copies.[15] Reportedly, the *Boletim da União Portuguesa do Estado de California* printed 2,500 copies during its first years at the end of the nineteenth century, a number that increased as this fraternal association increased its membership and influence in California.[16] Meanwhile, *Alvorada Diária* claimed to have a circulation of 4,000 copies at the start of 1922[17], right before renewing its printing machinery.

Other sources of data on the Portuguese-American press include reports prepared for the Portuguese government by members of the Portuguese diplomatic corps in the United States. In 1967, for example, in an effort to understand the impact of the Portuguese-American press, the Embassy of Portugal gathered the circulation numbers for every paper and rated them according to their level of identification with government policies. Here are some examples: *Jornal Português*, 7,000, "very good"; *Voz de Portugal*, 6,000, "good"; *Luso-Americano*, 8,000, "very good"; *Novos Rumos*, 5,000, "average"; *A Luta*, 10,000, "very good"; *Diario de Noticias*, 7,000, "good"; and *Familia Luso-Americana*, 750, "exclusively religious."[18]

As for more recent newspapers, according to data from Manoel da Silveira Cardoso, the *Luso-Americano* of Newark distributed 7,400 copies in 1974. This newspaper is currently said to have a circulation that reaches 40,000 readers in New Jersey, New York, Connecticut, Pennsylvania, California, and Florida.[19] One of the more recent newspaper publications in the Portuguese-American community, the ephemeral *Lusitânia News* (2006, Tracy, CA) mentioned in their first issue that they circulated 7,414 copies.

Table 4. Duration of Newspapers

Publication	Number of Years Published
Less than 1 year	43
From 1 to 2 years	29
From 3 to 5 years	11
From 6 to 10 years	19
From 11 to 20 years	17
From 21 to 50 years	13
More than 50 years	5
Unknown	30

Source: Calculated by the author.

Duration, or the lack of it, is another noteworthy factor for Portuguese-American newspapers. As can be observed in Table 4, the majority had an ephemeral existence. Seventy-two of the titles studied lasted less than three years, and forty-three of these never even made it to their first anniversary. The abundance of ephemeral publications is a constant in the American ethnic press, due to the financial difficulties of the editors, their lack of training, and, above all, small and variable audiences. Still, eighteen newspapers lasted for over twenty years. Of these, five exceeded fifty years: the *Luso-Americano* (weekly and biweekly, 74 years); *Jornal Português* (weekly, 65); *União Portuguesa* (weekly, 55); *O Heraldo Portuguez* (biannual and annual, 51), and the *Boletim da U.P.E.C.*, which was published for more than a century. The following newspapers fall in the range of 21 to 50 years: *O Independente* (weekly, 48); *Diario de Noticias* (daily, 46); *O Jornal* (weekly, 49); *Portuguese Times*, (weekly, 48); *As Novidades* (weekly, 41); *A Liberadade* (weekly, 37); *Aurora Evangêlica* (monthly, 30 or more); *A Tribuna Portuguesa* (weekly-fortnightly, 40); *A California Alegre* (weekly and fortnightly, 25); *O Heraldo* (monthly, 23); *The Lusitanian* (monthly, 23); *O Arauto* (weekly, 21); *O Popular* (weekly, 21). It is important to note that the duration of thirty newspapers is unknown, although it stands to reason that most of these would have been ephemeral.[20]

Table 5. Frequency of Publication

Periodicity	Number
Daily	4
Twice a week	1
Weekly	73
Every other week	15
Monthly	38
Three times per month	1
Every three or six months	5
Once a year	4
Single Issue	1
Irregular	4
Unknown	21

Source: Calculated by the author.

Table 5 breaks down the publications by periodicity. Due to the lack of surviving copies, calculating the frequency of publication for many titles included in this study was not an easy task. This was further complicated by publications that had variable periodicity or were published irregularly. For the purpose of elaborating the table, publications that had variable periodicity, such as the *Luso-Americano*, which was initially a weekly and became biweekly after 1988, the type of periodicity with longest duration was used. When it was not possible to track this information, the publication was classified under the periodicity of the first issues.

Due to the aforementioned limitations, the majority of Portuguese-American newspapers were not dailies (Table 5). But since it was difficult to survive economically without regular income, most opted for weekly publication, though in many cases the frequency was irregular. The remainder of the publications studied, many of which were more like magazines, relied on biweekly and monthly publication.

As for the dailies, the *Diario de Noticias* of New Bedford is the most important, as it was published without interruption between 1927 and 1973. Others include *Alvorada* (1919, MA), which was the predecessor of the *Diario de Noticias*; the ephemeral *Portuguese Daily* (1984, RI); and *24 Horas* (1999, NJ), which had its content supplemented by other newspapers from the Portuguese media group Cofina, such as *Correio da Manhã* and *Récord*. Other early daily newspapers include *O Correio Portuguez* (founded in 1895, MA), daily for approximately one month; *O Progresso* (founded in 1907, MA), daily for several weeks; and *A Liberdade* of Oakland, CA, published daily (except on Sundays) during some intervals between 1920 and 1926.

The type of content is another relevant element in the study of ethnic newspapers. Table 6 classifies the 167 newspapers on which this study is based into seven categories, according to the general characteristics of their contents. As can be seen, 72 of the publications, which amounts to about 43 percent, have been classified under the category of "general information" based on the fact that their content is predominantly journalistic. Although the articles and editorial line vary from one newspaper to the other, there is a series of recurrent topics that is common to all, with the following ten being the most important: 1) News of political, social, economic, and cultural events in

Table 6. Type of Contents

Type	Number
General Information	72
Variety	24
Religious	19
Political or Doctrinaire	12
Humorous or Satirical	4
Specialized Information	9
Unknown	27

Source: Calculated by the author.

Portugal. Due to the Azorean origin of most readers and editors, many of the newspapers had specific sections dedicated to news from the nine islands. Those hailing from Madeira also received significant coverage of their homeland. 2) Information related to public events within the community and the lives of Portuguese-Americans, including funerals, obituaries, weddings, business openings, accidents, work conditions, conferences, visits from celebrities, etc. 3) American political issues, especially those with the potential to affect the Portuguese-American community, Portugal, and its colonial empire, particularly issues related to the politics of immigration, education, health care, diplomatic relations with Europe, and Portuguese consular services. 4) Brief news items translated from other media or news agencies that focused on international issues, which could range from a column on a conflict in Africa to a news piece on a natural disaster in Asia. 5) Editorials penned by the editor almost always about controversial issues or topics of concern to the immigrant community, such as the preservation of the Portuguese language and cultural traditions in the United States. 6) Articles written by community members and letters to the editor from readers, which were typically about issues related to integration, Portuguese and American politics, and conflicts that involved institutions, associations, and individuals within the community. 7) Serialized works of literature by a variety of authors. 8) Literary compositions by readers, mainly poems extolling the value of Portuguese identity and culture. 9) Political and commercial advertisements, the majority Portuguese-American, which frequently appealed to Portuguese ethnic identity and solidarity in order to attract voters and clients. 10) *Ad hoc* sections related to campaigns to help members of the community with economic problems, to finance the opening of schools, churches, associations, clubs, etc., or to help compatriots back home in Portugal.

In general, the publications categorized under "variety" were illustrated monthly magazines that published a wide array of material, including literary commentary and articles on current or historical topics or events deemed to be of interest to a broad spectrum of readers. Stories about famous or mythological events and persons related to the history of Portugal were common.

Table 6 also shows that 19 of the titles were labeled "religious." The majority were newspapers founded by Catholic priests or members of other religious confessions in order to create a sense of community, spread moral values, and attract new parishioners to their congregations. The majority were Catholic priests, but there were also various Protestant ministers, especially Evangelicals and Baptists. The category includes general information newspapers founded and directed by editors whose official discourse closely identifies with the values and ideological assumptions of their own religion, such as the Fall River weekly *Novidades* (1907-1948), directed by John Baptista Machado, or the New York weekly founded by Father Joseph Cacella, *A Luta*. However, some publications with a clearly Catholic editorial line, such as the *Jornal Português* from California, are not included in this category because they were neither dependent on nor directly related to any religious institution. Some of the most influential Catholic newspapers were *O Amigo dos Cathólicos* (1888-1896), *Portugal-América* (1922-1923), *A Era Nova* (1923-1924), *O Portugal* (1929-1934), *The Lusitanian* (1932-1955), and *Novos Rumos Estados Unidos* (1961).

Political or doctrinaire newspapers (12) experienced their peak in the 1920s and 1930s, when heated debates erupted among various ideological currents that sought to change the world. The political life of the Portuguese-American community was not immune to anarchism, socialism, communism, fascism, liberalism, republicanism, and monarchism, among other political currents. Communist organizers, for example, played an important role in the Strike of 1928, which involved over 20,000 factory workers in New Bedford[21] and which is said to have contributed to the eventual downfall of the textile industry, where most Portuguese were employed. Some of the more socially committed members of the Portuguese-American community used print media to spread their ideas among their countrymen. Almost all of the newspapers of this type were linked to community institutions that promoted political and propagandistic actions in favor of their own ideology. One of the most prominent of these organizations was the Aliança Liberal Portuguesa of New Bedford, which published two newspapers, *Liberdade* and *A Emancipação*, as well as various manifestos against the Portuguese dictatorship in the 1930s.

Other specialized publications concentrated on a single issue, theme or audience. Some were the official newsletters of institutional organizations, like the *Boletim da U.P.E.C.* of the Portuguese Union of the State of California, but others were geared toward readers interested in particular topics. Among these, there are some that deserve mention. For example, *O Teatro* (1935-1936) was dedicated to informing the public about theatrical performances in the Portuguese-American community and the performing arts in general. Others included *Jornal das Senhoras* (1898) and *Jornal das Damas* (1919) of New Bedford, which were specifically directed at women. Humorous or satirical newspapers also had an audience among Portuguese immigrants. As many as four publications of this type were published, with interesting examples coming from California. These were *A California Alegre*, a weekly that was published irregularly by Cândido da Costa Nunes from Pico between 1915 and 1940 in Lemoore, Tulare, Hanford, Oakland, and Alameda; and the Hayward quarterly *O Companheiro da Alegria* (1961-1977), sometimes sold as a supplement to *A Voz de Portugal*.

"For the Good of the Community": Symbolic Features of Portuguese-American Journalism

As we bring the old *Luso-Americano* back into the ranks of journalism, it is appropriate that, in conformity with established norms, we tell our subscribers and readers what our intentions are or, in other words, what plan we intend to follow. We will fulfill this obligation in a very simple and brief way by stating that our plan is, and will always be, to dedicate our efforts to the development and progress of our community, which will always occupy a place of honor in the columns of our newspaper. This means that we will not put the interests of the few over the interests of the many, just as we will not sell our pens to the dishonest persons or dark interests that may be allowed to thrive among us, as a result of the naïve trust of some or the ill-justified complacency and protection of others. FOR THE GOOD OF THE COMMUNITY shall be our motto and to this goal shall the *Luso-Americano* dedicate itself. This is the plan we have prepared and for whose execution we ask the valuable cooperation of all our fellow countrymen. The Editors.[22]

"For the Good of the Community" was the motto most frequently used by Portuguese-American editors to justify the existence of their newspapers and to emphasize their profound identification with the interests of the Portuguese-American group. This type of rhetoric was not simply a crowd-pleasing commercial strategy. The majority of the editor-founders clearly felt that their business enterprise implied an obligation of public service to the members of the community, who, just like themselves, needed the spiritual nourishment provided by a Portuguese-language newspaper in order to maintain the patriotic flame that was essential to a sense of identity and social cohesion.

Despite this patriotic stance, Portuguese-American journalists were not always well regarded by Portuguese authorities. The freedom with which they could carry out their work, without the censorship commonly practiced in Portugal during the dictatorship period (1926-1974), was not to the liking of some consular representatives of the Portuguese government, who hoped to free the "community" from the "evil influence" of this type of press to which they attributed many of the ills plaguing Portuguese-Americans.[23]

The consuls of Portugal in Massachusetts and Rhode Island (New Bedford, Boston, Fall River, and Providence) tried to fight fire with fire by acquiring *O Independente*, but the plan was not as successful as they had expected.[24] According to Vasco Jardim, the project, which had been designed by Eduardo de Carvalho, was harshly attacked by *O Popular*, then the most widely known Portuguese-American weekly in the United States. *O Popular* had a team of some of the best journalists in the history of the community, such as João R. Rocha, Alberto Botelho, Inácio Santos, S. António Lemos, Affonso Mendes Ferreira, and Jardim himself.[25] Another illustration of the relationship between diplomacy and Portuguese-American journalism is provided by the consul of Portugal in Providence, José Agostinho Oliveira, who was the owner and editor of *Diario de Noticias* between June 1940 and 1943.

Creating a newspaper has never been an easy task, and it is even more difficult when the editor is an immigrant. Among the Portuguese newspapers in the United States, many were very good, and in some cases excellent within the context of the ethnic press, as was the case with the *Diario de Noticias* of New Bedford. But every one of them had a story to tell about effort, achievement, and dignity starring Portuguese individuals who, for various reasons, at one point made what Vamberto A. Freitas called the "quixotic" decision to found a newspaper.[26] Publishing a newspaper required a sustained and coordinated effort, often from people with little or no skills and experience. Although there were some exceptions, these newspapers were usually family-owned businesses based out of homes with two or three employees. The work was arduous and required investing many hours with little return, especially for those unable to secure sufficient advertising revenue.

Portuguese immigrants, like those of other ethnic groups, depended on their own publications for a series of emotional, cultural, political, and economic reasons. Immigrants wanted news about Portugal and about the Portuguese community in the United States, especially regarding the activities of their own associations and cultural organizations. In a sense, newspapers were also a kind of school, the main source of education in this new American life.[27]

António Mariano de Souza, in an article published in the newspaper *Novidades* in California, argued that the main task of the Portuguese-American press was to combat the "evil" of ignorance.[28] Although, on occasion, the cultural level of the immigrants may have been insufficient to understand fully certain types of content, the newspapers were a major stimulus for increasing the level of literacy in the community. Addressing the complaints of diplomats regarding the lack of formal education in the group, *A California Alegre* affirmed in 1937 that the Portuguese in California were "unpolished" because they were there to work; the community was neither cultured nor educated, but was patriotic and had a good heart.[29] *Diario de Noticias* also recognized both the excellent work ethic and the lack of cultural sophistication of the Portuguese immigrant, which was due to "the despicable and scandalous policies taking place in Portugal at the time."[30] Still, the press also pointed out that children of immigrants born in America generally failed to show any interest in learning Portuguese or in policies designed to stimulate an interest in learning. Moreover, speaking Portuguese often produced a feeling of inferiority, even among well-educated immigrants, as argued by the New Bedford daily in an editorial from July 31, 1940: "Ironically, it is the least educated who speak Portuguese the most, a fact that reveals the ridiculous inferiority complex that plagues the majority of those who are cultured or have college degrees."[31]

Nevertheless, it was usually those with some academic preparation who became involved with the Portuguese ethnic press, assuming public leadership roles. As noted by August Mark Vaz,

> Often these foreign publications sought to remind the immigrant that despite hardships and difficulties, and sometimes misunderstandings, he had something to be proud of, a cultural heritage, a history, a name. They did much, these early foreign language papers, to instill in the immigrant a sense of dignity, to lift his standing in the community, to give him self-respect and to remind him of the cultural pattern that had formed him."[32]

The feeling of belonging to the Portuguese community, which supported the Portuguese-language press, was also a factor that strengthened the group's capacity to defend its interests. During his visit to the

Portuguese-American community of California in September 1935, João António de Bianchi, ambassador of Portugal to the U.S. between 1933 and 1947, publicly acknowledged the value of the Portuguese-American press for the progress and dignity of the group:

> In general, the [Portuguese-American] press of California, in addition to the many services it has rendered to several generations of Portuguese, is a repository of the glorious history of the role of the Portuguese people in the stunning development of this prosperous state. Having developed along with the state itself and witnessed the first steps to overcome the barriers of such rapid progress, it contains the history of all life in California. I salute the Portuguese press, which deserves [such recognition] from the Portuguese homeland and from the Portugal of California, for the past that so dignifies it, and I wish it a future full of prosperity. I trust that it will continue its valuable work for the good of the people and the Portuguese nation.[33]

Despite the excellent service that the press provided to the community, this service was not always recognized; quite the contrary. Editors were often forced to demand respect for their work. In general, the only sources of revenue they could count on were the advertisements placed, often reluctantly, by Portuguese immigrants who wanted to promote their small businesses. The Portuguese ethnic press also felt abandoned by the government of Portugal. On November 16, 1938, the *Diario de Noticias* published an extensive editorial that criticized the traditional indifference and contempt of the Portuguese government toward the Portuguese press in the United States:

> Until now, the government of Portugal has completely neglected the Portuguese ethnic press in America. It has neglected, with unforgivable ingratitude, that powerful source of appeal and connection that are indispensable to keeping the love of Portugal alive in the hearts of the Portuguese. This press, although poor, has done a lot to keep the community intact ... What has Portugal done for the Portuguese emigrants who have come here? Absolutely nothing. But it's never too late to rectify an error.[34]

The appeal was well-timed[35] since the dissemination of propaganda in the United States by the Estado Novo was at an all-time high as a result of Portugal's participation in the 1939 World's Fair in New York. Even so, on August 11 of that year, the owner of the *Diario de Noticias* continued to complain about the lack of support and sensitivity on the part of successive Portuguese ministers of public education:

> The greatest fault should be attributed to our Ministers of Education in Portugal who have condemned us to oblivion, and have never rewarded, not even with words of encouragement, the efforts of those who have contributed so much to the promotion of Portugal in this country through the creation of both [Portuguese-language] newspapers and private schools.[36]

Portuguese-American newspapers also resorted to patriotic appeals in order to encourage subscriptions from readers who were frequently late with their payments. The American press, which offered better quality publications—more professional, with more content, and larger distribution—was stiff competition. On April 7, 1936, writing in the *Diario de Noticias*, António F. Cacella lamented that besides "depending on a relatively poor and dispersed community," the Portuguese ethnic press had to "fight against two powerful obstacles, namely: the newspapers of the country, information behemoths that cover all activities worldwide and, what is worse, the indifference of a large portion of the community who deny it the support it is owed."[37] Often editors reminded their readers of the difficulties they had to overcome in order to publish each issue, with lack of financing being one of the main problems that Portuguese-American newspaper businesses had to face. "The making of a newspaper, however small it may be, carries incalculable expenses, expenses that have to be paid," complained *A California Alegre* when readers asked them to continue publishing the popular humor section, "Tia Alegre."[38]

A Luta from New York published an editorial on February 2, 1938 praising the contribution of newspapers on behalf of the Portuguese-American community, calling for "justice" for the work carried out by the editors and criticizing those who did not appreciate the efforts and sacrifices that press workers had to make:

> The Portuguese press is the soul of the community! It announces our festivals, defends the interests of our compatriots, promotes our organizations, publishes news from our homeland, rekindles our patriotism, explores local issues, and communicates to the various Portuuguese settlements the sad news of those who drew their last breath of life in this country, away from the land of their birth. It is also the press that, in fulfilling its sacred obligation to the public, unmasks the cowards who come here to swindle the community. It is the press, in its service to our compatriots, that lends its pages to appeals to help those in need, the sick, and those who have been profoundly wounded by fate's cruelty. It is our newspapers that go from door to door collecting funds for the less fortunate, starting accounts, and otherwise working hand in hand with Charity! We do not ask for honors or excessive profits for the important role we play in the life of the community, but we ask for Justice, Consideration—and COOPERATION! It's time for the Portuguese community to assume its responsibility toward the Press. To shirk that responsibility is anti-patriotic, anti-Portuguese and demoralizing for those who are upholding the cultural values of a people in a foreign land. Research the history of Portuguese language newspapers in this country and you shall find that their publication is an odyssey of sacrifices, sorrows and disappointments, immolated on the altar of the Motherland and the Portuguese Language. And yet, there are fools who make fun of our newspapers, who read them for free and pride themselves in never having paid for a subscription—that insignificant amount that, over the course of a year, is hardly felt by those who spend it.[39]

The usually humorous weekly *A California Alegre* also addressed the matter with all seriousness, characterizing newspaper editors and publishers as "martyrs to the cause of duty and love of the country in which they were born,"[40] in their sacrifice, patriotism, and dedication to the Portuguese "race" and language. An editorial published on May 23, 1936, focused on the lack of commitment from members of the community to their newspapers and their dismissive view of the complex tasks of journalism. "Let them work if they want to eat, says the little mentality of some, as if they, those poor press workers, led an idle, extravagant, and self-indulgent life,"[41] complained the California newspaper, asking for more respect for the editors and their newspapers:

> Our press deserves more esteem and more respect from us, so that civilized people do not take us for savages. We have good Portuguese newspapers in California, and we should subscribe to them and support them for the prestige of our community and the good name of the Portuguese people of this State.[42]

In 1925, *A Colonia Portuguesa* noted that the lack of recognition for the work carried out by newspaper journalists was due primarily to the lack of understanding by a large portion of their countrymen who were incapable of appreciating the service that the Portuguese press was providing to the community, when, in fact, the press was the school of the people:

> Being a journalist is a thankless occupation because our people still do not understand its mission; they see in him, sometimes correctly, someone who makes a living out of criticizing others and tries to foist that work on the reader as if it were the sweat of the brow of a real worker. But no, there is no mission more sublime than that of nourishing the spirit of our people with wholesome reading that, after being digested, will leave behind something of value. The newspaper, with its many sections, must be a school where the people can drink the pure water of human knowledge, gathered and compiled by men who have studied or acquired that knowledge. Unfortunately, they say that there are no newspapers in California that have attained that desideratum. That is true, and the reason is that without the support of the people the newspaper cannot improve because it cannot retain competent staff. [43]

Portuguese immigrants, accustomed to manual labor, were largely unaware of the complex challenges of publishing a newspaper. In order to educate the public, in its 1946 special issue, the *Jornal Português* published an article entitled "O esforço na confecção do 'Jornal Português,'" which explained the disciplined effort that publishing a newspaper requires:

> The subscriber who, at the end of the day, sits down in a comfortable chair to read the newspaper, doesn't know, cannot imagine, has no idea of the effort, the aggravation, the toil of the poor Portuguese journalist in North America. He has no insight into how much pain and struggle were required by the pages that are now before his eyes. This job, my dear countrymen, from acquiring advertisers to the drawing of the illustrations, from the writing of the articles to the revision of the proofs and the pagination of the newspaper, involves an avalanche of willpower, a mountain of sacrifices and hard work, of "hard and tough" work, in the picturesque parlance of our people. And there are still people (Oh, Blessed Ignorance!) who say that if journalists want to eat, they should work![44]

Each paper published by Portuguese immigrants or their descendants represents not just a new business project for those who decide to publish it, but also the strength of the community's public expression, its shared values, identity, and dreams for a better life on American soil, while preserving its ancestral traditions.[45] According to August Mark Vaz, "They encouraged, they scolded, sometimes they quarreled and gossiped—but it was in the familiar tongue and with the familiar phrases and in the quiet of evening that they brought some comfort and encouragement and, above all, remembrance to their readers."[46] In the words of A. de Valverde, it was "por amôr á arte," "for the love of the craft," that the editors of the Portuguese ethnic press privileged the Portuguese language and culture in the United States and encouraged Portuguese-Americans to learn to read the language.[47] Time after time, certain newspapers expressed their desire to serve the community in promotional slogans, which often contained a strong sense of patriotism: "Honra é o lema dos Portuguezes/Honesty is the motto of the Portuguese" (*O Lavrador Portuguez*); "Jornal dedicado aos interesses da colonia portuguesa nos Estados Unidos da América" (Newspaper dedicated to the interests of the Portuguese colony in the United States of America) (*O Novo Mundo*) ; "Pela Pátria e pelo Povo" (For

Country and People) (*A Tribuna*); "A Bem de Portugal, a Bem da Colónia" (For the Good of Portugal, for the Good of the Community) (*A Pátria*) ; "Pela Pátria, Pela Raça" (For the Homeland, for the Race) (*O Portugal*); "Semanário independente ao serviço das comunidades de lingua portuguesa" (Independent Weekly at the Service of Portuguese-speaking Communities) (*The Portuguese Tribune*); "Jornal político e literário dedicado especialmente aos interesses da colónia portugueza de Hawaii" (Political and Literary Newspaper Specifically Dedicated to the Interests of the Portuguese Colony of Hawaii) (*A Sentinella*); "Órgão da Classe Operária Portuguesa no Território de Hawai" (Voice of the Portuguese Working Class in the Hawaiian Territory) (*O Popular*), etc.

The commitment of this type of press to the Portuguese language and values represented an "abraço fraternal" (fraternal embrace) for the popular poet Josefina do Canto e Castro. For her, newspaper staff, like those from the *Diario de Noticias*, were "a handful of poets" who, on a daily basis, wrote "the most beautiful love poem to the Portuguese homeland in the United States."[48] This opinion was shared by the journalist and poet Joaquim de Oliveira, who published a lyrical article entitled "Salvé 'Diario de Noticias' de New Bedford" (Hail to the Diario de Noticias of New Bedord).[49]

Strong patriotic commitment was also a recurring theme in the editorials of the Portuguese ethnic press. Like many others, the *Diario de Noticias* took on the role of representative of the community from the beginning, defending the Portuguese language and culture in the United States, as explained by João R. Rocha in an article published on January 20, 1930:

> Accordingly, we are interested in the existence of this newspaper—the *Diario de Noticias*—for which I work and from which I currently earn my living—because its life and expansion is connected to the name of the Portuguese community in the United States. Since it is the only newspaper in the East to advocate for our collective interests and to defend our rights, its disappearance, which is a matter of years (many or few, it doesn't matter when) will mark the beginning of the end for the Portuguese community in the United States, which is something that we, for all kinds of reasons and motives, must postpone, delay and uninterruptedly fight against until we are incapable of doing so.[50]

Ambassador João António de Bianchi recognized the importance of the Portuguese-American press in strengthening patriotic sentiment among immigrants. However, he also complained that despite the strong emotional bond the Portuguese maintained with their country, the condition of being a foreigner could be an impediment to the achievement of the "American Dream" that they all sought:

> Whenever he can catch a moment with the boss, friend, or neighbor, the following dialogue ensues: "Are you a citizen?" "I am a citizen," says the neophyte who passes from the fear of deportation to the feeling of being a candidate for Mayor of New York or even President of the United States—if not himself, at least his children, who he knows will have a guaranteed education and an "even chance" with the other millions of creatures that surround him and who, having begun life more or less the same way, are able to achieve great positions, through opportunities unparalleled in other countries. When this kind of revolution takes place in his heart, there are situations in everyday life that become difficult to face, like being told that since there are so many unemployed Americans they are unable to hire a foreigner, overcoming the inequalities between American and foreign workers, the barriers to exercising certain professions or going into businesses for themselves without resorting to subterfuge or the participation of Americans, and many other guarantees and opportunities.[51]

In fact, during the worst moments of the Great Depression there was a policy in New York City of rejecting Portuguese workers who were not naturalized, which led the consulate to complain to the local authorities.[52] Despite this, the Consul of Portugal Victor Verdades de Faria stated that there was widespread opposition to naturalization: "It is not usually done easily, not only because of love of the homeland, but also because of the atavistic resistance to acquiring a new language, habits and customs."[53] In California, where, according to the *Jornal Português*, the majority of the members of the community at the end of the 1940s were naturalized, there was conflict between those who had acquired American citizenship and those who preferred not to do so out of loyalty to Portugal. The latter accused the former of treason. In this debate, the *Jornal Português* tried to reduce tensions by claiming in an editorial that "The only true Americans are the Indians:"[54]

> The word "naturalized" or the act of becoming a naturalized U.S. citizen does not have the "black and ugly" or "terrifying" interpretation that it is given in Portugal. A Portuguese who becomes a naturalized citizen protects his civil rights and at the same time becomes useful in the affairs and goals of his community, in the administration of his state and in this great country in general. The United States is a new nation, less than two hundred years old, and was founded by people of different races and creeds, anxious for freedom; and if today it is the world's largest democracy and the richest, it is because of the amalgam that its people form... This is democracy. Rich or poor, their civil rights are equal.[55]

The lack of American citizenship did not impede the Portuguese from founding their own publications, even though most had limited resources and preparation. The lack of writing talent was sometimes replaced by the transcription of news from other newspapers, Portuguese and American. Three things were needed to create a newspaper: an idea, printing equipment, and the ability to write content. The last has always been the most challenging. The editorials in which newspapers offered their views on current issues were one of the elements most appreciated by immigrant readers.

One of the most skilled editorialists was the director of *A Colonia Portuguesa*, Arthur Vieira Ávila, who published hundreds of articles throughout his career. In "Apertos de un editor," Ávila acknowledged how difficult writing editorials could be:

> It's ten o'clock and the paper is going to press. One of the pages is incomplete. It's missing the editorial. Time is lost on various technicalities, the editorial is always the last part of the stew, and, often, the editor finds himself in a labyrinth without an exit, looking for a subject. Write. But write what, in ten or fifteen minutes? Oh! What difficulties the poor editor faces! But something has to be done, since it looks very bad if the

paper goes out without an "in-house article" as it is commonly called. I reach for an American newspaper looking for something sensational. Crimes, divorces, suicides. Good topics, no doubt, but ones that disgusts us to talk about, being what we read mostly about in the papers every day. . . But what the hell am I going to write?[56]

In addition to news about Portugal and the community, one of the most effective ways used by Portuguese-American newspapers to attract readers was the publication of serialized books, which were quite popular. Generally, these were sentimental novels with tragic plots about love stories, legendary heroes or saints. *A Liberdade*, directed by Guilherme Silveira da Glória, was one of the many newspapers that depended on this genre to attract readers. One of its most famous novels was *Florence. A Formosa Rapariga Da Fábrica Condenada Pelos Pecados Doutra. História Verdadeira de Duas Mulheres Parecidas: Uma Anjo e uma Demónio*, which was compiled and published in 1916 in the offices of *A Liberdade* (531 T Street, Sacramento) in four volumes, totaling 1,494 pages. On the back cover, the volumes displayed advertisements of various Portuguese businesses in California: Portuguese Hotel Co., Portuguese Mercantile Co., Ana L. Silveira—Ourives e Relojoeira Portuguesa, and the Portuguese American Bank of San Francisco.

Along with serialized novels, poetry was one of the usual contents of the Portuguese-American press. Guilherme S. Glória stood out in this category as well, since he published his own poems in every issue of his newspaper, eventually collecting them in *Poesias de Guilherme S. Glória*, which was printed at the press of his newspaper.[57] The work was favorably reviewed by the *Diario de Noticias*, which considered Guilherme S. Glória the Portuguese "bard" of California:

> In the POETRY of Guilherme Glória, there are not just feelings, abstract impulses, imperishable traces of a race; through the admirable form of the troubadour pass the details, the people, all aspect of the life of the Portuguese people in these parts. No one has been as gifted by inspiration in portraying the Portuguese soul with such enthusiasm and veneration.[58]

1. Cover of *A Liberdade*.
Copy of July 7, 1934.

However, lack of access to regular publications in Portuguese prompted some groups of immigrants to buy newspapers published in other Romance languages that could be more easily understood by them than English.[59] Thus, when the Spanish and Portuguese immigrant communities lived together in some areas of New York and New Jersey and the Portuguese press had an irregular distribution or insufficient content, newspapers in Spanish attracted Portuguese readers. This behavior irritated the editors of some newspapers of the Portuguese community, who saw in this attitude a kind of anti-patriotic felony, as stated by the *Diario de Noticias* on January 20, 1930:

We do not know to what we should attribute this show of bad taste in some Portuguese of New York and New Jersey. That fellow country-men become naturalized Americans for a variety of justified reasons, we already knew, but that there were also some who desire to be Span-ish, that cries Heavens, everyone!! . . . We do not accept excuses that are senseless, nor justifications which justify nothing. It is a fact known to all that our community newspapers are small and flawed in count-less ways. They lack very, very much. They leave much, much to be desired—according to critics. But these, our newspapers, are a reflec-tion of a small community, enfeebled by multiple and various setbacks. The modern newspaper is the mirror of the environment in which it operates. It reflects both the progress and the advancement of a people, just as it shows its stagnation or decay. How, then, can we demand more from this newspaper, which has only been a burden, an expense, and we might even say a loss, for those who stubbornly insist on publishing it? . . . Despite this small group of "Spanishized Portuguese," who prefer the more attractive table of their slicker neighbor to the poor but nourishing table of their loving mother, the vast majority, the vast entirety, almost all members of the Portuguese community living in the eastern states, support the Portuguese Press. They understand the need to maintain their own means of information, and if they do not do more, it is because they can't, it is because they lack the resources, the means or the condi-tions to do more.[60]

The publication of articles criticizing an institution or member of the community and of sensational news of all kinds was a recurring strategy for attracting new readers, as explained by Eduardo de Carvalho: "Chasing advertisements is not enough to meet the needs and appetites [of community newspapers]. Advertisers, noticing that the newspaper has a reduced circulation, stop giving them money. Readers lose interest . . . There is no other choice but to start a campaign, attract attention with sensational articles, stir up controversy."[61]

In order to attract advertisers, newspapers adorned their front pages with promotional slogans, which sometimes appeared in English, such as "Largest Circulation Guaranteed Among the Portuguese People of Fall River and All New England States" or "We reach a population of 300,000 Portuguese in America, 28,000 in Fall River," both published in *Novidades*. At the same time, they also attempted to get their readers engaged in making the newspaper a success by appealing to ethnic pride and responsibility—"*O Independente* should be read and disseminated by all Portuguese"—and presenting the publication as having an almost official role in the community—"A magazine devoted to the interests of the Portuguese, their descendants and their culture" (*O Mundo Lusíada*).

Despite these efforts, the majority of Portuguese-American newspapers were ephemeral, some lasting no more than a few numbers. Nevertheless, each one of them made a contribution to the advancement of the community. The Portuguese writer and composer Guilherme Pereira da Rosa, who made a business trip to the United States in the 1950s and had the opportunity to get in touch with the Portuguese-American community and their journalistic situation, certainly came to this conclusion. In his impressions of that trip, which were published in a series of articles for Lisbon's newspaper *O Século* and later gathered in a volume entitled *Estados Unidos*, he wrote vividly and poetically about the value of each newspaper, however ephemeral and unappreciated:

> Each newspaper dies every day. As soon as a number is put out, one has to be thinking about putting together the next. The reader glances over the millions of characters contained within its pages, gives them a few minutes of his morning or afternoon, and quickly abandons and forgets

them. Still, the newspaper lived its ephemeral existence, fulfilled its destiny before being swallowed into the vortex of time and events. Its fate is inescapable: king for twenty-four hours.[62]

As the foregoing suggests, newspapers in immigrant communities, as in all communities, must reinvent themselves every day to initiate public debate about issues of concern, to encourage consensus or dissent on certain topics, to portray reality through conscious, critical, and methodical representation, to strengthen their own identity through narratives that share common values, and ultimately to develop common objectives for their community. To succeed at this mission, immigrant publishers need irrepressible ambition, perseverance, energy, and the faith that it is possible to achieve the "American Dream" by producing and selling newspapers.

Pioneer Editors in the Portuguese-American Press

To better understand the role and background of Portuguese-American editors, it is necessary to work with some quantitative data, specifically regarding their geographical origin. From the 167 newspapers studied here, it has been possible to trace the origin of 91 founding owner-editors and 57 of them come from the Azores.[63] We know that 19 newspapers were founded by immigrants from Pico, 13 from São Miguel, 12 from Terceira, 6 from Flores, 3 from Faial, 1 from São Jorge, and 1 from Santa Maria. Two founders can be identified only as "Azorean." The remaining founding editors are from the following areas: continental Portugal, 23; Madeira, 7; Brazil, 2; Cabo Verde, 1; and Italy, 1.[64] The majority of editors from continental Portugal are from Lisbon (9), but other places of origin include Coimbra, Peniche, Ponte de Lima, Chaves, Monção, and Beira Baixa.

Many journalistic projects were the result of the efforts of a single individual (usually male) who developed the project alone or with the help of some family members or collaborators. In the majority of cases, the founders and owners were at the same time the publishers, editors, directors, managers, and printers. During certain periods, especially at the end of the nineteenth and beginning of the twentieth century, the founder was typically a typesetter who eventually became the editor. In working for a publication, they saw the possibility of increasing their income and gaining public influence and power in the community by becoming publishers themselves. Eduardo de Carvalho, the former consul of Portugal in Boston, was very critical of this type of editor, whom he describes as a kind of unscrupulous rogue who casts idealism aside in favor of profit. According to Carvalho, the process of creating a newspaper in the community at the beginning of the twentieth century emerged in a way that had little to do with romantic impulses in favor of Portuguese interests:

> Ordinarily, newspapers have been founded by printers, who, upon arriving in America, found it tedious to work in factories, or by some individuals with the ability to write, but without any special preparation. The two types of individuals put together could perform a very satisfactory job. But having a partner implies sharing profits. For this reason, a printer often works alone. Not knowing how to write, he puts all his efforts into acquiring advertisements. The text—which becomes simply a pretext—consists of stories borrowed at random from the first newspaper from the Continent or the Islands that falls into his hands, as well as letters and articles sent to him by whomever. It is not uncommon that to discourage the owner, an ambitious printer purposely messes up the appearance of the publication or causes administrative difficulties until he decides to leave, handing him the company for pennies. The printer, who was in charge of the printing and was the advertisement agent, becomes the owner, director, administrator, and undisputed head of the publishing company (in America, everything is considered a company or corporation, everything is Co. or Inc.).[65]

From Carvalho's point of view, the content did not always meet journalistic standards, but was subject, on occasion, to a mercenary attitude in the search for the income necessary to the survival of the paper. This was reflected in the commercial policies of some newspapers, which created issues by selling pages of the paper to other editors, making them in effect the owners of that space in exchange for sharing the advertising revenue.

"In a time and in a country in which space and time are incredibly valued, the Portuguese press of New England exhibited a strong sense of practicality and opened vast horizons for the exploitation of the printed page,"[66] Carvalho noted ironically. This commercial policy sometimes caused confusion for readers who could find contradictory opinions and information in the same newspaper. Carvalho explains this in a detailed and comic fashion:

> Just as diverse families and opposing beliefs and interests can be found under the same roof of many homes and offices; just as the most contradictory announcements and the most antagonistic political slogans can be plastered over the same wall or billboard; just as a field can be subdivided into lots in one of which you can dance, in the other play, in another build, in another sing prayers, and in another place a merry-go-round; just as modern life has become, in many ways, variety in uniformity, fraternity in rivalry, and reduced to a department store, where one finds everything from the gramophone needle to Bergsonian theory; so too we have the concentrated newspaper, the panoramic-encyclopedic-eclectic-newspaper, the guesthouse-newspaper, the kaleidoscopic-newspaper, the everything-newspaper, the pan-newspaper, with pages for all styles and all kinds of propaganda. On this point, the journalists of New England have taught a lesson to the journalists of Lisbon. Why can't a newspaper be independent on the first page, democratic-republican on the second, presidential on the third, nationalist on the fourth, constitutional monarchist on the fifth, integralist on the sixth, communist on the seventh, Catholic in one corner, Protestant in the other, Spiritualist before the theater section, Jewish at the end of the financial section, atheist here, freemason there, liberal over there, conservative further down? By doing this it would become—the newspaper from all Portuguese for all Portuguese.[67]

As indicated by the foregoing examples, the Portuguese-American newspaper press was an uncommon way of doing journalism.[68] Typographers, clergymen, doctors, lawyers, and public intellectuals, among others, all took part in its creation and production. Nevertheless, few made this activity their main occupation, not only because of the commercial challenges of the activity, but also because of its enormous professional and moral demands, as Rui A. Correia explains:

> The public exposure that characterizes journalism demands of its practitioners an irreproachable code of conduct. It is understood that a journalist should possess a set of personal characteristics, especially moral ones, above and beyond those of the average citizen. This view cannot be separated from the fact that, in its initial stages, the Portuguese language press in New England owed much to the work of religious groups and the personal efforts of clergymen who used newspapers as way of spreading their Christian message.[69]

They were attracted to an activity that seldom offered great economic benefits but that could offer opportunities for leadership within the community. Journalism could provide the prestige needed to start any type of enterprise within the community, but dependent as it was on the variable volume of individuals who read and advertised in Portuguese, it was a very precarious entrepreneurial activity.

Nevertheless, many newspaper owners, editors, and directors achieved a degree of success that deserves attention. Table 7 provides a list of the individuals that we consider to be the most important founder-owners and editors in the history of the Portuguese-American press, alongside the names of the newspapers they are associated with. The table also provides the editor's place of origin, when that is known and a column for other pertinent information.

Table 7. Selection of Relevant Founders and Editors of the Portuguese-American Press

Name	Place of Origin	Newspapers Associated With (as founders, editors, directors or owners at any time)	Year Founded	Notes
António Maria Vicente	Flores, Azores	O Jornal de Noticias	1877	Typographer
		O Progresso Californiense	1885	
		A União Portugueza	1887	
Manuel Stone	Brazil	A Voz Portugueza	1880	
		A Pátria	1891	
Manuel das Neves Xavier	Madalena, Pico, Azores	A Civilização	1881	Typographer
		Almanach Luso-Americano, Litterario e Recreativo	1884	
		O Novo Mundo	1891	
		O Correio Portuguez	1895	
		Aurora Luzitana	1900	
Manuel de Freitas Martins Trigueiro	Fazenda, Lajes, Flores, Azores	A União Portuguesa	1887	Owner-editor for more than 50 years
Francisco Caetano Borges da Silva	Lagoa, São Miguel, Azores	A Verdade	1893	Protestant minister
		O Progresso	1907	
		Alvorada	1909	
Joaquim Borges de Menezes	Terceira, Azores	A Revista Portugueza	1895	Teacher
		O Amigo dos Cathólicos	1888	
		O Arauto	1896	
		A Semana Portugueza	1903	
Mário Bettencourt da Câmara	Peniche, Portugal	A Chrónica	1895	Pseudonym of Lúcio da Silva Gonçalves
		Boletim da U.P.E.C.	1898	
		Aurora Lusitana	1900	
		A Chrónica Portuguesa	1926	

Name	Place of Origin	Newspapers Associated With (as founders, editors, directors or owners at any time)	Year Founded	Notes
Guilherme Silveira da Glória	Pico, Azores	O Amigo dos Cathólicos	1888	Catholic priest
		A Liberdade	1900	
Pedro Laureano Claudino da Silveira	Flores, Azores	O Arauto	1896	Co-founder with his wife Mary Nunes in the last two newspapers.
		Portugal-América	1905	
		Jornal de Notícias	1917	
		Jornal Português	1932	
Arthur Vieira Ávila	Lajes, Pico, Azores	O Lavrador Portuguez	1912	Co-owner of the Latin American Broadcasting Company
		A Colónia Portugueza	1924	
		Rose and Albert Magazine	1933	
		O Clarim	1934	
		O Portugal da Califórnia	1935	
Manuel B. Quaresma	Pico, Azores	O Amigo dos Cathólicos	1888	Founder of Irmandade do Espírito Santo (IDES)
		O Imparcial	1913	
Joaquim dos Santos Oliveira		O Popular	1914	Poet, son-in-law of João Escobar
		O Mundo	1915	
Cândido da Costa Nunes	Pico, Azores	O Lavrador Portuguez	1912	
		A California Alegre	1915	
		A Pátria	1916	
João Francisco Escobar	São Jorge, Azores	O Correio Portuguez	1895	
		O Progresso	1907	
		O Jornal do Povo	1916	
Guilherme Machado Luiz	Terceira, Azores	Alvorada	1919	Steamship agent and businessman in New Bedford
		Diario de Noticias	1927	

Name	Place of Origin	Newspapers Associated With (as founders, editors, directors or owners at any time)	Year Founded	Notes
Frederico A. Costa	Madeira	O Cosmopolitano	1922	
		O Colonial	1925	
João José Vieira Jr.	Madeira	A Aurora [then Aurora Evangêlica]	1918	Protestant minister
		O Heraldo	1936	
Alfredo Dias da Silva	Santo Amaro, Pico, Azores	O Lavrador Portuguez	1912	
		A Abelha	1924	
		O Progresso	1932	
João Rodrigues Rocha	Ponte de Lima, Portugal	O Independente	1897	
		Portugal-America Portuguesa	1926	
		Diario de Noticias.	1927	
Abílio Maria da Silva Greaves	Faial, Azores	Portugal-América	1922	Catholic priest
		A Cruz	1920s	
Joseph (José) Cacella	Fátima, Portugal	O Portugal	1929	Catholic priest
		A Luta	1936	
Luiz Antunes	Lisboa, Portugal	Luzo-Americano	1928	
		O Comércio Português	1932	
		O Mensageiro	1936	
		A Voz de Portugal	1942	
José Alves Rodrigues	Unknown	O Combate	1934	Notary and owner of the Portuguese Service Agency (N.Y.)
		O Bacamarte	1936	
		A Plebe	1936	
		O País	1950	
Vasco de Sousa Jardim	Madeira	O Vigilante	1915	
		Luso-Americano	1928	
		Esperança	1939	

Name	Place of Origin	Newspapers Associated With (as founders, editors, directors or owners at any time)	Year Founded	Notes
Alberto dos Santos Lemos	Rio de Janeiro, Brazil	Jornal Português	1932	Professional journalist, new owner and editor from 1957
Joseph (José) Capote	Unknown	Novos Mundos	1960	Catholic priest
		Novos Rumos Estados Unidos	1961	
Manuel Augusto Saraiva	Coimbra, Portugal	Portuguese Times	1971	Former archivist in Coimbra
		Almanaque do Emigrante	1970s	
		Factos e Gente	1970s	
José Cerqueira	Unknown	O Cartaz	1977	
		Portuguese News	1978	
João P. Brum	Pico, Azores	The Portuguese Tribune	1979	
		Noticia	1984	
		Portugal-USA	1986	
		Portuguese-American Chronicle	1997	

Source: Calculated by the author.

The biographical profiles compiled here are intended to be representative of Portuguese-American editors, but do not provide complete coverage. Biographical documentation regarding the members of this group is typically sparse and incomplete, but what does exist may suffice to rescue from oblivion the names of those who have contributed to the development of Portuguese-American journalism and the construction of the history of the Portuguese-American community.

Two of the most important figures of Portuguese-American journalism in its initial phase are Manuel das Neves Xavier and António Maria Vicente. Both fit the typographer-editor profile described by Carvalho. Manuel das Neves Xavier published five newspapers, four of which he founded, although all of them were short-lived and one of them was only an annual almanac. Xavier was born on March 28, 1852, in the town of Madalena on the island of Pico in the Azores. At nineteen, he embarked on an American whaling ship and landed in Provincetown, Massachusetts, in 1872. His main collaborator in print work was Miguel Maria Sereque, with whom he shared ownership of Tipografia Xavier & Sereque, based in Boston, where he began printing *A Civilização* in 1881. In order to improve the quality of the style and content of the paper, Xavier entered into a partnership with Manuel Garcia Monteiro, a poet and writer from the island of Faial in the Azores, who also had experience as a typesetter. Monteiro (born in

Horta on June 29, 1859; died in Cambridge, February 7, 1913) was one of the more prominent intellectuals in New England's Portuguese community in the late nineteenth century.[70] He emigrated to the United States to collaborate with the typographer António Maria Vicente on his editorial projects in California, but upon arriving in Boston (aboard the ship *Veronica*) he chose to stay there. Monteiro was already respected in the journalistic and literary circles of the Azores and Lisbon. The popular writer Fialho d'Almeida published an article about him in the literary supplement of Lisbon's *Correio da Manhã* on August 4, 1885, in which he lauds him as "the liveliest of Azoreans, and one of the most refined spirits that we have known."[71] On September 9, 1883, Monteiro founded the weekly *Açoriano* in the Azores, of which he was owner, edi-

2. Portrait of Manuel das Neves Xavier, editor of *A Civilização*

tor, writer, and typographer until he decided to sell his title and business to Jacinto Augusto de Bettencourt. He also founded the literary weekly *O Passatempo* on April 27, 1878, and published two volumes of poetry, *Versos* (Azores, 1884) and *Rimas de Ironia Alegre* (Boston, 1896).[72]

Together, Xavier and Monteiro decided to transfer the *A Civilização* to New Bedford, and give it a new name, *Luzo-Americano*, in an attempt to increase their audience by taking advantage of the large Portuguese population there. Monteiro was aware that his partner did not have the training necessary to edit the content of the newspaper alone, describing him as "a poor devil, deeply religious and honorable,"[73] who had put all of his passion into publishing the newspaper: "Even if he is dying of hunger, he will put all of his resources into it, because the newspaper is his pride and joy, his dream."[74] As a result of disagreements between the two, Xavier sold his interest in the newspaper to Monteiro in October 1884 and decided to open an antique shop. Despite the passion he had shown for the project, Monteiro faulted his partner for his lack of professional commitment:

> It is true, I bought the newspaper because Xavier is such a poor devil without energy, and I was not prepared to work just for him. I have met with difficulties, because the newspaper, as a result of its irregularity, insipid writing, and lack of news articles, did not generate enough subscribers to cover the costs. The *Luzo-Americano* has fallen into discredit and in order to raise its reputation among these generally ignorant and unsophisticated people, it will take some time; but I have hope for good results.[75]

Monteiro took on the responsibility of contributing to the "intellectual development" of the community through his newspaper, but he was pessimistic because his countrymen preferred news and gossip to modern ideas, which, he concluded, should be provided "in small doses."[76] In 1885, his dream of becoming a successful editor was dashed by his inability to continue publishing the newspaper in New Bedford. He had to return to Boston to work as a typesetter for the *Boston Herald*, while he studied medicine at the University of Baltimore (from which he graduated in 1890)[77] and continued to write poems for newspapers in the Azores and Lisbon.[78] In a letter sent to a friend on June 12, 1885, Monteiro expressed his frustration with his journalistic experience in the United States and provided some of the reasons for his failure:

> That fortune that was going to come from the newspaper was a ruin instead. I had hoped to find happiness in this country and instead I lived a sad and bitter life like never before. And not because I did not

push myself or put effort into achieving what I desired and still do. . . The newspaper is gone because, ultimately, I could not keep it going. I made sacrifices, to the point of feeding myself poorly, so that I could use all the money I had available on the most urgent expenses, which were composition, printing and paper. But even so, it was impossible to save it. I tried all kinds of contents. I even cut the subscription price in half. The number of subscribers was never even enough to pay the type-setter! . . . If you saw the way I worked, the way I lived, for the good of this community of ignoramuses, you would be amazed at how much this bohemian sacrificed.[79]

After splitting with Monteiro, Xavier created the *Almanach Luso-Amer-icano, Litterario e Recreativo* (1884) and, in 1885, bought *O Novo Mundo* in New Bedford, a newspaper founded by José Marques de Lima, a dentist from the island of São Miguel, Azores. Xavier transformed *O Novo Mundo* into *O Correio Portuguez*, which, in its initial issues, depended heavily on the contributions of a priest, Cândido da Vila Martins, from the island of Pico. He eventually sold *O Correio Portuguez* to fellow Azorean João Francisco Escobar. His last known periodical was the magazine *Aurora Luzitana* (1900), published only briefly. Manuel das Neves Xavier died in an automobile accident at the age of 89.[80]

As previously mentioned, other early printer-editors include António Maria Vicente, who was among a group of Portuguese immigrants who set-tled in Erie, Pennsylvania, in the 1870s. There, alongside his father, typogra-pher João (John) Maria Vicente, he founded in 1877 *O Jornal de Noticias*, which became the first newspaper in the history of the Portuguese-American press. Shortly thereafter, Vicente set out for California, where he intended to create a newspaper with the help of Manuel Garcia Monteiro, who eventually decided not to join him. Vicente went on to found *O Progresso Californiense* in 1885 and then *A União Portugueza* in 1887. The first lasted only two years, but the second became one of the longest-running newspapers of the Portuguese-American press, led for over half of a century by Manuel de Freitas Martins Trigueiro, to whom Vicente sold the business shortly after its creation.

Azorean João Francisco Escobar was an expert at transforming ail-ing newspapers into profitable businesses. He first acquired Xavier's *Correio*

Portuguez and then *O Progresso* from the Protestant minister Francisco Caetano Borges da Silva. He later bought *O Portugal* from Alberto Sousa da Cunha
e Moura (a native of Chaves), which he renamed the *Jornal do Povo*, a weekly
that was irregularly published between 1916 and 1923. He also published
one of the first manuals for learning Portuguese in North America: *The New
Method to Learn the Portuguese Language Without Teacher with Figurated Pronunciation of the Tones and Sounds.*[81]

Meanwhile, his son Eugénio Escobar Jr., owner of the Livraria Portugueza, took over *A Revista Portuguesa*, created in 1895 by Joaquim Borges de
Menezes, and founded the *Jornal das Senhoras*. João Vasco Jardim also attributes to Escobar Jr. the founding of *O Popular*,[82] although according *O Lavrador Português*, it was founded by Joaquim dos Santos Oliveira.[83]

Joaquim Borges de Menezes was born on March 6, 1866 in Altares (Terceira, Azores), the son of Francisco Borges de Menezes and Esperança Augusta
de Jesus. After attending the seminary, where he wrote for the Catholic Ter-
ceirense newspaper *O Amigo das Famílias*, he became a primary school teacher
in the town of Vila da Calheta on the island of São Jorge. After five months, he
abandoned teaching to focus on journalism. His articles were highly critical of
the local and national governments, which caused him political complications
that prompted him to emigrate. He boarded the ship *Vega* of the Companhia
Insulana de Navegação, embarking on March 1, 1892, in Calheta and arriving
in Boston on March 13. He worked with various Portuguese-American newspapers, including *O Colombo*, *O Português*, *A União Portuguesa,* and *A Chrónica*,
often using the initials J. B. as his byline. He translated literary works from
French and English to publish them as serials in *O Arauto*, including the works
of Jules Michelet and John Dix. Like Alberto Moura, Joaquim de Oliveira, and
the Protestant minister João José Vieira Jr., Menezes began his career on the
East Coast before moving to California. In New Bedford, Menezes briefly edited
A Revista Portugeza (1895). On July 27, 1896, he founded *O Arauto* in Oakland,
along with Francisco Inácio de Lemos, also a native of Terceira. *O Arauto* was
the successor to *O Amigo dos Católicos*, which had been founded in Irvington
in 1888 and which Menezes had directed for a few months in 1896. Menezes
also edited two ephemeral newspapers: *A Semana Portugueza*, founded on September 16, 1903, and *A Crítica Literária*, founded in 1905, of which he published

O ARAUTO.

Entered at the Post Office as Second class matter. J. de Menezei Editor and Proprietor, 1913 Myrtle St., near the 20 and 5th Public ave. Oakland, Cal.

XI ANNO   Published every Saturday   OAKLAND, CAL., 4 DE SETEMBRO DE 1909   Publica-se ao sabbado   NO. 13

AS NOSSAS SOCIEDADES

RIO VISTA, AGOSTO 17, 1909

Das flotas

Falando da mocidade

ENSINO GRATIS

RECREIOS

20 PREMIOS

VALIOSO PREMIO DO ARAUTO

OPPORTUNIDADE EXCEPCIONAL

Dinner Set
42 pieces

Trem de louça 42 peças

Valley Brew Bottling Company
PREMIADA COM MEDALHA DE OURO
1677 rua 7 W. Oakland.

The Oakland Bank of Savings

The First National Bank of Oxnard

PEOPLE'S STATE BANK

The Analy Savings Bank

Bank of Fruitvale

Merced Security Savings Bank

SAVINGS BANK and LOAN SOCIETY
STOCKTON CAL.

THE SAN JOAQUIN VALLEY BANK

3. Cover of *O Arauto*
Copy of September 4, 1909.

4. Cover of *A California Alegre.*
Copy of December 21, 1937.

one issue. Upon his death, his sons took over the management of *O Arauto* until Pedro Laureano Claudino da Silveira bought it and renamed it the *Jornal de Notícias*. At this time, Oakland was home to several important mainstream newspapers, including *Bay View News*, *The Oakland Telegraph*, *The Grove Street News*, *The North Oakland News*, *The Telegraphic*, *The Emeryville News*, and *San Pablo Avenue District Defender*, which were printed at *O Arauto*'s print shop.[84]

Other noteworthy figures from the beginning of the century in California include Pedro Laureano Claudino da Silveira (who will be discussed at more length when the *Jornal Português* is addressed), Manuel de Freitas Martins Trigueiro, and Cândido da Costa Nunes. Nunes was the founder and editor of the longest running humorous-satirical newspaper in the history of the Portuguese-American community—*A California Alegre*, published between 1915 and 1940. He was also the editor of *O Lavrador Portuguez* for some months in 1927 and reissued *A Pátria* (published by Manoel Stone between 1891 and 1897) in 1916.

Silveira and Trigueiro started working in California as employees of United States Laundry in San Francisco. Trigueiro, who combined his duties as a laundry employee with selling Portuguese works of literature, was focused on a single newspaper throughout his life, *A União Portuguesa*.[85] Although he was not the founder, Trigueiro was the paper's editor and director from 1889 until his death on January 8, 1940. After purchasing the newspaper from António Maria Vicente, he created the publishing company Editora União Portugueza, of which he was the sole owner throughout its existence. Between 1896 and 1906, Silveira worked for him as an editor and typesetter, an educational experience for which he publicly expressed his gratitude in the 50th Anniversary commemorative issue of the paper: "During that long period, I was treated courteously and kindly by the owner of *A União Portuguesa* and would not have left its service had it not been for the long-held burning desire to publish my own Portuguese-language newspaper."[86]

The great earthquake that devastated the city of San Francisco on April 18, 1906, destroyed *A União Portuguesa*'s printshop and archives, but some of the Portuguese-American newspapermen offered their help to Trigueiro in a show of solidarity. Joaquim de Menezes, owner of *O Arauto*, offered him the use of his printshop and office, and the Reverend Francisco Caetano

Borges da Silva, owner of *O Progresso* in New Bedford, opened a charity drive for *A União Portuguesa*.[87] The newspaper managed to rise from its own ashes and opened new facilities in Oakland weeks later.

One of the key figures among the pioneers of Portuguese journalism in California was Mário Bettencourt da Câmara, whose biography is marked by romance and tragedy. Câmara was the pseudonym of Lúcio Gonçalves da Silva, a native of Peniche, Portugal, where he was born on February 3, 1864. A Portuguese army officer with strong Republican convictions, he participated in the failed coup against the Portuguese monarchy in 1889, which forced him into exile, first in France, then in Italy, and later in Brazil, before coming to the United States. His musical talents allowed him to work as an opera singer and impresario of an opera company in Rio de Janeiro during part of his exile, until he contracted yellow fever, which damaged his voice. After working on the Panama Canal, he settled in San Francisco in 1892, where he started his journalistic career as a reporter and editor-in-chief of *A União Portuguesa*. On July 6, 1895, he founded *A Chrónica*, in San Francisco, publishing political criticism that, judging from the level of controversy it generated and the public stands it took, appears to have had a significant impact on the community, though only fourteen issues were published. He quickly integrated himself into the community by promoting numerous social initiatives. In 1895, he founded the Portuguese Bicycle Club of San Francisco. He also became part of the leadership of the União Portuguesa of the State of California, occupying the position of General Secretary and spearheading the publication of its official newsletter, the *Boletim da U.P.E.C.*, which began with four pages and a circulation of 2,500 copies.[88] His passion for music led him to found and direct the U.P.E.C. Band starting in 1906. As editor and director of *A Chrónica*, Câmara became known as a defender of the interests of the Portuguese community in California. When the *San Francisco Daily Report* implicated the Portuguese in several scandals related to prostitution, and the *San Francisco Chronicle* published, on November 14, 1895, a report criticizing the methods used by the Portuguese in the conquest of their African territories, M. Bettencourt da Câmara responded with a long editorial published in English on December 20, 1895,[89] and then published in Portuguese on February 1, 1896, under the title, "Uma Lição de História a alguns jornalistas sanfranciscanos. Carta Aberta ao Povo da Califórnia por um Jornalista Português," which translates as, "A History Lesson for Some San Franciscan Journalists: An Open Letter from a Portuguese Journalist to the People of California," in which he decried the attacks on Portugal by the English-language press:

> The frequency with which offensive references to Portugal and the Portuguese have been appearing lately in certain newspapers of this city imposes upon me the sacrosanct duty of coming today before the people of California to respond to the attacks of unprecedented brutality with which a few San Franciscan journalists have disrespected my glorious nation. If we were in Europe, where other processes are used to settle accounts of this nature, I would have already placed bits on the mouths of the donkeys who have trampled over the pages of history which have been so lavishly illuminated by the stupendous deeds with which the astounding heroism of my people has marveled the World. But here, where such processes are prohibited by the law, I am forced to resort to the only tool capable of putting an end to the gratuitous and insolent diatribes with which some of the pygmies of the San Francisco press have sought to diminish the old glories of my country, the value and virtues of the Portuguese people. This tool is the press, an institution from where I address today, to the people of California, this protest that is simple in its form, but most solemn in its intention. For some time now, I had been trying without success to discover the origin of such unexpected aggressions, when chance providentially bestowed upon me the answer to my question. On the 14th of last month, in the editorial section of the *San Francisco Chronicle* of that same day, I came across the following: "It is not in the habits of the Portuguese to achieve victories by the force of arms in Africa. They have obtained their colonial territories by trickery, taking a mile when they were given a yard. In this way they have acquired vast territories, but England has robbed them of much of this ill-gotten land. But nowadays we read that the Portuguese really defeated the natives of East Africa in a pitched battle. It must have been a pleasure for some of their soldiers to exchange beads for bullets."

. . . From this depressing picture of Portugal and the Portuguese, one can immediately infer the degree of ignorance of the editor of the *Chronicle*. Now, that someone may not know the past of a country and a people whose history has not had an impact beyond the limits of its borders is understandable and tolerable, even talking about a journalist, if he conceals his ignorance; but that someone who has had a basic education, that a journalist is unaware of Portugal's past and of the great achievements of her people is truly astonishing.[90]

His protest against the California press had an impact on public opinion in Portugal. The director of Lisbon's *A Vanguarda*, Faustino da Fonseca, expressed his support for the defense of Portuguese interests in California in the pages of his newspaper. According to the Lisbon daily, the text "moved the public deeply."[91] On the initiative of one of its readers, Joaquim Pedro Monteiro, who proposed recognizing the "heroic effort demonstrated by our countryman," *A Vanguarda* launched a charity campaign in order to buy a "pen of gold" for the director of *A Chrónica*:

> The article that we published the day before yesterday and in which we transcribed part of the proud and dignified response, which served as a protest to the insinuations made against the name of the Portuguese by two California newspapers, moved the public deeply. The homage provided to our colleague of the United States echoed in the spirit of the Portuguese people . . . We support the idea [of presenting him with a golden pen] as completely deserved, convinced that all patriots will respond to our appeal, thereby paying tribute to someone who, although far from the Motherland, knew how to honor her, defending her with the greatest pride. The amount of each contribution should not exceed 100 *réis*.[92]

Forty years later, on February 12, 1936, at age 73 and partially blind, after writing twelve letters to his family, friends, and the authorities, Mário Bettencourt da Câmara took his own life with a pistol.[93]

Another distinguished director of the Portuguese-American press was Arthur Vieira Ávila. He was born on March 5, 1888, in Lajes, Pico, and emigrated to the U.S. in October 1909.[94] He was one of the most prestigious figures in Portuguese journalism in California, not only in newspaper publishing, but also in the promotion of films and radio programs. For example, he owned the U.S. film rights to António Lopes Ribeiro's film *Gado Bravo* (1934), which was shot with the participation of several actors and technicians who had fled the Nazi regime and which was the third sound film in the history of Portuguese cinema.[95] But Ávila was best known for his work in radio. The creation of the pioneering radio club Castelos Românticos made him popular in California. His first paper was *O Lavrador Português*, founded with João de Simas Melo and Constantino Barcelos on December 3, 1912, in Lemoore, California. Ávila was the sole owner between 1915 and 1926, in addition to working as its editor and director at various times. His second major project was the founding of *A Colonia Portuguesa* on March 18, 1924, which later merged with *Jornal de Notícias* and *O Imparcial*. Ávila was its director for two periods from 1924 to 1925 and from 1928 to 1932.[96]

In January 1933, he and his wife Celeste Alice dos Santos, a native of Trás-os-Montes, Portugal, began the monthly publication of the *Rose & Albert Magazine* ("A production of the Latin-American Broadcasting Co.," "Hora Portuguesa-KROW"), which dealt with radio-related material and lasted until April 1934. The establishment of *O Clarim* followed on October 5 of that year, but survived only until August 15, 1935. Ávila co-founded and co-directed (with Leonel Soares de Azevedo) *O Portugal da Califórnia*, which resulted from the fusion of *O Clarim* and *Ecos de Portugal*. He also collaborated closely with the Portuguese diplomatic corps in California. For example, upon the death of the consul of Portugal on the West Coast, Francisco de Pina Aragão e Costa, he published an emotional tribute to the diplomat on the day of his funeral.[97]

Manuel B. Quaresma, a native of Pico, Azores, born in 1867, was another Portuguese-American owner-editor based in California. In 1913, he founded *O Imparcial* in Sacramento, which he published until 1932. In 1889, he bought *O Amigo dos Católicos*, in partnership with Francisco Inácio de Lemos, a partnership that Guilherme Silveira da Glória would later join. He was very active as a member of various fraternal societies and was the founder of the Irmandade do Divino Espírito Santo (IDES), which exists to this day. His

PORTUGAL na CALIFORNIA

Direcção e Redacção
JORDÃO MARQUES JARDIM

EDIÇÃO ESPECIAL
3 Secções—32 Paginas

Administração e Anuncios
MANUEL SOUSA ESPINOLA

Em Homenagem a Sua Excelencia o Sr. Dr. Bianchi, Ilustre Ministro de Portugal em Washington

HOSANA

A Alma Portuguesa da Costa do Pacifico está em festa...

Portugal, a Patria querida e saudosa, enviou até ela a pessoa ilustre do seu Ministro em Washington:

Hosana!... Hosana!... Hosana!...

E' o cantico, que neste momento, de norte a sul, de leste, a neste da California se faz ouvir, nos 200,00 portugueses que aqui vivem na esperança dum futuro prospero, mas de coração preso ao rincão amigo, ao berço inesquecivel onde abriram os olhos ao mundo, ou donde são oriundos por saudosidade.

Hosana!... Hosana!... Hosana!...

E' o testemunho da nossa gratidão por tão excelsa visita.

É' a prece do nosso patriotismo; é o grito de alegria por se encontrar no nosso seio, embora por uma curta visita, o homem, o português, que a Portugal tem oferecido uma brilhantissima pagina de serviços.

A nossa saudosidade pesa, trepida neste momento!... A nossa imaginação, curva-se com respeito e da nossa alma saltam lagrimas!...

Sim; são lagrimas de jubilo, são lagrimas de saudade pela nossa patria querida: são cruciantes recordações do nosso ultimo beijo, numa Santa Velhinha, que era nossa Mãi; são ainda os sorrisos de amigos da infancia, que lá deixamos e que, talvez, não mais voltaremos a gosar.

Ele é quadro...

Eis porque trepidamos neste momento na presença do mais alto e ilustre Representante de Portugal neste pais, que tão galhardamente nos recebeu, e onde aguardamos a realização dos nossos sonhos.

Senhor Ministro:

Perdoai a nossa simplicidade, e aceitai as nossas expressões humildes, como o mais sincero tributo do combatente que no campo da honra sabe nobremente morrer batalhando, pelo prestigio e honra da sua Patria e da sua nacionalidade.

Toda a Familia Portuguesa residente neste grande Estado, em vós—Senhor Ministro, deposita a caluroza saudação a Portugal.

Aceitai-a, Senhor Ministro, com o vosso cativante sorriso de Chefe e de Amigo, e religiosamente pedimos que a enviais á nossa Imortal e Nobre Nação Portuguesa.

Hosana!

JORDÃO M. JARDIM.

MOSTEIRO DA BATALHA

Este historico e lindo monumento foi mandado erigir por D. João I, em acção de graças á Virgem pela vitoria das tropas armas, na sangrenta luta travada no subterraneo da Espanha.

A sua construção principiou em 1387, tendo sido adicionadas no primitivo plano sucessivas alterações até á epoca do reinado de D. João III.

É' neste mosteiro que repousam os tumulos á varios reis de Portugal, e, é tambem aqui, que descansa o cansaco de heroi da Portugal na ultima guerra mundial—O Soldado Desconhecido.

O visitante, que uma vez no Continente, deixe de visitar o Mosteiro da Batalha (Convento de Nossa Senhora da Vitoria), é ter escavaco por ter furtado á vista uma das mais belas maravilhas da nossa Patria.

DR. JOÃO ANTONIO DE BIANCHI, Ministro de Portugal

Visitando varios pontos de interesse, e depois duma "rodagem" aclima de 15,000 quilometros, pelas estradas que cortam os Estados Unidos do Leste para o Oeste; até que num dos dias da presente semana, chegou a San Francisco, acompanhado por sua ilustre Esposa, D. Clara de Bianchi, o digno Ministro Plenipotenciario de Portugal em Washington, o sr. João de Bianchi.

O Sr. dr. João A. de Bianchi é um verdadeiro "sportman."

E a afirmá-lo, temos, já que outros dados não são necessarios, a persistencia para a jornada em estrada, se arrostar com as intemperies da estação que atravessamos, e ainda, com muitos outras contrariedades duma viagem tão comprida a morosa.

Felizmente Sua Excelencia chegou bem, embora, é certo, com ligeira indisposição.

Encontra-se, portanto, entre nós o sr. Ministro de Portugal em Washington!

E seja BEM VINDO, pelas suas belissimas qualidades de cidadão e de chefe.

Que seja BEM VINDO, porque da sua visita á California, um novo a risorte de união e entendimento, se há de espargir ademais da numerosa Colonia Portuguesa do Pacifico.

Que seja BEM VINDO, para que da sua permanencia e convivio com os seus irmãos de raça e nacionalidade, possam mais e mais estreitar-se os laços de consideração e respeito por Portugal, dessa colonia cujos membros, numa formidavel percentagem, já retornam, em segunda, terceira e quarta geração de ascendencia americana.

E são os amigos das suas tradições, que assinalados não necessita, desde já é pedimos afirmar, de ser horrificada com "gasolina"; mas sim, o que para nota se recomenda á

os conselhos dum bom chefe, dum bom orientador, que em Washington faça saber aos poderes centrais donde vimos e o que pretendemos.

Em sua Excelencia encontramos a bussola!

Portanto à sua hábil e distinta orientação nos entregamos, conscientes do seu superior carinho, por todo quanto nos anobrece e distingue.

Desde o primeiro instante em que chegou até nós a agradavel noticia da visita de Sua Excelencia, os varios nucleos da Colonia Portuguesa na America do Norte, sentimos a nossa alma de filhos de Portugal, orgulhar-se da escolha, que acertadamente, o Governo da Republica havia feito, para seu e nosso representante em Washington.

Ficamos contentes!...

E, hoje, que os factos falam sem paixões da barreiras, felicitamo-nos, e conhecendo então todos se portugueses.

Sim então todos os que sentem a necessidade de mais e mais se estreitar as amizades entre Portugal e América.

De mais a mais, se tornar ciente aos Portugueses da America que a Pátria Portuguesa, debruçada na sua tidão do Atlantico, olha com maternal carinho para todos os seus filhos.

Certos estamos, ainda, que a comprovada competencia do sr. Consul Geral de Portugal, em San Francisco, muito contribuirá para o completo estudo, que pretende fazer Sua Excelencia o Senhor Ministro, da situação social e economica dos portugueses do Pacifico.

O nosso digno Consul saberá, além de tudo, demonstrar com prova, o que a sua experiencia de 7 anos, no sobre,

Continua na pagina 2

DR. FRANCISCO FINA DE ARAGÃO E COSTA, Consul Geral de Portugal em San Francisco

5. Cover of *Portugal na California.*
Copy of September 1935.

death on October 14, 1929, generated a lot of controversy in the local press. Quaresma died of heart failure in Oakland, where he had gone to attend the annual convention of the União Portuguesa of the State of California, as the representative of that organization's 40th Council from Sacramento. Apparently, after suffering a heart attack on the street, Mr. Quaresma was detained by the police who believed he was intoxicated. They kept him at the station until a family member claimed him and took him to the hospital, where they were unable to save his life.[98]

Alfredo da Silva Dias (originally from Santo Amaro, Pico, Azores), was another prominent journalist who left his mark on the Portuguese-American press of California. He arrived in Sacramento in 1905 and later married Angelina da Rocha Homem in that city in 1915. He was the founder, owner, and editor of *O Progresso*, which was published in Sacramento between November 7, 1932, and 1940. He was also the editor, co-owner, and publisher of *O Lavrador Portuguez* from November 1915 until May 1926. He co-edited, in collaboration with António da Conceição Teixeira from Madeira, the humorous publication *A Abelha*, which was created in June 1924 in San Francisco, but which had a brief existence. He also worked in Oakland for *A Liberdade* and the *Jornal Português*. Later, he returned to Sacramento to work for *O Imparcial*. There he would found and edit *O Progresso*, which was published from his home with the help of his second wife, Mary Aurora Silva. His son, Alfred Dias da Silva, worked at the newspaper beginning at age seventeen as a typist and designer of advertisements.

Another influential journalist in the Portuguese-American community of California was Alberto Sousa da Cunha e Moura, better known as Alberto Moura, a native of Chaves, mainland Portugal. Moura was the founder of *O Portugal* in New Bedford before he moved to California in 1916. There, he worked for several months with the newspaper *O Mundo*, based in Oakland, and then, until 1918, was an editor for *A União Portuguesa*, where he replaced the owner, Pedro Laureano C. Silveira, in this role. Moura was the founder of the Sociedade Portuguesa de Instrução da Califórnia, which was created with the support of *A União Portuguesa*, following the publication of a series of articles in which he defended the value of this fraternal of organization. He was also the Secretary General of the União Portuguesa Continental and one of the first Portuguese immigrants to earn a law degree. He graduated in

1923 from St. Ignatius School in San Francisco. *A União Portuguesa* published a biographical article to celebrate the event.[99]

One of his first jobs as a lawyer was to manage the administrative and legal process for converting *A Colonia Portuguesa* into a shareholding company.[100] In March 1938, *A União Portuguesa* published a notice describing the professional profile of Moura and lauding his commitment to the Portuguese-American community:

> Who in the Portuguese community has not heard of Dr. Alberto Moura, who has his law office in the Bank of America Building on 12th Street and Broadway? Alberto Moura has played a very active role in our organizations, our celebrations, our enterprises, and the community owes him something of value, something that honors all of us. Through his work and dedication, Alberto Moura has earned a level of esteem that places him in a position of prominence and distinction among the Portuguese of California. Try, therefore, to seek his advice, when you need a lawyer.[101]

Many of the periodicals in the history of the Portuguese-American press were owned and published by men of the cloth. Among those run by Catholic priests, the best known were *O Amigo dos Católicos* (California) and *Novidades* (Massachusetts). But there were also significant Protestant newspapers competing for influence in the Portuguese community, often through the publication of religious articles meant to counteract the predominance of the Catholic faith.[102] Prominent among Protestant owners and editors was Francisco Caetano Borges da Silva, a Baptist pastor born in São Miguel, who founded three newspapers in New Bedford—*A Verdade* in 1893; the weekly *O Progresso*, which was a daily for a short while in 1907; and the weekly *Alvorada* in 1909. Another Protestant clergyman active in newspaper publishing was João José Vieira Jr., a native of Madeira, who first edited *A Aurora* in Cambridge in the 1920s and then *O Heraldo* in Oakland, California, between 1936 and 1959. Vieira also published three religious books: *A Voz da História* (1941),[103] *Eu Falo por Mim Mesmo. Autobiografia* (1963),[104] and *Aventuras no Eldorado. Novela Idealista* (1966).[105]

Predictably, the Catholic newspapers had a larger readership among Portuguese immigrants than those published by Protestants. One of the most popular editor priests was Guilherme Silveira da Glória who eventually left the priesthood in order to dedicate himself entirely to journalism, his true passion along with poetry. He was the co-owner and editor-in-chief of *O Amigo dos Cathólicos* between 1893 and 1896, and director of *A Liberdade* between 1900 and 1937. Born on June 6, 1863, in Candelária, Pico, Azores, Glória was the youngest in a family of seventeen children. He studied at the Seminary of Angra do Heroísmo, along with the Portuguese-American editor Joaquim Borges de Menezes. During that period of his life, Glória wrote for the newspapers *O Picoense* (Pico) and *O Católico* (Terceira). He heard about the Portuguese community in California through Fr. Manuel Francisco Fernandes, who had been placed at Mission San José and would go on to co-found *O Amigo dos Católicos*. Glória emigrated there and was ordained at the St. Thomas Aquinas seminary in Palo Alto. He celebrated his first mass on July 28, 1885, and due to the lack of Portuguese priests in many places, he passed through various parishes in California.[106] In 1895, he was named pastor for the town of San Pablo, and upon the death of Father Manuel Francisco Fernandes in Oakland, he was transferred to the San José church of that city.[107] While still a priest, he collaborated with several newspapers, including *O Progresso Californiense*, *A União Portuguesa*, and *O Amigo dos Católicos*, of which he became co-owner and editor-in-chief.[108]

Glória was also a popular poet who published hundreds of patriotic poems in the Portuguese-American press that he then collected in two volumes titled *Poesias de Guilherme S. Glória* and *Harpejos*.[109] Some of them were dedicated to relevant figures within the community. On December 11, 1939, for example, Glória welcomed the new Consul General of Portugal in San Francisco, Euclides Goulart da Costa, with a poem published in *A União Portuguesa*. His book *Poesias* was seen as a sort of elegy to Portuguese culture: "Portugal is our beloved path; we have left it behind, but no matter how far away we travel, we always carry it in our heart,"[110] wrote Carlos Fernandes, a regular contributor to the Portuguese press in California and president of St. John's Hospital, in the preface to the book,[111] which was promoted through an ad campaign by *A Liberdade*.

Fr. Joseph (José) Cacella, another influential Catholic editor, was born on September 21, 1882, in the village of Fátima, Portugal, and studied at the seminary of Santarém, where he was ordained in 1909. Cacella left Portugal during the Republican Revolution of 1910 to find a new life in the Americas as an assistant to the bishop of Manaus, Brazil, Frederico Costa. As a missionary among the indigenous tribes of the Amazon forest, he lived for six years in the jungle, and published a memoir in an illustrated book of literary beauty and anthropological interest entitled *Jungle Call* (New York, 1956).[112] He also published a book, *White Doves of Peace* (1949), about the miracle of the Virgin of Fátima. Due to health problems that arose from working in the jungle, he decided to come to the U.S. to spend some time with his siblings who had settled in New Bedford.[113] Once there, he collaborated with St. John's College until the archbishop of New York offered him the opportunity to become a priest of the Portuguese community in New York City where he founded St. Anthony's Welfare Center.[114] This is how he began his relationship with the Portuguese-American community for which he founded *O Portugal* (1929) and *A Luta* (1936). *A Luta*, published until the 1970s, became one of the most popular newspapers among the Portuguese-Americans of New York and New Jersey. New York Cardinal Patrick Hayes (1919-1938), referred to Cacella as "the apostle of the printing press."[115] In 1960, the Portuguese government, through the Consul General of Portugal in New York, José Manuel Fragoso, awarded him the medal of the Ordem de Benemerência for his work on behalf of the community.[116]

Other priests involved in newspaper publishing include Joseph (José) L. Capote and Abílio Maria da Silva Greaves. During the 1960s, Capote founded and edited the newspapers *Novos Mundos* and *Novos Rumos Estados Unidos* of Newark. Greaves, a native of Faial (Azores), was the editor of the magazine *Portugal-América*, founded in New Bedford by Joseph L. Laranjo in 1922, and later became pastor of the church of São João Baptista in Boston, where he published the religious newspaper *A Cruz*. According to Vasco Jardim, he loved to travel and was very creative. He invented the "termophone," an early type of fire alarm, and patented several inventions related to aviation.[117] After spending some time in New England, he spent sixteen years traveling through California and Hawaii, until Cacella invited him to work for *A Luta*.[118] He also worked with Vasco Jardim, who remembered Greaves as "a poor soul":

> I bought him clothes, from head to toe, and found him a home, but he died a week after the first edition of *O Luso*. He died suddenly, after climbing the stairs of a house on Elm St., where he lived. . . Father Greaves survived on a diet of sandwiches and pills. He had bowel problems. He was only 69 when he died. A day when he did not drink at least a gallon of wine was not a day for him.[119]

Sixteen patents registered in Washington were found in his room after his death. Greaves told Jardim that a rich woman from California once offered him $1.5 million for his patents, but he declined to sell.[120]

Although the vast majority of those who founded or directed newspapers were men, there were also several women who played important roles in the Portuguese-American press (see Table 8). Paradigmatic among them are the cases of Laurinda C. Andrade and Mary (Maria) Nunes da Silveira. The story of Andrade is found in her autobiography, *The Open Door* (1968),[121] which is written in English and offers an interesting story of personal growth and Portuguese culture in the United States. According to the book, Andrade was born on the island of Terceira, Azores, and was one of the first Portuguese women to graduate from an American university, receiving a degree in Philosophy from Brown University. Between April and December 1933, Andrade was the director and editor of *A Tribuna* of Newark. When she contacted the owner of the newspaper, the Italian typographer Joseph Merola, asking him for work after a series of personal vicissitudes in New York, he offered her the job with the following words: "I want to give you a break; I know that college degrees don't come easy, I earned one. The hours will be long and the pay small to start, but $10 a week is better than nothing."[122] Merola took the opportunity to get rid of his former director, Gil Stone, who had asked for a raise. Andrade describes the circumstances of this episode in the following manner:

> Gil Stone was a very likable young man, tall, slender, dark and handsome—the Gary Cooper type. Later I learned that he had been trying to

Table 8. Women Who Played Major Roles in the Portuguese-American Press

Name	Place of Origin	Publication	Period	Role
M. G. Rose		*A Colonia Portuguesa*	1924-?	Director of the edition at Tulare and Kings
Mary (Maria) Aurora Silva		*O Progresso*	1932-1940	Manager and editor
Celeste Alice dos Santos	Trás-os-Montes	*Rose and Albert Magazine*	1933-1934	Co-owner and co-editor with her husband, Arthur Vieira Ávila
		O Clarim	1934-1935	
Laurinda C. Andrade	Terceira, Azores	*A Tribuna*	1933	Director and editor. She left the newspaper to be the secretary of the new ambassador of Portugal
Louisa S. Trigueiro and Ângela B. Trigueiro	California	*A União Portuguesa*	1940-1942	Director-owners, daughters of Manuel de Freitas Martins Trigueiro
Mary (Maria) Nunes Silveira	Cholame, California	*Jornal Português*	1944-1957	Director, owner and manager
Carolina Matos		*The Portuguese-American*	1985-1995	Editor and owner with husband José Baptista
Filomena Rocha Mendes		*Tribuna Portuguesa*	1993-1994	Director
Maria Conceição Leal		*Jornal Português*	1994-?	Editor-in-Chief
Maria C. Odom		*Portuguese-American Chronicle*	1999-?	Editor
		Lusitânia News	2006-?	
Lurdes C. da Silva		*O Jornal*	2006-today	Editor

Source: Calculated by the author.

get more money for his services, but the enterprising Mr. Merola saw the opportunity to replace him with somebody who could do three jobs for the salary which Mr. Stone was getting just to edit the newspaper and, naturally, was anxious to take advantage of this.[123]

During her eight months as head of *A Tribuna*, Andrade had to overcome adversity as a woman leading a team of men. She also had to deal with limited resources when editing the paper:

> The next morning after introducing me to the other members of his staff, the boss gave me "carte blanche" to carry out my duties, with a clear understanding that the paper had to be printed on the usual date. "You know, the most important feature is the advertisements, and I can't collect for them until they are printed." With that practical reminder, he left the office. Invading the field of journalism was a daring feat, not likely to be accepted without trauma by the so-called superior sex. A woman editor was an oddity. To combat this prejudice, my first steps on to that shaky stage had to be carefully measured and well-balanced to establish the desired atmosphere for future performances. The office plant consisted of a combination of a banking establishment, a travel agency, two newspapers, and a printing firm, all under one roof and under the name of Vicarisi & Merola, managed by a refined and cultured young man from Lisbon, Luis Fonseca. There was a special area for the transaction of printing orders and two small compartments, in the back, for the Portuguese and the Spanish editors, Mr. Blanco, a Spanish immigrant, was in charge of "El Heraldo," another weekly publication. My first efforts were all directed at establishing a friendly relationship with my co-workers, by asking questions, soliciting advice and showing sincere appreciation. In the pressroom was my landlady, on whose support I could depend.[124]

In her work as director-editor, Andrade did everything possible to ensure that her gender was not an obstacle to performing her journalistic duties in a predominantly male world. She was humble when receiving the sometimes paternalistic support of her colleagues and staff, whom she knew how to manage wisely: "I have been accepted, on my own terms, in a community dominated by masculine minds rooted in the civilizations of the Iberian Peninsula."[125] Little by little, she discovered new ways and techniques to help her carry on her duties. She found, for example, that the most difficult task was to produce a good editorial, which was the most important section for most readers: "The importance attached to the editorial opened my eyes. That was the feature destined to make or break the image of the new editor. I proceeded to sound out my advisors, asking for suggestions as to fitting topics with which to introduce myself in that open market to my scattered readers."[126] For fear of the prejudice it might raise, Merola avoided placing Andrade's name on the first issue she edited. However, since the public response was favorable and circulation increased, the new director earned everyone's respect. Even her Spanish-speaking colleagues from *El Heraldo* admired her editorials: "I saw the day when my Spanish colleague sacrificed his proud 'hombria' to translate one of my editorials which was to appear in his 'El Heraldo'."[127]

Andrade's academic training allowed her to adapt quickly to journalistic routines, basing her narrative style on that of *The New York Times*.[128] Less than a year after she began her work at *A Tribuna*, at the end of 1933, Andrade left the newspaper's management to become secretary to the new ambassador of Portugal in Washington, D.C., João António de Bianchi. She was recommended for the job by the Consul General of Portugal in New York, Verdades de Faria, whom Andrade had met at an event organized by The New York Portuguese Club to honor the writer Alexander Lawton McKall, the author of *Portugal for Two* (1931), and during which she had delivered a speech.[129]

After leaving her activity as secretary to the ambassador, on January 26, 1942, Andrade became a teacher of Portuguese at New Bedford High School. In September 1944, with the help of the publisher of the *Diario de Noticias*, João Rodrigues Rocha, she founded the Portuguese Educational Society of New Bedford. This institution contributed to educational and cultural exchanges between Portugal, Brazil, and the United States, created the first Portuguese program in an American high school, and granted scholarships to Portuguese-American students.[130] Its three main objectives were: 1) to promote the learning and teaching of the Portuguese language by granting scholarships to students who had successfully completed two years of high school Portuguese; 2) to act as a center for the dissemination of information; 3) and to promote cultural exchange between United States, Portugal, and Brazil.[131] In 1950, the Portuguese Education Society was able, among other initiatives, to organize, in collaboration with the ambassador of Portugal in the United States, Pedro Teotónio Pereira, the first Luso-Brazilian Colloquium in the Library of Congress in Washington, D.C.

As for Mary Nunes Silveira, she was born in Cholame (Monterey County, California) on July 4, 1886, the daughter of immigrants from Flores, Azores, from whom she learned to speak Portuguese. Her relationship with the world of Portuguese-American journalism began in 1917 when her husband founded the *Jornal de Notícias*, where she performed administrative tasks until its merger with *A Colonia Portuguesa* and *O Imparcial.* With her husband, she not only ran *Jornal Português*, for which she was in charge of the newsroom and the administration, but she also acted as advertising manager and managed the printing of other community publications in the modern printshop they owned.[132] The new company encountered many difficulties with regard to the subscriptions of the previous newspapers, as Alberto Corrêa notes:

> Straightening out the subscriptions entailed much work and frustration. The records went through a great transformation: some names appeared two or three times. The same thing happened with the files. . . With lots of hours, lots of patience and a lot of drive on the part of the manager, we were able to get everything running smoothly and restore trust in an almost-perfect service.[133]

She belonged to various California women's societies and promoted strong philanthropic activity. From the *Jornal Português*, which she directed between 1944 and 1957, she ran several charitable aid campaigns for the needy and for social causes in the Azores, Brazil, and Portugal.[134] She also raised funds for the creation of a monument dedicated to Christ the King in Lisbon and the acquisition by the Portuguese government of the Palácio dos Condes de Almada, as a symbol of the restoration of independence in Portugal.[135] In 1955, when she was close to retirement, she received a public tribute in which the consular authorities and various organizations from the Portuguese-American community in California participated.[136] She died on May 9, 1960.[137] Her death shocked the readers of the *Jornal Português*, who sent letters of condolence and even poems dedicated to the former director, like this one by Adelina Lemos, which was published on the front page of the newspaper:

I still think it was a dream
Having heard the sad news
The mother of the poor is deceased
Our friend no longer exists!

Dona Maria Nunes Silveira
Was the first to give to the poor
With her captivating smile
Always came forward to help

May God give her the joys of heaven
While waiting for us to join her
All happy, all close together
Like little Angels in God's love.[138]

In a world in which women had enormous difficulties gaining influence and responsibility in certain areas of intellectual activity due to traditional forms of social discrimination that limited their educational and employment opportunities, some Portuguese women, either in association with their husbands or on their own initiative, dedicated themselves to journalism despite challenging circumstances. Beginning in the 1920s, several of them managed to occupy positions of authority in various newspapers, which served to make the professional activity of women visible beyond routine, unskilled jobs or domestic chores. In this context, cases such as those of Laurinda de Andrade, who had a short but intense experience leading *A Tribuna* in Newark, and Mary Nunes Silveira, who dedicated her life to journalism in California, provide pioneering examples of the professional integration and success of female journalists in the Portuguese-American diaspora.

Chapter 3
The Birth of the Portuguese-American Press, 1877-1929

The First Newspaper Publications, 1877-1889

The first known Portuguese newspapers appeared in the United States at the end of the nineteenth century. Between 1877 and 1900, thirty-three titles were published in Portuguese in the states of Massachusetts, California, and Hawaii, where several Portuguese communities had developed. During this period, immigrant groups began to organize fraternal societies, charitable institutions, recreational clubs, and associations of all kinds in the different places where they settled. The presidents and directors of these organizations, along with priests, soon became the most important public figures within these communities. As newspapers gained importance, their editors and journalists also became recognized as leaders,[1] who participated in the life of the community, narrating what happened within it, sometimes in hard competition with other papers to try to expand their audience. As Geoffrey Gomes points out:

> The Portuguese-language press was intimately involved in the daily life of the Portuguese-American community, chronicling the daily trials and tribulations and successes of its members. This intimacy, especially in a relatively small immigrant community, frequently led to intense rivalries among Portuguese language journals as they competed for a readership that never exceeded a few thousand.[2]

The weekly *O Jornal de Noticias* was the first newspaper published in Portuguese in the United States. Its founder and first editor, John (João) Maria Vicente, who settled in Boston after working on a whaling ship, began his journalistic career with the help of his eldest son, António Maria.[3] The Vincente family came to Erie from the island of Flores in the Azores to join the small community of Portuguese attracted by its booming economy. At the time, Erie was an important railway junction to Canada and the West, with job and business opportunities in the railroad and freight industries.[4]

O Jornal de Noticias was published until 1884, when António Maria Vicente, who had taken over the newspaper after the death of his father, decided to move to California to pursue other journalistic projects. As discussed earlier, like other Portuguese-American newspapers founded at the end of the nineteenth century, *O Jornal de Noticias* started as a project associated with typography. John Maria Vicente had founded a printing company in Erie, which his sons inherited along with the name, John M. Vicente's Son's. The newspaper was an important means through which to promote the business and to make extra income through advertising. *O Jornal de Noticias* advertised its typographical services with the following claims:

> This press performs any printing services: announcements, invitations, funeral notices, statutes, and documents relating to fraternities, organizations, and associations. Good printing and affordable prices are guaranteed. When our patrons in these states want work printed in Portuguese (and there are few, if any, presses in this country that print in languages they are not familiar with), they should remember that they have here someone who does the best job possible and for very low prices. *O JORNAL DE NOTICIAS* has an assortment of material and its printing equipment is all new. Send us your work, which will be carried out carefully and promptly. When you are in need of any printing work, consult us first.[5]

The American press directory Geo P. Rowel & Co., published in New York, describes *O Jornal de Noticias* in its 1878 edition as follows: "Saturdays; Portuguese; four pages; size 20x26; subscription $2, established 1877; J. M.

3.º ANNO.   ERIE, PA., SABBADO 26 DE JUNHO, 1880.   NO. 140.

O Jornal de Noticias.

O Christianismo.

GUERRA AOS HOMENS.

O HOMEM E A MULHER.

CAMÕES.

O MAJOR SERPA PINTO.

6. Cover of *O Jornal de Noticias* (Erie, Pennsylvania). Copy of June 26, 1880.

Vicente, editor and publisher."[6] It was distributed in the United States, but thanks to the connections provided by the railroad hub of Erie, it also reached the Azores, mainland Portugal, and Canada.[7]

Like most publications in Portuguese in the United States, *O Jornal de Noticias* attached great importance to the celebrations associated with the history and culture of Portugal. Its July 24, 1880 issue, for example, was dedicated almost entirely to the tercentenary of the birth of Luís de Camões, reproducing verses from the illustrious poet and publishing several articles related to the commemoration of the event in the United States. According to the newspaper's own account, this coverage was very well received by their readers, both within and outside the United States. Interest in some of the material was such that due to the large number of letters received, in its edition of February 21, 1881, *O Jornal de Noticias* decided to reprint some of its previous content "in order to please its readers." Among the stories republished was an article dated June 12, 1880, in Philadelphia, describing an event held in the home of Luiz H. da Silva that brought dozens of Portuguese immigrants together to share an evening of entertainment by pianist M.C. da Silva, who began her performance by playing the *Lusitania's Grand Constitutional March*.[8] Although the reprinting of stories like this one may indeed have been the result of popular demand, it is also true that because of scarce human resources, this type of press had serious limitations in gathering news and writing articles. One way of coping with this difficulty was to solicit content from readers, as illustrated by this announcement:

> When our readers have knowledge of any occurrence among our fellow countrymen: a marriage, death, disaster, whatever it is, we ask you to communicate this news to us as soon as possible, for which we would be very grateful. What we require are just the facts and the date, and we will write the article. Don't be afraid to write what you know.[9]

The second oldest Portuguese paper in the United States was the weekly *A Voz Portugueza*. It was founded in San Francisco on August 5, 1880. It was published by Manoel Stone, a Brazilian immigrant (possibly of Portuguese descent). Some authors attribute the founding of this newspaper to

António Maria Vicente,[10] but in the first issue of *A Voz Portugueza,* available at the Library of Congress, Manoel Stone is listed as the publisher. *A Voz Portugueza*, whose subtitle was, "Periódico da Colónia Portuguesa Político, Literário e Mercantil," (Political, Literary and Business Newspaper of the Portuguese Community) ran every Thursday until 1888. It had a format similar to *O Jornal de Noticias*, running between 4 and 8 pages, with news briefs of all kinds aimed at Portuguese immigrants. Its front page contained a message entitled "Expediente" (Mail), stating that the newspaper would publish letters and notices of general interest for free as long as they were "written in acceptable and decent language."[11] In contrast, it also warned on its cover that "writings on issues of personal interest will be accepted upon payment of $.10 per line, that is, if your language is proper and acceptable. If we do not express our opinion about what is written by others, our silence should not be taken as tacit support. We always reserve our opinion."[12]

Due to the lack of training in journalistic writing, the influence of English, and the limited resources available for editing work, grammatical errors were often inevitable. Some editors took advantage of the mistakes made by their competitors to criticize them and call attention to the better quality of their own Portuguese. Perhaps because his Brazilian Portuguese followed different conventions, Manoel Stone received scathing criticism over his ability to write in Portuguese. On June 29, 1887, Stone responded to one of his critics in an article entitled "Zig-Zag na Corda Bamba - Dez Minutos sem Maromba - Argumentum ad Ignorantiam - Resposta à Crítica à Crítica da Crítica" [*sic*]:

> After a thousand investigations and intensive study of his foxed and moldy tomes, after correcting more than twenty times an equal number of "proofs" of his "scribbles," after taking careful precautions, including "greasing the hands of the typesetter" so he would do the "final revision" inserting an 'l' here, deleting a 'p' there, and moving a comma over there, etc., and after being confident that not even Camillo Castelo Branco would be able to fault him for even one letter, finally, after five weeks, the man spit it out!! That's right, the man vomited the little he knows... and the very much he does not know!! That's right, the man showed how

7. Cover of *A Voz Portugueza* (San Francisco, California). Copy of June 29, 1887.

much he does not know, because right by the 15th line of the first paragraph he divides the word "producções" this way: "produc-ções." Rule: When two 'cc' occur at the same time and the second one takes a cedilla, they both belong with the vowel that follows them: *fa-cção, pro-du-cção*, etc. Oh Jesus! This one takes the cake! Look at what he says: "We inform the critic (and we are giving him the courtesy) that the word 'subjecto,' of Latin etymology, can be found in many dictionaries in place of "sujeito," just like "subjecção" in place of "sujeição." Well, now we also respond to Zig-Zag by informing him that "subjecto" is not a Portuguese word and cannot be found in any dictionary of the Portuguese language. Therefore, Zig-Zag is lying and spewing nonsense![13]

One of Stone's journalistic rivals was the biweekly newspaper *A Civilização*, founded in Boston on April 8, 1881, by the printer Xavier Manuel das Neves. It was the first newspaper in Portuguese in the state of Massachusetts and the third in the United States after *O Jornal de Noticias* and *A Voz Portugueza*. *A Civilização* (which would later become the *Luzo-Americano*) accused Stone of basic grammatical errors in his articles and claimed he was incapable of accepting criticism. Stone's recalcitrant attitude is criticized on April 5, 1884, in an editorial entitled "Maçada Inútil" (Waste of Time):

It's really a drag, and a big one at that, to put up with that colleague from *A Voz*. We are really getting tired of applying poultices that, unfortunately for us, have produced little effect, and only prove how truly consistent the great *orator*, *dictator*, and *writer* Mr. Stone is. However, our laboratory abounds in chemical preparations. Hence, let's persevere and go forward; let's find another *sedative* that will prove to be stronger and more effective. My dear colleague, for heaven's sake, enroll in night school! Accept our friendly advice, and you will see that you will reap great and numerous benefits from it. Besides, you must admit that you really need our advice as demonstrated by your flagrant abuses of the rules of grammar. The story "Um Intrigante" clearly shows Mr. Stone's journalistic incompetence. He wants to use fancy terms and chokes, he aims for rhetorical figures and, alas, gets stuck.[14]

A Civilização was published in Boston and New Bedford with the help of the poet Manuel Garcia Monteiro. The paper provided all types of news related to the Azores, often gathered from Azorean newspapers, as exemplified by the following piece about Terceira, published on May 7, 1881:

> The Deputy Civil Governor of the District [of Angra do Heroísmo] appointed a committee to collect donations for the victims of the violent earthquakes that took place on the island of São Miguel. Carnaval was celebrated in that city [Angra] without incident. The Sociedade da União Ginástica organized two soirées and the Assembleia Angrense three balls. All events were heavily attended. . . Mr. José de Bettencourt da Silveira left for Santa Maria, where he has been assigned as a county judge.[15]

A Civilização also published advice columns like "Observações sobre a Educação Moral dos Meninos" (Observations on the Moral Education of Children), which recommended moral principles to apply in the raising of children. These articles often referenced classic authors like John Locke to elaborate their arguments, such as in the article titled "o hábito é a faculdade de reprimir e domar as paixões" (habit is the capacity to suppress and tame passions), which proposed the following guidelines for teaching children good habits:

> They should get used, early on, to submit their whims to the reason of others, so that one day they will be able to listen to their own reason and follow its dictates. Habit is everything; children who, from a young age, get used to do as they please will grow up strong-willed, hotheaded, and stubborn. Later on, they may want to overcome their own passions, but it is too late. Subject, like slaves, to the force of habit, they will regret their weakness, and will have no control over themselves.[16]

Another topic *A Civilização* devoted itself to was the interests of the Portuguese immigrant community and the issue of Portuguese emigration itself. On May 3, 1884, for example, it expressed concern over increased Portuguese immigration to Hawaii, something that was attributed to the corruption of the Portuguese government:

Our patriotism extends from pole to pole. We care about the well-being of all Portuguese and, given our special mission, we cannot ignore the mistreatment of our countrymen who, much to our shame and that of our country, are being forced to emigrate to the faraway Sandwich Islands in order to flee the black specter of hunger caused by the indifference and corruption of the government, which though composed of intelligent men, is criminal and intolerable. No one but the government should be blamed for this; it's from the government we should demand accountability. We have large and very rich territories in Africa, Asia end even in Oceania, where we could send the workers who are being sent to enrich the inhospitable Sandwich Islands, whose indigenous people still have some time to go before being respected in civilized countries.[17]

A year after the disappearance of *O Jornal de Noticias* from Erie in 1885, António Maria Vicente founded the illustrated weekly *O Progresso Californiense* in San Francisco, which lasted two years. The paper was distributed throughout the United States, Canada, Portugal, Brazil, and other countries with a Portuguese presence.[18] One of its most frequent sections was the "Revista dos Açores." Like other papers whose readers were mostly of Azorean and Madeiran origin, *O Progresso Californiense* divided its content by islands, but it also had a section on continental Portugal. It had a fairly large short-news section, as well as a section for obituaries, and an occasional section on shipwrecks. Additionally, it provided frequent reports on the activities of the União Portuguesa da Califórnia, and published, with some frequency, literary pieces, especially poetry, such as the long and interesting one by Guilherme Augusto de Barros, entitled "A Sombra de Portugal" (Portugal's Shadow), which appeared on January 8, 1887, and began:

> T'was the shadow of a giant
> Its height showing how
> Powerful and mighty it was
> In the past, if not now.

Of the grandeur of its past
Only bad fate remains
His brave breast wounded
To save country and faith.[19]

After *O Progresso Californiense* failed, António Maria Vicente created a new newspaper, originally titled *A União Portugueza*, later spelled as *A União Portuguesa*. It was one of the three Portuguese-American weeklies, along with *Jornal Português* and the *Luso-Americano*, that was published for more than fifty years. From the beginning, the paper was very popular within the Portuguese community of California. Perhaps for this reason, in 1892 he decided to add the subtitle "Órgão da Colónia Portuguesa da Califórnia" (Organ of the Portuguese Community of California) to the paper's name.

In 1889, Vicente sold *A União Portuguesa* to Manuel de Freitas Martins Trigueiro, who then created the Empreza Editora União Portuguesa, where he worked as editor or director until his death on January 8, 1940. Mário Bettencourt da Câmara was its editor-in-chief for several years, and Joseph S. Marshall was its editor-publisher in the 1920s. Other members of its editorial staff included Constantino Leal Soares, Júlio Freitas, and the lawyer Alberto Moura. When Câmara left, Pedro L. Claudino da Silveira replaced him as editor and typesetter between 1907 and 1917. The last editor of *A União Portuguesa* was José T. Salgueiro, who directed it from February 3, 1940, to July 13, 1942, the date of its last issue. Trigueiro's daughters also served as owner-directors: Louisa S. between February 3, 1940, and November 30, 1941, and Ângela between December 1, 1941, and July 13, 1942.

A União Portuguesa had a permanent section dedicated to brief news from the Azores, with items like the following, taken from the September 1, 1888 issue. From São Jorge: "The mists and the winds of the last weeks of June have completely destroyed the English potatoes planted in May. The damage, however, does not have a large effect on public subsistence because the amount of that type of potato planted during that particular period is very small."[20] From São Miguel: "In the village of Santo António, Nordeste, a dead body was found in the forest next to a pile of wood. It was a poor man, head of a large family, who died suddenly as he gathered firewood."[21] *A União*

A União Portugueza.

JORNAL DEDICADO Á COLONIA LUSO-AMERICANA DA CALIFORNIA

ANNO 6.º   SAN FRANCISCO DA CALIFORNIA: QUINTA-FEIRA, 23 DE FEVEREIRO DE 1893.   NO. 241

Noticias de Portugal

REVISTA DO ESTRANGEIRO

AOS QUE SOFFREM

Mrs. Dr. A. D. Howe
1320 MARKET ST.
San Francisco, California.

REVISTA DAS COLONIAS

Noticias dos Açores

MRS. DR. A. D. HOWE,
1320 MARKET ST.
San Francisco, California.

Os melhores do Mundo

HUB RANGES STOVES

Mais de 100000 em uso.
A' venda no estabelecimento de
J. DELLA MONTANYA,
San Francisco.

---

8. Cover of *A União Portugueza*
(San Francisco, California).
Copy of February 23, 1893.

Portuguesa would also often transcribe news published by other newspapers, a common practice at the time. Serialized novels were also frequently included, with preference for Portuguese works. In the 1930s, the paper even published two novels simultaneously: Émile Richebourg's *Os Filhos da Milionária* (in Júlio de Magalhães's Portuguese version) and *Amores de Príncipe*.[22] In its early years, numerous advertisements, including those by travel agencies that promoted ocean travel, were published on the last page of the newspaper. One of them, published on January 17, 1895, announced the "Vapores Portugueses" (Portuguese steamships) with regular routes between New York, the Azores, Lisbon, and Porto, such as the *Olinda, Oevenum,* and *Donna Maria.* According to the advertisement, the captain of this last ship, Captain Marreiros, was "well known and respected by all Portuguese."[23]

On March 28, 1937, *A União Portuguesa* published a special issue entitled *A União Portuguesa (1887-1937). 50º Aniversário,* which was thirty pages in length and celebrated its own history. Shortly before ceasing publication on June 8, 1942, the newspaper declared itself to be against Salazar, adhering to the manifesto of Lúcio dos Santos, a professor at the University of Porto, which he published while in exile in Brazil.[24] In its last issue of July 13, 1942, the paper published an emotional farewell editorial that recalled the hard work entailed in producing each issue, published with the "punctuality of a stopwatch,"[25] interrupted only by the earthquake that struck San Francisco in 1906, which destroyed its facilities and forced the owner to open a new office in Oakland:

> Another tombstone rises in the vast field of journalism, announcing in just two words, two syllables only—HERE LIES—a long biography, the many hours of supreme pain and intimate joy that made up the more-than-half-century existence of the *União Portuguesa.* Yesterday it was a newspaper from Crockett, not too long before, one from Pinole, in this neighborhood, and further away in time and space, with a history of more than one hundred years, one of the major dailies of this country, the *Boston Evening Transcript.* And many others. Why? Because all of man's creations are mortal. Every week, for about 55 years, the *União Portuguesa,* the oldest newspaper in our community, paid a visit to its

subscribers. The only interruption was the week of the earthquake of 1906, during which the city of San Francisco was totally destroyed. Since then, as before, this newspaper has been published in Oakland with the punctuality of a stopwatch. The long life of this well-known weekly, which now leaves us, is owed to the tenacity of its owner and administrator, and the help of his genial brother Félix Trigueiro.[26]

O Amigo dos Católicos was established in the city of Irvington, CA, in 1888, but it was quickly transferred to Mission San Jose (now Fremont). As its name indicates, it was a Catholic weekly founded by the priests Manuel Francisco Fernandes[27] and João Francisco Tavares, natives of the island of Pico, Azores. In 1889, Francisco Inácio de Lemos (of Terceira) and Manuel B. Quaresma (of Pico) bought *O Amigo dos Católicos* and transferred its headquarters to Pleasanton, CA. In 1893, the priest Guilherme Silveira da Glória, from Pico, Azores, became the paper's co-owner and editor-in-chief, moving its headquarters to Hayward. Finally, in 1896, Joaquim Borges de Menezes became its editor for several months, renaming it *O Arauto* and moving its headquarters to Oakland.

O Amigo dos Católicos was a weekly paper intended to curb anti-clerical campaigns from the local press. It defined itself as "religious, commercial, and newsy," and "devoted to the Holy Mary." Its successor, *O Arauto*, based in Oakland under the direction of Menezes, became one of the most important papers in the Portuguese community between 1896 and 1917. The paper promoted itself with headlines that highlighted its wide distribution and the quality of its serials: "*O Arauto* is the newspaper with the largest circulation among the 100,000 Portuguese in the United States, as a result of publishing the most news and being the only paper that offers valuable prizes to its subscribers. *O Arauto* publishes novels of great interest, translated specifically for its pages."[28] Menezes himself translated some of the novels, such as *Vingança de uma Mulher Ciumenta* (Revenge of a Jealous Woman), published between 1908 and 1909. Like other newspapers of the time, it also featured personal news about well-known people in the community, such as the following from September 4, 1909: "Worse: The condition of Mr. José C. B. de Carvalho, currently in the Portuguese hospital of this city, has deteriorated."[29]

O Arauto often printed letters sent by members of the community about their own fraternal organizations, and responded to correspondence from readers through editorials.

A Unique Case:
The Portuguese Press in Hawaii, 1885-1927

The circumstances that gave rise to the emergence, survival, and vibrancy of Portuguese newspapers in Hawaii between 1885 and 1927, despite the islands' distance and isolation from Portugal, make this a special case in the history of the Portuguese-American press.

Just a year after the closing of *A Civilização* in 1884 in New Bedford, the Portuguese press would appear in the heart of the Pacific Ocean. The signing of the 1876 treaty between the United States and the Kingdom of Hawaii to open the U.S. market to Hawaiian sugar led to a boom in new sugar plantations and an increased demand for labor that attracted a flood of Portuguese contract workers.[30] Between 1878 and 1887 numerous ships arrived in Hawaii that brought approximately 10,700 Portuguese.[31] After that period, the arrival of Portuguese gradually decreasing until 1910, with a total of 16,000 new Portuguese immigrants. The wealthier classes of Hawaiian society tended to see the Portuguese as second-class citizens, which caused a grudge that stimulated their emigration to other continental territories of the United States, mainly California, in search of equality and new opportunities.[32] Despite this, many stayed, and according to the official census in 1910, the Portuguese accounted for 11.6% of Hawaii's population[33] of almost two hundred thousand people.[34]

Their arrival and settlement led to the emergence of Portuguese journalism in Hawaii. The first Portuguese newspaper in Hawaii was *O Luso Hawaiiano*, published in Honolulu between August 15, 1885, and 1890.[35] This was the first newspaper in a series of twelve titles, nine published in Honolulu and three in Hilo. Some of them proved quite durable: *O Facho* operated for more than twenty years, and *O Luso*, *A Liberdade*, and *A Setta* all lasted for more than ten years, but most others were of relatively short duration. This is not surprising given the fact that there was such a small number of immigrants.[36] In some cases, the newspapers were an effective instrument in the

HONRAE A PATRIA QUE ELLA VOS CONTEMPLA   PERIODICO HEBDOMADARIO   A UNIÃO FAZ A FORÇA

★O POPULAR★

ORGAO da CLASSE OPERARIA—PORTUGUESA NO TERRITORIO de HAWAII.

ANNO I.   HONOLULU, OAHU, QUINTA FEIRA, 5 OUTUBRO, de 1911.   PREÇO 5 CENTS.   No. 12

A NOVA BANDEIRA DA REPUBLICA PORTUGUEZA

9. Cover of *O Popular* (Honolulu,
Oahu, Hawaii). Copy of October 5, 1911.

10. Cover of *O Luso Hawaiiano*
(Honolulu, Hawaii).
Copy of December 13, 1890.

fight for workers' rights, for the labor conditions in the sugar plantations were harsh. The weekly *O Popular*, owned by the Popular Newspaper Co. based in Honolulu, was an outspoken defender of the rights of Portuguese workers. It was founded on July 20, 1911, by João de Sousa Ramos with the subtitle, "Órgão da Classe Operária Portuguesa no Território de Hawaii" (Organ of the Portuguese Working Class in the Hawaiian Territory) and was published until January 1913.[37]

O Luso Hawaiiano had several editors throughout its five years of existence: J. B. Marques, 1885-1888; Pedro Augusto Dias, 1888-1889; and José Augusto Monteiro Osório, 1889-1891.[38] According to his biographical sketch in George F. Nellist's *Men of Hawaii* (1935), Osório was born on November 13, 1858, in Celorico da Beira, Portugal, the son of Miguel Monteiro Osório and Maria Emília Nogueira Guimarães Osório. He was married to Maria Mathilde Sant'Anna, from Paulo do Mar (Madeira), on February 12, 1882.[39] Osório, who was the vice consul of Portugal in Hilo,[40] worked for A. Gonçalves & Company in Honolulu and for Grinbaum & Company and W.C. Peacock & Company. He owned a store in Kohala and was also associated with Hoffschlaeger & Company in Hilo.[41] In 1911, Osório, along with his thirteen children (one of whom is the Portuguese-Hawaiian novelist Elvira Osório Roll),[42] formed the Osório & Company, Ltd., which was "a leading mercantile establishment of Hilo." Osório was also a member of the Honolulu Rifles Company, under Captain Fisher.[43]

The second newspaper in Portuguese was the *Aurora Hawaiiana*, published in Honolulu from 1888 until March 28, 1891,[44] with the subtitle, "Jornal Litterário, Liberal, Mercantil e Instructivo, Consagrado á Colónia Portugueza das Ilhas de Sandwich."[45] Its owner was C. L. Brito, who printed the newspaper through the Sociedade Editora Aurora Hawaiana. Between 1889 and 1891, Manoel José de Freitas was the editor.[46] According to the Hawaiian Historical Society, a defamation lawsuit associated with an election campaign caused Brito to go bankrupt[47] and in 1891 the *Aurora Hawaiiana* merged with *O Luso Hawaiiano* to form a new paper—the weekly *A União Lusitana-Hawaiiana*, which became *A União Lusitana* after 1893. The subtitle for *A União Lusitana* demonstrated the paper's intention of becoming the voice of the Portuguese community in Hawaii: "Semanário Independente Dedicado Estrictamente aos Interesses Políticos, Moraes e Materiaes da Colónia

Portuguesa nas Ilhas de Sandwich."[48] It was published through a company named A União Lusitana and edited by August Jean Baptiste Marques (1891-1892) and G. Pereira (1892-1896).[49]

The weekly *A Sentinella* appeared in Honolulu in 1892 and was published until 1896 with an average length of 12 pages and a subtitle similar to that of *A União Lusitana:* "Jornal politico e litterario dedicado especialmente aos interesses da colonia portugueza de Hawaii."[50] The paper, which was owned by a group of Portuguese immigrants, adopted the slogan, "Pelo Direito se Pugna" (We fight for what is right). The director of the paper was J. M. Teixeira, who had the collaboration of the interpreter John (João) Marques Vivas.[51] Eventually *A Sentinella* merged with *A União Lusitana* as *O Luso,* which would appear in two periods—first between February 15, 1896, and October 30, 1897; and then from March 5, 1910, until March 27, 1924. The first editor was João de Sousa Ramos (1896-1911 and 1923-1924), followed by Godfrey (Godofredo) Ferreira Affonso (1912-1913), Manuel A. Silva (1913-1918), Manuel G. Santos (1918-1923), and A.H.R. Vieira (1923-1924).[52]

Three other newspapers appeared at the end of the century: *As Boas Novas*, edited by Augusto Honório R. Vieira (1896-1898; 1899-1905) and Ernest Gomes da Silva (1898-1899);[53] *O Direito*, edited by António José Rego (1896 and 1898);[54] and *A Liberdade*, published between August 17, 1899, and 1910, edited by C. Pereira (1900-1906 and 1907-1910) and Joseph Ferreira Durão (1906-1907).[55] The subtitle of this last paper invoked Portugal's colonial power: "Jornal Imperial, Literário e Noticioso Dedicado aos Interesses da Colónia Portuguesa em Hawaii" (Imperial, Literary and News-focused Newspaper Dedicated to the Interests of the Portuguese Community in Hawaii), but also had a promotional slogan in English: "The Independent Paper of the Portuguese Colony."

The Portuguese newspaper with the second longest duration, *A Setta*, was published weekly in Hilo between 1903 and 1921. It was edited by Manuel G. Santos (1903-1904), Godfrey Ferreira Affonso (1904-1911), Augusto Souza Costa (1911-1914), Manuel A. Silva (1915-1918), and Ernest Gomes da Silva (1919-1921).[56] Costa was a native of Angra do Heroísmo on the island of Terceira in the Azores. According to L. C. Newton, he was born on August 20, 1887, the son of Antonio Souza and Marie Neves Ribeiro Costa.[57] On June 16, 1927, he married Sylvia Pacheco in Honolulu. At age fourteen he worked in a store in Honohina, but his passion was newspapers. His first job in the field was at the *Hawaii Herald* in Hilo, where he worked for five years. Following this, he worked for *A Setta*, also in Hilo, and then for *O Repórter* in Oakland, California.[58] When he returned to Hawaii, he worked in the law offices of LeBond & Smith and as a Portuguese and Spanish interpreter for the District and Circuit Courts of Hilo from 1910 to 1912. For two years, he was the "Deputy Internal Revenue Collector in charge at Hilo Office."[59] In 1919, he became manager of the Wailea Milling Co., eventually becoming its president. On April 29, 1925, Governor W. R. Farrington named him a member of the Board of Public Lands of the Territory of Hawaii. He was elected in 1925 to the Hawaii County Board of Supervisors, and was reelected in 1927, 1930, 1936, and 1938.[60]

O Facho and *A Voz Pública* were two other newspapers with headquarters in Hilo. The weekly *O Facho*, which carried the English subtitle "The Intellectual Light of The Portuguese Colony," suggesting an educational intention, was published between 1906 and 1927, and was the longest-running newspaper in the archipelago. The founder and editor of the paper, António de Carvalho, known as Antone C. Oak, was a native of São Miguel, Azores. Little information exists on *A Voz Pública*. Edgar C. Knowlton[61] and Manoel da Silveira Cardozo state that it was published with an unknown frequency between 1899 and 1904.[62]

In his article "The Portuguese language press of Hawaii" (1960), Knowlton provides biographical information about early Portuguese-Hawaiian editors. According to Knowlton, the majority were from the Azores and Madeira, but there were also some from the mainland and even from other countries.[63]

August Jean Baptiste Marques, editor of the *União Lusitana*, was the first Portuguese editor in Hawaii. He was born in Toulon, France, on November 17, 1841, and arrived in Hawaii on December 25, 1878. He pioneered the digging of artesian wells in Honolulu in 1880. In 1883, he taught French at the Punahou School. Between 1890 and 1891, he was a member of the Hawaiian Parliament. He was a medical student in Paris and earned a PhD from the University of Lisbon. He was consul of France from 1912 to 1929 and also of Russia, Panama, and Belgium. He received the distinction of "Chevalier de la Legion d' Honneur" from the French government.[64]

As for the other editors, information is scarce and fragmentary. Pedro Augusto Dias, who was editor of *O Luso Hawaiiano* and manager of the Waipahu Store, was born in Funchal in 1855 and died in Oahu in 1908.[65] He arrived in Honolulu in September 1878 on board the *Priscilla*, with Godfrey (Godofredo) Ferreira Affonso, who, in addition to editing the *Luso,* also worked for the *Advertiser* in Honolulu. Affonso was born in Funchal on July 26, 1875, and died in Honolulu on November 7, 1950.[66] Joseph Ferreira Durão, editor of *A Liberdade*, was born in Lisbon on July 21, 1869, and died in Honolulu on February 26, 1942.[67] He had arrived in Hawaii with a group of Portuguese workers from New Bedford. Manoel José de Freitas, director of the *Aurora Hawaiiana*, came to the archipelago around 1886. He became a teacher of Portuguese and also taught in Honolulu's YMCA's racial integration school. On August 3, 1887, he became a member of Electoral District 6. On June 30, 189, he left for San Francisco aboard the *Albert*.[68] António de Carvalho (Antone C. Oak), founder of *O Facho*, was born in São Miguel on May 18, 1856 and died in Hilo on May 18, 1936. He owned a store on the island of Hawaii.[69] António (Antone) José de Rego, founder of *O Direito*, was born in São Miguel, Azores, in 1851 and died in Honolulu on August 14, 1929.[70] He came to Hawaii in 1881 and worked as a cabinetmaker. Manuel G. Santos, editor of *O Luso,* was born on September 23, 1871, in British Guyana and died on December 25, 1932.[71] He immigrated to Hawaii around 1900 and was ordained a minister in 1906.[72] Ernest Gomes da Silva, one of the editors of *A Setta,* was born in Madeira in 1875 and died in Hilo on March 9, 1955.[73] He came to Honolulu aboard the *Thomas Bell* in 1888 and became a minister of the Portuguese Christian Church of Hilo in June 1899.[74] Manuel A. Silva was born in Madeira in 1868 and settled in Hawaii in 1879.[75] He was contracted by the Hawaiian Sugar Planter's Association (HSPA) to recruit workers from the Azores, Madeira, continental Portugal, and Spain.[76] Augusto Honório R. Vieira, the founder of *Boas Novas,* who was born in Funchal, Madeira, on April 24, 1874, arrived in Honolulu in 1883.[77] He was a primary school teacher, worked for the jewelry company H.F. Wichman for seven years, and later became a jeweler.[78] He died in October 1934. João (John) Marques Vivas, who was a writer for *A União Lusitana*, was born in Madeira in 1863 and died in Wailuku, Maui, on November 5, 1912.[79] He landed in Hawaii in August 1879 aboard the passenger ship *Ravenscrag*.[80]

He served in the military in Macau, studied law, and became a successful law-yer.[81] Finally, João de Sousa Ramos, the founder of *O Luso*, was a native of São Miguel, Azores, where he was born in 1857.[82]

New Voices of Portuguese-American Journalism, 1890-1909

Between 1890 and 1909, Portuguese journalism thrived in the United States. As migration from Portugal continued to grow, so did the demand for infor-mation in Portuguese, providing business opportunities for immigrants with publishing experience or strong educational backgrounds. Forty newspapers were founded during this period. Most were short-lived, but some managed to gain a lasting foothold. In addition to what was happening in Hawaii, strong journalistic projects emerged in California and Massachusetts during this period, such as *O Repórter* (Oakland, San Francisco, 1897-1916), *A Liber-dade* (Sacramento, 1900-1937), *O Independente* (New Bedford, 1897-1945), *A Alvorada* (1909-1923?), and *Novidades* (New Bedford, 1907-1948). Along with the 1930s, this was one of the most successful historical periods in terms of the number of titles founded. In California alone, sixteen newspapers were published during this period, in addition to the *Boletim da U.P.E.C.*

At this time, California was growing rapidly, with a multiethnic, multicultural, and multilingual social structure that included a wide range of religious beliefs and political affinities. The massive influx of immigrants from diverse backgrounds caused conflicts that could lead to clashes. Racist attitudes and religious intolerance were not rare. It was an historical stage in which political structures and labor relations needed to adapt to a new context. It was a time of change and political debate, but it also of intense cultural learning and social integration in which the Portuguese-American newspapers were intricately involved.[83]

Struggles for leadership were commonplace within each immigrant community, and the press was often the most effective means of propa-ganda for the contenders. In the case of the Portuguese, there were recur-rent controversies involving Republicanism against Monarchism, clericalism against anti-clericalism, and policies within fraternal societies. In some cases, personal-level conflicts acquired a public dimension through the press, such as the one between Mário Bettencourt da Câmara and Guilherme Silveira da Glória. The latter, through *O Amigo dos Católicos*, attacked the former's criticisms of Catholicism while editor-in-chief of *A União Portuguesa*; the row went on for years. Then, in the first issue of the critical and satirical magazine *A Chrónica*, which Câmara founded in San Francisco on July 6, 1895, he again picked up the dispute with Glória in an editorial entitled "Ao Povo Português" (To the Portuguese People), accusing the priest of seeking to increase his popularity at Câmara's expense.[84] The editorial, preceded by the title "Private Court of the Public Conscience – Father Glória and I,"[85] was accompanied by a letter, published in both Portuguese and English, addressed to the highest Church authority of the area: "Open Letter to the Most Illustrious, Most Excellent, Most Reverend Archbishop P. W. Riordan, Most Eminent Prelate of the Catholic Diocese of San Francisco, California."[86] The letter stated that he was forced to abandon *A União Portuguesa* and found *A Chrónica* to defend himself against a smear campaign launched by Glória:

> Illustrious Prelate, for two years, Father Guilherme Glória, editor-in-chief of a weekly that is a pseudo-advocate of the interests of the Catholic Church, has been spitting at me the vilest of insults, rendered in no less humiliating language. This behavior has discredited me to the point where I had to found this publication in order to defend myself before the eyes of my countrymen who may not know us, so that they may judge for themselves between the *religious* and the *secular* writer, between the *clergyman* and the *layman*.[87]

Câmara laid the responsibility for the insults he had received at the feet of the archbishop because, as he said,

> given the fact that on the first page of that weekly there is a statement claiming "This newspaper is approved and recommended by His Excellency the Most Reverend P. W. RIORDAN, Archbishop of San Francisco," it is clear that either you are in agreement with Father Glória with regards to the insults that newspaper has hurled at me or you have been and are being

deceived, and are unaware of what has been written in that weekly as well its true mission.[88]

The dispute between Câmara and Glória spread to other newspapers and other issues. When, for example, *O Eco Açoreano*, of which Constantino C. Leal Soares was part owner, campaigned against the Portuguese Republican Party and the Republican movement, the director of *A Chrónica*, an exiled Republican, took it as a personal attack. In it, he again saw the hand of Glória, since Soares worked for him as editor of *O Amigo dos Cathólicos*.[89] Câmara did not attribute Glória's attacks to a religious motivation, in defense of Catholic interest, but rather to other ideological and journalistic rivalries:

> Therefore, it was not "religious zeal" intended to stamp out misconception or heresy that forced Father Glória to attack us because, up to then, Catholicism and its ministers had received better and greater support from *A União Portugueza* than from *O Amigo dos Cathólicos*. What was it, then? That is the question! Let's go back to the first articles written about me by Father Glória. It's clear that when he referred to the editorial office of the *União*, he was talking about me, since I was the one charged with the honor of shaping that newspaper into a publication that more clearly reflected the interests of our country and our immigrant community. Perhaps by examining those texts, and exposing some facts and documents associated with them, we can discover something illuminating about this murky question.[90]

The controversy also affected other priests who defended Glória against Câmara's accusations. One of them was Fr. Alfredo A. M. Santos, who intervened in the journalistic duel in *O Amigo dos Cathólicos* on July 27, 1895, after Câmara accused him of having lied when he assured him that Glória no longer wrote articles for *O Amigo dos Cathólicos*.[91] The conflict between Câmara and *O Amigo dos Cathólicos* did not cease when Joaquim Borges de Menezes became its editor and owner, shortly after the paper was transformed into *O Arauto*. The Republican journalist settled accounts with the new editor of the religious newspaper, ridiculing his professional skills as a journalist.

Câmara first mocked Menezes for an article entitled "De New Bedford, Mass., a Hayward, Cal.," about his journey between the two North American cities, which he had published in *O Amigo dos Cathólicos*. After Menezes responded, referring to Câmara by the nickname "Cabotino," (Vaudeville actor) and calling him envious, the director of *A Chrónica* punched back: "Just as this donkey in human form classified us, this fisherman of murky waters, this starving dog that ran to the first bone thrown to him (...)."[92] Câmara further ridiculed his opponent by mentioning a case in which, in his capacity as editor-in-chief of *A União Portuguesa*, he had rejected an article by Menezes:

> On June 10, 1893, the owner of *A União Portugueza* placed on my desk, in the editorial office of that newspaper, an unsolicited article titled "St. John in Boston and St. John in the Azores." The article was written by Mr. Joaquim de Menezes. I read the prose and the verse—it also contained verse—and read it again once or twice. As I turned to inquire about the author, the writer [sic], I saw two faces looking at me and, drawn upon them, the question, "What do you think?" It was the owner of *A União* and the unfortunate Mr. Ferreira D'Ávila, who worked for the paper at the time. "Who is this scholar?," I asked. "It's a village schoolteacher who is now on the East Coast, where he fled to because of political problems at home." "Ah!... For a schoolteacher... it's good; for a newspaper writer deserving of the honor of political persecution by anyone other than a poor village mayor, it leaves a lot to be desired." I did another reading, this time aloud, stressing certain incorrections that would be forgivable were it not for the literary pretensions of the article, and placed St. John in the reserve box.[93]

Câmara's anti-monarchist rhetoric provoked clashes with other prominent figures in the California community, such as the consul of Portugal in San Francisco, Ignácio R. da Costa Duarte, who was offended by the portrait of him published in *A Chrónica* as part of a text that was critical of the Portuguese monarchy. In a letter published in the weekly *A Pátria*, the consul of Portugal showed his public displeasure with *A Chrónica* for its "deplorable abuse." Câmara responded by denigrating Portuguese royalty in a new article aimed at the diplomat:

So the Consul classifies as violent attacks and insults to the king and queen the fact that we have said that Queen Amelia is committed to transforming the country into a den of scoundrels from various sub-sections and both sexes of Jesuitism, even though her active collaboration in filling that poor land with all the tramps and lay brothers that exceed the holding capacity of the French lairs of the black sect is clear and unfortunate proof of that. Is this not true? How, then, is this an insult to the queen? Doesn't she implement this reactionary policy, semi-officially, with the passive tolerance of the king?[94]

Other Portuguese-American newspapers published in California during this period include *A Pátria*, printed by Manoel Stone in Oakland between 1891 and 1897 on an irregular basis; *O Eco Açoreano*, managed by Constantino C. Leal Soares in San Francisco in 1890; *O Progresso*, edited by Frank Silva in 1894; and *Nova Pátria* in Oakland.

The longest-running of these Portuguese-American periodical publication—the *Boletim da União Portuguesa do Estado da Califórnia*—was founded in San Francisco on August 1, 1880, and it was initially edited by Câmara. The *Boletim da U.P.E.C.* is the only newsletter of an institution included in this study because of its longevity, its institutional prestige, its impact on the Portuguese-American community in California,[95] and because at times it utilized a journalistic approach in the way it dealt with issues affecting the Portuguese immigrant community. It was published in two periods, one running from March 1, 1898, to June 1967, and another beginning in January 1968, when the newsletter was recast as *U.P.E.C. Life*.[96] It was published under this title until the creation of the Portuguese Fraternal Society of America (PFSA) in January 2010.[97] The *Boletim da U.P.E.C.* started with a circulation of 2,500 copies, which expanded as its membership increased.[98] It was published monthly, quarterly, and semi-annually in different periods, with a variable format, generally of a magazine type.[99] Its language was Portuguese, though English was occasionally used, and its subtitle was "Órgão Oficial da União Portuguesa do Estado da Califórnia" (Official Organ of the Portuguese Union of the State of California).

Between 1968 and 1995, Carlos Almeida was the director, and from 1995 until 2009, it was edited by Duarte Batista. In its first issues, it was limited to reproductions of official statements regarding the operation of the institution, with a "president's letter" that chronicled the visits of the president of the U.P.E.C. to the local boards (known as "subordinate councils") throughout the state, as well as resolutions by the board of directors, treasury reports, acknowledgments, activities, parties, ceremonies, members' deaths, organization directories, etc. After the April 1940 issue,[100] the *Boletim* introduced advertisements. Its reporting format would adapt to the needs of its time. During the Second World War, for example, it adopted a more propagandistic discourse in support of the U.S. government and the numerous Portuguese-American soldiers on the frontlines. After the 1950s, information of a more journalistic or cultural character increased. With the April 1960 issue, the newsletter began to include informative content provided by members of the U.P.E.C.[101]

In 1960, the *Boletim da U.P.E.C.* started being printed at the presses of the *Jornal Português*. From July 1961, it was printed by *A Voz de Portugal* of Hayward, and later by the Bay View Printing Service in San Leandro. In June 1967, the newsletter ceased publication, and news about the U.P.E.C. was transmitted instead through Portuguese radio, but this lasted only for about six months. In January 1968, publication resumed under the name *U.P.E.C. Life*, in a magazine format, printed in color and displaying the promotional motto, "A fraternal insurance society serving humanity since 1880." Reports on Portuguese culture and community activities organized by the U.P.E.C. or other Portuguese-American institutions were published in this new phase.[102] The Freitas Library[103] was founded at this time, and its director-founder, Carlos Almeida, also acted as secretary-treasurer of U.P.E.C. and director of *U.P.E.C. Life*. The newsletter was published twice a year after 1978 and it appeared regularly until 1995, when Carlos Almeida retired after thirty-six years of service. With the new director, Duarte Batista, *U.P.E.C. Life* became a profusely illustrated magazine providing news about the institution. The magazine went out of print when negotiations began to integrate all the Portuguese-American fraternal organizations in California into a single body, and the project ended on January 1, 2010, with the creation of the Portuguese Fraternal Society of America, directed by Timothy Borges.[104]

Besides the long-lived *Boletim da U.P.E.C.*, there was a series of newspapers that emerged at the beginning of the last century, including the weekly from San Jose *A Semana Portugueza* (1903) and the magazine *A Crítica Literária*, both founded by Joaquim Borges de Menezes; Pedro L. C. da Silveira's magazine *Portugal-América* (1905) in Fresno; and *A Voz da Verdade* (1908-1909) in Oakland. However, all of these were short-lived. Besides *A União Portuguesa* and *O Arauto*, the only newspaper that was able to establish itself for a longer period of time was Guilherme Silveira da Glória's popular *A Liberdade*, published between October 1, 1900, and 1937, first in Sacramento (until 1920) and then in Oakland, where it was printed on a daily basis "for a while."[105] In 1926, *A Liberdade* claimed to be the only Portuguese newspaper in California and boasted in its header that "We reach all of the Portuguese population on the Pacific coast. There are more than 100,000 in the state of California; one third in the Bay Cities; 18,000 in Greater Oakland. Advertise in this paper if you wish to secure Portuguese trade [*sic*]. They like to read your 'ads' in their own language." The following phrase recurs throughout the 1930s: "Dedicado aos Interesses da Cólonia Portuguesa na Califórnia" (Dedicated to the Interests of the Portuguese Community in California). In December 1934, a new promotional slogan appeared in the header: "O Jornal de Maior Circulação entre os Portugueses da Califónia e Hawai" (The Newspaper with the Largest Circulation among the Portuguese in California and Hawaii).[106]

A Liberdade was managed and edited by Glória. In his editorials, he often invoked great heroes and myths from Portuguese history in order to increase the papers educational value. On July 7, 1934, in an article about one of the more important female fraternal societies of the community, the Sociedade Rainha Santa Isabel, Glória recalls the virtues of the queen to which the association owed its name, the consort of the great King Dinis, and emphasizes the king's life as a farmer, poet, and founder of the first university in Portugal:

> No other king of the Portuguese Nation, either before or after, lived as much with the people and for the people as King Dinis. His popularity was such that it came down through the centuries and even today it resonates gently in the memory of the people. Farmers, seeing his interest in their labors, called him, proudly, "the Farmer King," and the commoners seeing how he challenged the privileges of the nobles and the clergy, checking their lawless ambitions and forcing them to stay on the path of

justice with regards to the men of the plow and the hoe, would exclaim with delight, "King Dinis achieved all his goals![107]

Glória stopped publishing *A Liberdade* after the loss of his son and wife. When his wife, Ana Beatriz Glória, died in January 1937, the news appeared on the cover of *A Liberdade*, with her photo and an ode, in Portuguese and English, entitled "Mea Máxima Culpa" ("The Prayer").[108] Before closing the newspaper, he tried to find a buyer by running ads explaining that he wished to sell because of his old age and recent bereavement: "This sale is necessary, due to my old age, and especially as a result of my state of depression caused by the irreparable loss of my wife, who was the soul of this business, and the painful loss of my son, the only hope I had left in this bitter and scabrous life path."[109]

In Massachusetts, eighteen newspapers emerged during this period. During the 1890s alone, nine were founded. Among them, *O Independente* appeared from 1897 until 1945; *Novo Mundo* lasted four years; and *Correio Português* lasted more than twelve years. All the others failed to reach their first anniversary: *O Colombo* (1892-1893), created by Joaquim Maciel; *O Português* (1893), published by the Catholic priests Cândido Martins Neves and Claudio Vieira e Pimentel; *A Verdade* (1893), founded by Francisco Caetano Borges da Silva, who also edited *O Progresso* in 1907;[110] *A Revista Portuguesa* (1895), founded by Joaquim Borges de Menezes;[111] *Jornal das Senhoras* (1898), a newspaper dedicated to women, founded by Eugénio Escobar;[112] and the illustrated weekly *Açores-América* (1903), which was based in Cambridge—the only one of these papers not based in New Bedford—created by Eugénio Vaz Pacheco do Canto e Castro, a former teacher and principal of Antero de Quental High School in Ponta Delgada (São Miguel, Azores), which published thirteen issues between February 14 and March 16, 1903. It was distributed in Portugal and Brazil, and published some articles written in English by Burton Holmes.[113]

O Correio Português was founded on August 15, 1895, with the subtitle, "Jornal Dedicado à Colónia Portuguesa na Nova Inglaterra" (Newspaper Dedicated to the Portuguese Community in New England). According to H.W. Kastor & Son's directory of the American press, *O Correio Português* had an average circulation of 2,500 copies in 1906.[114] The founder and editor in its initial years, Manuel das Neves Xavier, published content similar to that of his previous newspaper, *A Civilização*, with articles discussing moral issues. In January 1896, he published an editorial entitled "Moral," which exemplifies his moral philosophy on the relation between conservatism and altruism:

> Even today, many people think that killing is simply the taking of someone's life with a knife or a gun; that stealing is simply the taking of something that belongs to another. Nothing could be further from the truth. People are killed when someone takes away their ability to take care of themselves, when they are forced to work beyond their physical ability, when they are not fed, clothed or housed properly; or when their reputation is damaged by slander... Ultimately, all personal gain that is obtained at the expense of others, be it in commerce or in industry, is always a theft, and sometimes murder as well. In contrast, by virtue of the instinct for the conservation of the species, every time we help someone we feel an intimate satisfaction, and that satisfaction is greater the greater the number of those helped and the greater the help provided, with maximum satisfaction coming from helping the whole species forever.[115]

O Independente was one of the most successful weeklies in the community's history.[116] Though few copies have been preserved, the paper deserves its own study because of the richness of its content and its nearly fifty years of existence in the "capital" of the Portuguese community on the East Coast, New Bedford. Although its foundation is traditionally attributed to João Francisco Escobar,[117] Miguel F. Policarpo,[118] in fact, founded it as a biweekly on March 30, 1897, with the help of his brothers David and Joaquim.[119] Beginning with issue number five, Frederico Pacheco Macedo joined Miguel F. Policarpo, and the newspaper thereafter became a weekly as the property of Policarpo's & Co. After a few months, the paper was transferred to the firm Bartholo & Co (owned by the public notary Alípio Coelho Bartholo[120] and the priest António Claudio Vieira), where Policarpo worked as a printer and typographer.[121] *O Independente* would later be purchased by the consuls of Portugal in Providence, Fall River, Boston, and New Bedford who intended to use it as part of their campaign to indoctrinate Portuguese immigrants in New England. The project failed, and in November 1923, José M. Almeida and typographer

António Fernandes Fortes acquired the paper. The latter would eventually assume full ownership.

Between 1926 and 1932, Fortes hired Aníbal Branco as an editor (with a salary of $15/week) and Delfina Sousa as a linotypist. In June 1932, Fortes resold the paper to João Rodrigues Rocha (director and editor from 1933 to 1940) and the printing equipment to Joseph Merola of Newark, who would use it to found *A Tribuna*.[122] During Rocha's administration, the paper was owned by the Portuguese Newspaper Company. Journalists and other contributors included John E. Neves (editor of the Section of Greater Boston), Carlos Domingues (editor of the Section of Blackstone Valley), Manuel de Freitas Junior, Jose Serrano, Dr. Madureira e Castro, Ezequiel S. Cardoso, and V. J. Deponte, among others. In 1920, Joaquim dos Santos Oliveira was the editor.

O Independente, which came out on Thursdays, was for many years "the oldest Portuguese newspaper in New England," as its first page announced, and it was one of the most professionally produced, especially during Rocha's time as director. It contained various sections and its contents dealt with all kinds of issues associated with the Portuguese-American community, as seen in the following examples, extracted from copies found at various archives. The June 18, 1936 edition featured front page stories about the lack of Portuguese priests in the United States and the death of the consul general of Portugal in California, Francisco de Pina Aragão e Costa.[123] On January 14, 1937, the paper published a story about the trip that the journalist and editor Arthur Vieira Ávila took to New England to promote António Lopes Ribeiro's film *Gado Bravo*.[124] On the cover of the same issue, a photo of Salazar appeared with the caption "Right or wrong?," which was accompanied by the following text: "Prime Minister Oliveira Salazar, the person responsible for the latest international actions taken by the Portuguese Government, who, by virtue of his great and ascendant importance, will, in the words of many— make or break Portugal!!"[125] On February 8, 1940, the weekly reported on the inauguration of a monument dedicated to Henry the Navigator in Fall River and on the possible reopening of the Portuguese pavilion at the 1939 New York's World Fair.[126] Like most Portuguese newspapers, *O Independente* published serialized novels, including *O Conde de Malvar ou a Filha de um Pirata* by D. Torcuato Tárrago y Mateos.

Printers, editors, and contributors frequently moved from paper to paper. Immigrant journalists, like other professionals, worked where the pay was best or where they could access the most direct path to their own version of the "American Dream." This caused quite a few rivalries and misunderstandings, especially when an employee left to join a direct competitor, as when Rocha left the *Diario de Noticias* to become the editor and owner of *O Independente* in July 1932. Rocha was a self-made man, full of energy, initiative and entrepreneurial ability. He had been one of the most valuable employees at *Diario de Noticias*, helping to manage the company and accompanying the owner, Guilherme Machado Luiz, in August 1931 on an official visit to Lisbon, where he was able to interview the President of the Republic, Óscar Carmona, General Norton de Matos, and Republican member of parliament Francisco Manuel Homem Cristo.[127] The two papers had a history of exchanging criticisms through the articles of their various columnists, but this was usually done with a certain prudence and elegance. When Rocha took over *O Independente*, however, the tone underwent a drastic change. As noted by Rui Antunes Correia,[128] the *Diario de Noticias* even hinted that Rocha had left because of irregularities detected in the advertising revenues and published a story about Policarpo's arrest for supposedly engaging in illegal gambling. These reports were a *casus belli* for *O Independente*. On February 16, 1934, the *Diario de Noticias* published an article entitled "*O Independente*, Esterqueiro Colonial" ("*O Independente*, Community Dump"), which continued the personal attacks on Rocha and Policarpo:

> *O Independente*, a newspaper whose owner António Fernandes Fortes, upon leaving the U.S. and liquidating his business, threw into the trash barrel because there was nobody interested in continuing to publish that weekly which, under his ownership, had but one merit—that of being clean and honorable; that title, headline or shingle was picked up from the pile of useless things, from the pile of filth, by the dirty hands of a certain J. R. Rocha, "Rochinha" to himself and to the group of hustlers who make up the gang that is continually preying on this poor community. . . All the scum, all that is base, cheap, and despicable was able to find a hiding place there. . . The scoundrels did not waste any time. Right away, as was to be

expected, *O Independente* became the dump of the community... But then came the case of the raid on the gambling house, which was kept by that loud paladin from the firm of the morally "independents." Miguel Policarpo the "chaste," Miguel Policarpo the "moralist," Miguel Policarpo the brain of that den of thieves, had been caught in the act by the police.[129]

The *Diario de Noticias*'s public claims about Rocha's leaving the newspaper had little in common with the version of events that Rocha himself sent to the Portuguese authorities. On February 18, 1939, in a confidential letter to the director of the Secretariat of National Propaganda (SPN), António Ferro, he attributed his resignation to politics, arguing that his departure from the *Diario de Noticias* was the result of his clashes with the newspaper's management in defense of the Estado Novo's policies.[130] Rocha affirmed in the letter that he had maintained a secret alliance with the Consul of Portugal in Providence, José Agostinho de Oliveira, to defend the policies of the dictatorship in New England with all the means of propaganda at his disposal.[131] In support of his testimony, he noted that he had entrusted the political orientation of his weekly to Consul José Agostinho de Oliveira, who was also responsible for an editorial section.[132] According to Rocha, from 1929 until 1932, the period in which he was employed by the daily, he had several clashes with the owner and staff of the newspaper: "And all this because I held firm in my defense of Portugal's political situation and refused to take part in the attack they wanted to launch against Consul Oliveira by any means necessary."

In 1934, Rocha declared himself the winner of the fight initiated against him and his colleagues at *O Independente*:

For two weeks I was the target of the vilest of attacks, which, indirectly, was also intended to hurt Consul Agostinho de Oliveira. But I knew the men of the *Diario de Noticias*, and in our defense we crushed and reduced to ash all the slander and lies that they threw at us. Shortly after, we published a special issue dedicated to the Minister of Portugal in Washington in which more than 400 leading figures from the community, such as members of the clergy, etc., showed their support.[133]

Rocha's statements in support of the Estado Novo must be placed in context. His letter of alleged support was part of a request he had sent to the SPN, asking to collaborate with the Portuguese government's publicity campaign during the 1939 New York World's Fair.[134] Rocha was now a businessman and was not about to miss an opportunity to make extra income for reasons of political affiliation. Rocha aligned himself with the Estado Novo during its early years, until 1936, but then adopted positions that were more critical of the dictatorship, as is clear from his correspondence.[135] It seems that he tended to be pragmatic, pursuing public relations strategies that would benefit his paper.

Alongside *O Independente*, another celebrated weekly emerged during this period—*As Novidades*, or just *Novidades*. It was founded on June 14, 1907, in Fall River and was published until 1948. According to Vasco S. Jardim, Joaquim Braz, a pharmacist from Goa, was the founder of the newspaper. Manoel da Silveira Cardozo, however, attributes its founding to John (João) Baptista Machado.[136] Despite the fact that much of its content was related to the activities of the Catholic Church, it also included a wide range of general information. The first editor was Camilo Câmara, a native of Madeira. Braz offered him the position of editor and then publisher, allowing Câmara to quit his job at a textile factory. Câmara breathed new life into *Novidades*, which began to compete with *O Independente*,[137] whose management he would, in turn, take over in 1922 after leaving the post of Vice-Consul of Portugal in Boston.[138] From the data available, it appears that when Fr. Joaquim Braz died in 1919, he left the newspaper to Fr. António Silva, parish priest of Santo Cristo in Fall River, who hired his sexton, João Baptista Machado, from the island of Terceira, as editor and manager. He later became its owner. Thereafter, *Novidades* adopted a more religious tone, showing a special interest in the situation of Portuguese priests in the United States. Along with other Catholic-leaning newspapers like the *Jornal Português* in California, it advocated for a greater presence of Catholic priests to increase missionary work in the Portuguese communities throughout the United States. In a February 29, 1940 editorial entitled "Um Acto de Patriotismo Digno de Imitar-se" (An Act of Patriotism Worthy of Imitation), *Novidades* praised the Portuguese immigrants of California for donating to a collection to finance the stay of two missionary priests. It uses their example to encourage the Portuguese of New England to become more involved in solving the problem of a lack of priests: "When, among us, will we do the same? We are in need of priests to continue the great religious and patriotic work built by the efforts of our ancestors in this area. The venerable Bishop of this Diocese has tirelessly pointed out, time and time again, the urgent need of the Church for priests who can serve our parishes."[139]

One of the more interesting cases of political journalism at the beginning of the twentieth century in Massachusetts featured a small newspaper with a newsletter format that was briefly the political voice of the Cabo Verdean diaspora in the United States. *A Alvorada* was founded by the great poet of Cabo Verde Eugénio Tavares, who arrived in New Bedford as a political exile on the ship *B. A. Brayton* on July 11, 1900.[140] *A Alvorada* began publication a month later on August 9, 1900. Tavares is recognized as one of the key figures for the understanding of Cabo Verdean culture and national identity.[141] In issue no. 2, dated August 16, 1900, *A Alvorada* published a front page editorial entitled "Autonomia," a polemic against the Portuguese monarchy that advocated the territorial independence of Cabo Verde.

Other titles were either short-lived or published irregularly, including *Aurora Luzitana*, edited by Manuel das Neves Xavier between 1900 and 1901; *Jornal Português*, founded by Manuel Benevides Raposo in 1900; *O Semeador*, published by Augusto B. Pimentel from 1906 to 1909; *O Progresso*, directed in 1907 by Francisco Caetano Borges da Silva and José Escobar; *A Alvorada*, a religious weekly created in 1909 by the Protestant minister Francisco Caetano Borges da Silva, which was published until the early 1920s; and *A Pátria*, edited by Avelino de Abreu in 1909 and then reissued between 1935 and 1936 by the Madeiran Carlos Alberto Supico,[142] a former editor for *O Independente*, using the presses of *Diario de Noticias*.[143]

The Expansion of the Portuguese-American Press, 1910-1929

Between 1910 and 1929, the Portuguese-American press reached its high-water mark in the number of titles established with a total of fifty-two new newspapers, nearly one third of the Portuguese-American newspapers ever published. At some point during this period, New England was home to five contemporaneous newspapers: one daily, *Alvorada*, and four large, general information weeklies, *O Independente, Novidades, O Popular* and *O Colonial*. In Massachusetts thirty-three new titles were created in this span of time, almost all in New Bedford. Among them was *O Portugal*, founded by Alberto de Sousa da Cunha e Moura in 1914. When he moved to California to try other projects in 1916, he passed the paper on to João Francisco Escobar, who served as editor and publisher and who changed the title to *Jornal do Povo*.[144] After his death on January 21, 1923, he was succeeded by his son Eugénio, who closed the paper a few months later. Joaquim dos Santos Oliveira was its editor between October 1921 and June 1922.[145]

Joaquim dos Santos Oliveira founded one of the best papers in New Bedford, the weekly *O Popular*, published between 1913 and 1936, first in New Bedford and then in Providence. *O Lavrador Português* described its first issues as containing a lot of news, and being "very well-written and without political and religious ideas."[146] However, Oliveira quickly abandoned *O Popular* to travel to California, and the priest António Cláudio Vieira, who abandoned pastoral work for journalism, just as Guilherme Silveira da Glória had done in California, became the owner, editor, and publisher. Miguel F. Policarpo, the founder of *O Independente*, was appointed administrator. One of the owner's sons, Eduino Vieira (a graduate of Harvard's school of medicine) inherited the paper in the 1930s when it was relocated to East Providence, Rhode Island.[147] Several important writers in the history of Portuguese journalism in North America worked at *O Popular*, including João Rodrigues Rocha, Manuel C. Botelho, Vasco Sousa Jardim, Affonso Gil Mendes Ferreira, Inácio Santos, and António S. Santos. *O Popular* was the first Portuguese-American newspaper to create special local editions, with autonomous management, administration, and editorial direction. The owner of each edition or section was a renter who paid the newspaper a percentage of the advertising revenue they collected. *O Popular* had editions in Boston, Fall River, Bristol, and Providence. Other newspapers, like the daily *A Alvorada*, imitated this commercial strategy in the 1920s.[148]

It was also during this period, more specifically in 1919, that a new magazine aimed at a female audience, *Jornal das Damas*, was published in New

Bedford by a "committee of ladies" led by Virginia C. Escobar, thought to be the wife or daughter of João Francisco Escobar, the editor of *Jornal do Povo*. The *Jornal das Damas*'s promotional campaign included the following message:

> A new magazine dedicated to Portuguese ladies titled *Jornal das Damas* (Ladies Journal), will soon be published in this city. It will contain beautiful short stories, novels, and splendid engravings on fine paper. This magazine will be published by a committee of women headed by Mrs. Virginia C. Escobar. All who wish to obtain the first issue of this magazine for free, kindly fill out the following coupon and mail it, as soon as possible, to the address below.[149]

Portuguese newspapers also appeared in a number of other cities in Massachusetts. *O Micaelense* emerged in Taunton in 1915 as the official organ of the Associação Real Autónoma Micaelense, and it was directed by the association's secretary Alípio Galvão. Membership in this mutual aid society was open only to men of São Miguel origin, which irked many in New Bedford and led other associations to retaliate by barring persons from that island.[150] The religious newspaper *Aurora* emerged in Cambridge in 1918 with the subtitle "Jornal Evangélico Inter-Denominacional" (Interdenominational Evangelical Journal), and it was published bimonthly by the Portuguese Evangelical Federation until the 1930s.[151] *Aurora* mixed religious information with social content related to the community. In Fall River, Manuel Correia Botelho founded *O Vigilante* in September 1915.[152] In Boston, the magazine *A Luzitania* emerged in 1917, and in Lowell, Domingos J. F. Spinney (Spínola) from Terceira founded *A Paz* in 1919.[153]

The most important newspaper of this period was the daily *Alvorada*, originally founded by the Reverend Francisco Caetano Borges da Silva as the weekly *A Alvorada*, as noted above.[154] When businessman Guilherme Machado Luiz bought it in 1919, he decided to maintain the commitment to former subscribers by keeping the weekly, while editing a new daily newspaper (except for Sundays) beginning on January 25, 1919, which he called *Alvorada*. Initially, *A Alvorada,* the weekly, had a circulation of 5,500 copies and *Alvorada*, the daily, 3,000.[155] The confusion that having two papers with very similar titles generated for mailmen, who could not tell one from the other, forced the owner to change the name of the daily to *Alvorada Diária* on March 6, 1919.[156] The newspaper explained that "the present title—*Alvorada Diária*—was suggested to us by the postal authorities, due to the fact that the other title—*Alvorada*—which is very similar to that of the weekly—*A Alvorada*—was causing confusion in that department."[157] Along with the change in name, Luiz changed the format, going from six to seven columns, and added the caption "Jornal Imparcial e Noticioso" (Impartial, news-focused paper), later altered to "Jornal Diário Imparcial e Noticioso" (Impartial, news-focused daily newspaper), which remained unchanged until December 31, 1926, when the paper gave way to its successor, the *Diario de Noticias*.[158] Before that happened, however, the title continued to change. On January 1, 1920, it was renamed as *A Alvorada*; on March 6 of that year the title *Alvorada Diária* returned, and on November 1, 1923, it became *A Alvorada* again.

During this period the paper advertised itself with a variety of messages, including "This is a Portuguese daily with a circulation in New Bedford and Fall River larger than all Portuguese weeklies combined," "The only Portuguese daily in the United States," "Advertise in the *Alvorada* because it helps your business," and "Member of the American Association of Foreign Language Newspapers of New York City" (incorporated in May 1919). From 1923 on, the title page in its Fall River edition featured new promotional ads that stated, "This is the Paper Where Your Ads Are Worth Money" and "A third of the population of Fall River is Portuguese. Advertise in this daily newspaper if you want Portuguese trade." In the meantime, the paper was growing and updating its equipment and facilities. On December 8, 1922, it announced that in addition to other equipment it now possessed a new press that printed up to 25,000 copies per hour and reached 350,000 persons throughout the country, including 35,000 in New Bedford.[159] Four years later, in its last edition as *A Alvorada*, the board of directors of its publisher, the Alvorada Publishing Company, Inc. (which would become the Portuguese Daily News Publishing Co. in the 1930s), published a front page editorial, highlighted in bold, announcing the final change of name:

At a general meeting of its members, the management of Alvorada Publishing Company, Inc. decided that, after January 3, 1927, this newspaper

Assinai a "Alvorada" Jornal de Grande Informação e Unico Diario Portuguez nos Estados Unidos da America

THE ONLY
PORTUGUESE DAILY
IN THE
UNITED STATES

Alvorada

Jornal Diario

ADVERTISE
IN THE
"ALVORADA"
BECAUSE IT
HELPS YOUR
BUSINESS

ANO I — No. 16   NEW BEDFORD, MASS. Quarta-feira Fevereiro 12, 1919   NUMERO AVULSO 2 cents

PORTUGUEZES DIPLOMADOS DO LICEU DESTA CIDADE

A SITUAÇÃO EM LAWRENCE

NEM CORTEJO NEM MEETING PUBLICO

As Autoridades Recusam-se dar Permissão

CONTRA ALMIRANTE HERBERT OMAR DUNN

ROUBO DE 340 CONTOS DO BANCO DE PORTUGAL

Medico Morto pelo Seu Cliente

Presa por Matar o Filho

Salvou a vida da esposa centra sua vontade

Quasi tantas bebidas como Anteriormente

Voltam Para o Trabalho

Mobilia de Superior Qualidade

Este é o melhor estabelecimento de Mobilia que os Portuguezes podem encontrar nesta cidade.

FOGOES

Fogões de Gaz

Fogões de Petroleo .... $5.40 - $8.10
Fogões de Petroleo Miller $7.43

Tem os Empregados Portuguezes em todos os
DEPARTAMENTOS

VINDE AQUI

The C. F. Wing & Co.

790 PURCHASE STREET.

Defronte do Five Cents Savings Bank.
HENRY COSTA, Empregado Portuguez.

11. Cover of *Alvorada*
(New Bedford, Massachusetts).
Copy of February 12, 1919.

142   Alberto Pena Rodríguez

will be published under the name *Diario de Noticias* [Daily News]. This decision was based on the fact that this seems to be the most appropriate name, given the role that the newspaper plays within the Portuguese community, where, each business day, it brings to the home of most of its families the latest news of what is going on in the world and is the only means by which business owners, both national and Portuguese, can advertise their products to its numerous readers and the Portuguese community in general. This Company is convinced that the Portuguese public will welcome the *Diario de Noticias* with the same good will with which it has been welcoming *Alvorada*, since our approach under the new name will be the same we took with *Alvorada*, while attempting to make as many improvements as possible. Just like *Alvorada* has been until now, the *Diario de Noticias* will undeniably be the number one Portuguese newspaper in North America, not only in terms of its circulation, which in New Bedford and Fall River exceeds that of all other publications put together, but also in its quality as a purveyor of news and information.[160]

A number of individuals were involved in the growth and success of the newspaper. The first editor of the newspaper was Joaquim Maciel.[161] In the 1920s, his Guilherme M. Luiz' son-in-law, the Madeiran António Vieira de Freitas Jr., became the director while Joaquim Maciel took over management of the newspaper.[162] In August 1924, Frederico Rosa replaced Freitas, who would go on to become the manager of Luiz' Casa Bancária.[163] Its first major editors were Alípio Coelho Bartholo and the poet Quirino de Sousa, under whose supervision and direction worked several others, including Jaime Lopes and Raul M. Pereira. Over the years, as it expanded, *A Alvorada* opened sections or editions in Boston (João Luso, director), Fall River (Alberto Freitas, director, and Manoel I. Câmara, administrator), Newark (Lucindo de Freitas), Taunton (Antonio Fournier), and Bristol, RI.

A Alvorada published news about the community and Portugal's political situation, but serialized novels were also a popular feature of the newspaper, especially among women. These tended to be popular classics of Portuguese literature or well-known, popular foreign works in translation. The first was *Coração de Criança* by Carlos Vitis,[164] followed by many more, including *Mistérios de Lisboa* by Camilo Castelo Branco, *O Canário da Fábrica* by Quirino de Sousa, *A Volta ao Mundo: Jack e Francinet* by Henry de la Vaux and Arnould Galopin, *As Pupilas do Sr. Reitor* by Júlio Diniz, *O Conde de Monte Cristo* by Alexandre Dumas, *A Esposa* and *Os Filhos da Milionária* by Emile Rechebourg, and *A Rosa do Adro* by Manuel Maria Rodrigues. In August 1924, due to the growing popularity of movies, *A Alvorada* started a section entitled "Pelos Palcos e Cinemas" (Through stages and cinemas), which included ads from movie theaters in New Bedford, such as the Olympia and the Empire.

In the 1920s, an explosion of Portuguese-American newspaper titles occurred in the state of Massachusetts with the publication of twenty-three new newspapers, the majority in New Bedford. This was due to the great influx of immigrants during the previous decade and the first half of the 1920s (See Fig. 1) as Portugal struggled during the political crisis that ensued after the establishment of the Republic on October 5, 1910, with serious implications for its economy. This was a period of great instability, with forty-six different governments between 1910 and the coup of May 28, 1926. Many sought relief from the country's economic and political troubles by emigrating, and the U.S. was one of their major destinations until the restrictive immigration laws of the 1920s went into effect. In the early 1920s, about 30,000 people of Portuguese origin resided in New Bedford, a figure that would increase to 35,000 in the 1930s. In the neighboring city of Fall River, the figure was around 26,000. At that time, the number of Portuguese living in the United States was approximately 250,000.[165]

It was a time of great change, legally, politically, and socially. The U.S. economy, including the textile industry, had begun to falter, and the whaling industry, which had attracted the first Portuguese immigrants, had disappeared. The U.S. government began to apply immigration restrictions. First, through the literacy requirement, which only allowed entry to those over sixteen who could read and write, and then, after 1921, through national quota restrictions.[166] Then the Great Depression came in 1929. The cities of New Bedford and Fall River were greatly affected. Portuguese immigrants who lived off the sea or worked in the textile mills were forced to find employment in other sectors. Some moved to other areas of the country and many returned to Portugal.

The burgeoning of the publishing industry in the Portuguese-American community during the 1920s reflected this dynamic process of economic, political, and social change taking place in the United States as well as in Portugal and many other parts of the world. It was a historical moment in which political clashes that pitted the Republican movement against the monarchy and liberalism against conservatism had a major impact on the Portuguese community. Each faction's propaganda became part of a public debate that was largely conducted through newspapers, then the most effective means of political influence. New political movements associated with ideologies like communism, socialism, Nazism, and fascism sparked debates that only intensified during the 1930s with the advent of the Estado Novo and the international implications of the Spanish Civil War, the Great Depression, and the Second World War.

The importance of Portugal in the United States, in terms of its representation, perception, and influence, was becoming a matter of concern to Portuguese Americans. Political and religious indoctrination, intellectual experimentation, and leadership in the community were the three most important motivations driving the development of new papers. *O Talassa* and *A Restauração* were among the political publications affiliated with the Portuguese monarchist movement in the United States. The first, published every two weeks between 1923 and 1924, was the organ of the Centro Monárquico Português (Portuguese Monarchist Center) of New Bedford, which was directed by Captain Carlos Augusto de Noronha e Montanha, a political exile who had been a collaborator of Henrique Paiva Couceiro, leader of the royalist raids against the Portuguese Republic in 1911, 1912, and 1919.[167] According to Eduardo de Carvalho, Captain Noronha e Montanha was also the promoter of *Portugal*, a monarchist newspaper published in the 1920s in Cambridge by António S. Lemos and managed by José Maria Bettencourt.[168] The irregular weekly *Restauração* was the successor to *O Talassa* as the mouthpiece of the Monárquicos Portugueses da América do Norte (Portuguese Monarchists of North America). It was owned by Manuel Pinho Ribeiro, but directed by Noronha e Montaha, with António Augusto Lopes as editor and Quirino da Fonseca as editor-in-chief.[169]

In 1923 and 1924, the socialist newspaper *O Combate*, led by the bookseller Diamantino Teixeira, was published in Fall River. *A Luta*, a sort of flyer that was the newsletter of the Ateneu de Estudos Sociais,[170] was distributed throughout New Bedford and Fall River. *A Luta* defended anarchist and anti-clerical principles, which caused it problems with the United States authorities. Three of its editors, António da Costa, António Alves Pereira, and Diamantino Teixeira, were arrested in 1926 and deported to Portugal, accused of revolutionary, anti-clerical propaganda.[171]

The anticlericalism of the era led to the publication of several religious publications aimed at counteracting its ideas, including *A Cruz*, which was printed in Boston by Father Abílio Maria da Silva Greaves, and *A Era Nova*, founded in 1923 by Father João F. Ferraz, pastor of the São Miguel Arcanjo Church, with collaboration from the typographer Manuel Capeto. A few months after its creation in 1924, Ferraz was named monsignor by the Vatican, and Capeto died, causing the newspaper to close, but its printshop, Era Nova Printing Company, continued operations. According to Vasco Jardim, the newspaper was an ambitious but ruinous project:

> Father Ferraz, who was a renowned orator and highly cultured, aspired to produce a well-made and well-written newspaper. He did. Unfortunately, it did not appeal to his colleagues. Ferraz and Capeto upgraded the printshop. They bought two linotypes, a "Ludlow," the machine that was known in Portugal as a "tituleira," and a rotary. Capeto had good taste in graphic art. However, the newspaper never made enough to meet its expenses. Everybody liked *Era Nova* but no one, except for factory workers, paid for it.[172]

Aurora Evangêlica, founded in 1918 in the greater Boston area, was the longest running religious publication, surviving until the late 1970s. The Protestant minister João José Vieira Jr. from Madeira edited the newspaper, and Francisco Silva took over when he moved to California to found the Evangelical newspaper *O Heraldo* in 1936. Eventually, *A Aurora* was transferred to the Baptist pastor João G. Loja and then acquired by the Episcopalian minister João Cristiano da Rosa. In December 1963, Reverend António Monteiro of the Presbyterian Church of São Paulo announced the intention to restart the paper with the help of the Brazilian journalist José Ricardo Aquilino, former director of the *Folha do Povo* in the city of Bauru in the state of São Paulo, Brazil. [173] Between 1926 and 1927, the Baptist minister Francisco Silva also published *A Imprensa*,[174] with editorial offices in Cambridge and the administration based in New Bedford.[175]

Between 1921 and 1922, Francisco A. Santos directed *A Crítica*, a magazine specializing in humor and political criticism.[176] Engravings of the consuls of Portugal in New York, New Bedford, and Fall River were published in its first issue.[177] Santos, popularly known as "Xico," was also an editor for *A Alvorada*, *O Talassa*, and *O Independente* in New Bedford, and *O Século* in Lisbon. Later, he would move to Newark, where he founded the short-lived *O Portugal* in 1927.[178] While in Newark, he collaborated with the surgeon José Dias to create the Grémio Literário Português (Portuguese Literary Guild). In the 1930s, he returned to Lisbon, and then attempted to return to the U.S. in 1939 as a stowaway on the ship *Vulcania*. The *Diario de Noticias* ran a story about his arrest in which they cite an unidentified source as stating:

> The famous Francisco Santos tried weeks ago to go over there [to the U.S.] by embarking clandestinely on the *Vulcania*. Two hours after the ship weighted anchor, however, he was discovered and handed over to the authorities in Ponta Delgada. He was later sent to Lisbon under arrest and turned over to the international police who took him back to prison where he is still detained awaiting trial. Since he has been in Lisbon, the scoundrel has been involved in a number of shady exploits, tricking and cheating all those who get close to him. Not too long ago, one of his victims was one of the brothers of the late Fr. Carmo of Fall River, and involved a typewriter, etc., etc..[179]

On December 3, 1925, Frederico da Costa, a native of the island of Madeira, who worked as a notary public, founded the weekly *O Colonial*, based in Fairhaven.[180] It was one of the most successful newspapers, publishing for almost twenty years, until 1945. It had an edition in New York, directed by António Pires, and relied on a wide range of contributors, among whom were some illustrious figures, such as former Portuguese minister João Camoesas, a supporter of the Portuguese Republican Party, who used the newspaper to publish articles against the Estado Novo regime. *O Colonial* billed itself as "The only Portuguese weekly printed in Greater New Bedford," and a "Member of the Portuguese American Chamber of Commerce of New Bedford," stating "We reach a population of 200,000 Portuguese in America; over 100,000 in New England; Largest Circulation Guaranteed." It was a general information newspaper of Republican leanings, printed in a broadsheet format, eight pages long, illustrated, and carrying many ads from Portuguese-American businesses and others.[181] In the 1930s, *O Colonial* campaigned against the dictatorship in Portugal, publishing front page editorials denouncing Salazar's politics.[182]

Another important Portuguese-American journalist was Affonso Gil Mendes Ferreira. In 1925, while working in a textile factory, he founded *O Heraldo Portuguez*, one of the first free newspapers in the history of the Portuguese press. Financed exclusively by advertisements, *O Heraldo Portuguez* ran until 1976. An eminently commercial biannual publication with a broadsheet format that used photography and illustrations for large advertisements, its objective was to promote immigrant businesses in New England, particularly in Taunton, MA, where its headquarters was located. He also used it to advertise his popular radio show "A Voz Portuguesa."[183] The two annual issues came out during the times of the year with the most commercial activity—Easter and Christmas—with a variety of content that included some articles in English.

12. Portrait of Affonso Gil Mendes Ferreira, editor of *O Heraldo Portuguez* (Taunton, Massachusetts).

In addition to these major newspapers, there were other short-lived publications in New Bedford and Fall River. For instance, Alexandre Miranda founded *Pé de Vento* on January 15, 1921; Miranda managed and edited the paper until October of that year with the help of the Lisbon typographer José Augusto Laranjo.[184] In 1921, Vasco S. Jardim published a few issues of *Esperança* in Fall River. In 1922, José L. Laranjo founded, in New Bedford, the illustrated Catholic-leaning magazine *Portugal-América*, which was managed by Abílio Maria Greaves, a priest

VI ANNO   SEXTA-FEIRA, 3 DE ABRIL DE 1931.   NUMERO 215

O COLONIAL

OFFICINAS
191 NORTH WALNUT STREET
FAIRHAVEN, MASS.

ASSIGNATURAS

PROP. E EDITOR, FREDERICO A. COSTA   SEMANARIO PORTUGUEZ   TEL.— NEW BEDFORD, CLIFFORD 1052

Novo Sistema Educativo

A Universidade de Chicago Vae Inaugurar Um Método de Ensino Inteiramente Moderno

O AUTOMÓVEL DE SUA SANTIDADE

Notas da Arcada

O Padre Palhaço

(Auto lirico ou fita-falada, ultra-moderna.— Música de canto Gregoriano e motivos de "Jazz-Band".— Libreto, inspirado nas Sagradas Escrituras e nas chronicas dos "Dois Companheiros" immortal creação do jornal cómico-religioso as "Novidades" de Fall River.)

PROLOGO

SOLDADO DESCONHECIDO PORTUGUEZ

A DISCUSSÃO Á VOLTA DO PACTO NAVAL

A SITUAÇÃO DOS NATURALISADOS NO BRAZIL

OS PREJUIZOS DA REVOLTA DE FEVEREIRO DE 1931

O QUE OS ESTADOS UNIDOS EMPRESTAM

VISCONDE D'ALTE

A RUSSIA E A TURQUIA

---

13. Cover of *O Colonial.*
Copy of April 3, 1931.

O HERALDO PORTUGUEZ

O QUE FIZEMOS

A NOSSA LINGUA

DEDICADO AO POVO E COMERCIO DE TAUNTON

ANNO VIII AFFONSO FERREIRA Editor e Proprietario Distribuição Gratuita P. O. BOX 392 Taunton ,Mass. No. 11

Saudação

Os Portuguezes Em Taunton

Os Amigos de Joaquim Ferreira Esperam Que Elle Proponha a Sua Candidatura ao Municipio D'aquela Cidade

A Lição da Primavera

Joaquim F. Ferreira

União Portugueza Continental

Pierce Hardware Co.

TAUNTON

A maior venda nesta cidade esta sendo realizada presentemente na nossa loja.

Uma excelente ocasião para adquirirdes, por preços relativamente baratos, todos os artigos e utensilios que dese jardes para

As Vossas Casa e Jardins

Talvez a venda esperada com mais anciedade das que temos realizado.

Ancinbos Bamboo 39c

Dobadouras $2.00

Arame Farpado Um Rolo $2.20

Lawn or Flower Bed Guard

Mangueiras

Sementes de Registadas de

Garden Barrows Special $5.45

Turf Edger $1.25

Sachador Dandelion 85c

GRATIS

Vasilhas para Borrifar

Sementes de Ervas

Fertilizadores

Fertilizador para Batata

Aperelhos Conductores de Ar Comprimido

Luma

Vigoro

Sementes de Flores para Jardins

Lawn Rollers De $11.00

Sheep Dressing

Scalecide

Qualidades de Cebolas

Gratis a Todos os Nossos Freguezes

Pierce Hardware Co.

Phone 57 TAUNTON 15 Main St.

14. Cover of *O Heraldo Portuguez* (Taunton, Massachusetts). Copy of May 1, 1931.

from Faial.[185] In 1924, the quarterly magazine *Varões Assinalados* appeared in New Bedford. In 1925, António Lopes's *A Tradição* was published; and the magazine *O Cosmopolitano*, by Frederico A. Costa, was printed between 1922 and 1925. During this period, João Gonçalves published *A Voz da Madeira*, created specifically for the Madeiran community. In 1926, the illustrated magazine *Almanaque da Colónia Portuguesa* by Leonídio Cabral appeared. In the 1920s, Quirino de Sousa founded *Sem Pés Nem Cabeça*, a humor newspaper, which became part of *O Independente* in February 1927 as a supplement. Sousa, who also had briefly edited *A Borboleta* in 1906, then became the literary editor of *O Independente*.[186]

Outside of New Bedford and Fall River, new publications also sprang up. It was during this period, for example, that, after working as a janitor and shopkeeper in Cambridge, João R. Rocha created his first major journalistic project, the *Revista Portugal-América Portuguesa*, which was published between October 6, 1926, and 1929 in Cambridge.[187] The following were also part of the magazine's management team: Branco de Torres (literary editor), Anthony Cabral (head of the illustrated section), and Eduino F. Furtado (director of circulation for New England). It was an illustrated monthly magazine of high quality with sophisticated intellectual content, mainly literary articles and reports on cultural issues. Women were the primary audience, and there was a section in English.[188]

The flourishing of journalistic activity among Portuguese immigrants in New England also expanded to California, where in addition to the weekly humor newspaper *A California Alegre*, numerous weeklies appeared from 1910 on. Among them were *O Lavrador Português* (published between 1912 and 1927), *O Imparcial* (1913-1932), and *Jornal de Notícias* (1917-1932), which were rough contemporaries of three other influential newspapers: *O Arauto*, *A Liberdade*, and *A União Portuguesa*. In 1915, Joaquim dos Santos Oliveira, who moved to California after founding *O Popular* in New Bedford, founded and edited the weekly *O Mundo*.[189] In 1916, Alberto Moura worked for the newspaper as an editor. The paper ceased publication when Oliveira returned to Massachusetts, where he worked as editor of *O Independente* and *Jornal do Povo*.

O Lavrador Português was founded on December 3, 1912, and published until September 23, 1916, during its first run. About five years later, it resumed publication on June 6, 1921, only to be suspended again in 1924.

Two years later, in 1926, it re-emerged for a third and final time, lasting until September 23, 1927. It was a biweekly from 1921 until 1924, and it changed cities multiple times: it was first located in Lemoore, 1912-1913; then in Hanford, 1913-1915; then in Tulare for two periods, 1915-1916 and 1921-1924; and, finally, in Oakland between May 1926 and 1927.[190] Its mottos were: "Honra é o lema dos Portugueses/Honesty is the aim of Portuguese colony;" "Fundado para pugnar pelos interesses do trabalhador português da California" (Founded to fight for the interests of the Portuguese worker of California); and "The Paper with Largest Circulation." It was a general-interest newspaper designed for readers who worked as farmers or ranchers in California, particularly in the San Joaquin Valley, hence the abundance of advertisements related to agricultural activities such as land, plows, etc. The paper published a large number of brief news articles dispersed in several sections such as "News from Portugal," "Abroad," "The Portuguese in San Joaquin," "Azores," "Agriculture," "Telegrams and other News from the Warfront," and "Serialized Novel," among others. The first editorial explains its objectives:

> Most of our farmers already like to read; they are studious and are always ready to take advantage of new ideas. So, as we publish our little newspaper in the San Joaquin Valley, where ninety percent of the Portuguese are farmers, we dedicate it—*O Lavrador Português*—to them. Our newspaper has no ambitions to be a literary publication. No, it is simply a newssheet that will bring to the Portuguese of the San Joaquin Valley news from their hometowns, from the United States and from all over the world. [191]

Throughout its history, *O Lavrador Portuguez* (which would become *O Lavrador Português*) experimented with its format, beginning as a broadsheet with 4 to 8 pages, but then reducing in size. For some issues, the header was adorned with the Portuguese and United States flags. In 1914, the faces of Luís de Camões, Teófilo Braga, and George Washington were added, but they disappeared after September 1915. The paper was owned by the Lemoore Publishing Co., which changed hands several times. João de Simas Melo Jr., Constantino Ávila Barcelos, and Arthur Vieira were the founders. In March 1913, the paper moved to Hanford, where the number of ads increased significantly, and

Ano 2.º   Hanford, Cal., Sabado 22 de Agosto de 1914   N.º 81

O LAVRADOR PORTUGUÊS

Direção: 529 W. 8th St.   *Redactor e Proprietario:* ARTHUR V. AVILA   Telefone: Main 434 Y

Um Amigo dos Portugueses

THOMAS F. GRIFFIN

Acompanham estas palavras uma fotogravura do sr. Thomas F. Griffin, que aspira á nomeação para Senador Democratico dos Estados Unidos, pelo Estado da California.

O sr. Griffin é natural da California, e actual residente de Modesto, Cal., e vem perante os eleitores deste Estado com uma carreira de cidadão prestimoso. Foi eleito membro da Assembleia Legislativa do Estado da California em 1911, e desde então tem lutado sempre para melhorar a situação do homem e da mulher das classes trabalhadoras principalmente.

Ele foi o autor da lei das oito horas de trabalho para mulheres, uma das melhores leis adoptadas nos ultimos dez anos, e que protege as mães dos cidadãos de amanhã contra os rigores do trabalho excessivo e rigoroso. Foi igualmente o autor da lei do Tribunal das Creanças, e da lei que elevou a idade escolar até 15 anos e a idade do trabalho dai para cima, leis estas que protegem os interesses e garantem um futuro condigno á geração nova.

Por tudo isto se pode avaliar os sentimentos altruistas que caracterisam o caracter de Thomas F. Griffin e que o recomendam ao eleitorado da California nas proximas eleições.

Alem disso, o sr. Griffin é um abastado lavrador de Modesto e Turlock, muito devotado a tudo que tende a beneficiar o campo, e a sua moção no Senado dos Estados Unidos, uma vez eleito, será de grande proveito e segura garantia do bem estar dos agricultores do Estado da California.

Thomas F. Griffin recomenda-se de um modo especial aos Portugueses da California, por ser um membro do conselho Modesto, No. 59 da I. D. E. S., e por tomar sempre a parte pelos Portugueses quando os interesses da Colonia reclamam os seus serviços.

Especialmente os membros da Comissão de Recepção ao Conselho Supremo da I. D. E. S., que teve a reunir em Modesto na segunda semana de setembro proximo, devem a Mr. Griffin muitos e assinalados favores, e podem dizer com verdade que, só não fizes este prestimoso cidadão Thomas F. Griffin, a comissão não poderia fazer mantaçe dos entretenimentos que vão haver, em honra do Conselho Supremo, Representantes, suas Familias e visitantes.

Por tudo isto, pois, Thomas F. Griffin pode contar com o auxilio certo dos Portugueses da California, que rogam tambem a todos os Portugueses em geral do Estado da California que, quando forem exhibir as suas listas nas proximas eleições, não se esqueçam de dar um voto por Thomas F. Griffin para Senador Democratico dos E. Unidos, pelo Estado da California.

Exposição Panamá-Pacifico

Comissão Executiva
A' Colonia Portuguesa

A vossa Comissão Executiva, atendendo ao brilhante e patriotico esforço dos seus delegados enviados a Portugal, srs. dr. José de Sousa Betencourt, F. I. de Lemos e Joaquim A. da Silveira, e ao successo da sua missão, querendo testemunhar-lhes a gratidão da Colonia representada na vossa Comissão Executiva, pelos desinteresse, devoção e sacrificios materiaes na importante comissão, resolveu oferecer-lhes um banquete no Hotel Oak Land desta cidade, sabado, 29 do corrente, ás 8 horas da noite, convidando todos os membros da colonia e suas familias a associar-se á vossa Comissão nesta pequena manifestação de reconhecimento da justa gratidão áquelles cavalheiros.

O preço por talher é $2.75, e o restaurante perfeitamente á vontade dos convivas.

Os nomes das pessoas que desejarem assistir ao banquete devem ser enviados a Mr. F. J. Cunha, 1231, Magnolia St., Oakland, Calif., até sexta-feira, 28, antes do meio dia, acompanhado da importancia respectiva.

A Comissão de Banquete
     F. J. Cunha, pres.
     M. B. da Camara, sec.
     Manuel Fraga

Chegou o dia!...

A era de terror e do sangue chegou enfim, e o mundo inteiro se abala perante a grande guerra europea.

Uma segunda era Napoleonica apparece despontando no horizonte das nações europeas.

Os povos de Alem-Atlantico preparam-se para entrar numa das maiores lutas que a historia nos mostra.

Waterloo e Trafalgar são pequenos atomos perante a luta presente. Willington e Nelson são dois certmes relativamente aos vencedores que decidirão num futuro mais ou menos curto os destinos das grandes potencias europeas: Alemanha, Russia, França, Austria e Inglaterra.

Realizar-se-ha a profecia de Bismark?

A França vingará agora 1870?

A Alemanha anequilando a esquadra ingleza conseguirá o seu ambicionado sonho?

A Austria resolverá o intrincado problema Slavo?

A Inglaterra ficará sempre dominando nos Oceanos?

Eis as perguntas que constituem o X do grande problema que estas grandes nações teem de resolver quando como lapis os grandes cutelos e como papel o solo europeu a a superficie dos mares.

Ondas de sangue correrão de parte a parte, milhares de vidas cobrirão ceifadas pela mão futilista e cruel da guerra, milhares de mães ficam sem filhos, milhares de esposas...

(Continua na quarta pagina)

Dona Maria C. Tavares

Ha muito que a minha humilde prosa não apparece no jornal, e, hoje ao traçar o que segue, não venho com pretensões de escritura. Nunca as tive. Simplesmente o que dá a ousadia de, neste semanario, vir dizer o que sinto a respeito duma senhora como é D. Maria C. Tavares.

Não posso, porque não sei, escrever longo elogio, em boca ninguem o dê com mais fé de que ele é merecido.

Direi somente:

Portuguezes, eis uma senhora que honra a nossa colonia. Eis uma dama que luta pela educação civica e moral do nosso povo, eis uma amiga dos portuguezes.

E' ela, a apresentada, vice-presidente suprema da S. P. R. S. I.

Foi eleita para tam elevada posição na ultima sessão annual do Conselho Supremo desta sociedade.

A honra e gloria do povo portuguez na California está nas suas sociedades.

A S. P. R. S. I., uma tam bela quam util instituição, muito terá a lucrar com a eleição da sua vice-presidente.

Não se poupara ela, estou disso certa, a nenhum sacrificio, logo que desse sacrificio venha para a sociedade de que ela é vice-presidente, algum beneficio.

Decorra um anno e veréis D. Maria C. Tavares ocupar a mais alta posição que a uma mulher portugueza, na California é dado alcançar, e continuar a ser o que até hoje tem sido—amiga de tudo o que é portuguez—incansavel propagandora da S. P. R. S. I.

Hanford, Calif., 18 de Agosto de 1914.

Maria P. C. de Barcelos

A Justiça num pais está na razão inversa do numero das suas leis. Os povos serão tanto mais felizes quanto mais renuidos forem os seus codigos.

---

15. Cover of *O Lavrador Português*
(Hanford, California).
Copy of August 22, 1914.

Arthur V. Ávila became the sole owner.[192] In Tulare, Alfredo Dias da Silva joined as co-owner and co-editor. In Oakland, Cândido da Costa Nunes acquired the paper in 1927, and Ávila and J. T. Salgueiro were the editors. The paper always had an extensive network of correspondents and contributors.[193]

On March 18, 1924, the owners of *O Lavrador Português* transformed the paper into the biweekly *A Colonia Portuguesa*, which was published in Oakland until June 24, 1932.[194] Although one newspaper was meant to replace the other, *O Lavrador Português* reappeared briefly between 1926 and 1927. *A Colonia Portuguesa*, "bi-seminário independente" (independent bi-weekly), was directed and edited by Ávila from 1924 to 1925 and from 1928 to 1932. João da Cunha Valim (from São Jorge, Azores), who also worked for *A Revista Portuguesa* in Hayward, took Ávila's place during the years 1925-1926. Other figures holding positions in the initial management team were Alberto Moura and Abílio Reis (editors), António Martins da Silva (administrator), M. P. Silva (artistic director), A. D. Silva (office manager), M. R. Homem (attorney), and M. G. Rose (publishing director for Kings County and Tulare).

On December 3, 1925, it was announced that the paper would become a corporation (A Colónia Portuguesa, Inc., a shareholding company) with initial capital in the amount of $50,000: "This means that *A Colonia Portuguesa* will no longer belong to a half dozen individuals, but will be the property of all of its subscribers."[195] The newspaper pitched the change as a step toward turning *A Colonia Portuguesa* into the official newspaper of the Portuguese-American community:

> *A Colonia Portuguesa* belongs to the Portuguese people. To serve them, to entertain them, to enhance their visibility. The majority of the current owners do not expect to live off the profits of this company. They are men who, thanks to their honest work, intelligence and energy have been able to accumulate considerable amounts of wealth and occupy prominent positions within our community.[196]

To increase circulation, the firm acquired a new rotary press as well as new installations, which enabled them to offer all kinds of printing services.[197] The organizational structure of the newspaper consisted of the following: M.

16. Cover of *A Colonia Portuguesa.*
Copy of March 25, 1924.

Gaspar (president), A. M. Carvalho (vice-president), M. S. Soares (treasurer), A. V. Ávila (secretary), and M. P. Silva (director). *A Colonia Portuguesa* wanted to become the newspaper of reference for the Portuguese community in California. According to its promotional motto, it was founded "to fight for the rights of the Portuguese People of this State and to strengthen, whenever possible, the political and trade relations between Portugal and the United States."[198]

A Colonia Portuguesa was a broadsheet-type newspaper with an average of eight pages and many advertisements,[199] photos, and engravings. The paper offered extensive coverage of the Portuguese-American community and Portugal, and its header was adorned with the flags of Portugal and the United States. The paper had various sections such as "Notas da Semana" (Weekly Notes), which consisted of notices on the departures and arrivals of members of the community, the opening of businesses, illnesses, and obituaries, among other items; "O Correio da Colónia" (letters from readers); and "Carta de Lisboa do Nosso Correspondente Especial Sr. J. André de Freitas, Antigo Senador pelo Distrito da Horta" (Letter from the paper's correspondent in Lisbon: political news). It was one of the first newspapers to publish articles in English. In 1927, at the urging of the Portuguese American Society of California, the management team decided to print 1,000 copies of the newspaper in English, specifically for the 23rd Avenue district of Oakland, as explained:

> This is one of the thousand copies of the Twenty-third Avenue, Oakland, section of the "Portuguese colony" printed in English at the request of the Portuguese-American Society of California. This request was made as a mark of respect to the hundreds of American readers of that district, who it is hoped through this means will become better acquainted with the Portuguese of that district.[200]

O Imparcial was founded on October 7, 1913, and published until 1932 in Sacramento (1913-1930) and then in Alameda (1930-1932).[201] The paper was subtitled "Semanário Independente e Noticioso" (Independent News Weekly). *O Imparcial* was founded and directed by Manuel B. Quaresma, a native of Pico, while Mary A. Silva worked as editor and administrator. In 1930, shortly after the death of the director, *A Colonia Portuguesa* bought the newspaper and named António Azevedo its director (1930-1932). The following message was posted at the top of the frontpage, "You must buy from the companies that advertise in this newspaper and tell them that you saw the announcement in O *Imparcial*. At no cost to you, you will be doing us a favor that will greatly help us."[202] Its contents were similar to those of its competitors, often delivered in a highly descriptive and emotional narrative style, as in the article "José V. Mendonça de San Leandro Suicida-se" (José V. Mendonça takes his own life):

> On the afternoon of October 1st, José V. Mendonça, who for many years operated a restaurant at the corner of Callan Ave. and East 14th St. in San Leandro, was found dead in one of the rooms of the Elmer Hotel of which he was the owner. A mourning wreath on the door of that establishment, which had closed on the 2nd, a card explaining the closing as being due to the sudden death of J.V. Mendonça, and a short notice in the local papers noting, superficially, a history of murder [sic] attempts—five in the last week—is all that is publicly known about the tragedy, which is probably the result of domestic issues. Mr. Mendonça was a very decisive and strong-willed person. It appears that he had decided to end his life, and did it.[203]

The weekly *Jornal de Notícias*, founded by Pedro Laureano Claudino da Silveira, began publication in San Francisco on March 28, 1917. The paper was later transferred to Oakland and then to Alameda, where the last issue was published on June 24, 1932. Initially, the paper came out on Wednesdays, but this changed to Fridays. It had the subtitle "Semanário Imparcial Dedicado à Colónia Portuguesa dos Estados Unidos" (Impartial Weekly Dedicated to the Portuguese Community in the United States). On its frontpage, it displayed the following informative note in English, "This paper publishes all the news and has a large circulation among the Portuguese colony in California and the United States." It had a section dedicated to news from the Azores and another with weekly columns featuring local information on cities with large Portuguese populations. Eventually, a section was created specifically for the Santa Clara Valley, possibly to meet the specific interests of those who worked as farmers and ranchers in that area. The newspaper also included brief articles about Portugal and other countries as well as the customary serialized novels. The following advertisers appeared frequently in the paper: Newman Hospital, John Day Motor Car Company, Glover Hotel, Lucindo Freitas – Notário Público, Freitas & Bunce – Canalizador, Luís Jerónimo – Roupas e Calçado, Mrs. Christina Bertão – Roupas e outros artigos, Metropolitan Meat Market of Honolulu, and Cosulich Line – Serviço directo de New York e Boston para Açores e Lisboa.[204] As was common with other Portuguese-American newspapers, charity collections to raise money for social or humanitarian purposes were also frequently featured in its pages. In 1921, for example, *Jornal de Notícias* launched a campaign to cover the construction of a new orphanage in Angra do Heroísmo (Terceira). In an article entitled "Um Apelo aos Bons Portugueses/Appeal to all Good Portuguese," the paper appealed to fellow countrymen with the following emotional message:

> An orphanage in Angra do Heroísmo is home to forty little children, ages four to ten, whom adversity, after having robbed them of the tender breast of a mother and the strong arm of a father to guide them on the path of life, is now, once again, threatening to deprive them of that charitable roof under which they receive the sustenance of life and spirit. The old building where these unfortunate children are housed is falling apart, ruined, in need of significant repairs in order to make it habitable. Moreover, the increase in the cost of living has been such that, without an increase in income, it will be impossible to keep that institution going. Fellow Portuguese of the vast and rich state of California, please make a donation to help our little brothers and sisters, who, from so far away, are reaching out to us with their little, fragile hands. Fellow Portuguese, remember that Christ himself said "suffer the little children to come on to me." If you want to be worthy of His sublime teachings, help the little children that, through this newspaper, are now imploring your protection. Hear their prayers! Here, thus, is now open the collection to raise funds to help the orphanage of Angra do Heroísmo and the little orphans who live there.[205]

The humor weekly *A California Alegre*, published between 1915 and 1940, also had a nomadic existence. It was founded in Lemoore, but then changed locations several times: Tulare, Hanford, Oakland, and Alameda.[206]

Cândido da Costa Nunes, a native of the island of Pico, Azores, was the founder, publisher, and editor from 1915 to 1938. After 1938 he was succeeded by M. J. Vieira and A. M. G. Nunes became the manager. The paper's header included a passage from *As Farpas* by Ramalho Ortigão, a nineteenth-century journalist famous for his criticism of Portuguese society:

> Let's hit them hard and strong
> Let's hit them where it hurts
> Let's whip all those jackasses
> No pain, no gain, the saying goes
> So, let's cure them of their flaws.
> Let's laugh, too. Laughter can be punishment, laughter can be a philosophy, often, laughter is salvation.[207]

The newspaper was published every Saturday and financed by the ads bought by local merchants, including St. John's Hospital, Fábrica de Linguiça de António Ferreira da Cruz, Caporgno & Company – Casa Funerária, Luis Correia – Pintor e empapelador, and Hanrahan & Wadsworth – Casa Funerária, among others.[208] It was a satirical newspaper, but occasionally it took on a serious or even dramatic tone, such as when Cândido da Costa Nunes's youngest son died. On October 14, 1937, the following headline covered the entire front page, "Um Anjinho para o Céu" (A Little Angel for Heaven). The newspaper described the death of Nunes's twelve-year-old son, Joseph:

> On September 17, after coming home from school and while playing with other children, our young son had the misfortune to step on a nail. The nail went through the sole of his shoe and punctured his right foot. After pulling out the nail himself, he came home and told his mother what had happened. His worried mother treated him with the home remedies suggested by some people who were present. The problem seemed to go away and José went back to playing. In the days that followed, he went back to school and did not complain of any symptoms. On the night of Saturday, September 25 to Sunday, September 26, the little boy began to complain of pain in the neck and back. Early Sunday

morning, we called a doctor, the distinguished surgeon Dr. Abílio Reis, who upon entering the sick boy's room advised us to take him to the hospital immediately. Poor José writhed with pain and his cries pierced our hearts. It was the terrible tetanus.[209]

The director of *A Liberdade*, the former priest Guilherme Silveira da Glória, was the uncle of the deceased boy. To express his solidarity, he published a poem in *A California Alegre* entitled "Hino Elegíaco. À Memória do Jovem José da Costa Nunes, Meu Sobrinho, que Faleceu a 28 de setembro de 1937" (Elegiac Hymn. To the Memory of the Young José da Costa Nunes, My Nephew, who Passed Away on September 28, 1937). The poem lamented the tragic loss of the young boy's life, snuffed out by a rusty nail, at an age when he had so much to look forward to.[210]

A Revista Portuguesa was published monthly in Hayward between 1914 and 1925 with the subtitle, "Agrícola, Comercial e Literária" (Agricultural, Commercial, and Literary), and the following promotional message in English: "This is the ONLY Magazine Published in the interest of the 100,000 Portuguese of California."[211] It was a quarter-page, general-interest magazine with more than twenty pages per issue and color on the cover, first green, then red. *A Revista Portuguesa* was founded and edited by João de Simas Melo Jr., from Pico. F. E. Adams was the Business Manager, Joaquim Rodrigues da Silva Leite was the Literary Editor, and João da Cunha Valim and F. C. Serpa were its major editors.[212] The paper paid special attention to issues of commerce and cultural activities related to the community. *A Revista Portuguesa*, according to its self-promotional messages, saw itself as being different from the other Portuguese newspapers:

> Our magazine is simple, but at the same time attractive and accurate, which will certainly make it unique among current Portuguese newspapers, for the novelty and variety of its articles. This, in and of itself, is enough to earn us your high and valuable support. But we will spare no effort and sacrifice in order to serve our readers and will strive to improve the magazine as best we can. Subscribe to the *Revista Portuguesa* and you shall have plenty to read during the long winter nights.[213]

The publication featured a permanent editorial section under "Notes from the Editor," and from 1918 on, it had an opinion section with articles on local and international topics.[214] In February 1915, the paper informed its most loyal readers that those who bought the annual collection would receive the following two books as gifts: *O Homem Misterioso*, set in the Azores, and the novella *Benita*. The magazine had many advertisements and they were of high quality, both creatively and graphically. As with many papers, *A Revista Portuguesa*'s header featured the crossed flags of Portugal and the United States, along with symbols that referred to emigration (a ship) and agriculture (crop fields). After 1920, the title changed, eliminating the definite article "A" and adding the slogan, "The Silent Partner of the Portuguese Farmer." An editorial welcoming readers explained its journalistic philosophy this way:

In naming our monthly publication *Revista*, it was not our expectation that our readers would find in its first issues all that the title may bring to mind. In order to publish a Portuguese "revista" with the same format and number of sections found in magazines published in Portugal or Brazil, or one that, in the words of our dear friend Valim, would encompass the "eight commandments," we would have to have a fabulous amount of capital at our disposal. Capital to buy machinery, capital to keep the most experienced typesetters, capital to hire good writers and be able to depend on their "promises." –Capital. Three times capital! But since that "earthly god" never shed his grace on us, we had to make do with the little training and experience in the printing arts that we possessed, as well as the help of our friends Valim and Serpa, in order to put into practice an idea the latter and I had been hatching for a long time. We had to come up with an affordable way of offering the Portuguese community a monthly publication that would attract their interest; that would awaken them from their indifference to reading; that would show them how good they are and how much better they can be; and that would inspire them to love all things Portuguese. Then, after many sleepless nights and days of enormous labor, we were able to offer this *Revista*, which is as good as we were able to come up with, but not the best we wished for. Just like Rome was not made in a day, so it may take months, maybe years, before our magazine is exactly what one would expect a publication of this type to be.[215]

The news about the various towns in the Azores published by *A Revista Portuguesa* tended to be telegraphic in style. In the issue cited above, one could read, for example, that on Pico, Mr. Fortunato Sebastião's brother, a teacher in Prainha de Cima, was robbed of about 40,000 *reis*; that Vasco Terra Furtado, a teacher in Santo Amaro, had joined the political party created by Dr. Manoel Francisco Neves; that the collection made on behalf of the Red Cross in Pontas Negras raised 8,500 *reis*; and that repairs to the streets of Lages were under way.

In addition to the aforementioned examples, there were other short-lived publications in California, including *A Crónica Portuguesa*, the self-styled "Revista Crítica da Sociedade Portuguesa dos Estados Unidos" (Critical Magazine of the Portuguese Society of the United States), which published only two issues in 1926. With offices in San Leandro, this was a failed attempt by Mário Bettencourt da Câmara to revive a journal that he had founded in the late nineteenth century. The *Gazeta Portuguesa* (Portuguese Gazette) was founded in 1926 by Francisco Fialho, a native of Pico, and edited by Eduardo Correia in Newark, California (Alameda County) and San Leandro.[216] In 1922, Constantino de Barcelos published *As Novidades* in Newman;[217] and in June 1924 the illustrated newspaper *A Abelha* appeared. It was edited in San Francisco and Oakland by Alfredo Dias da Silva and António da Conceição Teixeira, ex co-owner of *O Repórter* and a native of Madeira.

In New York City, *O Luso-Brazileiro* emerged in 1918 with the subtitle "Portuguese Weekly Newspaper." Taking on the role of "Defensor dos Interesses da Colónia Portuguesa e Brasileira" (Defender of the Interests of the Portuguese and Brazilian Communities), it was the property of O Luso-Brasileiro Publishing Co., whose management team consisted of Joseph Silva Jr. (president;) Manuel S. Chuva Ramos (editor); and Julio Pereira ("business manager"). It was a tabloid newspaper with a large format, 8 pages long, and published information of every kind with few ads. It was organized into sections on literature, poetry, "letters from abroad," news from Portugal and Europe, etc. There was also a section for learning English, which included practical exercises.[218] Also in New York, the Catholic priest José (Joseph) Cacella founded

O Portugal, which was published irregularly between 1929 and 1934 and subtitled "Semanário da Colónia Portuguesa da América do Norte" (Weekly of the Portuguese Community of North America). It included the following notice in English: "We reach all the Portuguese Population of New York State, the State of New Jersey, Boston, Mass., R. Island, California, Penn. and Conn. Our Paper has a good list of Subscribers in Portugal [and] Brazil."[219] It was printed in a tabloid format with four pages and, like the *Luso-Brazileiro*, had a section in English. To attract more subscribers, *O Portugal* published a patriotic message asking for support: "Subscribe to *O Portugal*. It is the duty of every good Portuguese to help the Portuguese press that week in and week out works to keep the sacred language, memory, history and traditions of our Homeland alive. Patriotism or love of Country is demonstrated with deeds."[220]

In the late 1920s, the movement of large numbers of Portuguese from New England to New Jersey[221] led to the expansion of Portuguese journalism there with the founding of two titles, *O Portugal* (1927-1928) and *Atlântico* (1928). The first was an illustrated weekly founded by Francisco Santos and two Italian printers, the Buffardi brothers. They were the driving force of *Atlântico*, which emerged as the successor to *O Portugal*, edited and published by António Rebelo Martins, who only managed to publish two issues. 1928 was also the year of the birth of the *Luso-Americano*, which was reissued in December 1939 by Vasco S. Jardim and has endured until the present day, as we shall see in chapter five.

In Rhode Island, Portuguese newspapers first appeared in the 1920s. *O Inquérito* was founded, published, and edited in Providence by José Martins da Cunha, a native of Terceira (Azores). The *Jornal Português* was owned by João Soares de Vasconcelos, originally from São Miguel (Azores). In Bristol, João Cristiano da Rosa founded *A Voz da Colónia* on March 13, 1926, but moved it shortly thereafter to Providence.[222] It would last until the 1940s, coming out on Thursdays with the subtitle: "Semanário Imparcial, Instrutivo e Noticioso" (Impartial, Educational and News Weekly).[223]

Chapter 4

New Challenges: Portuguese-American Newspapers, 1930-2015

Crisis and Consolidation, 1930-1939

The 1930s constituted an important historical period for the Portuguese-American community's journalistic production. Restrictions on the entry of Portuguese into the U.S., the end of the whaling industry at the beginning of the century, and the closing of the textile mills of New Bedford, Fall River, and other New England towns in the late 1920s forced some immigrants to return to Portugal or to relocate within the U.S.[1] A decade earlier, a similar process had occurred in Hawaii. After the territory stopped sponsoring contract labor from Portugal in the first decade of the twentieth century, immigration ceased and many Portuguese left the archipelago for the U.S. mainland, especially California.[2] These demographic changes, along with the loss of Portuguese language skills among the new generations in traditional areas of settlement, led to a decline in the number of new newspapers founded in Massachusetts and Hawaii and a significant increase in California (11), New Jersey (5), and New York (4), states that attracted new settlers from areas undergoing economic restructuring.

This was the period in which the Portuguese-American community intensely debated the political situation in Portugal and its change of regime, which was fueled in part by the arrival of political exiles from Portugal, such as the former Minister of Public Education João Camoesas, who settled in Taunton, Massachusetts. The end of the Republican era and the establishment of the Estado Novo regime ignited propaganda battles between supporters and opponents of the authoritarian state led by António de Oliveira Salazar. It was in these years that the two most important titles in Portuguese-American journalism in the twentieth century came into being: the *Diario de Noticias*, founded in New Bedford in 1927, and the *Jornal Português*, founded in Oakland in 1932. The latter, which resulted from the merger of the *Jornal de Notícias, O Imparcial,* and *A Colonia Portuguesa*, became the most popular Portuguese news medium on the Pacific Coast. Due to their extraordinary importance, both papers will be analyzed in detail in Chapter 5.

The first newspaper founded in Massachusetts in this decade was a weekly from Fall River, *Portugal*, created by Marcelino de Melo in 1933 with the help of the Consulate of Portugal in the city. It published only four issues.[3] Despite economic problems, New Bedford maintained a social, political, and cultural vitality that allowed for the publication of five new newspapers in addition to *Diario de Noticias*. The Aliança Liberal Portuguesa of New Bedford, a political club of progressivist tendencies, published two newspapers: *Liberdade* and *A Emancipação.* The former was created at the end of 1933 through a statutory mandate, inspired and driven by the editor-in-chief of the *Diario de Noticias*, Ferreira Martins. It was a weekly of eight illustrated pages in a tabloid format that came out on Thursdays. It was edited by a committee consisting of Alfredo Gaspar, Francisco Rebelo, and Jaime Fonseca, and featured the typical blend of articles, political criticism, educational information, and serialized novels, as well as advertisements from local merchants. The Aliança Liberal published a single edition of *A Emanicpação* in May 1934, with the subtitle, "Órgão da Aliança Liberal Portuguesa" (Organ of the Aliança Liberal Portuguesa). Two sentences appeared by the title, one by Jesus and the other by Karl Marx. The first was given in the form of spiritual advice—"Always tell the truth and the truth will set you free."[4] The second was a call to action—"Workers of the world, unite!"[5] This single issue contains the article "A Aliança Liberal Portuguesa e o que Tornou Necessária a sua Criação" (A Aliança Liberal Portuguesa and What Made its Creation Necessary), a bitter, somewhat literary, reflection on the causes and consequences of the First World War:

Vivid as a deep, unfadable scar left by a monstrous scalpel on the bronzed face of History, that macabre and hideous bacchanalia known as the

Great War is still engraved on the heart and soul of humanity! Conceived and carried out by cruel and debauched old capitalists who, moved by unlimited greed and ferocious selfishness, did not hesitate to sacrifice millions of innocent lives in order to satisfy their depraved and orgiastic vices. The war, with all its attributes, represented symbolically by the Four Horsemen of the Apocalypse, left the indelible mark of its passage everywhere: hunger, pestilence, destruction, death!"[6]

The monthly newspaper *O Teatro*, dedicated to the performing arts, was founded by António Pereira in New Bedford and directed by António Santinho between October 1935 and June 1936. The paper was, according to its promotional slogans, "dedicado aos Grupos Dramáticos Portugueses da América" (dedicated to the Portuguese drama groups of the U.S.) and was a "membro da Câmara de Comércio Portuguesa de New Bedford" ("member of the Portuguese Chamber of Commerce of New Bedford). It covered artistic activities, with an emphasis on Portuguese-American theatre.[7]

Between December 1936 and January 1937, the monthly newspaper *O Mensageiro*, "dedicado ao comércio e colónia portuguesa dos Estados Unidos d'América" (dedicated to commerce and the Portuguese community of the United States of America), came out. It was published by The Messenger Press,[8] which was owned by Luiz Antunes, who, according to Vasco S. Jardim, was a former policeman from Lisbon with monarchical leanings.[9] *O Mensageiro*, which was a newspaper with a semi-handmade print dedicated to publishing a variety articles, ceased production in January 1937 after a fire in the print shop destroyed its facilities.[10]

Luiz Antunes had also been an editor of the *Luso-Americano* in Newark in 1931, and went on to publish *O Comércio Português,* which was printed irregularly in that city throughout 1932. Having no press of their own, they paid to use the equipment of other papers, including the *Luso-Americano,* *Pátria Portuguesa* (owned by Manuel Nascimento), and *A Tribuna* (owned by the Merola brothers).[11]

O Evangelista appeared in Fall River on December 7, 1934. It was founded by the Protestant minister João Pacheco dos Santos and directed by José de Lima. On its frontpage, it displayed the following subtitles: "Mensário

Fundamentalista de Propaganda Evangélica" (Monthly Fundamentalist Publication of Evangelical Propaganda) and "Órgão e Propriedade da Juventude da Igreja Batista Portuguesa de Fall River, Mass" (Organ and Property of the Youth of the Portuguese Baptist Church of Fall River, Mass). The editor-in-chief of the newspaper was Manuel A. Oliveira Jr. and the administrator was M. Rebelo.[12] *O Evangelista* was financed by donations from church members and by advertisements. It was distributed for free.[13]

In California, *A Colonia Portuguesa, Jornal de Notícias,* and *O Imparcial* all closed and were later combined as the *Jornal Português* with the intention of developing an even more ambitious and stable paper, thus ending a cycle during which many popular newspapers were published. Other significant closings included Guilherme S. Gloria's *A Liberdade*, which ended in 1937, and *A União Portuguesa*, which ceased publication in 1942, two years after the death of Manuel de Freitas Martins Trigueiro.

The first new newspaper created in California during this decade was *O Portugal*, founded in Oakland on July 28, 1930, by the editor and publisher João Roldão, who was also one of the founders of the União Portuguesa Continental.[14] It was published irregularly as a "Quinzenário Dedicado à Propaganda de Portugal nos Estados Unidos" (Biweekly Dedicated to the Promotion of Portugal in the United States) and had a heavy proportion of advertisements.[15] The paper published news about Portugal and the Portuguese community in America in small sections, many of them created *ad hoc* for each new issue, such as "News from Aveiro," "News from Madeira," or "To those who Suffer."

The newspaper reported on the activities of the União Portuguesa Continental and provided news related to the immigrants from Ílhavo (Portugal).[16] It also included poems, like this one dedicated "To the Portuguese Children of California," published on September 7, 1935, which began and ended with these, freely-translated, stanzas:

> Oh, pretty children, beautiful and winsome
> What endless grace God shed on you!
> Sweet stars and roses in sparkling dew
> Angels from heaven, holy and handsome.
>
> . . .

17. Cover of *O Portugal*.
Copy of October 5, 1933.

Of California the brave discoverer, who was he?
Although he was sailing for proud Spain
Forevermore he shall remain
João Cabrilho, a Portuguese, like you and me.[17]

The biweekly magazine *Portugália* was published in Oakland between December 1931 and June 1932.[18] It was founded and edited by Joaquim Rodrigues da Silva Leite, a native of continental Portugal, and it would merge briefly with *O Portugal*. It included reports on Portuguese culture, advertisements from businesses in the community, and a course for learning English. Not long after *Portugália*'s closing, the weekly *O Progresso* was founded in Sacramento by Alfredo Dias da Silva on November 7, 1932. It was published until 1940. It carried the subtitle "Jornal dedicado à colónia Portuguesa dos Estados Unidos da América do Norte" (Newspaper dedicated to the Portuguese community of the United States of North America) and claimed to be "the only newspaper in the Sacramento Valley."[19]

In 1932, *The Lusitanian* began publication in Oakland, and it ceased production in 1955. It was founded and edited by Zósimo S. Souza from São Jorge, Azores. Anthony Sousa was the associate editor and Phil Cantal was the assistant editor. As the voice of the Lusitania Club, it was a monthly magazine that defended Catholic values.[20] It was aimed at Portuguese Americans who had difficulty speaking or understanding Portuguese.[21] Its subtitle was "The Monthly Messenger of the Lusitania Club," but after September 1939 it changed to "The Monthly Messenger of the Lusitanians in America."

Promoted initially by a network of California social clubs dedicated to upholding the prestige of the Portuguese navigator João Rodrigues Cabrilho, *Cabrillo – Commentator Discoverer of California* was a monthly magazine written in English that was founded and published by Manuel F. Sylva in San Francisco and San Leandro.[22] The magazine accompanied its title with an informative note that stated: "This publication is dedicated to the memory of John Rodrigues Cabrillo (João Rodrigues Cabrilho), Portuguese Navigator in the service of Spain, who discovered California on September 28th, 1542. Died and was buried on San Miguel island, Santa Barbara Channel on January 3rd, 1543." Sylva edited the magazine from April 1937 until Joaquim Rodrigues da Silva Leite, a native of continental Portugal, became editor in 1938. In an editorial in the first issue, Sylva explains the reason for its existence:

> [T]he reason behind this magazine is the lack of interest manifested by most Californians in the great maritime deeds and navigational feats of the discoverer of California, John Rodrigues Cabrillo. This man deserves a more prominent place on the pages of our histories. Not only was he a daring mariner and soldier, but he was also possessed of kindness and consideration for human lives. During the epoch of his discovery, some explorers were ruthless toward the Indians and killed them at the slightest provocation. Not so with Cabrillo, he was kind to them and earned their gratitude. Another educational motive is that this great navigator was a Portuguese in common with other mariners who came to the shores of California, but of course in the service of Spain which had led many to believe that they were Spaniards. Further, Portuguese contributions to California and to civilization in general is such wonderful lore that it is worthy of publication.[23]

The Reverend John (João) José Vieira Jr. (originally from the island of Madeira), who had been editor of *A Aurora* in Cambridge, founded *O Heraldo*, an organ of the Portuguese Methodist church, published from January 1936 to 1959 in Oakland, whose title was accompanied by the biblical quotation "And you shall know the truth and the truth shall set you free."[24] *O Heraldo* included content critical of the Catholic Church, which generated controversy with other newspapers affiliated with Catholicism, as in November 1936, when an article was published that condemned the role of the Catholic hierarchy in the Spanish Civil War:

> On the first page of the September issue of *O Heraldo*, there was a little article about the Spanish Civil War that really caught the attention of the editor of the *Portugal da Califórnia*. The article in question, which was based on statements by a Spanish Socialist priest named João Garcia Morales, accused the Catholic Church of being the instigator of the terrible civil war that is causing so much misery to that country. Indeed, that

piece was of so much interest to the editor of the *Portugal da Califórnia,* that in a most waspish way he used his newspaper to accuse us of having forged the story, which we had said had been provided by the Associated Press. ...We did not invent; we simply published facts. Facts cannot be denied. Ignorance, Dear Editor, can be overbold. Let this be a lesson.[25]

In New Jersey and New York, Portuguese-American journalism was marked by the appearance of a series of publications related to the anti-Salazar political activity of José Alves Rodrigues, who served for several years as a correspondent for *O Colonial* in Newark. He was also the editor of *A Tribuna,* a notary public, and, in the 1940s, owner of the Portuguese Service Agency, located in the neighborhood of Jamaica, in Queens, New York.[26] José Alves Rodrigues, as noted in Chapter 2, also published *O Combate* in 1934, *O Bacamarte* between 1936 and 1937, *A Plebe* from 1936 to 1938, and *O País* in the 1950s.

On the opposite side of the ideological spectrum was the biweekly *A Luta,*[27] which emerged on December 15, 1936, and was published until 1970. It was owned by the Catholic priest Joseph (José) Cacella.[28] Except for a brief period in 1937, when Gil Stone was hired as director after leaving *A Tribuna,* José Cacella was responsible for managing and editing the newspaper. In the various subtitles adopted by *A Luta* over the years, it announced that it was "The Portuguese Newspaper in the Empire State;" "Imparcial, Recreativo, Noticioso" (Impartial, Recreational, News-focused); and the "New York–New Jersey Portuguese Weekly News." Its motto, a call for unity and coexistence, was "Sem União é Lutar em Vão" (Without Unity We Fight in Vain). Its commercial ads claimed the newspaper had a wide circulation among the 500,000 Portuguese in the United States beyond the 10,000 in New York. It published articles about Portugal and Portuguese Americans, especially those living in New York and New Jersey.[29] Its editorial line favored the Estado Novo regime, and Cacella maintained numerous contacts with its leaders. He even met and interviewed Salazar, while accompanying the Archbishop of Indianapolis, Paul Schulte, on a visit to Portugal in the spring of 1949. After the trip he published an extensive report praising the Portuguese dictator.[30]

A Tribuna was a weekly founded by the Italian typographer Joseph Merola in Newark on July 2, 1931.[31] The newspaper was launched with old linotypes bought from António Fortes, former owner of *O Independente* in New Bedford. Merola also hired *O Independente*'s linotypist, Delfina Sousa, and Gil Stone as editor and director. Stone also edited a special page dedicated to the Portuguese community (in Portuguese) in the Anti-Franco Spanish newspaper *La Voz*, founded in New York during the Spanish Civil War.[32] Between April and December 1933, the editor, director, and publisher of *A Tribuna* was Laurinda C. Andrade, who would leave to become the secretary to the new ambassador of Portugal in Washington, João António de Bianchi. When Merola moved to Paterson, NJ, he sold the paper to a company owned by Luis Gomes, Gil Stone, José Alves Rodrigues, and António Pires, but it lasted for only one more month.[33] During those Depression years, according to Vasco S. Jardim, "neither Bianchi's (the ambassador) money, nor Verdades' (consul general of New York), or even that of a Ford would have been enough"[34] to keep it afloat. One of the goals of *A Tribuna* was to raise awareness about the culture, commerce, and industry of Portugal in the United States, which, according to an editorial of March 15, 1934, could be done by having the Portuguese authorities invest more in advertising:

The French Parliament has just approved the spending of $2,167,440 to promote France in North and South America. That fabulous amount that France is spending on advertising is a sign of common sense and shrewdness; it will return, multiplied many times, to the coffers of the French government and the businesses that, as a result of those advertisements, will sell their products abroad. . . .These facts should open the eyes of the Portuguese government and our complacent merchant-exporters so that they too would do something more than those perennial meetings, with conference after conference, that produce no results, no Portuguese participation—OTHER THAN THROUGH ENGLISH FIRMS—in this vast and wealthy American market! Some time ago, a contract was "almost" signed between our country and a commercial advertising company from New York. The contract was for the promotion of Portuguese products and involved the total sum of $25,000, if I'm not mistaken. But the contract never saw the light of day because in Portugal they deemed the amount to be FABULOUS! It did not occur to them that, nowadays, you cannot sell anything without advertising, that spending that amount to promote our products would bring to the commerce and industry of Portugal MANY, MANY TIMES the amount spent.[35]

Between 1931 and 1932, *A Pátria Portuguesa* was published in Newark. It was founded by Manuel Nascimento, a native of Santa Maria, Azores, and owner of Iberic Press, with António Mora as editor and Crisostónio Cruz as director.[36] Prior to coming to the U.S., Cruz had lived in Rio de Janeiro where he founded *A Voz de Portugal*. In its initial phase, *A Pátria Portuguesa* attempted to occupy the space left in the New Jersey community by the closure of *O Portugal* and the *Luso- Americano*, but the decline in advertising revenues caused by the Great Depression led to the demise of the paper.[37] Beset by debt, Nascimento ended his life by turning on the gas at the newspaper's headquarters on April 5, 1933.[38] Vasco S. Jardim wrote the following about the circumstances surrounding the death of the founder of *A Pátria Portuguesa*:

> Manuel Nascimento was a very decent and competent man. He was familiar with Portuguese and American laws and had been a translator in New York. His wife and children lived in Pawtucket. It was at that time that they moved to New York. There was a man, Francisco Ribeiro, who offered to help the struggling Nascimento family. How? By making the payments Nascimento owed on his life insurance policy under the conditions that he be named the beneficiary. Nascimento died and Ribeiro paid all the debts of the couple and gave the balance to Nascimento's widow and children. Francisco Ribeiro was a giant of a man, and was even more of a giant in his philanthropic work. He learned how to read and write after he was 52.[39]

According to a report on the Portuguese press in the United States published by the *Diario de Noticias* in August 1933, José Dias Escobar published the magazine *A América* in New York City sometime in the early 1930s.[40] In 1939 in Danbury, Connecticut, Joaquim de Oliveira, author of a book of verse entitled *Do meu Coração ao Vosso (From my Heart to Yours)* that was dedicated to the "Mocidade Humilde da sua Pátria" (Humble Youth of his Country), founded *O Trabalho*, one of the last Portuguese-American papers to appear during the 1930s.[41] On February 1, 1940, the *Diario de Noticias* reported the following about the publication:

> Today we received the third issue of *O Trabalho*, which is published in Danbury, in the state of Connecticut, under the leadership of our dear contributor Mr. Joaquim de Oliveira who is its editor. The third issue of this well-written newspaper displays on its front page a beautiful photoprint of the great native son of São Miguel Dr. Teófilo Braga of blessed memory, who was the first president of the Portuguese Republic (provisional government). This issue commemorates the historic date of January 31, 1891 and had contributions from the well-known Dr. João Camoesas and Dr. José Rodrigues Miguéis. We thank *O Trabalho* for their gift, and we hope for its prosperity as well as that of its director and editor to whom we send our sincere greetings.[42]

New Newspapers in a New Stage, 1940-1969

Succeeding at newspaper publication during the 1920s and 1930s, following the passage of immigration restrictions, was a great achievement for any Portuguese-American publisher, but doing so in the 1940s was even more challenging, due to the drastic reduction in subscriptions and the decrease in commercial advertising revenue. Nevertheless, some did survive. In Massachusetts, there was the *Diario de Noticias*, which experienced a change in ownership due to its delicate financial situation; *O Colonial* and *O Independente*, which continued until 1945; and the semi-annual *O Heraldo Português*, which lasted until 1976. In California, *A California Alegre* and *O Progresso* both closed in 1940, leaving only the *Jornal Português* and the *Boletim da U.P.E.C.* By contrast, in New Jersey, the *Luso-Americano*, which had been edited by Vasco Jardim since 1939, experienced a rebirth, perhaps as the result of a new influx of immigrants that relocated from New England to the Newark-New York region. By the late 1940s, the formerly crowded Portuguese-American media landscape was essentially reduced to three general-information newspapers, two on the East Coast—the *Diario de Noticias* and the *Luso-Americano*—and one on the West Coast—the *Jornal Português*.

Nevertheless, the reduced number of immigrants did not prevent the appearance of three new titles in the 1940s. In New Bedford in 1942, Luiz Antunes launched the weekly *A Voz de Portugal*, which was published irregularly until 1949. It was a tabloid newspaper of four pages that had a list of delegates and contributors in various Massachusetts locations. In Cambridge, its correspondent was Porfírio Bessone; in Arlington, Maria J. Duarte; and in Somerville, Sérvio Ribeiro. Invited contributors included Gil Stone, José Caçoilo Rocha, Theotónio I. Martins, José de Matos, and M. Cabral.[43] *A Voz de Portugal* offered news related to the community and to Portugal. In 1945, it had an issue dedicated to "Greater Boston."[44] *A Palavra,* a biweekly magazine of political and social commentary was also published at this time in New Bedford. In September 1949, a new magazine was published in New York, the illustrated quarterly *O Mundo Lusíada*.[45] With the subtitle "The Portuguese Word" and the slogan "A magazine devoted to the interests of the Portuguese, their descendants and their culture," it was founded and edited by José Dâmaso Fragoso, who was also listed as "president," "publisher," and "former member of the faculties of New York University, Hunter College and Queens College of the City of New York." Antone S. Pimentel appears as "vice president," and Manuel L. da Silva as "secretary and assistant editor." *O Mundo Lusíada* was also distributed in New Jersey, Massachusetts, and Rhode Island.[46] Its content was mainly political and cultural, with a nationalist, anti-Communist, and pro-Estado Novo editorial line. The first editorial outlines its patriotic agenda:[47]

> If talent and skill will not fail us,[48] this magazine proposes: first, to fight for Portuguese and for Luso-Brazilian culture. Second, to increase the teaching of Portuguese in the public schools of this country and develop the love for Portuguese literature and Luso-Brazilian culture among American students. Third, to honor the most enlightened and cultured minds of the Lusophone Family by publicizing their best works of literature, philosophy, science, music and art. Fourth, to correct each and every injury perpetrated by the Press against our people, whether they live here,

in Europe, in Africa, in Asia, or in Oceania. And, finally, to point out the merits or demerits of those of Portuguese heritage because we believe that both the good and the bad deeds of citizens must be made public so that the first receive proper reward and the second suppressed.[49]

In the 1950s, the situation remained dire for the Portuguese press in the United States. To our knowledge, only two new publications were founded, the short-lived biweekly *O País* in 1950 and *Portugal Today*. The first is believed to be the last newspaper published by José Alves Rodrigues in New York. The second was a high-quality magazine distributed monthly (irregularly) from Manhattan and written entirely in English.[50] The magazine had a large editorial team with correspondents in several countries, and produced a variety of in-depth political, social, and cultural reports about the Portuguese community in the United States and Portugal (including its overseas territories).[51] Its content targeted Portuguese Americans born in the U.S. who did not speak Portuguese, and its goal was to increase American tourism to Portugal and enhance the image of Portugal in the U.S. Its editorial discourse was favorable to Salazar's government, with a message intended to reach out to the new generation of Portuguese Americans, as is clearly apparent in this excerpt from its first issue:

> You can go away from Portugal, but you can't put Portugal out of your heart. This sentiment, echoed by thousands of tourists who return to colorful Iberia again and again, is felt even more keenly by those who have emigrated from Portugal to seek new opportunities in other parts of the world. It is reflected in the nostalgia which second and third generation Portuguese abroad feel for the country which they may never even have seen but to which they are still so strongly tied in blood and spirit. To all those who are absent from Portugal... to those who long to return or who look forward to going... we direct this first issue of *Portugal Today*.[52]

In the 1960s, five new newspaper titles were created. On September 1, 1960, a newspaper published irregularly three times per month called *Voz de Portugal* (Voice of Portugal) was founded in Hayward, California, by Gilberto Lopes de Aguiar (a native of continental Portugal and a former typesetter for *Jornal Português* and the Lisbon-based *Diário de Notícias*, who served as editor and director until his death in January 1975. He was succeeded by his son Lourenço da Costa de Aguiar, who managed to publish the paper until 1985. Subtitled "Trimensário Independente, Noticioso, Recreativo e Cultural" (Independent, News, Recreation, and Culture Trimonthly), it employed the slogan "Engrandecendo os Estados Unidos; prestigiando a raça lusitana" (Honoring the United States; dignifying the Lusitanian Race).[53] Aguiar justified the emergence of *Voz de Portugal* to readers by explaining that the news available in California was not enough to meet the needs of the community:

> A new publication written in the melodious language of Camões has just come into existence in this prodigious state of California. ... As far as we know, no proprietor or editor of a Portuguese-language newspaper in this state has ever become rich, or even lived comfortably, off the profits of such an enterprise. On the contrary, their prospects were never the best, and, in general, most of them ended up going into other activities in order to meet their economic needs. Hence, those who, for better or for worse, have been able to bring the Portuguese voice to the community should be considered heroes and patriots. We are completely aware of this, but we are also aware that the Portuguese community of California is in dire need of a press that meets its just aspirations. In our view, two newspapers are not enough to serve the half million Portuguese living in the richest and most progressive state of the American Union. The fact that we have only one small-circulation Portuguese-language newspaper to serve a community as vast as ours clearly illustrates the stagnation into which the Portuguese press in California has fallen in recent years. Therefore, we think that this is a good step, not only for the Portuguese community of California, but also for the press itself, which will benefit from having more than just one representative and, as a result, will attract more general interest.[54]

A year after the founding of *Voz de Portugal*, Aguiar launched a humor-satirical publication called *O Companheiro da Alegria*, also known as "Partner of Cheer," which was printed in the same printshop as *Voz de Portugal* and sometimes sold with it. It was published monthly in Portuguese until 1975, and then quarterly until 1977, the year of its final issue.[55]

On May 1, 1961, the biweekly newspaper *Novos Rumos Estados Unidos* emerged in Newark and was edited until the 1970s through the Church of Fátima by Fr. Joseph (José) Capote, in collaboration with Fr. John S. Antão. It was subsequently sold to Almadir Correia.[56] Although it was a Catholic-affiliated newspaper, it reported on a variety of issues regarding the Portuguese community in the United States.[57] Capote was also responsible for editing *Novos Mundos*, another newspaper produced in Newark at the time. Finally, the weekly magazine *A Chama* appeared in New Bedford in 1968. It was founded by Manuel Medeiros, a lighthouse keeper from Faial, Azores, who was the president of the general assembly of the Club União Faialense, a social club associated with persons from the island of Fayal, Azores. Originally intended to be that club's newsletter, differences among its members led Medeiros to turn it into an independent publication, printed without interruption until 1978.[58] It subtitle was "The Portuguese Language Magazine" or "Weekly magazine, independent of any party affiliations, founded in 1968."[59] In the beginning, Manuel Medeiros was the director, Manuel Maria Duarte and Heldo Teófilo Braga, the editors, and Santiago Gomes, editor-in-chief.[60]

The Reawakening of Portuguese-American Journalism, 1970-1989

Toward the end of the 1950s Portuguese immigration to the U.S. began to increase. First, the Azorean Refugee Act of 1958 allowed an influx of immigrants fleeing volcanic eruptions and earthquakes in the Azores into the country. Then the Immigration and Naturalization Act of 1965, which put an end to the policy of national origin immigration quotas, gave rise to a new wave of Portuguese immigrants that was even higher in number than the previous one at the beginning of the century, totaling 243,994 immigrants between 1960 and 1999 (Figure 1).

The renewal of Portuguese immigration in this period spurred an increase in journalistic production, with the founding of twenty-six new newspapers. Illustrated variety magazines became particularly popular at this time, sometimes even more popular than newspapers. Among these was *For the People*, a monthly magazine written in English, which was published between 1970 and 1981 in Fall River to "express new ideas and to record the experiences of the people, and to spread this to the people." In a similar vein, Manuel Augusto Saraiva founded the short-lived magazines *Factos e Gente* (1975?) and *Almanaque do Emigrante* (1970s) in Newark, New Jersey, where José Cerqueira published some issues of *O Cartaz* (1977) and *Portuguese News* (1978), which was also the name of a magazine founded by Alfred DiJulio (a native of continental Portugal) and Anthony D. Azevedo in San Leandro, California, of which five issues were published in 1979. In Newark in 1979 Bernardino Moutinho directed *Tic-Tac*, subtitled "revista para os jovens de todas as idades" (magazine for young people of all ages). It had the pedagogical and didactic goal of teaching Portuguese history and culture to young Portuguese Americans. The great commercial magazine of the 1970s, however, was *Oportunidades* (1970s), edited monthly in Kearny, New Jersey, with two subtitles: "Revista do Emigrante Português" (Magazine of the Portuguese Emigrant) and "Revista da Comunidade Portuguesa dos E.U.A. e Canadá" (Magazine of the Portuguese Community of the United States and Canada). Although it covered a wide range of topics, founder and editor José B. Moreira's primary purpose was promoting community businesses.[61]

In the 1970s, despite the closure of *Diario de Noticias* in 1973, which ceased publication with the retirement of its owner and director, João Rodrigues Rocha, three newspapers emerged that have continued publishing until the present day: *O Jornal de Fall River* (named simply *O Jornal* from 1981 onwards, in Fall River, MA), *A Tribuna Portuguesa* (originally *The Portuguese Tribune*, first in San Jose and then in Modesto, CA), and the *Portuguese Times* (founded in Newark, NJ, and moved to New Bedford, MA). The latter, which attracted most of *Diario de Noticias*'s audience, will be analyzed further in Chapter 5. The free weekly *O Jornal de Fall River*, written in Portuguese and English, was founded in 1970 by Raymond Canto e Castro. In 2012 it was published by Ric Oliveira, with Lourdes C. Silva as editor.[62] It was owned by Portuguese-American Publications, which was part of Ottaway Newspapers, a business communication group that also owned the *Standard-Times* of New Bedford. A member of the New England Press Association & International

Newspapers Marketing Association, *O Jornal* publishes abundant advertising and a wealth of information related to the activities of the Portuguese, Cabo Verdean, and Brazilian communities. Currently, *O Jornal*, which continues to thrive as a free bilingual newspaper financed exclusively through advertisements, is owned by GateHouse Media and, according to its website "remains a vibrant piece of the Portuguese-speaking communities in Massachusetts and Rhode Island... [and] continues to be a powerful tool utilized by businesses, agencies, political leaders and others to reach the largest ethnic group in Southeastern Massachusetts."[63]

Another bilingual newspaper, *A Tribuna Portuguesa/The Portuguese Tribune* ("semanário independente ao serviço das comunidades de língua portuguesa"/"independent weekly at the service of the Portuguese language communities"), was founded in July 1979 by João P. Brum in the area of San Jose known as "Little Portugal."[64] It began as a weekly and, since 1994, has been published fortnightly, except in January.[65] In 1986, *A Tribuna Portuguesa* was purchased by Alberto Soares, who was its editor between 1986 and 1993. John Rodrigues da Silveira and Arthur Thomas reorganized the company in 1989, placing editorial direction in the hands of the Azorean writer and member of the European Parliament Artur da Cunha Oliveira, and journalistic direction in the hands of the radio personality Filomena Mendes Rocha (1993-1994). A new team formed by Azoreans Jaime Lemos, Armando F. Antunes, and Helder Antunes entered in 1991, modernizing the structure and content of the paper. Coverage regarding activities of the community increased as news from Portugal decreased, since digital and television media already provided extensive information on continental Portugal and the islands.

In 2002-2003, The Tagus Group, presided by José Ávila, took ownership of the publication, which was transferred to Modesto in the San Joaquin Valley.[66] In its early days, it featured news from Portugal and the Azores, with numerous advertisements, especially from travel agencies and airlines. In its first issues, it published a section in English titled "Luso-American Tribune." Current issues are printed in color in a tabloid format; it is also available in a digital format.[67] Its content focuses on social activities and events in the Portuguese community in the United States, mainly in California, with a profusion of photographs and advertisements.

In Rhode Island, Portuguese-American journalism also gained strength, launching three newspapers almost simultaneously: *A Comunidade*, *The Azorean Times*, and *Jornal Português*. *A Comunidade* was begun by Daniel Manhães in Pawtucket between 1974 and 1978 as a monthly publication, though in 1978 it was distributed fortnightly for a few issues. *The Azorean Times*, which was published every other week, was founded in Bristol in 1975 as "The Azorean Voice in the USA," owned by the Azorean Committee 75-Non Profit Corp,[68] with an editorial team that promoted the independence of the Azores.[69] In the 1980s, José Baptista and Carolina Matos acquired the paper and changed its name to *The Portuguese-American Journal*, transforming it into a bilingual weekly of news related to the Portuguese community. The paper was published in Providence and Bristol between 1985 and 1995, and it had three editions: Fall River, New Bedford, and Greater Boston. Lastly, at the end of the 1960s, and perhaps during the 1970s as well, Manuel T. Neves[70] published the monthly *Cape Verdean Newspaper*,[71] which aimed to be the voice of the Cabo Verdean immigrant community.

In the 1980s, six new publications appeared: one in Massachusetts, three in California, and one in New York and Rhode Island, respectively. The continued flow of immigrants, which reached 42,685 in this decade,[72] permitted the consolidation of various titles founded in the previous decade and stimulated the creation of new ones, although the majority, as had always been the rule, were ephemeral. In 1982, *Novo Mundo em Revista* came to light in New Bedford as a weekly Catholic magazine whose founder, Fr. Manuel Garcia, from Faial, Azores, edited the magazine from May 21, 1982, until the last issue on December 27, 1983.[73] In San José, the weekly *Noticia* emerged on December 5, 1984, directed and edited by the popular radio announcer João José Encarnação (a native of São Miguel) with the support of radio entrepreneur Batista S. Vieira, president of Portuguese Publications of California, which owned the paper.[74] In April of 1986, João P. Brum acquired *Noticia* and became its director and editor. In its first issue, the reborn newspaper was presented to its readers in these terms:

It was a difficult birth. Not everyone liked that I was to be born. There was a bit of everything to prevent my appearance. Cries and tears.

Lamentations and screams. Suicide threats. Meetings and agreements. They experimented with the pill, they suggested abortion, and even went to a witch. There have been a lot of changes. Because of me, some people who could not stand the sight of each other are now the best of friends. Others, who felt despondent, got a new lease on life. And all that for what? For a simple newspaper—a business that no one wants. (At least in other people's hands.) If this kid was undeserving of this merit, the fact that it created so much interest in newspapers in this community would be more than enough to justify and be grateful for its birth. Until now, creating newspapers has been the business of poets, of idealists, of the penniless who couldn't punch their way out of a paper bag. Now, for the love and hate of this child, the rich have entered the race. "But why another newspaper?" some ask. "For what?" we ask ourselves. Three restaurants, three travel agencies, three men's clothing stores, three jewelers in the Portuguese commercial center alone? Why so many philharmonics, so many fraternities, so many brotherhoods and so many clubs? Eurico Mendes from *The Portuguese Times* told me in a letter, "Certainly, they have already told you that there is not enough space for another Portuguese newspaper in California." Maybe you would like to know that, in reference to a similar situation, a friend of mine said, "We are the space that we create." We liked the phrase and we are determined to create our own space. We will not beg for subscriptions or blame the community for our inabilities and incompetence.[75]

On August 6, 1986, Brum reestablished the weekly *Noticia* in San Jose, launching it as the successor to *Portugal-USA* with the subtitle "Voz Independente da Comunidade" (Independent Voice of the Community). It was published until November 4, 1987, by Portuguese Publications of California, Inc.[76] In Tulare, the magazine *A Novidade,* founded and edited by Pedro Valadão da Costa (Terceira, Azores), was published monthly between 1983 and 1986 and was released as a supplement to *A Tribuna Portuguesa* between 1985 and 1986. In its last issue the title was changed to *Revista*.[77] In New York City, Martin Avillez launched the biannual illustrated magazine *Lusitânia* ("A Journal of Reflection & Oceanography") in February 1988. Its content was predominantly literary and cultural, publishing texts by prestigious authors like Fernando Pessoa and Roland Barthes. And in East Providence, Tomás Veiga and Luís Pires founded the *Portuguese Daily* in 1984, published on weekdays and touted as "the only daily newspaper of the community."[78]

The Portuguese Press at the Turn of the Twenty-First Century, 1990-2010

Four new newspapers appeared in the 1990s, but none on the East Coast, where the market was dominated by the *Portuguese Times* of New Bedford, *O Jornal* of Fall River, and the *Luso-Americano* of Newark. The latter, through its publishing company Luso-Americano Publishing, directed by António Matinho, expanded into California by founding the weekly *Luso-Americano California* in the city of Hayward on September 9, 1992. The paper was published independently on Wednesdays until May 31, 1995.[79] The *Portuguese-American Chronicle* began publication in Tracy (San Joaquin Valley) on December 22, 1997. It was founded by João P. Brum and agricultural entrepreneur Frank J. Silva, first as a weekly, then as a biweekly. In 1998, Tony Matinho replaced Brum as director, and in 1999 John de Melo became the director and Maria del Carmen Odom the editor, publishing the paper with the help of Mary L. Silva, wife of Frank J. Silva. Tracy Press acquired it in June 2005 and closed it in February 2006.[80]

On November 4, 1991, Portuguese Americans newly settled in Florida founded a fortnightly tabloid written entirely in English titled *Portuguese Heritage Journal* and subtitled "The biweekly newspaper for Portuguese and Brazilian Americans," in the city of Coral Gables. Its owner/publisher was António V. Cavaco, and Merwin Sigale the editor.[81] After September 1993, it became a monthly variety magazine,[82] paying special attention to the activities of the Portuguese community in Miami.[83] With an interest in bringing Portuguese culture closer to the descendants of Portuguese immigrants who have moved away from their heritage, *Portuguese Heritage Journal* reflected in its inaugural issue on the situation of the Portuguese immigrant community and its cultural identity within American society:

One has to be realistic. Life in America is full of ethnic strife due to the rapid growth of minorities in the past three decades. The idealistic image of a melting-pot society in the United States appears to be far from reality, as it hasn't worked up to now, and ethnic and racial differences are everyday facts of life. The problem cannot be ignored, and those differences cannot be suppressed, so they must be dealt with positively. We cannot ignore the real differences of the various ethnic groups, and acceptance of a melting-pot image can hurt this country because it distracts us from teaching the values that hold Americans—whatever their background—together in the greatest nation on Earth. Portuguese immigrants integrate themselves quickly into the communities where they live and accept the melting-pot theory without much ethnic strife, but we cannot ignore our cultural identity and the values that bind us together as the ethnic group—religion, family unity, food, etc.—in this great nation. . . As the number of immigrants increases, great efforts have been made for the preservation of cultural identity through the proliferation of clubs and associations throughout the country, wherever there are a few Portuguese-speaking families that can get together. Much credit must also be given to the various Portuguese-language weekly newspapers published in the largest Portuguese-speaking communities of California, New England, and New Jersey, which strive to keep their readers informed of local community events and news of the motherland. Much has been achieved on the local level. But much more must be done *at the national level to maintain and preserve the identity* of the people of Portuguese ancestry, regardless of their ability to speak the language and wherever they have chosen to reside—in a community with a large Portuguese-speaking population or not—or whether their country of birth was Portugal, Brazil, or the United States of America. There has to be a meeting of the minds of all, be it in the North or South, on the East or West coast. There has to be a common goal to defend our interests as a minority group and to develop means of assistance to promote the welfare of our people. Like other well-organized ethnic groups, our clubs and associations of the East, center, and West must work together through a Federation of Portuguese Clubs and Associations of America. Being published in English, the *Portuguese Heritage Journal* wants to reach those who, because of language or distance from the Portuguese-speaking communities, have separated themselves and become aloof from their heritage. With the publication of feature articles written by distinguished journalists and university professors about important historical events, concise and accurate reporting of current news, as well as economic and financial information, community events, and sports, we aim at arousing their interest to become more involved.[84]

In 1999, a new daily emerged in Newark, *24 Horas*, which, in 2012, was edited with the promotional slogan, "o vício diário" ("the daily vice") and the subtitle "Portuguese Daily Newspaper." *24 Horas* was founded by Victor M. Alves, who also served as its director and administrator. It was initially developed by local entrepreneurs associated with the Portuguese company Prodiário, S.A., which owns the "24 Horas" brand. At first, the paper was integrated into the Lusomundo Group, after it became allied with PT Multimedia, and later on it belonged to Controlinveste/Global Notícias, which in mid-2010 stopped publishing the parent edition of *24 Horas* in Portugal. This situation affected the American edition, which had to close for two weeks until it associated itself with the group Cofina, owner of nine newspapers and five magazines in Portugal, including the general-information daily *O Correio da Manhã* and the popular sports newspaper *Record*, which provided content to *24 Horas*. It published news, articles, and reports about Portuguese immigrants, and issues related to Portugal, Brazil, and Lusophone African communities. The newspaper itself emphasized its role as a newspaper of reference within the community and as the only daily newspaper published in Portuguese in the United States, currently with circulation in the states of New York and New Jersey.[85]

After the turn of the twenty-first century, the Portuguese media landscape in the United States experienced a sharp decline in the emergence of new titles. Only three new publications—a limited-impact magazine in Massachusetts, a newspaper in California and a monthly magazine in Virginia—have been recorded. All three have since ceased publication. In March 2002, Deodato Faria and Orlando Guimarães, both from São Miguel, founded the

Luzonet Magazine in Fall River and published it until December 2004. With simple editing and an abundance of ads from the community, its content mixed cultural topics with sections on family entertainment.[86] The biweekly newspaper *Lusitânia News* was founded by Rui Jacinto on April 7, 2006 in Tracy, California with an initial print run of 7,414 copies.[87] It included some articles in English, and was edited by Maria C. Odom.[88] The most recent title, as far as we known, was the bilingual monthly magazine, *ComunidadesUSA*, which was founded and directed by João José Morais in Manassas, Virginia, in December 2006. It published reports and interviews related to the culture of Lusophone societies, as well as articles related to the immigrant communities and Portugal. It dedicated special interest to issues relevant to the problem of emigration/immigration.[89] Since 2006, there has been no new Portuguese-American newspaper of significance.

Currently, the Portuguese-American community publishes five newspapers: two in New Jersey (*Luso-Americano* and *24 Horas*), two in Massachusetts (*Portuguese Times* and *O Jornal*) and one in California (*Tribuna Portuguesa*). The oldest of these is the Newark biweekly *Luso-Americano*, which has expanded its audience on the East Coast with content directed at the Brazilian community that has settled in this region in the past few decades.

Chapter 5

Four Newspapers that Made History

The Flagship Newspaper of New England: The *Diario de Noticias*

The *Diario de Noticias*, founded on January 3, 1927, by Guilherme Machado Luiz in New Bedford, was probably the most important newspaper in the history of Portuguese journalism in the United States and a major landmark in the history of Portuguese immigration and the expansion of Portuguese language and culture in America. Rui Antunes Correia's pioneering M.A. thesis[1] is the only specialized study dedicated to this extraordinary title, which deserves a monograph-length study. The *Diario de Noticias* was published for over half of a century, between 1919 and 1973, counting the span of its predecessor, *A Alvorada*. It offered rich and varied content about the Portuguese-American community with a clear commitment to the language and other cultural expressions and symbols of Portuguese identity. It was, no doubt, based on the conviction of its value to the group as a whole that, in 1966, when the paper struggled to survive, it appealed to the community's patriotism to help save it: "If you are Portuguese and feel the need to keep the 'Diario de Noticias' alive, help us find new subscribers."[2]

The *Diario de Noticias* was not only a beacon of Portuguese culture and language in the U.S., but also one of the strongest agents of the political, economic, and cultural development of the Portuguese-American community in New England. The *Diario de Noticias* was more than a newspaper; symbolically, one could say it was a school, a home, a mirror, a breath of freedom, and, above all, a dream come true. It was a school for immigrants who wanted to learn how to navigate the American socio-economic environment, who wanted to understand the ways of the new society, but also for the children of immigrants who felt the need to learn Portuguese and the culture of their parents in order to forge their new Portuguese-American identity. It was a home that, on a daily basis, connected immigrants to their roots, to their neighbors on the other side of the Atlantic, to those with whom they shared not only a common heritage, but also a real interest in the political life of their country of origin. It was a mirror because, more than any other media, the newspaper was a reflection of what happened in the community, and systematically published articles and letters from immigrants that made their opinion known to their fellow countrymen on whatever issues preoccupied them at the time. And it was a breath of freedom. Its long publishing period nearly coincides with the Portuguese dictatorship, which lasted from 1926 to 1974, but while strict censorship of the press was imposed in Portugal during this period, the *Diario de Noticias* became a champion for freedom of expression. Although it was subject to pressure from the Estado Novo,[3] and even experienced ideological wavering and political docility at some points, it was essentially an independent and free newspaper that could only circulate clandestinely in Portugal. Some letters from readers on the other side of the Atlantic attested to persecution by the political police, who considered those who read the newspaper subversive.[4]

In its pages there was room for all political currents, the most passionate debates, and the most diverse array of contributors from the community. The readers, owners, and journalists of the *Diario de Noticias* made it a collective dream come true, both for those who sought in their pages the emotional comfort of reading news about Portugal in their own language and for those who made the decision to risk their capital in a bold business venture. The *Diario de Noticias* reported with a spirit of community and even with patriotic pride. It is true that most newspapers had similar discourses, but the *Diario de Noticias* was different because its circulation, public impact, prestige, and influence were enormous.

The history of the *Diario de Noticias* is dominated by two singular figures—Guilherme Machado Luiz and João Rodrigues Rocha. Guilherme

O TEMPO
SEBULOSO, CHUVA

Diario de Noticias

THE ONLY PORTUGUESE DAILY NEWSPAPER PUBLISHED IN THE UNITED STATES SINCE 1919

Member of Pan-American Board of Commerce — NEW ENGLAND HOME EDITION

Director, João E. Rocha

ANO XXVIII — Entered as Second Class Matter — NEW BEDFORD, MASS., SEXTA-FEIRA, 28 DE NOVEMBRO DE 1947 — P. O. Box 931 — Número Avulso, 5c. — No 8674

Marshall e a nova fronteira polaco-germanica

A CELEBRAÇÃO DO "THANKSGIVING" NA AMERICA

O povo americano compartilhou a sua abundancia com os necessitados de féra

Foi salientado o espirito de Caridade nos templos de todos os crêdos. Os menos afortunados aqui tambem tiveram motivo de dar graças a Deus

Rejeita as afirmações de Molotov de que o caso foi solucionado em Potsdão

Leu um paragrafo do acôrdo de Potsdão que refuta a alegação de Molotov.—Concordam que uma Govêrno democratico alemão é cousa necessidade urgente

VÃO TOMAR PARTE NA CELEBRAÇÃO DO 1.o DE DEZEMBRO

Ao senhoras Castro, Nacelo e Castta Alves nos Fra...

VOLTA À CALIFORNIA

Foi Encontrado o Cadaver Duma Rapariga Que Estava Desaparecida

★ ★ ★

A Festa Comemorativa Da Independência de Portugal no Proximo Domingo

A Russia Protesta Contra A Expulsão de 19 Agentes Soviéticos

57 Pessoas Perderam A Vida no Dia do "Thanksgiving"

Adverte da Possibilidade De Falta de Pão Neste Paiz

Um Congressista propõe que o Plano Marshall seja posto a votação

Sugere um referendum nacional para que o povo americano registe a sua vontade quanto ao auxilio a dar ás nações europeias

Os soviétes governam a sua zona da Alemanha por métodos de terrorismo

Estes processos são postos em prática por alemães treinados em Moscou, dizem os democratas liberais

E' Lá Possivel!

(Especial para o "Diario de Noticias")

Pelo Pe. J. Alves Correia

"Diario de Noticias"

18. Cover of *Diario de Noticias*
(New Bedford, Massachusetts).
Copy of November 28, 1947.

Machado Luiz was one of the wealthiest and most powerful Portuguese businessmen in New England, where he created in the early twentieth century a thriving business agency that offered financial, insurance, and travel services to the Portuguese community. Luiz soon discovered that the newspapers in Portuguese were the best means of marketing to potential customers. At the beginning of the twentieth century, the influx of Portuguese who came to New Bedford to work in the textile mills created opportunities for his businesses, especially for his travel agency, which served as "steamship agent" on behalf of the Compagnie Française de Navigation à Vapeur Cyprien Fabre & Compagnie (better known as the *Fabre Line*) in the ports of New York and Boston and of the Portuguese Transportes Marítimos do Estado (including the ship *Mormugão*).[5] He also played an important role as a financial intermediary between Portuguese immigrants and their families in Portugal, collecting money from Portuguese-Americans to send to their relatives. His knowledge of the Portuguese community in New England was extensive, and his close contacts with immigrant networks and his media influence made him more than competitive with the numerous shipping companies operating between the United States, the Azores, and Europe.[6]

According to the detailed description given by Rui Antunes Correia, who collected the testimony of relatives and close friends, Luiz was born on June 4, 1879, in Angra do Heroísmo, Terceira.[7] He arrived in New Bedford on February 24, 1893, to work in the textile industry, like many of his fellow immigrants. Until 1909, he worked as a loom fixer in the "Dartmouth Mill" (probably Dartmouth Manufacturing Company, built in 1895, which was located on Cove St., New Bedford, MA). Afterwards, he dedicated himself to marketing travel tickets and transferring money between Portugal and the United States. According to Correia,

> The problem of foreign exchange rates for a mostly uneducated or even illiterate population gave rise to numerous opportunities for fraud, so much so that it was felt necessary to establish a reliable group of trustworthy Portuguese persons who could serve as intermediaries, on the issue of currency exchange values as well as on the process of helping immigrants bring over other members of their families.[8]

Although aware of his enormous lack of qualifications for developing a newspaper, since he did not know how to read or write when he came to America, Luiz founded the daily *Alvorada* in January 1919, following the purchase of the weekly magazine of the same name from Protestant minister Francisco Caetano Borges da Silva. Because of its resounding success, the demand for information related to Portugal and the community, and advertisements from Portuguese businesses, Luiz decided to relaunch the paper. After meeting with and getting the approval of the representatives of Alvorada Publishing Company, Inc, which owned *Alvorada*, the paper became known as *Diario de Noticias*, beginning on January 3, 1927.[9] It was the continuation of *Alvorada*, but with a more ambitious professional agenda that would make it the standard for journalism in the Portuguese-American community for over forty years. According to Vasco Jardim,

> Luiz was not interested in whether the name of his daily was this or that. His greatest desire was that the newspaper went into many homes and was a news-filled publication for the thousands of readers spread throughout the American territory. He was not mistaken, this man of low literacy skills. If he had been [a man of higher literacy skills], the daily would have had a wider and more fruitful life, given his effort and persistence. But even so, the daily was the longest-running newspaper in New Bedford.[10]

The expansion of the *Diario de Noticias* in the 1920s was soon to come to a halt. The sharp decline in immigration after the mid 1920s, the Great Depression, the rising costs of paper and taxes meant smaller profits for the *Diario de Noticias*. Nevertheless, whether because of his personal commitment to maintain a daily in Portuguese in the United States for the public influence it enabled, or because it was necessary for his other businesses, Luiz continued to publish the *Diario de Noticias* until 1940, despite the losses that it caused him during the 1930s.[11] "It was an expensive adventure that has cost me an arm and a leg," he said when he put the paper up for sale.[12] This was confirmed by some of his employees, who publicly recognized the efforts of the businessman "who has spent thousands of dollars so this source of global information in the beautiful language of Camões did not disappear from this American context."[13] The financial challenges, and perhaps a lack of real interest in journalism, made Guilherme M. Luiz sell the paper on June 8, 1940, to the consul of Portugal in Providence, José Agostinho de Oliveira, who immediately became its director.[14] Shortly before the sale, the ambassador of Portugal in Washington, João de Bianchi, sent a letter to his minister on October 20, 1938, in which he explains the importance of the *Diario de Noticias* and its owner:

> The only daily and, therefore, the most important newspaper is the *Diario de Noticias* of New Bedford, which belongs to Mr. Guilherme M. Luiz, the banker of Portuguese immigrant remittances par excelence; ticket agent to and from Portugal and the Islands; owner of other types of businesses that have earned, in good times, a sizeable fortune, nowadays very reduced, to some extent, by the very strategies he used to make that fortune, some of which have been reported to this Ministry.[15]

Despite his ownership of the major Portuguese media venue in New England, his media appearances were minimal. In his only known interview, published in the August 11, 1939 issue of the *Diario de Noticias* that commemorated the 30th anniversary of his bank and travel agency, he responded to questions about his business. An excerpt of this interview follows:

> How many Portuguese have travelled to and from Portugal using the services of your agency, and how much was sent in terms of immigrant remittances?
> – I don't know the exact number, but it's in the thousands. As for the remittances sent by our countrymen through our banking services both to the mainland and to the Adjacent Islands, it reaches the millions of dollars! . . . I would like to note that despite the tens, if not hundreds of thousands of transfers that we have handled, some of them involving very large sums, no Portuguese ever had reason to regret the trust placed in me.
> Over the course of the past three decades, you must have helped many of our countrymen...

– I don't like to boast about how much I have done for our people because I believe it is everybody's duty to help each other.

We appreciate your modesty, but we insist.

– Well, then. Yes, I have helped many people both here and in Portugal. In my trips to the mainland and the islands I have filled out the legal papers for hundreds of our compatriots who wanted to emigrate to America and loaned many the money they needed to pay for tickets and other expenses to come here. I did not ask them for any guarantees for that money; they were Portuguese and that was enough. Here, I have helped many who were undocumented legalize their status, and I have helped many by becoming their guarantor, some of whom did not live up to the trust I placed in them.[16]

In his last issue as owner of the newspaper, *Diario de Noticias* announced the change in ownership and management, and recognized the work done by Luiz:

If for twenty-two years we have been able to enjoy a daily newspaper in Portuguese, we owe that to the admirable perseverance and tenacity of Mr. Guilherme M. Luiz. It cannot be emphasized enough that it was through all sorts of sacrifices that he, like no other Portuguese, was able to keep alive the love of the motherland, using the press to communicate to his countrymen the value of that noble virtue. To him, and to all those who do the same, Portugal owes a great debt of gratitude.[17]

Luiz was a self-made man of Republican convictions and a member of the Portuguese Republican Club of New Bedford. He was not an intellectual, but had great business and entrepreneurial acumen, according to Manuel Calado, who was editor-in-chief of the *Diario de Noticias* between 1949 and 1973.[18] He possessed a tenacious yet approachable character that helped him succeed at defending the interests of the Portuguese in the United States, to the point of financing the trips of dozens of compatriots who settled in New Bedford. His philanthropy afforded him great popularity in the community, to such an extent that he was even called "the father of the Portuguese."[19] In addition, he was the first owner of the only bookstore in New Bedford selling books in Portuguese, founding the Livraria Colonial in the same building as the *Diario de Noticias*. The bookstore sold works of classic authors translated into Portuguese, dictionaries, maps of Portugal, and the English-language handbooks that immigrants demanded. On his frequent trips to Portugal, he would bring back books to supply local demand.[20]

Luiz died on November 25, 1965, at the age of 87. The *Diario de Noticias* remembered its founder on the day of his funeral by running a portrait of him on its front page. The man who was his first editor, as well as his son-in-law, António Vieira de Freitas, recalled the courage he showed in founding the newspaper:

> Without his "daring," without his particular "temperament," it is very possible that the foundation on which the *Diario de Noticias* was based would never have been built. And for that alone, even if he had done nothing else in his entire life, and making allowances for his human limitations, the Portuguese community owes Guilherme Machado Luiz a great debt of gratitude. This is a feeling shared by all of us who are carrying his work forward.[21]

The Portuguese government recognized his work by awarding him the Ordem de Santiago.[22] The influence of the *Diario de Noticias* made him a respected and even revered figure in New Bedford, as can be seen in the poem "Ao *Diario de Noticias* " by community poet António Batalha, published on January 31, 1940:

> For successive years you have been
> Delivering news without prejudice.
> For this reason, you deserve our affection,
> Worthy propagator of the voice of Portugal!

> There is no other newspaper in America
> Whose reading gives us as much delight
> As you, beautiful *Diario de Noticias*,
> Herald of our language, unrivaled!

May your voice last for many years!
That was the desire of your founder
Who made superhuman sacrifices for you.

We congratulate then, let there be no doubt,
The meritorious Guilherme Machado Luiz
Who honors this community of Lusitanians![23]

Shortly after the *Diario de Noticias* was purchased by Oliveira, João Rodrigues Rocha, editor of *O Independente* between 1933 and 1940, acquired a share of the newspaper, and in 1942 Oliveira was listed as "publisher" and Rocha as "editor and field manager." But in 1943, after paying $6,000 to his partner, Rocha assumed full ownership of the *Diario de Noticias*, becoming "publisher & general manager."[24]

João Rodrigues Rocha was another major figure in the history of the Portuguese-American press. Born on January 25, 1899, in Ponte de Lima, he first emigrated to Brazil at the age of thirteen and then arrived in the United States in 1920. His first job in this country was as a sweeper in a factory in Cambridge, MA, until he managed to open a small clothing store, which he sold when he had saved enough to start his career as a journalist and editor.[25] To better defend his business interests, he became a citizen in 1926.[26] His first publication was the magazine *Revista Portugal-América Portuguesa*, published in Cambridge between 1926 and 1929. After its closure, he became the circulation manager for the *Diario de Noticias*, a position he occupied until June 1932, when he became the owner of the weekly *O Independente*, which ran for several years between 1933 and 1940.[27] "João R. Rocha was the surprise of Portuguese journalism abroad,"[28] according to Vasco Jardim, who complimented his perseverance and professional abilities:

From store clerk to journalist is a big step. After having failed with the magazine and "lived" with *O Independente*, Rocha takes off his jacket, rolls up his shirtsleeves and at six o'clock in the morning takes up the fight in the newsroom... Even though he knew nothing about graphic arts, João Rocha achieved a very successful position. Before stopping publication of the daily, he paid all his bills, and refunded his subscribers a few thousand dollars for the subscriptions that had been paid in advance. Nobody was able to brag about buying his business while he was in the last days of his life.[29]

Throughout his career, he published hundreds of editorials and conducted interviews, some quite exclusive, with figures of historical significance, such as the one with António de Oliveira Salazar for his May 2, 1958 issue,

19. Portrait of
João Rodrigues Rocha

whose front-page headline was "Dr. Oliveira Salazar Expressed Strong Interest in the Portuguese of America."[30] He always tried to maintain contact with U.S. government authorities and cultivate relationships of mutual respect. His personal archive, donated to the Ferreira-Mendes Portuguese-American Archives at the University of Massachusetts Dartmouth, includes telegrams and letters from several politicians, both Democrats and Republicans. He corresponded with Senator Ted Kennedy and President-elect Richard Nixon, who sent him an autographed letter on December 2, 1968, recognizing his leadership in the Portuguese-American community and asking him to propose names of qualified people who could work in his administration. [31]

One of the first things that Rocha did when he stopped publishing the *Diario de Noticias* was to donate the newspaper collection, whose historic value he recognized, to the library of Southeastern Massachusetts University (SMU), the institution that preceded the current University of Massachusetts Dartmouth.[32] He would subsequently donate personal documents as well as documents on the history of the Portuguese-American community, which form part of the collection of the Ferreira-Mendes Portuguese-American Archives at UMass Dartmouth. On November 3, 1975, SMU offered him, along with his family, an honorary luncheon.[33] Rocha died in February 1977 at his home in Dartmouth, MA. The owner of *The Standard Times* sent a letter to his wife in which he affirmed that Rocha's work "on behalf of Portugal and the Portuguese people of our area will be remembered for many years to come."[34]

The figure and career of João Rodrigues Rocha marked an era in which Portuguese-American journalism might possibly have reached its best moments, both for its circulation and influence among immigrants and for the quality of its contents. Rocha was the right person to transform the journalistic project that Guilherme Machado Luiz had started in 1919 with *A Alvorada* into a profitable and professional business. The *Diario de Noticias* inherited *A Alvorada*'s infrastructure, office equipment, press, office on 93 Rivet St.,[35] editions in other cities, and its newsroom staff. The director, António Vieira de Freitas Jr., stayed on until 1940. Nevertheless, technically, the two should be considered as independent papers, not only because of the change in title, but also because there were substantial changes in the design, content, and commercial strategies of the paper, as well as the ownership of the company after 1940 (The Portuguese Daily News Publishing Company) and its business philosophy. In its first issue, for example, the successor to *A Alvorada* informed the readers of Fall River that a special edition would be substituted for the pages customarily dedicated to them.[36]

After 1950, the paper was subtitled "The Portuguese Daily News" and it started to carry some ads and articles in English, which would be progressively incorporated into its regular content, though Portuguese was and remained the primary language of the *Diario de Noticias*. Throughout its long life, it used several commercial slogans in its header. Initially, it read "Two thirds of the homes of 35,000 Portuguese in New Bedford and of 30,000 in Fall River are daily visited by the Newspaper." In 1939, it used the motto "The Only Portuguese Daily Newspaper Published in the United States," and in 1960 it featured the slogan "America's Only Daily Published in Portuguese." Its format would change over time as well, though its size tended to be tabloid, between 8 and 16 pages, illustrated with photographs and engravings. Over its lifetime, it published thousands of ads, many of high quality, for dozens of businesses, institutions, and individuals who wanted to get their messages to members of the Portuguese community. Periodically, the *Diario de Noticias* would encourage readers to read the ads and buy from the merchants who sponsored the newspaper in order to ensure its continuity:

> There are many reasons why those who advertise in *Diario de Noticias* deserve the support of our community. One of them, and the most

important one, is that in order to let the members of our community know that they desire their business, they use the columns of this newspaper that is published in our language to advertise their products, and in so doing they help a Portuguese company whose existence enhances the prestige of our group in these parts.[37]

Rocha was one of the main architects of the increasing growth and circulation of the newspaper.[38] During his time as sales representative from 1929 to 1932, he was responsible for a major "expansion campaign."[39] As a special agent for the newspaper, Rocha made several trips, the first one between September 1929 and January 1930, that took him to dozens of towns with residents of Portuguese origin in New England, where he managed to establish a network of sixty-two correspondents that extended to the states of New York, New Jersey, and Pennsylvania.[40] Touring cities with large Portuguese populations gave Rocha valuable knowledge about the Portuguese community on the East Coast as well as direct contact with its most prominent figures.[41] The exhaustive nature of this commercial campaign can be deduced from this description:[42]

> During his trip to these centers he had the opportunity to visit all the associations and clubs, where he introduced the *Diario de Noticias*, the Portuguese newspaper with the widest range of information and circulation in the United States. But it was not only the clubs that João Rocha visited; he also went to the private homes of many Portuguese, where he recruited new subscribers. João Rocha does not rest, and there he goes again, headed to other cities and towns he had not had the time to visit before, carrying out the noble mission he was charged with.[43]

In addition to the several thousand subscribers who received the newspaper by mail, the *Diario de Noticias* set up eighty vending sites in seven states in the late 1930s.[44] In Massachusetts, the newspaper was sold in fifty-six places in ten cities: Fall River, Lowell, Plymouth, Framingham, Holyoke, Boston, Cambridge, Peabody, Gloucester, and New Bedford; in Rhode Island there were thirteen, in Bristol, River Point, Providence, and Pawtucket; in

Connecticut, six, located in Waterbury, New Haven, Hartford, and New Britain; in New Jersey, three, in Newark, Hudson, and Carney's Point; in Pennsylvania, three, in South Bethlehem, Philadelphia, and Hallerton; in New York it was distributed throughout Brooklyn and Manhattan; and in Illinois, in Prospect Heights. According to data reported to Rui Antunes by Manuel Calado and Raimundo Luiz, printer of the newspaper between 1939 and 1973, the paper's circulation averaged between 9,000 and 10,000 copies in the 1930s and 1940s, and 10,000 to 15,000 between 1950 and 1970, with some editions of up to 20,000 copies.[45]

When Rocha retired from the ownership and management of the *Diario de Noticias*, he named Manuel Calado editor-in-chief and António A. Cacella, brother of Fr. José Cacella (founder of *O Portugal* and *A Luta* in New York City), editor. In 1950, the newspaper's team consisted of António F. Costa, António Santinho, Álvaro D. Carreiro, and José V. Carreiro as typesetters; João Alves as stereotypist; Luciano Mota as office manager; José Luiz as head of distribution in New Bedford; Simão C. Tenreiro as editor; Frank Cavanaugh as head of advertising; Laura Alves in accounting; and Raimundo Luiz and Ronald Correia in shipping and distribution.[46] During 1960, António F. Costa also assumed editorial duties. Although individuals and positions changed with time, Rocha had inherited an established editorial and printshop team with the *Diario de Noticias*.[47] It was a kind of homeschooling in Portuguese-American journalism that had been developing since the creation of *A Alvorada*. One of its most emblematic figures in its early years, between 1927 and 1935, was the brilliant journalist Domingos Ferreira Martins, who joined *Diario de Noticias* as chief editor after the closure of the consulate of Portugal in Bristol, Rhode Island, where he had held the post of consul since October 1925, after having been nominated to a similar post in Valladolid, Spain.[48] Ferreira Martins wrote dozens of editorials and opinion pieces in an original style, characterized by an intelligent, sharp, and ironic rhetoric. A Portuguese Republican who was vehemently opposed to the Estado Novo, he was a staunch defender of democratic principles.[49]

The *Diario de Noticias* had many contributors. Most of them were readers of the newspaper who wanted to see some of their literary or journalistic creations published in its pages, but there were also those who wanted

[No último sábado, vespera do Natal, os emprega-
fos do "Diário de Noticias" reuniram-se, a exemplo dos outros anos, na sala da redacção, numa
pequena mas expressiva festa de confraternização,
que teve a honrá-la a presença do fundador deste
jornal e seu proprietário durante cerca de vinte
anos, sr. Guilherme M. Luiz e o director do mesmo durante esse longo periodo de tempo, sr. Antonio Vieira de Freitas. De pé, a contar da esquerda, vêem-se: Antonio A. Costa, linotipista; José V.
Carreiro, linotipista; Luciano Mota, chefe das ofi- cinas; Antonio A. Cacella, editor; João R. Rocha,
director; José Luiz, chefe da distribuição em New
Bedford; Simão C. Tenreiro, redactor; Antonio
Santinho, linotipista; Manuel Calado, chefe da redacção; Frank Cavanough, Advertising Manager.
Sentados: o sr. Freitas; Miss Laura Alves, da contabilidade; o sr. Guilherme Luiz; e Mrs. Maria Alves, chefe da contabilidade. Faltam na gravura os
srs. Alvaro D. Carreiro, linotipista; João Alves, es-
teriotipia; Raimundo Luiz e Ronald Correia, ex-
pedição.

20. Photo-news from the
Diario de Noticias "O Natal
dos empregados do Diario de
Noticias" [The Christmas of the
Diario de Noticias employees].
Copy of December 27, 1950.

influence in the community. Its list of contributors included well-known Portuguese politicians and intellectuals, such as former Republican Minister João Camoesas; the writer José
Rodrigues Miguéis; the Director of the Secretariat
of National Propaganda of Portugal (SPN), Antó-
nio Ferro; the leader of the Aliança Liberal Portuguesa, Manuel Moutinho, who
was the director of Casa de Portugal in New York; the journalist Gil Stone; and
the Vice-Consul of Portugal in Providence, Manuel Caetano Pereira.[50]

The contents of the *Diario de Noticias* fell under four main themes:
news about Portugal, news about the Portuguese-American community, international information, and issues related to American society. Much of the
international information was taken from news agencies or from stories published in other newspapers. Despite its limitations and scarce resources, the
coverage of national and international issues of relevance provided by the

Diario de Noticias was more extensive and professional than that of some of the major newspapers in Lisbon during the same period, and free from the censorship of the Estado Novo. The editorial published by Conceição Junior on February 7, 1936, titled "Liberdade de Imprensa," clearly and precisely addressed this issue:

> As a rule, dictatorships are governments that do not express the will of the people, but rather that of a group or party that tramples on all constitutional rights to impose its authority. . . We believe that in all governments and parties there are well-intentioned people who do not fear having their actions discussed and informed by public opinion. If the leaders of a country would like the people to believe them when they talk about their intentions, announce their achievements or call attention to the way they are rebuilding the economy, then they should not fear fair criticism of their work. Quite the contrary, they should take it as a deserved reward for their efforts in serving the Nation well. Censorship is always an odious and absurd gag that those in power place over the mouth or the pen of those who are capable of judging facts dispassionately. It is an oppressive and excessive insult to intelligence.[51]

Its reports on Portuguese politics tried to demonstrate independence, offering on occasion two competing views of the same controversial topic in the same issue. The *Diario de Noticias* followed the professional model of American journalism, defending freedom of the press, speech, and thought as fundamental rights of a democratic society.[52] It respected the right of its readers to express their views in its pages, provided that they were written in respectful language and the identity of the writer was made known to the management team. Since some readers hid their identity, the paper saw it necessary to specify the conditions for publication:

> For some time now, we have been receiving requests to publish articles, some of them very serious, doctrinaire and opportune. Much to our regret, we had to refuse some of those requests because the articles in question came signed by pseudonyms or initials without their authors identifying

themselves, as is their obligation and a requirement of journalistic practice. For this reason, and in order to give the articles in question the publicity that they deserve, it is absolutely necessary that all authors provide us with their name and address, which we will keep in absolute confidentiality.[53]

Of all the sections that the *Diario de Noticias* published in its nearly half-century of existence, there are two that, because of the frequency and longevity of their publication, had a great impact and were quite popular among readers: the editorial section and serialized novels. The latter had already achieved great success in *A Alvorada*. The *Diario de Noticias* continued this popular tradition, publishing such novels as *Os Exploradores da Desgraça* and *O Poder dos Humildes* by A. Contreras; *Os Milhões do Criminoso* and *As Mulheres de Bronze* by Xavier de Montepin; *A Toutinegra do Moinho* by E. Richebourg; *Maria da Fonte* by Rocha Martins; *Os Dois Garotos* by Pierre Decourcelle; and *Margarida a Mártir* by Lorenzo Bassi.

Generally, the editorials focused on issues of concern to members of the Portuguese-American community. They provided information on the operation of institutions and on the rights and duties of immigrants in America, attempted to engage readers in critical thinking, encouraged commitment to projects that enhanced personal or collective development, and defended Portuguese interests. Hundreds of editorials analyze, interpret, discuss, and criticize social, political, economic, and cultural issues at different historical moments. Some look like political manifestos in support of their compatriots;[54] while others are more similar to political reporting.[55] There are complaints,[56] philosophical, anthropological, and literary reflections;[57] health advice,[58] discussions of fraternal organizations;[59] expressions of political views;[60] discussions of Iberian relations;[61] commemorative pieces;[62] discussions of emigration;[63] editorials on religious themes;[64] pieces on education;[65] discussions of economics and banking;[66] expressions of immigrant solidarity;[67] responses to detractors;[68] pieces on immigrants;[69] editorials on world peace;[70] editorials recognizing Portuguese-American successes, etc.[71] The *Diario de Noticias* believed it had a moral duty to defend the community, sometimes challenging diplomatic authorities from Portugal:

Just because people occupy high positions, that does not grant them immunity [from criticism] when it comes to the press. Just because chance placed them outside the common realm where other citizens live, and way above them in social standing, those circumstances do not protect them from criticism, quite the opposite, their actions are more likely to be the object of scrutiny. Those who represent a foreign nation in a particular country are required to fulfill their duties. They are not placed in state capitals just for ceremonial purposes. They should devote careful attention to the interests of the nation that they represent and to the immigrants from that country. Those who take that obligation seriously do not create conflicts in the community or in the press. They are treated with respect by all. Those who do not fulfill their duty should not be surprised by the recriminations they receive.[72]

The *Diario de Noticias*'s contribution to the expansion of the Portuguese language and culture in the United States, its role in shaping public opinion and protecting the collective interests of the Portuguese-American community in New England, make it one of the most important institutions in the history of the Portuguese diaspora in North America.

The *Jornal Português*: The Flagship of Portuguese Journalism in California

The Portuguese diaspora in California underwent, as it did in Massachusetts in the early 1930s, a process of change and transformation as a result of economic and demographic crises within the community, forcing many newspapers to reformulate their business strategies in order to cope with the challenges. The case of the *Jornal Português* was, in this sense, typical of other newspapers of the time, but also different in some aspects. Whereas the *Diario de Noticias* was the result of an ambitious plan, consciously created to expand it into the great daily that it became after 1927, taking advantage of the still-favorable economic situation on the East Coast at the time, the creation of the *Jornal Português* was fueled by the need for survival in the face of almost opposite circumstances. It was born from the fusion of three failing Portuguese-American weeklies—*O Imparcial* (Sacramento, 1913), *Jornal de Notícias* (San Francisco, 1917), and *A Colonia Portuguesa* (Oakland, 1924)—that, upon realizing that the competition among them threatened to ruin them all, decided to take advantage of the potential synergy of joining forces and becoming one.

The weekly *Jornal Português* was born on July 24, 1932, and was published without interruption until September 25, 1997. It was first based in Oakland and then in San Pablo after 1978.[73] Its official language was Portuguese, although English was used to attract Portuguese-American readers who had difficulty reading Portuguese. The paper used two subtitles: "Semanário Português Publicado à Sexta-feira" (Portuguese Weekly Published on Fridays) and "Portuguese Journal," along with several promotional slogans: "O Semanário Português de Maior Circulação na Costa do Pacífico e Hawai" (The Portuguese Weekly with Widest Distribution on the Pacific Coast and Hawaii); "The Only Portuguese Newspaper in the Western States – Founded in 1888;"[74] and "O Jornal Português Mais Antigo e de Maior Tiragem da Costa do Pacífico" (The Oldest Portuguese Newspaper with the Largest Circulation on the Pacific Coast). After August 16, 1957, it added the slogan "Reaching Over 500,000 People of Portuguese Origin;" and in the 1990s it added "Membro Honorário da Ordem do Infante D. Henrique" (Honorary Member of the Order of Prince Henry). Since September 13, 1935, the header was adorned with new notices for its readers such as: "ALWAYS INTERESTING IN ALL OF ITS SECTIONS—This newspaper strives to inform its readers of the most interesting events in this country and abroad, and especially in Portugal and its territories. Our community always gets special attention,"[75] and: "A GOOD MEDIUM TO ADVERTISE YOUR BUSINESS—The 'Jornal Português' offers to the business man the best advertising field because it reaches a Portuguese population of over 200,000, and has a circulation exceeding that of many other Portuguese publications in California and other States. Our people like to read your advertisements."

Its founder, first owner, and director was Pedro Laureano Claudino da Silveira, who counted on the collaboration of his wife, Mary (Maria) Nunes Silveira, whom he had married in 1903.

Pedro L. C. Silveira, born on December 7, 1870, in Fajã Grande, Flores, arrived in California on August 5, 1886. He worked with his father in the gold mines of Oregon and North Carolina. His literary interests led him to seek employment in Guilherme S. Gloria's weekly, *A Liberdade*, where he worked between 1900 and 1902, when he decided to try his luck as a publisher. First, he founded the short-lived *Portugal-América* in Fresno (1905) and then the *Jornal de Notícias*, which was the successor of *O Arauto*. Guilherme S. Glória, with whom Silveira got into some disagreements while directing the *Jornal de Notícias*, published the following profile of him:

> He was a good-looking young man, very personable, well dressed, and attractive and courteous in manner. He spoke Portuguese well and seemed to know something about typography. . . Right from the beginning, he started to show his intelligence and energy by performing his typographical work promptly and correctly and, in his spare time, by doing some writing and translating for the paper, with admirable correction. Sometimes, while I was away taking care of financial matters for the paper, and at my request, he wrote some little editorial articles, which met with my approval and praise, and were well received by the readers. . . Everything was going well. Pedro respected me and obeyed me like one would a father, I treated him with the care and affection with which one treats a brother or a son. . . You can imagine my surprise when one day (I cannot remember what month in 1902), our good Pedro, pale and with his head down, came to tell me to look for another man to replace him.[76]

When Silveira died in 1944, his wife, Mary, assumed the functions of "director-manager" and editor of the *Jornal Português* between 1944 and 1945. She then became "director and owner" until August 2, 1957, when she sold the newspaper to Alberto dos Santos Lemos. Journalist and lawyer Alberto Corrêa worked for her as editor, while J. S. Marshall, Leo L. Broucier, and Raulino Nunes, among others, worked as typesetters. Mary developed her newspaper enterprises at the same time that she directed a branch of the American Trust Co. bank in San Francisco.

After buying the newspaper, Alberto dos Santos Lemos became the managing editor and his brother Afonso Lemos the assistant editor.[77] Lemos expanded and modernized the paper, both typographically and with regard to content. He created new sections, including a sports page, increased the number of articles in English, reduced the number of opinion pieces, and added stories from Portugal's official news agency National Agency of Information (ANI) as well as community news, especially those pertaining to the activities of fraternal organizations. The always-popular "Romances" section,[78] however, remained unchanged throughout the paper's entire existence.

Throughout its history, the paper had a variety of formats and typographic designs. It began as a broadsheet and ended as a tabloid. The design of the header also underwent various changes. After some modifications, in November of 1962, the font was changed; and in the 1970s, another change was introduced: the symbol for the San Francisco Bay, the Golden Gate, was used as the background for the title. In the 1980s, it reverted to its original typographical format. In its first phase, the average number of pages was 8, and it increased to 16 when Lemos acquired the paper. In the 1970s, the quality of the design and content decreased, with fewer articles and pages. The *Jornal Português* was available to subscribers in the Azores, Madeira, and continental Portugal.

Lemos, who edited and directed the newspaper until 1994, was born in Rio de Janeiro on September 9, 1921, the son of Portuguese immigrants. He was raised in Portugal and studied at the Commercial Institute of Lisbon and the British Institute. His Anglophile training allowed him to work for four years at the British Embassy in Lisbon during the Second World War. He also worked for the Bank of London and South America for ten years before emigrating to the United States in 1955. In 1974, he took a course in journalism at Laney College, and in 1976 he earned a bachelor's degree in mass communications and Latin American studies from California State University at Hayward. He died on July 7, 2011 at his home in El Sobrante, California.[79] Lemos directed the *Jornal Português* for 37 years, assuming all kinds of responsibilities, as he himself declared: "Besides being a small publisher, editor, photographer, sweeper, bag carrier, sales promoter, gatherer of subscriptions, etc., I also have to be manager, administrator, and one of the most careful."[80]

Lemos was able not only to shore up the project started by the Silveiras, but also to transform it into the newspaper of reference for the Portuguese community on the West Coast. His work in the paper was accompanied by his commitment to fraternal organizations, including his participation in the founding of the Federação Fraternal Luso-Americana. His contribution as director of the *Jornal Português* to the preservation of Portuguese identity and culture in the United States and his information and public relations efforts aimed at showing American politicians and local authorities the strength and dynamism of the Portuguese community in California earned him recognition from the government of Portugal, which honored him with several awards, including the Comenda do Infante D. Henrique and the Medalha do Mérito das Comunidades Portuguesas.[81]

On April 28, 1994, the *Jornal Português* was tranferred to Alberto Matos Soares Pacciorini, who assumed its direction with Alberto Lemos as editor and Maria Conceição Leal as editor-in-chief.[82] On September 25, 1997, the administrative board, composed of Magda Cita Bettencourt, Fernando José Brum, Nilza Cardoso Langley, and Rosa Pinto Vilão, announced its sale and ceased publication, thus ending its sixty-five-year history. Nevertheless, it had existed for nearly a century if one takes into account the publications that preceded it, which date back to the creation of *O Amigo dos Católicos* in 1888.

The *Jornal Português* became the voice of the Portuguese community in California almost from its foundation, especially after the disappearance of *A União Portuguesa* in 1942. It was a weekly newspaper with Catholic leanings that offered wide journalistic coverage on what happened on the Azores, Madeira, and other places in Portugal, as well as in the Portuguese-American community in California itself. It also contained several specialized sections. In the 1930s, Mary N. Silveira ran a supplement entitled "Revista Feminina," which featured poems, fiction, and tips on health and beauty. She also published a page of "Notícias Agrícolas e de Laticínios," (Farm and Dairy News) specifically aimed at the great number of readers who worked as farmers and ranchers in California. Serialized novels were a major component, and the paper ran multiple series in each issue. *Os Dois Garotos, Madame Sans-Gene,* and *Aura* were some of its first titles. Its editorial page and comments section gave voice to contributors who wished to express their opinion. Generally, the *Jornal Português* addressed contemporary issues related to Portuguese or North American politics or community problems in the editorial section, but in the opinion section all types of public interest issues were included.[83] In the first phase, directed by the Silveira family, the paper attempted to project a cordial and friendly image of the Portuguese-American community, avoiding political controversies. Although it did not shun public debates, the paper's editorial line was marked by its ideological proximity to the politics of the Estado Novo, with which it maintained a relationship of information exchange through the publication of speeches and press releases from the SPN.[84] The usual official statements that the government of the dictatorship sent to the press to clarify any question or to respond to any detractors appeared very prominently within its pages, sometimes in bold characters and in the most visible place on the cover.[85] This close relationship with the dictatorship government continued after the change of ownership in 1957, when Lemos assumed its direction. Under the premise that "those who hate Portugal cannot be true friends of America,"[86] laudatory articles on the policies of Salazar's government were frequent. In January 1954, for example, it published an extensive ode of 19 stanzas, composed by Manuel S. Azevedo and dedicated to the Portuguese dictator:

> In this rich California
> Living far from the homeland!
> About the glories of Portugal
> I am proud to write.
>
> . . .
>
> Portuguese from around the world
> Came to our capital!
> In tribute to Salazar
> A hero son of Portugal.
>
> . . .
>
> Be proud, oh Portugal,
> Of your shining son!
> Who saved you from the abyss,
> Who kept your heart beating.
>
> . . .
>
> Half a century has passed
> Of your heart, Salazar!
> Of your brilliant government
> The whole empire celebrates!

. . .

With the greatest heroism
He brightens the nation!
Our Lusitanian land
With love in his heart.

. . .

Salazar, in the palace
He received the crowd!
Long live Salazar
In immortal memory.[87]

There is abundant documentation on the cooperation between the management of the *Jornal Português* and Salazar's government in the archives of the Portuguese embassy in the United States.[88] Lemos even participated in a propaganda campaign aimed at informing the American public about "Portugal's great overseas civilizing work"[89] in Africa, where he traveled in 1966 with the financial support of the Portuguese government.[90] Although this collaboration conditioned the editorial discourse of the *Jornal Português*, which was transformed into a propagandistic voice of the regime, it also had economic and commercial motivations: it allowed the newspaper and its owners to obtain subsidies from and to do business with the Portuguese administration.[91]

Between 1937 and 1953, the *Jornal Português* published sixteen special issues to celebrate each anniversary of the newspaper, assembling its best contributors to write on leading topics, take stock of the past year, and congratulate the paper's workers and administrators on reaching another anniversary. These special issues, fully illustrated with high-quality prints, reached more than one-hundred pages in some years. In addition to standard content related to the Portuguese diaspora and its most popular figures in California, each one of these special supplements was dedicated to a central theme. Their contents are of historical significance. They showcase the best qualities of the *Jornal Português* and provide a good portrait of the Portuguese community in California. The complete list of these special issues is provided in Appendix C.

Jornal Português claimed 1888 as its founding date, for this was when priests Manuel Francisco Fernandes and João Francisco Tavares created *O Amigo dos Católicos*, the predecessor of *O Arauto* and of Silveira's *Jornal de Notícias*. For this reason, the weekly celebrated its fiftieth anniversary in 1938. During the celebration, president Franklin D. Roosevelt conveyed his congratulations to the director in a personal letter that was published in the commemorative issue of that year.[92] The *Jornal Português* also published portraits of the president of the Portuguese Republic, Óscar Fragoso Carmona; the president of the Council of Ministers, António de Oliveira Salazar; and the ambassador of Portugal to the U.S., João António de Bianchi, who highlighted this as a great moment for Portugal and recognized the contributions and the virtues of Portuguese immigrants:

> There are no differences of opinion when it comes to recognizing their fear of God, their love of family, their industriousness, their parsimony and sobriety, their spirit of sacrifice, their law-abiding conduct, their conscientious voting. They have made many spiritual and material contributions to this great country in the fields of public administration, justice, music, industry, fishing, farming and many other activities, even though the Portuguese are still far from having realized their full potential in the United States.[93]

These special issues were sponsored by the community's businesses, which seized the opportunity to increase their visibility. One of the institutions that stood out in the advertising sponsorship of the *Jornal Português* was Saint John's Hospital of San Francisco, led by Dr. Carlos Fernandes, who was a regular contributor to the weekly. [94]

Vasco de Sousa Jardim and the *Luso-Americano* of New Jersey

Vasco Jardim arrived in Providence in June 1920 aboard the ship *Britannia*, from Ponta Delgada, Madeira, where he was born on January 24, 1900. His memoir as an immigrant begins with the eight days of sea travel, which he describes as a journey in which a romantic feeling of adventure was mixed with outrage for the poor condition of the boat and the accommodations of those of lesser means who traveled on it:

I was disappointed at not having been able to rub shoulders with the beautiful Spanish and mountain girls. I took my meals in first class and slept (when I slept), on a divan at the entrance to the dining room. The ship rocked like crazy. It made me sick to go into steerage and see how the immigrants were packed one on top of the other on metal frames. The most putrid filth I have ever seen. It had been only two years since the end of the war. The ships were antiquated, and France was ruined by debt. At night, life was more attractive, more glowing and even more poetic. When the wind was mild and the ocean shimmered, the men would play guitar, mandolin and other instruments. The Portuguese, with their concertinas and guitars, would gather on the deck late into the evening. The girls from the Beira region competed with those from Andalusia and Italy. Fun was not what was on people's minds. Everyone came with the idea of saving some money for the family in as short a time as possible. But the music brought inspiration, and the skirts the scent of human seduction. From the bridge, we could only be observers of this scene which usually ended up in a brawl.[95]

Vasco Jardim started his career in Fall River, where he lived for eight years. There, he studied graphic arts and, along with Leonel Lima, founded in July 1921 the short-lived weekly *Esperança*, which he printed on an old rotary press he had acquired in Boston.[96] After a few months, he decided to sell everything for $300 to typographer António Francisco Almeida, though he claimed that he "received only $50."[97] In 1923, he began contributing to the *Fall River Globe*, and in 1925, while also working with *O Popular* and *A Alvorada*, he decided to try his fortune again as an editor by buying from Manuel C. Botelho the weekly *O Vigilante* and the printshop A Lealdade from Leonídio Cabral & Brothers.[98] After a hiatus of a few weeks, *O Vigilante* resurfaced briefly, on April 11, 1925, under the direction of Vasco Jardim,[99] who described Manuel Botelho's process of putting out the paper and the circumstances surrounding his own frustrated attempt to revive it:

He founded the four-page weekly, which he composed without any original in front of him. He printed one page at a time, folded it by hand

and distributed it himself throughout the city. Botelho was not interested in the four Portuguese churches being built in Fall River. What he was interested in was the women because all they cared about was gossip and intrigue. The newspaper was sought after and commented upon. Manuel Botelho, with three type cases of sizes 8, 10 and 12 did the composition and printed the paper at a shop on South Main St., almost in front of the Monte Pio Club, although Ramos did not want to have anything to do with him. He was afraid of gossip, the terror of the presidents of organizations, said Ramos himself. One day, almost on a whim, I bought the paper and all the equipment from him, at the same time that I bought [the Lealdade print shop] from Leonídio Cabral. . . I quickly found out that Botelho only printed 300 copies of the newspaper per week. I combined the equipment of the two print shops and set myself up on the second floor of a shack owned by D. Casey. I thought of giving a new life to the *Vigilante,* with a larger format, a new title, some photo engravings, and Botelho working for a fixed salary of $22 a week. Botelho, Cabral, a young Irish typesetter apprentice and I took three weeks to put together the first issue. I paid Aníbal Branco six dollars for two humor articles. In the end, I threw all twelve pages of that issue into the stove. The paper did not look at all like I wanted it to. On the third issue, I published an editorial on the front page announcing that *O Vigilante* would cease publication due to the fact that it only had 82 paid subscriptions and to other issues that don't matter now. I was not ready to suffer the fate of a Botelho and give up on my commitments to the *Fall River Globe* and the *Diario de Noticias.* I returned $37 to the subscribers, I learned, and I had fun.[100]

After closing *O Vigilante* in 1928, Vasco Jardim moved to Newark, New Jersey. He sold his rotary press to the founders of *Luzo-Americano,* assuming the technical and commercial management of the publication. Between 1932 and 1939, he was chief correspondent for the *Diario de Noticias* in New York and New Jersey. Jardim's biography is inseparable from the history of the *Luzo-Americano,* his major journalistic project, which he managed to turn into one of the longest-running titles of the Portuguese-American press. It remains in circulation today.

The history of the newspaper can be divided into three phases. It was founded on May 28, 1928, with the title of *Luzo-Americano*, and its first phase ended in November of 1929. In a second phase, it was re-issued for several months in 1931. In its third phase, which began on December 7, 1939, it was titled *New Jersey Luso-Americano* and subtitled "Portuguese-American Newspaper," and then changed to *Luso-Americano*. Its permanent headquarters were on 88 Ferry Street, Newark, from 1944 until 1998 when production moved to more modern facilities on 66 Union Street.

The paper was created in 1928 by José Paulo Lobo (who returned to Lisbon in 1930), M. Conceição Jr. (who graduated from the University of Coimbra with a degree in literature), and the merchants Francisco de Castro and Valentim Rocha. Vasco Sousa Jardim said in his memoirs that José Paulo Lobo was a physician—an internist, originally from Goa, who had worked in Fall River. He also noted that Dr. John Silveira Enos, who had a clinic in Providence, was involved with the creation of the paper.[101] The title ceased publication in November 1929, when the effects of the Great Depression began to be felt. In late 1931, driven by Luiz Antunes and Casimiro Moraes (a native of Monção), the paper reappeared, but suspended publication when U.S. Immigration Services arrested Moraes for residing illegally in the United States. Upon returning to Portugal, Moraes worked as a typesetter for *O Primeiro de Janeiro* for twenty years.[102]

According to the official history of the *Luso-Americano*, at the time of its founding there were 6,209 Portuguese in New Jersey and 4,411 of them had been born in Portugal.[103] Many of these, and those who joined in subsequent years, did not come directly from Portugal; they were former textile workers from New England, especially from "Massachusetts, who were forced to leave that state when the textile industry collapsed in the 1920s and 1930s."[104] Capitalizing on this influx of new immigrants into New Jersey and the neighboring states of New York and Pennsylvania as well as the institutional growth of the community, with the founding of institutions such as the Associação Fraternal Luso-Americana and the Sport Club Português, Jardim restored the newspaper and became its new owner and director in the late 1930s. He published the first issue of the last phase of the *Luso-Americano* on December 7, 1939.[105] As the community expanded with new immigration in the late 1950s and especially after 1965, Jardim remained at the helm of the paper. In 1979 he was replaced by his son-in-law António Matinho, who would eventually become the owner.[106] Throughout his life Jardim participated in many Portuguese-American institutions, where he frequently played leadership roles. He was vice president of the Associação Protetora Madeirense of New Bedford, became president of the Conselho Fiscal do Sport Club Português of Newark in 1932, and was appointed by mayor Ralph Villani to the Human Rights Commission of Newark in 1952. Vasco de Sousa Jardim died on October 5, 1983.[107]

Giving a rundown of the contents of the *Luso-Americano* throughout its more than seventy-five years of existence would take us beyond the scope of this study. In general, it resembled the newspapers that have been analyzed, with a concern for what affected the economic and social development of the community, as well as their political and cultural activities in different contexts. A sense of the paper as it began publication can be obtained by looking at the first issue, which included the following items: the approval of the purchase of the headquarters of the Sports Club Português in Newark for $6,500; the approval of the statutes of the Associação Fraternal Luso-Americana of the same city; a recital by Professor Ricardo Freitas at the headquarters of the Club Português of New York; the Portuguese government's ban on the export of mineral fuels and lubricants from Angola; the attacks on sheep by wolves in Foz Côa; the celebration of the feast of São Miguel de Tarouca, etc.[108]

At first, the *Luso-Americano* was a weekly edited in Portuguese and addressed exclusively to the Portuguese community, but after 1988 it was published twice a week (Wednesday and Friday) with some articles in English for an audience that included readers from various Lusophone origins, despite its subtitle of "Portuguese-American Newspaper." Although its dimensions varied over time, its most common standard format has been the tabloid. In the beginning, the number of pages did not exceed four. Currently, however, most issues have forty pages. Color printing was first used in 1988, on the front page of the Saturday issue.

At the present, the *Luso-Americano* combines a focus on social events in the community with outstanding national and international coverage, paying particular attention to Portuguese affairs. Due to an increase in the number of Brazilians in the U.S. from the 1980s and 1990s to the present,[109] the *Luso-Americano* has been devoting more attention to issues related to this community. It contains various sections including "classified ads," "social networks" pages, and an "English Section," with news in English.

According to Manoel Cardoso da Silveira, the newspaper had a circulation of 7,400 copies in 1974. It had correspondents in the towns of Danbury, Hartford, New Haven, and Waterbury (Connecticut); Chicopee, Ludlow, New Bedford, and Taunton (Massachusetts); Elizabeth (New Jersey); Oakland (California); Bethlehem (Pennsylvania); Mineola and Tarrytown (New York); Lisboa, Ílhavo, and Murtosa (continental Portugal); and the Azores. According to information from the newspaper itself, its circulation today reaches 40,000 readers. The states with the largest distribution are, in order, New Jersey, New York, Connecticut, Pennsylvania, California, and Florida.[110] Since 2010, the *Luso-Americano* has had an online edition (www.lusoamericano.com). It claims to be the only Portuguese-American newspaper with distribution in all the states where there is a significant Portuguese or Brazilian presence.

The *Portuguese Times* and the New Journalism of New Bedford

The *Portuguese Times* was originally founded in 1971 in Newark, NJ, where it competed directly with the *Luso-Americano*. Its founder was Manuel Augusto Saraiva, a native of Coimbra, where he worked as an archivist at the university. António Alberto Costa, a native of Lisbon, bought the *Portuguese Times* when he was the general director of the Portuguese radio station WGCY New Bedford, a post he left in the summer of 1973 in order to devote himself entirely to the paper.[111] That same year, shortly after the closure of the *Diario de Noticias,* the paper took up headquarters in New Bedford, where it remains to this day.[112] According to M. Adelino Ferreira, the decision to move the *Portuguese Times* to New Bedford was not directly related to the closure of the *Diario de Noticias,*[113] but the truth is that this coincidence was favorable to the commercial interests of the newspaper, since it filled the information gap left by João Rodrigues Rocha's newspaper.

When it first opened in New Bedford in 1973, the *Portuguese Times* was led by António Alberto Costa, with Manuel Adelino Ferreira as managing editor and Eurico Mendes among its most prominent editors.[114] The paper presented itself to readers by publishing an infomercial that showed it as a modern newspaper equipped with the best technological resources for the production of each issue, including electric typewriters, computers, and photocopiers. The human resources included a network of correspondents in several states on the East Coast, including Connecticut, New York, Pennsylvania, New Jersey, Rhode Island, and Massachusetts.[115] Among its many contributors were such intellectuals and prominent academics as Professor Eduardo Mayone Dias of the University of California Los Angeles and Professor Onésimo T. Almeida of Brown University, who contributed to the paper from its first issues.[116] Over the years, Costa developed and expanded the company's media structure to include a television channel, The Portuguese Channel. In 1979, Manuel Adelino Ferreira, from the island of São Miguel, Azores, succeeded Costa as publisher and editor, and since 2012 its director has been Francisco Resendes, who is also a native of São Miguel.

Once in the Whaling City, the weekly inaugurated a new journalistic style created after the new wave of Portuguese emigration to the United States in the second half of the twentieth century. Speaking of "new journalism" may sound excessive or pretentious, but when discussing the *Portuguese Times*, one cannot avoid mentioning the Portuguese journalistic tradition and culture of New Bedford and how this newspaper added to and transformed that tradition.

Although its title is in English, Portuguese has always been the official and primary language of the *Portuguese Times*, which in its first years had an English-language section. Published in tabloid format, it has used two subtitles: "Jornal de Informação e Cultura Popular" (Information and Popular Culture Newspaper), in the beginning, and "O Jornal da Comunidade Portuguesa dos Estados Unidos" (The Newspaper of the Portuguese Community of the United States), later on. Its promotional slogan is "O Jornal de Língua Portuguesa de Maior Tiragem dos Estados Unidos" (The Portuguese Newspaper with the Largest Circulation in the United States).

The *Portuguese Times* has traditionally included numerous opinion pieces and an editorial section that offer comments not only on issues related to the community, but also on national and international politics. Currently, it publishes content in color with photographs and illustrations accompanying the various sections: obituaries, cooking, social commentary and criticism, horoscopes, community celebrations, summaries of the chapters of the current "telenovelas" (Television series and soap operas) on the Portuguese Channel, educational materials, such as "O Leitor e a Lei" (The Reader and the Law) and "Segurança Social" (Social Security), and study guides to prepare for the U.S. citizenship exam.[117]

The *Portuguese Times* Reacts to the Carnation Revolution

The *Portuguese Times*' coverage of the Portuguese community in New England and Portuguese politics represented a new stage in Portuguese-American journalism. Its founding coincided not only with the closure of the *Diario de Noticias*, but also with one of the most important political events in the history of Portugal, which further helped increase its circulation and consolidate its distribution. This was the Carnation Revolution of April 25, 1974, which marked the collapse of the Estado Novo and the beginning of the political transition to democracy. This historic event, which attracted much international media attention,[118] had an enormous impact, both politically and emotionally, on Portuguese immigrant communities. The *Portuguese Times* responded to it by intensifying their activity and production, publishing issues that sometimes ran over forty pages. This situation was propitious for the development of a campaign in 1975 to attract new subscribers entitled the "20,000 subscription campaign."[119] From the outset, the *Portuguese Times* was actively committed to democracy in Portugal, because, as noted by its director, António Alberto Costa, "we cannot believe that there is a single Portuguese (or descendant) in the world, who is not concerned about the situation in Portugal."[120] He explained that those who acquired American citizenship, as he had, had every right to try to influence the future of Portugal, "because professionally, commercially, and socially we have always been connected to the Portuguese-speaking community of the United States."[121] In an emotional appeal to Lusitanian loyalty, he used the American civics model as an example to follow:

What we are today is nothing more than an amalgamation of what we have learned throughout our lives. The lessons I learned in my first 19 years were all from Portugal back then. North America has given me the opportunity to understand good and evil with a clearer vision and sense of justice. It was here, in this nation that grants to all the same rights and opportunities, that I began to understand the full significance of Democracy, Liberty and Justice.[122]

The *Portuguese Times* was not a spectator of the political developments of the transition process taking place in Portugal, especially during the Constituent Assembly elections of April 25, 1975. During this period, the newspaper expressed its doubts, its fears, and its disappointments in advocating for a democratic model for Portugal and opposing attempts to establish a new authoritarian regime. This line followed the appeal made by the president of the Portuguese Republic, Francisco da Costa Gomes, when in February 1975 he warned the political parties that they had to "avoid dictatorships."[123] The *Portuguese Times* was very concerned about this issue, fearing that the communist affiliation of some of the leaders of the revolutionary movement could transform Portugal into a new dictatorship, this time under a leftist ideology. On February 20, the newspaper published an exclusive interview with Senator Ted Kennedy, who expressed confidence in the "good sense of the Portuguese."[124] And on the cover of the same issue, the significance of the word "Totalitarian" was explained: "It indicates the unlimited power of a dictatorial government or a single party. A government is arbitrary when it decides, arbitrarily and abusively, everything regarding life (and death!) of the citizens."[125]

In a celebration of democratic freedom in early 1975 the *Portuguese Times* invited its subscribers to vote for the person that they considered most qualified to lead the country in those difficult times. According to the paper, they received seven hundred ballots in a few days. Some of them were disqualified for various reasons, including those that contained the name Salazar, Carmona, or Lenin. The winner was António de Spínola, who had led the government between May and September 1974.[126] When the provisional government resigned in mid-March 1975 and negotiations were underway to create a new cabinet amidst confusion and political instability, the paper's director, António Alberto Costa, begged for prudence and calm from his readers. The influence of the Portuguese Communist Party in the process led the *Portuguese Times* to print an editorial on March 27, 1975, urging all members of the Portuguese community in the United States to pressure American political leaders to become directly involved:

> The events of Portugal, as we interpret them, convince us that it is time we take conscious and aggressive action. Before it is too late—if it is not already. More than any other consideration at the moment, we want Portugal to become an authentic democracy, to oppose extremisms from the left and from the right, safeguarding the sacred rights of the individual. Convinced that the U.S. government can do much to prevent Portugal from reaching the point of no return, we believe it behooves each of us—those that believe in true political democracy—to act immediately to pressure the leaders of the U.S. to use all of their influence with the current interim government of Portugal, so that it does not continue to violate the right to freedom of association, the freedom of the press, and the right to vote freely (without any kind of coercion). The "Portuguese Times" has taken the initiative to address Senators Kennedy, Brooke, Pastore, Pell, and Buckley in the following telegram translated into Portuguese for the benefit of our readers: "We urge strong opposition to Communism in Portugal. We know that journalists who criticize governmental policies are fined and detained. Anti-Communist publications are being suspended. The United States has to take a public stand." We suggest today that all of our readers who can, send their senators and congressmen identical telegrams to make them aware of the fears experienced by all good Portuguese-Americans, regardless of their political affiliation. It seems to us, too, that it would be useful to organize a mass demonstration at the Embassy of Portugal in Washington and at the White House. This is just a well-intentioned suggestion. Everything depends on how this well-intended idea is received by our readers.[127]

But the pressures of the *Portuguese Times* were not merely rhetorical. Its committed attitude went beyond issuing a public outcry to fellow compatriots to fight for a democratic regime in Portugal and lobbying American political representatives. The New Bedford weekly organized a campaign to lobby President Gerald R. Ford by publishing a cutout coupon with a letter to President Ford so that all of its readers could ask the U.S. government for help. "If you are concerned about the possibility of a dictatorship in Portugal, participate,"[128] announced the paper in its campaign, affirming that "the biggest enemy of Democracy is the totalitarian Communist regime."[129] The letter to the U.S. president stated the following:

> To: Gerald R. Ford
> President of the U.S.A.
> Washington, D. C.
>
> I, the undersigned, appeal to you to use the power of your office in aiding the people of Portugal to institute a truly democratic system in their native land.
> All reports indicate the possibility of a leftist takeover which, if it occurs, will eventually lead to serious repercussions for the Western World.
> Elections are scheduled to take place in Portugal on April 25.
> The provisional government of Portugal has announced that the people will freely choose "the socialist system which they desire." This, in itself, indicates a biased and false meaning of Democracy.
> Please use all your diplomatic influences to ensure that Portugal will not become another Soviet "Satellite."

Costa wrote several articles during the revolutionary process in which he highlighted the "gullibility of the Portuguese people," a phrase that opens one of his longest articles on the theme, published on April 3, 1975, in which he observes the effectiveness of the Communist propaganda in persuading the Portuguese. According to his argument, the popular success of the communists "is no more than a reflection of a state of mind caused by selfish despotic men who, for five decades, took advantage of a situation that benefitted them to the point of scandal. . . The communists did no more than take advantage

(although dishonestly) of the general discontent and of the lack of awareness of the Portuguese people."[130] The *Portuguese Times* argued that the provisional government of the Armed Forces Movement had steered increasingly
away from the "rudimentary principles" of democracy with no clear division
of power between the executive, legislative, and judiciary branches. "The arbitrary decisions of Portugal's provisional government are all the more repre-
hensible given the fact that a provisional government cannot, however much
it tries, justify itself as representing the will of the people who have not had
the opportunity to express that will through a secret and free vote."[131]

The newspaper's editorial line was resented by immigrants more
sympathetic to communist ideas, who saw in these comments a reactionary
attitude. According to Costa, the communist party of the community was
"small in number, but very active. Very dedicated to the cause, to the international Marxist conspiracy."[132] The pro-communist community engaged in
propaganda against the *Portuguese Times*, including the publication of a pam-
phlet linking the newspaper to the C.I.A.[133]

Amid this heated debate, the *Portuguese Times* also reported on the
Movement for the Autonomy of the Azorean People (Movimento para a Auto-
determinação do Povo Açoriano / MAPA), whose foundation in June 1974
created a new source of political instability for the Portuguese government.
The *Portuguese Times* believed that many of MAPA's demands were reasonable, given the lack of public investment in the islands by the Portuguese government. According to Manuel Adelino Ferreira, who interviewed José de
Almeida, one of the founders of the movement,[134] the situation had worsened
because the frequent changes in the Portuguese government made it incapable of managing the situation properly. Furthermore, the São Miguel-born
journalist pointed out, most Azorean immigrants and the Azorean press were
against the independence of the archipelago.[135]

As the majority of immigrants in America were of Azorean origin,
this question further stirred political debate in the community. Some readers, such as the Azorean Jorge M. Silva of Pawtucket, Rhode Island, called
for the independence of the Azores rather than a communist dictatorship.
In order to prevent the Azorean people from being subjugated by a communist regime, he believed that the best option was to separate from Portugal,

arguing that the strategic position of the archipelago guaranteed "naturally advantageous economic aid from other countries, notably from the United States and France, which were already installed [on the islands]."[136] The unexplored natural resources and remittances from immigrants are mentioned as other sources of wealth that would give the Azores the economic autonomy needed to become a free country. In an op-ed article published by the *Portuguese Times*, Silva called for a fight for the freedom of the Azorean people:

> BETTER TO DIE FREE THAN IN PEACE BE SUBJUGATED.[137] At this time of danger for our islands one could find no better words than these to claim our freedom. But complete freedom as expressed in these words that for many years have reflected the will of the Azorean People. These people who, ignored and exploited, always lived isolated from true civilization. These people who, as they got poorer, made the rich richer. These people who have always suffered their misfortune in silence. These people who long for freedom since the past, in the present, and for the future. These people who without rulers to protect them have sought shelter in this free and friendly nation. It's from these unprotected and abandoned people that I come. It's for these abandoned people that I send out a cry of alarm and an appeal to fight. Let us fight so that our isolated Atlantic brothers can have the freedom they deserve.[138]

José Afonso Rocha (San Jose, CA) also wrote in favor of Azorean independence. While acknowledging that the islands were discovered by the Portuguese, he complains that, "nevertheless, since the day of their discovery, the Azores have been purely and simply enslaved by the Moors of Lisbon."[139] In contrast to these emotional appeals, other readers such as Assunção Santos (Providence, RI) prayed for more caution and common sense.[140]

The appeals of the *Portuguese Times* for mobilization for a democratic regime in Portugal led to several demonstrations organized by immigrants in the United States and sensitized non-immigrants to the situation and how Portuguese Americans felt about it. The *Portuguese Times* reported, for example, that some politicians of Portuguese origin were reacting favorably to the campaign. One of those was Fall River city councilor John Medeiros who filed a motion against the "possibility of a leftist takeover in Portugal."[141] Some of the campaigns succeed in bringing large numbers of people to demonstrate at strategic places. On April 5, 1975, more than three thousand protested outside the headquarters of the United Nations in New York to seek international support for the establishment of a democracy in Portugal.[142] The organizing committee of the demonstration also sent a telegram to Portugal's President Costa Gomes, Prime-Minister Vasco Gonçalves, and the Minister of Foreign Affairs, Ernesto Melo Antunes, declaring their opposition to the establishment of a new dictatorial political system:

> Portuguese residing on the East Coast of the United States of America demonstrated today, April 5, 1975, outside the United Nations in New York their wish for the fulfillment of the promise of the Armed Forces Movement to give Portuguese people free elections on April 25, for the establishment of a Democracy in our beloved Portugal, and the repudiation of dictatorial regimes of any ideology.[143]

On April 19, 1975, more than five thousand Portuguese Americans from New England traveled to Washington to protest outside the White House. The event was coordinated by Drs. José Lopes da Costa (from Hartford, Connecticut) and Joseph Nunes Costa, who lived in the U.S. capital. José Nunes Costa spoke on behalf of the protesters who were there to defend the "original program" of the Armed Forces Movement, which had "predicted a bright future for Portugal and a dignified life for the Portuguese."[144] Costa denounced the changes to the MFA's (Armed Forces Movement) initial objectives stating that "it was so deeply adulterated that when we compare it with today's program, we find that they are two totally different programs, if not opposites."[145] The ideological neutrality and impartiality of the MFA in the early days of the revolution had been diluted, according to the protesters:

> Thus, we find ourselves here in Washington to publicly express our great anxiety for the future of Portugal and also to declare ourselves against any form of censorship. Against elections that are not completely free or that do not respect the will expressed by the people. Against imprisonment

without proof of guilt. . . We are against the installation in Portugal of any single party, whether from the right or from the left. Fellow Portuguese, we have come to Washington because we love the land where we were born. We want Portugal to be a free nation in a free world in which all Portuguese can live in peaceful freedom. Long live Portugal![146]

The demonstration ended at the Portuguese Embassy, where Ambassador João Hall Themido received the organizers. They told the ambassador that they were offended by the way they had been portrayed in some Lisbon newspapers, which had claimed that the participants in the movement for democracy in Portugal within the Portuguese-American community were "fascists" and accused them of disseminating propaganda against the spirit of April 25th. When the *Portuguese Times* was criticized by the prestigious Lisbon weekly *Expresso* for its lobbying the U.S. government, the director of the *Portuguese Times* responded by asking why *Expresso* had not denounced the censorship of the press and the arrests of journalists in Portugal:

What we and all good democrats want to know is: What has become of the ten Portuguese journalists who were arrested in Angola and sent to Lisbon? By what right were the magazine *Notícia* and the newspaper *Liberdade* suspended? How can you justify the arbitrary arrests, without probable cause, of individuals who are put in dungeons, without so much as having the right to receive visits from their defense lawyers? These are just three questions that deserve clarification from *Expresso* or from the provisional government that wants to become permanent for the "good of the people."[147]

The Carnation Revolution through the Eyes of Readers of the *Portuguese Times*

In its Letters to the Editor section, the *Portuguese Times* published numerous letters debating the role that should be taken by Portuguese Americans with regard to the revolutionary process.[148] Some, irritated by the committed attitude of the newspaper and its propaganda in favor of democracy, criticized its "anti-democratic action" in trying to interfere in Portuguese national politics.[149] Judite Dias, a reader from Newark, requested respect for the Portuguese living in Portugal, arguing that many of the protests that were happening within the community were reactionary in nature:

> Dear Reactionaries:
> Let the Portuguese people be. Let the people who live in Portugal, the people who in their day to day lives suffer and feel, the people who did not need us to make April 25th happen, let them choose what is best for them.[150]

In a similar vein, some attacked the *Portuguese Times* for having the audacity to promote foreign intervention in "internal Portuguese affairs." This was the view expressed by Ilídio Gomes (Central Falls, RI), who rejected the weekly's campaign for democracy in Portugal. According to this reader, the pressure exerted by the *Portuguese Times* on the U.S. president and other American politicians amounted to an "anti-Portuguese" movement led by the editor:

> The way in which you refer to Portugal and the members of its current government convinces me that you are involved in a task that aims to establish within the Portuguese Community a climate of distrust and discredit for everything that the government of Portugal is doing for its people. Not satisfied with all of these affronts, you were the architect of the message sent to President Ford asking for the INTERFERENCE IN INTERNAL PORTUGUESE AFFAIRS by a foreign power: the United States. Of course, I cannot call you a traitor because you are a U.S. citizen, but I know what one calls individuals like you. For all I have seen you do, I protest; and also protest against the fact that you use your newspaper as a means to influence the Portuguese into adopting anti-patriotic attitudes, using for this purpose the same "slogans" used in Portugal during fascist times.[151]

And there were readers such as Z. Quintela (New Bedford), who expressed his love for Portugal and his anti-communist feelings in a poem titled "Portugal":

For you, I feel something
That blurs my eyes...
Look at you then and look at you now!
Why is God punishing you?

If you always knew how to love.
THE VIRGIN descended upon you.
Why are you being crush by
An atheistic communism?

Oh, my beloved homeland,
Of such infinite beauty,
You are now being profaned
By a damned bunch of crooks.

And the "Castro" with boldness
Presses rewind,
And calls you a new Portugal,
Turning you inside out.[152]

Yet others, proclaiming themselves socialists, like this reader from Vila do Porto, Azores, wrote to make clear that socialism did not mean dictatorship:

TO BE SOCIALIST is to believe in the revolutionary power of freedom; it is to believe in the creative and progressive power of our People through freedom of thought, freedom of speech and freedom of association. . . It's admitting that each and every one of us has the right to publicly write and say what we think about political and social life, without being persecuted or having our rights and duties curtailed.[153]

Throughout the transition period, the *Portuguese Times* was a political actor and shaper of public immigrant opinion regarding the developments that took place after the Carnation Revolution. Its pro-democratic and anti-communist position stimulated debate and provoked reaction from the Portuguese-American community and some American politicians in a pivotal moment for the future of Portugal.

Currently, despite serious competition from *O Jornal* of Fall River, which has been distributed for free for almost fifty years, the *Portuguese Times* continues to be a paper of reference among Portuguese immigrants in New England. The continual migration of readers to digital media, however, is making the profitability of print newspapers increasingly difficult, especially those with small audiences. In the Internet era, immigrants have various sources of free information through networks that reduce the prominence and relevance of traditional media. The great cyber showcase and the phenomenon of digital applications has created a virtual universe that presents great challenges to the survival of the paper-based press, forcing it to adapt to this new disruptive environment. Faced with these challenges, Portuguese-American newspapers have adapted in a variety of ways. The *Luso-Americano*, for example, offers a paid digital edition, while the only Portuguese newspaper published today in California, *A Tribuna Portuguesa*, which turns forty in 2019, offers a free digital edition that allows it to increase its media projection and reach a greater number of readers. The future of the Portuguese press in the United States will, therefore, depend on its ability to remain a useful source of information for immigrants in this new communications context.

Conclusion

The history of the Portuguese-American press has received little attention from those investigating the cultural, social, and symbolic aspects of immigrant life. Despite their potential to provide a representative view of immigrant life, with very few exceptions, the creation of newspapers and the journalistic and commercial activities of the Portuguese media in the United States have not attracted the interest of immigration historians. Taking this lacuna into account, this study investigates the causes, consequences, characteristics, protagonists, and extent of the phenomenon of the immigrant press to demonstrate its importance to Portuguese communities in the United States.

The appearance of Portuguese newspapers in different areas of the United States depended on the presence of a Portuguese community that was significant enough to constitute a potential audience. The earliest titles to be published were edited by immigrants who had knowledge of typography and who used their technical resources to print a modest newspaper for the community. This was the case in Erie, Pennsylvania, where the first Portuguese newspaper in the United States, *O Jornal de Noticias*, was founded by António Maria Vicente in 1877. Vicente, who owned a printing press, published his paper in this city that was then experiencing great economic development due to its strategic position as the railway junction for the *Pennsylvania Railroad*, which connected the ports of the Atlantic with all of the Western states and Canada.

The massive influx of immigrants into the United States, including 218,246 Portuguese during the period from 1890 to 1930, drove the emergence of Portuguese journalism, a phenomenon that would be consolidated as the years went on. With migratory flows continuing over these four decades and with the establishment of communities of Portuguese origin in different territories, dozens of periodicals published in Portuguese began to appear. According to the data collected for this research, which is summarized in Appendix A, between 1877 and 1930, Portuguese Americans founded at least 101 newspapers. Thirty-four of these were first published during the 1920s, the most productive period for Portuguese journalism in the United States. A chronological study of Portuguese newspapers in the United States shows clearly how periods of decline in Portuguese journalistic activity coincided with decreases in migration, as happened between 1940 and 1960, when immigration was negligible and only five newspapers were founded.

The emergence and rapid expansion of Portuguese-language radio was another disruptive factor that caused the press to lose prominence from the 1930s onward and forced some newspapers to reinvent themselves to attract new readers. Despite the complications involved in keeping their companies afloat due to the lack of new audiences and competition from new media, some newspapers persisted for several decades. Among the 167 newspapers listed in Appendix A about 72 of them did not survive for more than two years, which indicates the enormous difficulties faced when trying to build a commercially stable paper among immigrant communities. Nevertheless, 30 papers managed to survive for more than 10 years, 13 lasted for more than 20 years, and five, surprisingly, were published for more than half a century.

Among the more significant cases are the *Diario de Noticias* (New Bedford, MA), the weekly *Jornal Português* (Oakland, CA), and the biweekly *Luso-Americano* (Newark, NJ). All three papers were published with great effort by self-taught editors, who assumed the status of spokespersons for their respective communities. The successor to the *Diario de Noticias* as the paper of reference of the Portuguese press in New England was the *Portuguese Times*, which inherited many of the readers of João Rodrigues Rocha's paper when it ceased publication. The *Portuguese Times* played a prominent role for Portuguese Americans during the Carnation Revolution, for it expressed a political stance in favor of democracy and against the dictatorship, calling on members of the group to participate in social mobilization in order to pressure U.S. politicians to intervene in the revolutionary process taking place in Portugal. Today, the *Portuguese Times* and the *Luso-Americano* continue to serve as the papers of reference for Portuguese immigrants in the United States.

The Portuguese-American press has historically served to promote the Portuguese language and culture, while being an instrument of civic education. It also promoted and supported social cohesion, political consensus, and associative projects. Through its press, the Portuguese-American community succeeded in creating a public opinion expressed in its own voice that resisted the dominant mainstream discourse in English. The dissemination and duration of some of these newspapers, as well as the dialogue they maintained with their readers, show that the Portuguese-American press contributed significantly to the development of a sense of belonging among the group and increased their visibility within the American social context by promoting Portuguese traditions and culture.

Overall, the history of the Portuguese-American press can be subsumed under four defining characteristics. Its development was the result of private initiative connected, at least in the early stages, to immigrant typographers who saw in the publication of a newspaper a business opportunity with the potential for attaining their American Dream through the practice of their trade. The vast majority of the founders and editors of papers came from the Azores, the origin of the majority of their fellow immigrants. In general, it was a press that published irregularly and whose audience varied according to the ebb and flow of Portuguese immigration. Finally, due to the bi-coastal pattern of settlement that characterizes Portuguese immigration to the U.S., whereby most Portuguese have traditionally lived in Massachusetts and California, the majority of Portuguese newspapers were published in these two states.

Many of the immigrants who took the step of founding a newspaper believed that their calling to public service on behalf of their compatriots was implicit in their entrepreneurial initiative. They sought, as did their compatriots, the emotional and social support provided by a newspaper in Portuguese, which was a symbol of patriotic affirmation that helped to forge emotional and social bonds within the community. In general, immigrant editors claimed informative and instructive, as well as representative, roles in their communities. They were also aware of their important function in helping their readers understand local social, political, cultural, and economic dynamics. This type of press was, therefore, also a means of providing information and encouraging integration.

Within each community, a struggle for leadership was commonplace, and the press was the most effective means of promoting ideological positions. For the Portuguese-American press, issues such as republicanism versus monarchism or clericalism versus anti-clericalism, or the support for or opposition to certain policies in fraternal societies, were sources of controversy in the late nineteenth and much of the twentieth century. In some cases, ideological intolerance caused personal confrontations to assume a public dimension because of the amplifying effect of newspapers. This can be seen in the quarrel between Mário Bettencourt da Câmara and Fr. Guilherme Silveira da Glória.

From analysis of their content, it can be inferred that newspapers taught immigrants to relate to each other and to the local society, affirming their position within the complex ethnic diversity of North American society, in which the Portuguese risked being easily assimilated. The creation of a public space for information and debate allowed the emergence and consolidation of lines of cooperation between the main concentrations of Portuguese-American communities across the United States and the development of an integrated social network that fostered community protection projects and policies within a multicultural social fabric.

In the newspapers published in Portuguese, immigrants found a narrative that connected them to their origins through news related to Portugal and Portuguese life. Occasionally, what the immigrants sought in these kinds of publications was simply the spiritual inspiration that nourished their emotional attachment to the community through language. Portuguese-language newspapers offered transcendence, through rhetoric that was usually laden with patriotic language, to immigrants and their families in the United States. Although the percentage of illiterate Portuguese immigrants that came to North America was quite high, it is possible that the need to maintain contact with Portuguese culture through the press could stimulate their learning to read. In fact, data exists that seems to indicate awareness of this phenomenon within the Lusophone community.

In these papers, the immigrant public found information in Portuguese about their associations, commercial life, traditions, festive celebrations, community events, and other activities that resonated with their shared linguistic or cultural contexts. But the press also informed readers about life in the U.S. and labor or legal issues. It often performed a pedagogical function: it made recommendations about community life, disseminated advertising messages, taught English and Portuguese, helped readers look for work, and offered ideas for the founding of new businesses. For this reason, some newspapers were committed to promoting and encouraging socio-educational initiatives among immigrants, while criticizing the Portuguese government for its failed education policies and its lack of support for the Portuguese press in its educational endeavors.

Throughout its history, the Portuguese press in the United States has been an influential mass medium that has represented, supported, stimulated, and given cohesion and meaning to the unique situation of immigrants in a social environment that was alien to their native cultural traditions. Many Portuguese editors felt they were misunderstood by their communities; a lack of journalistic culture among immigrants meant that readers did not appreciate the tireless effort that was required to publish a newspaper on a regular schedule. However, for some of them, Portuguese-American journalism was an effective means of achieving their own American Dream.

Appendixes

Appendix A

Catalog of the Portuguese Press in the United States (1877-2013)

Abbreviations: B: Bulletin; D: Only data about the publication, no copies; F: Fusion of several periodicals; I: Irregular; O: Other titles used; P: Predecessor; M: Magazine; S: Successor.

No.	Title	City (State)	Founder(s) and Origin	Periodicity and Type of Contents	Issuing Period	Sources – Archives
1 (M)	(A) Abelha,	S. Francisco, Oakland (CA)	Alfredo Dias da Silva (S. Amaro, Pico) and António da Conceição (Madeira)	Monthly, satirical	1924	Freitas Library (CA) (D)
2 (M)	(A) América,	New York City	José Dias Escobar	-	1930s	Diario de Noticias (MA); Ferreira-Mendes Archives (MA) (D)
3	Atlântico	Newark (New Jersey)	António Rebelo Martins (publisher)	-	1928	Diverse hemerographic sources
4	Açôres-America	Cambridge (MA)	Eugénio Vaz Pacheco do Canto e Castro (São Miguel)	Weekly, several types of contents	1903	Regional Archive of Ponta Delgada

No.	Title	City (State)	Founder(s) and Origin	Periodicity and Type of Contents	Issuing Period	Sources – Archives
5 (M)	*Almanach Luso Americano, Litterario e Recreativo*	Boston (MA)	Manuel das Neves Xavier (Madalena, Pico)	Annually, several types of contents	1884	Ferreira-Mendes Archives (MA)
6 (M)	*Almanaque da Colónia Portugueza*	Fall River (MA)	Leonídio Cabral	Annually, several types of contents	1926	*A Alvorada* (MA); Ferreira-Mendes Archives (MA) (D)
7 (M)	*Almanaque do Emigrante*	Newark (NJ)	Manuel Augusto Saraiva (Coimbra)	Single Issue, several types of contents	1970s	Ferreira-Mendes Archives (MA) (D); *Portuguese Times*
8	*Alvorada*	New Bedford (MA)	(Rev.) Francisco Caetano Borges da Silva (Lagoa, São Miguel)	Weekly, of Protestant inclination	1909-1923?	*A Alvorada, Diario de Noticias* (MA)
9	*(A) Alvorada*	New Bedford (MA)	Eugénio Tavares (Brava, Cabo Verde)	Weekly (I), of political inclination	1900	http://www. eugeniotavares. org [consulted in 2013]
10	*Alvorada* (O: *Alvorada Diaria, A Alvorada*) (S: *Diario de Noticias*)	New Bedford (MA)	Guilherme Machado Luiz (Angra do Heroísmo, Terceira)	Daily, general information	1919-1926	Boston Public Library, Ferreira-Mendes Archives (MA); Library of Congress (MD) (D)
11	*(O) Amigo dos Cathólicos* (S: *O Arauto*)	Irvington, M. San José, Pleasanton, Hayward, Oakland (CA)	(Priests) Manuel Francisco Fernandes and João Fran-cisco Tavares (both from Pico)	Weekly, of Catholic inclination	1888-1896	County of Los Angeles Public Library (CA); Library of Congress (MD) (D)

No.	Title	City (State)	Founder(s) and Origin	Periodicity and Type of Contents	Issuing Period	Sources – Archives
12	O Arauto (P: O Amigo dos Cathólicos; S: Jornal de Notícias)	Oakland (CA)	Francisco Inácio de Lemos and Joaquim Borges de Menezes (both from Terceira)	Weekly, of Catholic inclination	1896-1919	Harvard College Library, Ferreira-Mendes Archives (MA); Bancroft Library, Freitas Library, California State Library (CA)
13	A Aurora	Cambridge (MA)	(Rev.) João F. de Oliveira (President)	Monthly, of Evangelical inclination	1918-1941?	Freitas Library (CA)
14	(A) Aurora Evangélica	Newark (NJ), New Bedford (MA)	(Rev.) João G Loja?	Monthly and bimonthly, of Evangelical inclination	1941-1970s	Eduardo de Carvalho (1931); Diario de Noticias (MA); Biblioteca Municipal do Funchal
15	Aurora Hawaiana	Honolulu (HI)	C. L. Brito	Weekly, general information	1888-1891	The Hawaiian Historical Society (HI); Library of Congress (MD) (D)
16	Aurora Luzitana	New Bedford (MA)	Manuel das Neves Xavier (Madalena, Pico)	Monthly (I), several types of contents	1900-1901	Ferreira-Mendes Archives (MA); Diario de Noticias (MA)
17	Azorean Times (S: The Portuguese-American Journal)	Bristol (MA)	Albert Silva (director)	Bimonthly, general information	1975-1983	Freitas Library (CA)
18	(O) Bacamarte	Newark (NJ)	José Alves Rodrigues	Monthly, political	1936-1937	Historic Diplomatic Archive (Lisbon)

No.	Title	City (State)	Founder(s) and Origin	Periodicity and Type of Contents	Issuing Period	Sources – Archives
19	*(As) Boas Novas*	Honolulu (HI)	A. H. R. Vieira	–	1896-1905	Edgar C. Knowlton (1960); Manoel S. Cardozo (1976)
20 (B)	*Boletim da U.P.E.C.* (O: *UPEC Life*)	S. Francisco, San Leandro, Atwater, Oakland (CA)	Mário Bettencourt da Câmara (pseudonym of Lúcio Silva Gonçalves, from Peniche)	Monthly, institutional information	1898-1967; 1968-2010	Freitas Library (CA)
21	*(A) Borboleta*	New Bedford (MA)	Quirino de Sousa	Bimonthly, several types of contents	1906	Duarte Mendonça (2007)
22 (M)	*Cabrillo Commentator. Discoverer of California*	S. Francisco, San Leandro (CA)	Manuel F. Sylva	Monthly, institutional information	1937-1938	Freitas Library (CA)
23	*(A) California Alegre*	Leemore, Tulare, Oakland, Alameda (CA)	Cândido da Costa Nunes (Pico)	Monthly, humor and satire	1915-1940	Freitas Library (CA); Ferreira-Mendes Archives (MA)
24	*Cape Verdean Newspaper*	Lynn (MA)	Manuel T. Neves	Monthly	1970s	Ferreira-Mendes Archives (MA) (D)
25	*(O) Cartaz*	Newark (NJ)	José Cerqueira	–	1977	Ferreira-Mendes Archives (MA) (D)
26 (M)	*(A) Chama*	New Bedford (MA)	Manuel Medeiros (Faial)	Weekly, several types of contents	1968-1978	Ferreira-Mendes Archives (MA)

No.	Title	City (State)	Founder(s) and Origin	Periodicity and Type of Contents	Issuing Period	Sources – Archives
27 (M)	*(A) Chrónica* (S: *A Chrónica Portuguesa*)	San Francisco (CA)	Mário Bettencourt da Câmara (pseudonym of Lúcio Silva Gonçalves, from Peniche)	Monthly, general information	1895-1896	Freitas Library (CA)
28 (M)	*(A) Chrónica Portuguesa* (P: *A Chrónica*)	San Leandro (CA)	Mário Bettencourt da Câmara (pseudonym of Lúcio Silva Gonçalves, from Peniche)	Monthly, general information	1926	Freitas Library (CA) (D)
29	*(A) Civilização* (O: *Luzo-Americano*)	Boston, New Bedford (MA)	Mário das Neves Xavier (Madalena, Pico)	Bimonthly (I), general information	1881-1884	Ferreira-Mendes Archives (MA)
30	*(O) Clarim* (S: *Portugal na California*)	Alameda, Oakland (CA)	Arthur Vieira Ávila (Lajes, Pico) & Celeste Santos (Trás-Os Montes)	Weekly, radio information	1934-1935	Freitas Library (CA)
31	*(O) Colombo*	New Bedford (MA)	Mr. Joaquim Maciel	Weekly (I), several types of contents	1892-1893	*Diario de Noticias* (MA)
32	*(A) Colonia Portuguesa* (P: *O Lavrador Portuguez*; S: *Jornal Português*)	Oakland (CA)	Arthur Vieira Ávila (Lajes, Pico)	Bi-Weekly, general information	1924-1932	Bancroft Library, Freitas Library, California State Library (CA); Ferreira-Mendes Archives (MA)

No.	Title	City (State)	Founder(s) and Origin	Periodicity and Type of Contents	Issuing Period	Sources – Archives
33	*(O) Colonial*	Fairhaven (MA)	Frederico A. Costa (Madeira)	Weekly, general information	1925-1945	New Bedford Whaling Museum (MA); New York Library (NY); Historic Diplomatic Archive (Lisbon).
34	*(O) Combate*	New York City	José Alves Rodrigues	Weekly (I), political	1934	*Diario de Noticias* (MA)
35	*(O) Combate*	Fall River (MA)	Diamantino Teixeira	(I) Political, doctrinarian (socialist)	1923-1924?	Ferreira-Mendes Archives (D); *Diario de Noticias* (MA)
36	*(O) Comércio Português*	Newark (NJ)	Luiz Antunes (Lisbon)	(I) Commercial information	1932	*Diario de Noticias* (MA)
37	*(O) Companheiro da Alegria*	Hayward (CA)	Lourenço da Costa Aguiar	Monthly, humor	1961-1977	Freitas Library (CA)
38	*(A) Comunidade*	Pawtucket (RI)	Daniel Manhães	Monthly, general information	1974-1978	Ferreira-Mendes Archives (MA) (D); diverse hemerographic sources
39	*Comunidades USA*	Manassas (VA)	José João Morais	Monthly, several types of contents	2006-?	www.comu-nidadesusa. com [consulted in 2013]
40	*(O) Correio Portuguez* (S: *O Novo Mundo*)	New Bedford (MA)	Manuel das Neves Xavier (Madalena, Pico)	Weekly, Daily (1 month), general information	1895-1907?	Ferreira-Mendes Archives (MA); *Diario de Noticias* (MA)

No.	Title	City (State)	Founder(s) and Origin	Periodicity and Type of Contents	Issuing Period	Sources – Archives
41 (M)	*(O) Cosmopolitano*	Fairhaven (MA)	Frederico A. Costa (Madeira)	Monthly (?), several types of contents (?)	1922-1925	*Diario de Noticias* (MA)
42	*(A) Crítica*	New Bedford (MA)	Francisco A. Santos (Lisbon)	Weekly, several types of contents	1921-1922	Ferreira-Mendes Archives (MA) (D); *Diario de Noticias* (MA)
43 (M)	*(A) Crítica Literaria*	(CA)	Joaquim Borges de Menezes (Terceira)	Several types of contents	1905	Freitas Library (CA) (D)
44	*(A) Cruz*	Boston (MA)	Father Abílio Mª da Silva Greaves (Faial)	Religious, of Catholic inclination	Decade of 1920	*Diario de Noticias* (MA)
45	*Diario de Noticias* (P: *A Alvorada*)	New Bedford (MA)	Guilherme Machado Luiz (Terceira)	Daily, general information	1927-1973	Ferreira-Mendes Archives, Boston Libray (MA); Library of Congress (MD); Historic Diplomatic Archive (Lisbon)
46	*(O) Direito*	Honolulu (HI)	A. J. Rego	General information (?)	1896-1898	Edgar C. Knowlton (1960)
47	*(O) Eco Açoreano*	San Francisco (CA)	Manuel José Ferreira de Ávila (Terceira)	Weekly, general information	1890	*Diario de Noticias*; Geoffrey L. Gomes (1983)
48	*(A) Emancipação*	New Bedford (MA)	Aliança Liberal Portuguesa	Special Issue, political	1934	Ferreira-Mendes Archives (MA)
49	*(A) Era Nova*	Fall River (MA)	João F. Ferraz	Weekly (?), of Catholic inclination	1923-1924	*Diario de Noticias*

No.	Title	City (State)	Founder(s) and Origin	Periodicity and Type of Contents	Issuing Period	Sources – Archives
50	*Esperança*	Fall River (MA)	Vasco de Sousa Jardim (Ponta Delgada, Madeira)	Weekly (I), several types of contents	1921	Vasco Sousa Jardim (1989)
51	*(O) Evangelista*	Fall River (MA)	João Pacheco dos Santos	Monthly, Evangelical	1934	Freitas Library (CA) (D); Ferreira-Mendes Archives (MA) (D)
52	*(O) Facho*	Hilo (HI)	António de Carvalho o Antone C. Oak (São Miguel)	Weekly, general information	1906-1927	The Hawaiian Historical Society, The University of Hawaii at Manoa (HI); Library of Congress (MD) (D)
53 (M)	*Factos e Gente*	Newark (NJ)	Manuel Augusto Saraiva (Coimbra)	Monthly, several types of contents	4-5 numbers issued, 1975 (?)	Ferreira Mendes Archives (MA) (D); *Portuguese Times* (MA)
54 (M)	*For the People*	Fall River (MA)	-	Monthly, several types of contents	1970-1981	Ferreira Mendes Archives (MA) (D)
55	*Gazeta Portuguesa*	Newark, San Leandro (CA)	Francisco Fialho (Pico)	General information	1926-(?)	*Diario de Noticias* (MA)
56	*(O) Heraldo*	Oakland (CA)	(Rev.) João José Vieira Jr. (Ponta Delgada, Madeira)	Monthly, of Evangelical inclination	1936-1959	Freitas Library (CA)

No.	Title	City (State)	Founder(s) and Origin	Periodicity and Type of Contents	Issuing Period	Sources – Archives
57	*(O) Heraldo Portuguez*	Taunton (MA)	Affonso Gil Ferreira Mendes (Barroca do Zêzere, Beira Baixa)	Biannually, Commercial information	1925-1976	Ferreira-Mendes Archives (MA)
58	*(O) Imparcial* (S: *Jornal Português*)	Sacramento, Alameda, Oakland, Chico (CA)	Manuel B. Quaresma (Pico)	Weekly, general information	1913-1932	California State Library, Freitas Library (CA); Center for Research Library of Chicago; Ferreira-Mendes Archives (MA)
59	*(A) Imprensa*	Cambridge, New Bedford (MA)	(Rev.) Francisco Silva	Religious, of protestant inclination	1926-1927	*Diario de Noticias* (MA)
60	*(O) Independente*	New Bedford (MA)	Miguel F. Policarpo (Faial)	Weekly, general information	1897-1945	Boston Public Library, New Bedford Whaling Museum (MA); Historic Diplomatic Archive (Lisbon)
61	*(O) Inquêrito*	Providence (RI)	José Martins da Cunha (Terceira)	Weekly (?)	Decade of 1920	Ferreira-Mendes Arquives (MA) (D)
62 (M)	*Jornal das Damas*	New Bedford (MA)	Virgínia C. Escobar	Monthly (?), several types of contents	1919- ?	*Diario de Noticias* and various hemerographic sources

No.	Title	City (State)	Founder(s) and Origin	Periodicity and Type of Contents	Issuing Period	Sources – Archives
63	*Jornal das Senhoras*	New Bedford (MA)	Eugénio Escobar (Azores)	Monthly (?), several types of contents	1898	Ferreira-Mendes Archives (MA) (D) and *Diario de Noticias* (MA)
64	*(O) Jornal de Fall River, O Jornal*	Fall River (MA)	Raymond Canto e Castro	Weekly, general information	1970-present	Ferreira-Mendes Archives (MA)
65	*Jornal de Notícias (P: O Arauto; S: Jornal Português)*	San Francisco, Oakland, Alameda (CA)	Pedro Laureano Claudino da Silveira (Flores)	Weekly, general information	1917-1932	California State Library, Freitas Library, Bancroft Library (CA); Ferreira-Mendes Archives (MA), Library of Congress (MD) (D)
66	*(O) Jornal de Noticias*	Erie (PA)	João Maria Vicente and António Maria Vicente (Flores)	Weekly, general information	1877-1884	Ferreira-Mendes Archives (MA); Library of Congress (MD); Regional Archive of Ponta Delgada
67	*Jornal do Povo (P: O Portugal)*	New Bedford (MA)	João Francisco Escobar (Azores)	Weekly (I), general information	1916-1923	Eduardo de José Carvalho (1931); diverse hemerographic sources
68	*Jornal Português*	Cambridge (MA)	Manuel Benevides Raposo	-	1900-1901?	*Diario de Noticias* (MA) and other hemerographic sources

No.	Title	City (State)	Founder(s) and Origin	Periodicity and Type of Contents	Issuing Period	Sources – Archives
69	*Jornal Português* (F: *A Colonia Portuguesa, O Imparcial*, and *Jornal de Notícias*)	Oakland, San Pablo (CA)	Pedro Laureano Claudino da Silveira (Flores)	Weekly, general information	1932-1997	Bancroft Library, California State Library, Freitas Library (CA), Center for Research Library at Chicago, Library of Congress (MD)
70	*Jornal Português*	Providence (RI)	João Soares de Vasconcelos (São Miguel)	General information	1920s	*Diario de Noticias* (MA)
71	*(O) Lavrador Portuguez* (S: *A Colonia Portuguesa*)	Leemore, Hanford, Tulare, Oakland (CA)	João de Simas Melo Jr., Constantino Barcelos, and Arthur Vieira Ávila (Lajes, Pico)	Weekly, biweekly (1921-1924), general information	1912-1927	Freitas Library (CA); Ferreira-Mendes Archives (MA)
72	*(A) Liberdade*	Honolulu (HI)	C. Pereira	Weekly, general information	1899-1910	HI State Public Library; Library of Congress (MD) (D)
73	*(A) Liberdade*	Sacramento, Oakland (CA)	(Priest) Guilherme Silveira da Gloria (Pico)	Weekly, Daily (1920-1926), general information	1900-1937	California State Library, Freitas Library (CA); Ferreira Mendes Archives (MA); Library of Congress (MD) (D)
74	*Liberdade*	New Bedford (MA)	Aliança Liberal Portuguesa	Weekly, political	1933-1934?	Historic Diplomatic Archive (Lisbon)

No.	Title	City (State)	Founder(s) and Origin	Periodicity and Type of Contents	Issuing Period	Sources – Archives
75 (M)	*Lusitânia*	New York City	Martin Avillez	Biannually, several types of contents	1988- ?	Freitas Library (CA)
76	*Lustitânia News*	Tracy (CA)	Rui Jacinto	Bimonthly, general information	2006- ?	Freitas Library (CA)
77 (M)	*The Lusitanian*	Oakland (CA)	Zósimo S. Souza (São Jorge)	Monthly, several types of contents (of Catholic inclination)	1932-1955	Ferreira-Mendes Archives (MA)
78	*(O) Luso* (F: *A União Lusitano-Hawaiana* and *A Sentinella*)	Honolulu (HI)	João de Sousa Ramos (São Miguel)	Weekly, general information	1896-1897; 1910-1924	The Hawaiian Historical Society (HI); Library of Congress (MD) (D)
79	*Luso-Americano* (*Luzo-Americano, Luzo-Americano NJ*)	Newark (NJ)	1928-1929: José Paulo Lobo (Lisbon), M. Conceição Jr., Francisco de Castro and Valentín Rocha; 1931: Luiz Antunes (Lisbon) and Casimiro Morais (Monção); 1939: Vasco Sousa Jardim (Madeira)	Weekly, biweekly (since 1988), general information	1928-1929; 1931; 1939-present	Franklin D. Roosevelt Library (Hyde Park, NY); Free Public Library of Newark, South River Public Library (NJ); Ferreira-Mendes Archives (MA); Library of Congress (MD) (D)
80	*Luso-Americano California*	Hayward (CA)	António Matinho	Weekly, general information	1992-1995	Freitas Library (CA)

No.	Title	City (State)	Founder(s) and Origin	Periodicity and Type of Contents	Issuing Period	Sources – Archives
81	*(O) Luso-Brazileiro*	New York City	Joseph Silva Jr.	Weekly, general information	1918- ?	New Bedford Whaling Museum (MA)
82	*(O) Luso Hawaiiano* (S: *União Lusitana Hawaiana*)	Honolulu (HI)	A. Marques	Weekly, general information	1885-1890	The Hawaiian Historical Society (HI); Library of Congress (D) (MD)
83	*(A) Luta*	Fall River, New Bedford (MA)	-	(I), political, doctrinary	Decade of 1920	*Alvorada, Diario de Noticias* (MA)
84	*(A) Luta*	New York City	Joseph (José) Cacella (Lisbon)	Weekly and Bimonthly, of catholic inclination	1936-1970?	Harvard College Library (MA); Historic Diplomatic Archive (Lisbon)
85 (M)	*A Luzitania*	Boston (MA)	-	Annually	1917- ?	Diverse hemerographic sources
86 (M)	*Luzonet Magazine*	Fall River (MA)	Deodato Faria and Orlando Guimarães (São Miguel)	Monthly, several types of contents	2002-2004	Ferreira-Mendes Archives (MA)
87	*(O) Mensageiro*	New Bedford (MA)	Luiz Antunes (Lisbon)	Monthly, several types of contents	1936-1937	Ferreira-Mendes Archives (MA)
88	*(O) Micaelense*	Taunton (MA)	Alípio Galvão (São Miguel)	Monthly (?)	Issued in 1915	Various hemerographic sources
89	*(O) Mundo*	Oakland (CA)	Joaquim dos Santos Oliveira	Weekly, general information	1915-1916	*Diario de Noticias* (MA) and various hemerographic sources

No.	Title	City (State)	Founder(s) and Origin	Periodicity and Type of Contents	Issuing Period	Sources – Archives
90 (M)	*(O) Mundo Lusíada*	New York City	José Dâmaso Fragoso	Quarterly, several types of contents	1949-1952?	Ferreira-Mendes Archives (MA)
91	*Noticia* (S: *Portugal-USA*)	San José (CA)	José João Encarnação (São Miguel) and Batista S. Vieira	Weekly, general information	1984-1986	Bancroft Library, Freitas Library (CA)
92	*Nova Pátria*	Oakland (CA)	-	-	1894- ?	Geoffrey L. Gomes (1983)
93	*(A) Novidade*	Tulare (CA)	Pedro Valadão da Costa (Terceira)	Monthly, general information	1983-1986	Geoffrey L. Gomes (1983)
94	*(As) Novidades*	Fall River (MA)	Joaquim Braz (Goa)?	Weekly, of Catholic inclination	1907-1948	Boston Public Library (MA); Center for Research Library at Chicago; Historic Diplomatic Archive (Lisbon)
95	*(As) Novidades*	Newman (CA)	Constantino Barcelos	Weekly, general information	1922	*Diario de Noticias* (MA); Geoffrey L. Gomes (1983)
96	*(O) Novo Mundo* (S: *O Correio Portuguez*)	New Bedford, Boston, Fall River (MA); Providence (RI)	José Marques de Lima (São Miguel)	Bimonthly, general information	1891-1895	Ferreira-Mendes Archives (MA) (D)

No.	Title	City (State)	Founder(s) and Origin	Periodicity and Type of Contents	Issuing Period	Sources – Archives
97	*Novos Mundos*	Newark (NJ)	(Priest) Joseph (José) L. Capote	Monthly ?, of Catholic inclination	Decade of 1960	*Diario de Noticias* (MA); Ferreira-Mendes Archives (MA) (D)
98	*Novo Mundo em Revista*	New Bedford (MA)	(Priest) Manuel Garcia (Faial)	Weekly, of Catholic inclination	1982-1983	Ferreira-Mendes Archives (MA)
99	*Novos Rumos Estados Unidos*	Newark (NJ)	(Priest) Joseph (José) L. Capote	Bimonthly, of Catholic inclination	1961-1970?	Historic Diplomatic Archive (Lisbon)
100	*Oportunidades*	Kearny (NJ)	José B. Moreira	Monthly, Commercial information	Decade of 1970	Ferreira-Mendes Archives (MA)
101	*(O) Pais*	New York City	José Alves Rodrigues	Bimonthly	1950?	Ferreira-Mendes Archives (MA) (D); diverse hemerographic sources
102 (M)	*(A) Palavra*	New Bedford (MA)	-	Bimonthly	1942?	Ferreira-Mendes Archives (MA) (D); diverse hemerographic sources
103	*(A) Pátria*	Oakland, San Francisco (CA)	Manoel Stone (Brasil); 1916: Cândido da Costa Nunes (Pico)	Weekly (I), general information	1891-1896; 1916	Library of Congress (MD) (D); Freitas Library (CA) (D); diverse hemerographic sources
104	*(A) Patria*	New Bedford (MA)	Avelino de Abreu; 1935: Carlos A. Supico	Weekly, general information	1909; 1935-1936	New Bedford Whaling Museum (MA)

No.	Title	City (State)	Founder(s) and Origin	Periodicity and Type of Contents	Issuing Period	Sources – Archives
105	(A) Pátria Portuguesa	Newark (NJ)	Manuel Nascimento (Santa Maria)	Weekly, general information	1931-1932	Diario de Noticias (MA)
106	(A) Paz	Lowell (MA)	Domingos J. F. Spinney (Spínola) (Terceira)	-	1919- ?	Alvorada Diaria (MA)
107	(O) Pé de Vento	New Bedford (MA)	Alexandre Miranda and José Augusto Laranjo (Lisbon)	Bimonthly and Weekly	1921	Various hemerographic sources
108	(A) Plebe	New York City	José Alves Rodrigues	Monthly, political	1936-1938	Historic Diplomatic Archive (Lisbon)
109	(O) Popular	Honolulu (HI)	J. S. Ramos	Weekly, general information	1911-1913	Hawaii State Library, The Hawaiian Historical Society, University of Hawaii at Manoa, Historical Society of Hawaii; Library of Congress (MD) (D)
110	(O) Popular	New Bedford (MA); East Providence (RI)	Joaquim dos Santos Oliveira	Weekly, general information	1913-1931	Widener Library; Library of Congress (MD) (D); Diario de Noticias (MA) and various hemerographic sources; Eduardo de Carvalho (1931)

No.	Title	City (State)	Founder(s) and Origin	Periodicity and Type of Contents	Issuing Period	Sources – Archives
111	*(O) Portugal* (S: *Jornal do Povo*)	New Bedford (MA)	Alberto de Sousa da Cunha e Moura (Chaves)	Weekly, general information	1914-1916	*Diario de Noticias* (MA); Eduardo de Carvalho (1931)
112	*(O) Portugal*	Newark (NJ)	Francisco A. Santos (Lisbon)	Weekly, general information	1927-1928	*Diario de Noticias* (MA)
113	*Portugal*	Cambridge (MA)	António S. Lemos	-	1920s	Eduardo de Carvalho (1931); diverse hemerographic sources
114	*(O) Portugal*	New York City	(Priest) Joseph (José) Cacella (Lisbon)	Weekly (I), of Catholic inclination	1929-1934	Freitas Library (CA)
115	*(O) Portugal*	Oakland (CA)	João Roldão (continental Portugal)	Bimonthly (I), general information	1930-1937?	Freitas Library (CA); Ferreira-Mendes Archives (MA)
116	*Portugal*	Fall River (MA)	Marcelino de Melo	Weekly	1933	*Diario de Noticias* (MA)
117 (M)	*Portugal-América*	Fresno (CA)	Pedro Laureano Claudino da Silveira (Flores)	Bimonthly (?), general information	1905	*Diario de Noticias* and other hemerographic sources
118	*Portugal-América*	New Bedford (MA)	José Laranjo (Lisbon)	Monthly (?), general information	1922-1923?	*Diario de Noticias* and other hemerographic sources
119	*(O) Portugal da California* (F: *O Clarim* and *Ecos de Portugal*)	Oakland, Alameda (CA)	Arthur Vieira Ávila (Lajes, Pico) and Leonel Soares de Azevedo	Weekly (I)	1935-1937	Freitas Library (CA)

No.	Title	City (State)	Founder(s) and Origin	Periodicity and Type of Contents	Issuing Period	Sources – Archives
120	*Portugália*	Oakland (CA)	Joaquim Rodrigues da Silva Leite	Bimonthly	1931-1932	Freitas Library (CA) (D); various hemerographic sources
121	*Portugal na California*	Oakland (CA)	Jordão Marques Jardim	Special Issue (about the ambassador's visit), political	1935	Freitas Library (CA)
122 (M)	*Portugal Today*	New York City	George Rossen (publisher)	Monthly (I), several types of contents	1959-1961	Freitas Library (CA)
123	*Portugal-USA* (P: *Noticia*)	San José (CA)	João P. Brum (Pico)	Weekly, general information	1986-1987	Bancroft Library, Freitas Library (CA)
124	*(O) Português*	New Bedford (MA)	(Rev.) Cándido Martins Neves and (Rev.) Claudio Vieira e Pimentel	-	1893	*Diario de Noticias* (MA)
125	*The Portuguese-American Journal* (P: *Azorean Times*)	Providence, Bristol (RI)	José Baptista and Carolina Matos (São Miguel)	Weekly, general information	1985-1995	Rhode Island Historical Society Library (RI)
126	*Portuguese-American Chronicle*	Tracy (CA)	João P. Brum (Pico) and Frank J. Silva	Weekly and bimonthly, general information	1997-2006	Freitas Library (CA)
127	*Portuguese Daily*	East Providence	Tomás Veiga	Daily (except Saturdays and Sundays), general information	1984	Ferreira-Mendes Archives (MA) (D)

No.	Title	City (State)	Founder(s) and Origin	Periodicity and Type of Contents	Issuing Period	Sources – Archives
128	*Portuguese Heritage Journal*	Coral Gables (FL)	António V. Cavaco	Bimonthly and Monthly, general information	1991-1994?	Freitas Library (CA)
129 (M)	*Portuguese News*	Newark (NJ)	José Cerqueira	Monthly (?), general information	1978-?	Ferreira-Mendes Archives (MA) (D)
130 (M)	*Portuguese News*	San Leandro (CA)	Alfred Dijulio (continental Portugal) and Anthony de Azevedo	(I), general information	1979	Freitas Library (CA) (D)
131	*Portuguese Times*	Newark (NJ), New Bedford (MA)	Manuel Augusto Saraiva (Coimbra)	Weekly, general information	1971-present	Boston Library, Ferreira-Mendes Archives (MA); Rhode Island Historical Society Library (RI); University of Scranton Library (PA); Library of Congress (MD)
132	*(O) Progresso*	(CA)	Frank Silva	-	1894	Geoffrey L. Gomes (1983)
133	*(O) Progresso*	New Bedford (MA)	(Rev.) Francisco Caetano Borges da Silva (Lagoa, São Miguel)	Weekly, Daily, of Catholic inclination	1907	*Diario de Noticias*; Eduardo de Carvalho (1931)
134	*(O) Progresso*	Sacramento (CA)	Alfredo Dias da Silva (Santo Amaro, Pico)	Weekly, general information	1932-1940	Freitas Library (CA); Ferreira-Mendes Archives (MA)

No.	Title	City (State)	Founder(s) and Origin	Periodicity and Type of Contents	Issuing Period	Sources – Archives
135	(O) Progresso Californiense	S. Francisco (CA)	António Maria Vicente (Flores)	Weekly, general information	1885-1887	Freitas Library (CA); Ferreira-Mendes Archives (MA)
136	(O) Reporter	Oakland, San Francisco (CA)	Constantino Cândido Leal Soares and Frank Joseph	Weekly, general information	1897-1916	Freitas Library (CA); Ferreira-Mendes Archives (MA); Library of Congress (MD)
137	(A) Restauração	New Bedford (MA)	Manuel Pinho Ribeiro	Weekly (I), political, doctrinary	1924-1925	New York Public Library; Library of Congress (MD) (D); Ferreira-Mendes Archives (MA) (D); Diario de Noticias (MA)
138 (M)	(A) Revista Portuguesa	New Bedford (MA)	Joaquim Borges de Menezes (Terceira)	–	1895	Ferreira-Mendes Archives (MA) (D); Diario de Noticias (MA)
139	(A) Revista Portuguêsa	Hayward (CA)	João de Simas Melo Jr.	Monthly, several types of contents	1914-1925	Freitas Library (CA)
140 (M)	Revista Portugal-America Portuguesa	Cambridge (MA)	João Rodrigues Rocha (Ponte de Lima, Trás-Os-Montes)	Monthly, several types of contents	1926-1929	Freitas Library (CA)
141 (M)	Rose and Albert Magazine (S: O Clarim)	Oakland (CA)	Arthur Vieira Ávila (Lajes, Pico) and Celeste Santos (Trás-Os-Montes)	Monthly, radio information	1933-1934	Freitas Library (CA)

No.	Title	City (State)	Founder(s) and Origin	Periodicity and Type of Contents	Issuing Period	Sources – Archives
142	*(A) Semana Portugueza*	San José (CA)	Joaquim Borges de Menezes (Altares, Terceira)	Weekly, general information	1903	Harvard College Library (MA); Library of Congress (MD) (D)
143	*(O) Semeador*	Cambridge (MA)	Augusto B. Pimentel (Angra do Heroismo, Terceira)	Evangelical	1906-1909	Ferreira-Mendes Archives (MA) (D); Eduardo de Carvalho (1931)
144	*Sem Pés Nem Cabeça*	New Bedford (MA)	Quirino de Sousa	Weekly, humor	Decade of 1920	*Alvorada, Diario de Notícias* (MA)
145	*(A) Sentinella (S: O Luso)*	Honolulu (HI)	J. M. Teixeira	Weekly, general information	1892-1896	The Hawaiian Historical Society (HI); Library of Congress (MD) (D)
146	*(A) Setta*	Hilo (HI)	M. G. Santos	Weekly, general information	1903-1921	Hawaii State Library, The Hawaiian Historical Society, University of Hawaii at Manoa; Library of Congress (MD) (D)
147	*(O) Talassa*	New Bedford (MA)	Centro Monárchico Portuguez	Bimonthly, political	1923-1924	New York Public Library; Library of Congress (MD) (D); Ferreira-Mendes Archives (MA) (D)

No.	Title	City (State)	Founder(s) and Origin	Periodicity and Type of Contents	Issuing Period	Sources – Archives
148	*(O) Teatro*	New Bedford (MA)	António Pereira	Monthly, arts and entertainment	1935-1936	Historic Diplomatic Archive (Lisbon)
149 (M)	*Tic-Tac*	Newark (NJ)	Bernardino Moutinho	Monthly, didactic information	1979-1980?	Ferreira-Mendes Archives (MA)
150	*(O) Trabalho*	Danbury (CT)	Joaquim de Oliveira	Monthly, general information	1939-1940	*Diario de Noticias* (MA)
151	*(A) Tradição*	New Bedford (MA)	António Lopes	-	1925	*A Alvorada, Diario de Noticias* (MA)
152	*(A) Tribuna*	Newark (NJ)	Joseph Merola (Italy), publisher: Gil Stone	Weekly, general information	1931-1934	Historic Diplomatic Archive (Lisbon); *Diario de Noticias* (MA)
153	*(A) Tribuna Portuguesa (O: The Portuguese Tribune)*	San Jose, Modesto (CA)	João P. Brum (Pico)	Weekly and bimonthly (since 1994), general information	1979-present	Freitas Library (CA); Ferreira-Mendes Archives (MA)
154	*(A) União Lusitana -Hawaiana (O: A União Lusitana) (F: Luso Hawaiano and Aurora Hawaiana)*	Honolulu (HI)	A. Marques	Weekly, general information	1891-1896	The Hawaiian Historical Society (HI); Library of Congress (MD) (D)

No.	Title	City (State)	Founder(s) and Origin	Periodicity and Type of Contents	Issuing Period	Sources – Archives
155	(A) União Portuguesa (O: A União Portugueza)	San Francisco, Oakland (CA)	António Maria Vicente (Flores)	Weekly, general information	1887-1942	California State Library, Freitas Library (CA); Center for Research Library at Chicago; Ferreira-Mendes Archives (MA); Kansas State Historical Society at Topeka
156 (M)	Varões Assinalados	New Bedford (MA)	-	Quarterly	1924	Ferreira-Mendes Archives (MA) (D); diverse hemerographic sources
157	(A) Verdade	New Bedford (MA)	(Rev.) Francisco Caetano Borges da Silva (Lagoa, São Miguel)	Religious, of protestant inclination	1893-?	Diario de Notcias; Eduardo de Carvalho (1931)
158	(O) Vigilante	Fall River (MA)	Manuel Correia Botelho (São Miguel)	Weekly (I), general information	1915-1928	Ferreira-Mendes Archives (MA) (D); A Alvorada, Dario de Noticias (MA)
159	(A) Voz da Colonia	Bristol, Providence (RI)	João Cristiano da Rosa	Weekly, general information	1926-1945?	Ferreira-Mendes Archives (MA) (D); Diario de Noticias (MA)
160	(A) Voz da Madeira	New Bedford (MA)	João Ferdinando Gonçalves (Madeira)	-	Decade of 1920	Diario de Noticias (MA)

No.	Title	City (State)	Founder(s) and Origin	Periodicity and Type of Contents	Issuing Period	Sources – Archives
161	*(A) Voz da Verdade*	Oakland (CA)	Manuel Clemente de Simas	-	1908-1909?	*Diario de Noticias* (MA); Geoffrey L. Gomes (1983)
162	*(A) Voz de Potugal*	New Bedford (MA)	Luiz Antunes (Lisbon)	Weekly, general information	1942-1945	New Bedford Whaling Museum (MA)
163	*(A) Voz de Portugal*	Hayward (CA)	Gilberto Lopes de Aguiar (continental Portugal)	Tri-Monthly (!), general information	1960-1985	Freitas Library (CA)
164	*(A) Voz Portugueza*	San Francisco (CA)	Manoel Stone (Brasil)	Weekly, general information	1880-1888	Freitas Library (CA); Ferreira-Mendes Archives (MA)
165	*(A) Voz Pública*	Hilo (HI)	G. F. Affonso	Weekly (?), general information	1899-1904	Edgar Knowlton (1960)
166	*La Voz* (Portuguese edition)	New York City	Gil Stone	Weekly, political	1938- ?	Historic Diplomatic Archive (Lisbon)
167	*24 Horas*	Newark (NJ)	Victor M. Alves	Daily, general information	1999-present	www.24horas-newspaper.com

Appendix B

Table 9: Newspapers Published by Decade with Place(s) and Year(s) of Edition

Decade	Number	Titles (and Cities of Edition)	State	Date
1870-1879	1	*O Jornal de Noticias* (Erie)	PA	1877-1884
1880-1889	8	*A Civilização* (Boston-New Bedford)	MA	1881-1885
		Almanach Portuguese Americano, Litterario, Recreativo para o Anno de 1884 (Boston)	MA	1884
		A Voz Portugueza (San Francisco)	CA	1880-1888
		O Progresso Californiense (San Francisco)	CA	1885-1887
		A União Portuguesa (San Francisco)	CA	1887-1942
		O Amigo dos Cathólicos (Irvington-Fremont-Pleasanton-Hayward-Oakland)	CA	1888-1896
		O Luso Hawaiiano (Honolulu)	HI	1885-1890
		Aurora Hawaiana (Honolulu)	HI	1888-1891
1890-1899	23	*O Novo Mundo* (New Bedford-Boston-Fall River-Providence)	MA/ RI	1891-1895
		O Colombo (New Bedford)	MA	1892-1893
		O Português (New Bedford)	MA	1893
		A Verdade (New Bedford)	MA	1893
		A Revista Portuguesa (New Bedford)	MA	1895
		O Correio Portuguez (New Bedford)	MA	1895-1907?
		O Independente (New Bedford)	MA	1897-1945
		Jornal das Senhoras (New Bedford)	MA	1898

Decade	Number	Titles (and Cities of Edition)	State	Date
1890-1899		*A Pátria* (Oakland-San Francisco-Auburn)	CA	1891-1897, 1916
		O Eco Açoreano (San Francisco)	CA	1890
		O Progresso (unknown city)	CA	1894
		Nova Pátria (Oakland)	CA	1894-?
		A Chrónica (San Francisco)	CA	1895-1896
		O Arauto (Oakland)	CA	1896-1917
		O Repórter (Oakland-San Francisco)	CA	1897-1916
		Boletim da U.P.E.C. (Atwater-Oakland-San Leandro)	CA	1898-1967 1968-2009
		A União Lusitana-Hawaiiana, A União Lusitana (Honolulu)	HI	1891-1896
		A Sentinella (Honolulu)	HI	1892-1896
		O Luso (Honolulu)	HI	1896-1897 1910-1924
		O Direito (Honolulu)	HI	1896-1898
		As Boas Novas (Honolulu)	HI	1896-1905
		A Voz Pública (Hilo)	HI	1899-1904
		A Liberdade (Honolulu)	HI	1899-1910
1900-1909	17	*A Alvorada* (New Bedford)	MA	1900
		O Jornal Português (Cambridge)	MA	1900?
		Aurora Luzitana (New Bedford)	MA	1900-1901
		Açôres-América (New Bedford)	MA	1903
		A Borboleta (New Bedford)	MA	1906
		O Semeador (Cambridge)	MA	1906-1909
		(As) Novidades (Fall River)	MA	1907-1948
		O Progresso (New Bedford)	MA	1907
		A Pátria (New Bedford)	MA	1909, 1935-1936
		Alvorada (New Bedford)	MA	1909-1923?
		A Liberdade (Sacramento-Oakland)	CA	1900-1937
		A Semana Portugueza (San Jose)	CA	1903

Decade	Number	Titles (and Cities of Edition)	State	Date
1900-1909		*Portugal-América* (Fresno)	CA	1905
		A Crítica Literária (unknown)	CA	1905
		A Voz da Verdade (Oakland)	CA	1908-1909?
		A Setta (The Arrow) (Hilo)	HI	1903-1921
		O Facho (The Torch) (Hilo)	HI	1906-1914
1910-1919	18	*O Portugal* (New Bedford)	MA	1914-1916
		O Popular (New Bedford-East Providence)	MA/ RI	1914-1935
		O Vigilante (Fall River)	MA	1915-1928
		O Micaelense (Taunton)	MA	1915
		O Jornal do Povo (New Bedford)	MA	1916-1923
		A Luzitânia (Boston)	MA	1917-?
		Aurora (Cambridge)	MA	1917-1934?
		A Paz (Lowell)	MA	1919-?
		Jornal das Damas (New Bedford)	MA	1919-?
		Alvorada/Alvorada Diária/A Alvorada (New Bedford)	MA	1919-1926
		O Lavrador Portuguez (Leemore-Hanford-Tulare-Oakland)	CA	1912-1927
		O Imparcial (Sacramento-Alameda-Oakland)	CA	1913-1932
		(A) Revista Portuguêsa (Hayward)	CA	1914-1925
		A Califórnia Alegre (Leemore-Tulare-Hanford-Oakland-Alameda)	CA	1915-1940
		O Mundo (Oakland)	CA	1915-1916
		Jornal de Notícias (San Francisco-Oakland-Alameda)	CA	1917-1932
		O Luso-Brazileiro (New York City)	NY	1918-?
		O Popular (Honolulu)	HI	1911-1913
1920-1929	34	*Esperança* (Fall River)	MA	1921
		O Pé de Vento (New Bedford)	MA	1921
		A Crítica (New Bedford)	MA	1921-1922

Decade	Number	Titles (and Cities of Edition)	State	Date
1920-1929		*Portugal-América* (New Bedford)	MA	1922-1923?
		O Cosmopolitano (Faihaven)	MA	1922-1925
		A Era Nova (Fall River)	MA	1923-1924
		O Combate (Fall River)	MA	1923-1924?
		O Talassa (New Bedford)	MA	1923-1924
		Varões Assinalados (New Bedford)	MA	1924
		Aurora Evangêlica (Boston)	MA	1924-1970s
		A Restauração (New Bedford)	MA	1924-1925?
		A Tradição (New Bedford)	MA	1925
		O Colonial (Fairhaven)	MA	1925-1945
		O Heraldo Portuguez (Taunton)	MA	1925-1976
		A Imprensa (Cambridge)	MA	1926-1927
		Revista Portugal-América Portuguesa (Cambridge)	MA	1926-1929
		Almanaque da Colónia Portugueza (Fall River)	MA	1926-?,
		Diario de Noticias (New Bedford)	MA	1927-1973
		A Luta (Fall River-New Bedford)	MA	1920s
		A Cruz (Boston)	MA	1920s
		A Voz da Madeira (New Bedford)	MA	1920s
		Portugal (Cambridge)	MA	1920s
		Sem Pés Nem Cabeça (New Bedford)	MA	1920s
		As Novidades (Newman)	CA	1922-?
		A Abelha (San Francisco-Oakland)	CA	1924
		A Colónia Portuguesa (Oakland)	CA	1924-1932
		A Chrónica Portuguesa (San Leandro)	CA	1926
		Gazeta Portuguesa (Newark-San Leandro)	CA	1927-?
		O Portugal (Newark)	NJ	1927-1928
		Atlântico (Newark)	NJ	1928
		Luzo-Americano/ Luzo-Americano New Jersey/Luso Americano (Newark)	NJ	1928-1931 1939-Present

Decade	Number	Titles (and Cities of Edition)	State	Date
1920-1929		*O Inquêrito* (Providence)	RI	1920s
		A Voz da Colónia (Bristol-Providence)	RI	1926-1945?
		O Portugal (New York City)	NY	1929-1934
1930-1939	27	*Portugal* (Fall River)	MA	1933
		Liberdade (New Bedford)	MA	1933-1934?
		O Evangelista (Fall River)	MA	1934-?
		A Emancipação (New Bedford)	MA	1934
		O Teatro (New Bedford)	MA	1935-1936
		O Mensageiro (New Bedford)	MA	1936-1937
		O Portugal (Oakland)	CA	1930-1937?
		Portugália (Oakland)	CA	1931-1932
		O Progresso (Sacramento)	CA	1932-1940
		The Lusitanian (Oakland)	CA	1932-1955 ·
		Jornal Português (Oakland-San Pablo)	CA	1932-1997
		Rose and Albert Magazine (Oakland)	CA	1933-1934
		O Clarim (Alameda-Oakland)	CA	1934-1935
		Portugal na California (Oakland)	CA	1935
		Portugal na California (Oakland-Alameda)	CA	1935-1937
		O Heraldo (Oakland)	CA	1936-1959
		Cabrillo–Commentator. Discoverer of California (San Francisco-San Leandro)	CA	1937-1938
		A Tribuna (Newark)	NJ	1931-1934
		A Pátria Portuguesa (Newark)	NJ	1931-1932
		O Comércio Português (Newark)	NJ	1932
		O Bacamarte (Newark)	NJ	1936-1937
		O Combate (New York City)	NY	1934
		A Plebe (New York City)	NY	1936-1938
		A Luta (New York City)	NY	1936-1970?,
		A América (New York City)	NY	1930s

Decade	Number	Titles (and Cities of Edition)	State	Date
1930-1939		*La Voz* (Portuguese edition) (New York City)	NY	1938
		O Trabalho (Danbury)	CT	1939-1940
1940-1949	3	*A Palavra* (New Bedford)	MA	1942?
		A Voz de Portugal (New Bedford)	MA	1942-1945
		O Mundo Lusíada (New York City)	NY	1949-1952?,
1950-1959	2	*O País* (New York City)	NY	1950
		Portugal Today (New York City)	NY	1959-1961
1960-1969	5	*A Chama* (New Bedford)	MA	1968-1978
		Voz de Portugal (Hayward)	CA	1960-1985
		O Companheiro da Alegria (Hayward)	CA	1961-1977
		Novos Mundos (Newark)	NJ	1960s
		Novos Rumos Estados Unidos (Newark)	NJ	1961-1970?
1970-1979	15	*For the People* (Fall River)	MA	1970-1981
		O Jornal de Fall River, O Jornal (Fall River)	MA	1970-present
		Cape Verdean Newspaper (Lynn)	MA	1970s
		Factos e Gente (Newark)	NJ	1970s
		Almanaque do Emigrante (Newark)	NJ	1970s
		Portuguese Times (Newark-New Bedford)	NJ/MA	1971-present
		Portuguese News (Newark)	NJ	1978
		O Cartaz (Newark)	NJ	1977
		Tic-Tac (Newark)	NJ	1979-1980?
		Oportunidades (Kearny)	NJ	1970S
		The Portuguese Tribune, A Tribuna Portuguesa (San Jose-Modesto)	CA	1979-present
		Portuguese News (San Leandro)	CA	1979
		A Comunidade (Pawtucket)	RI	1975-1985
		Azorean Times (Bristol)	RI	1975-1983
		Jornal Português (Providence)	RI	1970s

Decade	Number	Titles (and Cities of Edition)	State	Date
1980-1989	7	*Novo Mundo em Revista* (New Bedford)	MA	1982-1983
		A Novidade (Tulare)	CA	1983-1986
		Noticia (San Jose)	CA	1984-1986
		The Portuguese-American Journal (Providence-Bristol)	RI	1985-1995
		Portugal-USA (San Jose)	CA	1986-1987
		Lusitânia (New York City)	NY	1988-?,
		Portuguese Daily (East Providence)	RI	1994
1990-1999	4	*Luso-Americano California* (Hayward)	CA	1992-1995
		Portuguese-American Chronicle (Tracy)	CA	1997-2006
		Portuguese Heritage Journal (Coral Gables)	FL	1991-1994?
		24 Horas (Newark)	NJ	1999-present
2000-2013	3	*Luzonet Magazine* (Fall River)	MA	2003
		Lusitânia News (Tracy)	CA	2006
		ComunidadesUSA (Manassas)	VA	2006

Source: Calculated by the autor.

Appendix C

Special Issues of the *Jornal Português*

1937: "(1887-1937): 50° Aniversário" [(1887-1937): 50th Anniversary].

1938: "Número Especial: Os Portugueses da Califórnia (1888-1938) [Special Issue: The Portuguese of California (1888-1938)].

1939: "Anniversary Number Dedicated to the Sons and Daughters of Portugal".

1940: "Número Comemorativo dos Centenários de Portugal" [Commemorative Issue of the Centenaries of Portugal].

1941: "Número Comemorativo da Exposição Mundo Português em Lisboa e do Aniversário do Nosso Jornal" [Commemorative Issue of the Exposition of Portuguese World in Lisbon and of the Anniversary of our Newspaper].

1942: "Número Comemorativo: Quarto Centenário da Descoberta da Califórnia por João Rodrigues Cabrilho. Bodas de Oiro da Igreja Portuguesa de S. José de Oakland" [Commemorative Issue: Fourth Centennial of the Discovery of California by João Rodrigues Cabrilho. 50th Anniversary of the Portuguese Church of S. José of Oakland].

1943: "Fifty-fifth Annual Edition. Número Especial: Servindo os Estados Unidos" [Fifty-Fifth Annual Edition: Serving the United States].

1944: "Fifty-Sixth Annual Edition. Número Dedicado aos Nossos Jovens no Serviço Militar dos Estados Unidos" [Fifty-Sixth Annual Edition. Issue Dedicated to Our Youth in the United States Military Service].

1945: "Fifty-Seventh Annual Edition. Número Dedicado às Mães dos Militares e Marinheiros nas Forças Armadas dos E.U.: Victoria" [Fifty-Seventh Annual Edition. Issue Dedicated to the Mothers of the Soldiers and Sailors of the United States Armed Forces].

1946: "Fifty-Eighth Annual Edition: 58 Years of Continuous Publication. Número Especial de 1946" [Special Issue of 1946].

1947: "Fifty-Nineth Annual Edition: Uma Festa do Espírito Santo em Oakland. Número Especial de 1947" [Fifty-Nineth Annual Edition: The Feast of the Holy Spirit in Oakland. 1947 Special Issue].

1948: "Sixtieth Annual Edition. Número Especial Dedicado à Sociedade Portuguesa Rainha Santa Isabel. Jubileu de Oiro, 1898-1948" [Sixtieth Annual Edition. Special Issue Dedicated to the Portuguese Society of Queen Saint Isabel. Golden Jubilee, 1898-1948], and "Convenção Anual em San Jose; Peregrinação a Portugal. Número Especial de 1948" [Annual Convention in San Jose; Pilgrimage to Portugal. 1948 Special Issue].

1949: "Sixty-first Annual Edition: Gold Rush Centennial. Número Especial de 1949" [Sixty-first Annual Edition: Gold Rush Centennial. 1949 Special Issue].

1950: "Sixty-Second Annual Edition. Os Portugueses na Guerra da Independência. A História de Meio Século da Igreja Católica; História e Milagres da Rainha Santa Isabel, Protetora de Coimbra. Número Especial de 1950" [Sixty-Second Annual Edition. The Portuguese in the War of Independence. The History of a Half Century of the Catholic Church; History and Miracles of Queen Saint Isabel, Protector of Coimbra. 1950 Special Issue].

1951: No issue was published.

1952: "Sixty-fourth Annual Edition. História e Façanha dum Herói Português que em 1866, perante os maiores perigos, cavalgou centenas de milhas sobre a neve para trazer reforços a um forte sitiado pelos índios. O Centenário da Cidade de Oakland: Perto das margens do Lake Merrit levanta-se o edificio do Tribunal e Arquivos do Condado de Alameda, considerado um dos mais finos nos Estados Unidos. As principais repartições do Condado têm ali as suas sedes" [Sixty-Fourth Annual Edition. History and Achievement of a Portuguese Hero that in 1866, facing the greatest dangers, rode hundreds of miles on horseback through snow to bring reinforcements to a fort besieged by Indians. The Centenary of the City of Oakland: Near the shores of Lake Meritt rises the new building of the Alameda County Court and Archives, considered one of the finest in the United States. The main offices of the County have their headquarters there].

1953: "Sixty-fith Annual Edition: Dedicado aos Homens de Portugal que se têm distinguido no Governo e Orientação da Nação. Reportagem Gráfica da Visita do Embaixador de Portugal a Núcleos Portugueses da California. A Voz das Bandeiras: O Homem de Portugal que recebeu o voto do povo do Império Português, pela voz de milhares de bandeiras – na mais bela, na mais digna, na mais expressiva das manifestações até hoje realizadas em homenagem a Salazar. Número Especial de 1953" [Sixty-fifth Annual Edition: Dedicated to the Men of Portugal that have distinguished themselves in the Government and Direction of the Nation. Graphic Report of the Ambassador of Portugal's Visit to Portuguese communities in California. The Voice of the Flags: The Portuguese Man who received the vote of the people of the Portuguese Empire, by the voice of thousands of flags – in the most beautiful, the most dignified, and the most significant of demonstrations held in honor of Salazar. 1953 Special Issue].

Notes

Introduction

[1] Original: A imprensa portuguesa é a alma da colónia! É ela que anuncia as nossas festas, defende os interesses dos nossos compatriotas, faz propaganda das colectividades, publica noticias da nossa Pátria, aviva o patriotismo, ventila questões locais e leva a través dos núcleos portugueses as notícias tristes dos que exalaram neste país o último sôpro de vida, longe da nossa terra que lhes serviu de berço. ... Investiguem a existência de todos os jornais portugueses neste país, e encontrarão que a sua publicação é uma epopeia de sacrifícios, de desgostos e de desilusões, imolados no altar da Pátria e da Língua Portuguesa. "A imprensa portuguesa é a alma da colónia," *A Luta*, no. 10.2 (2 February 1938), 1.

[2] See M. Glória De Sá, Sonia Pacheco, and Judy Farrar, "Preserving and Promoting Ethnic Heritage, Identity and Representation in the U.S.: The Ferreira-Mendes Portuguese-American Archives," http://conference.ifla.org/ifla77 (World Library and Information Congress: 77th IFLA, 2009).

[3] This term was coined by James Truslow Adams in his book *The Epic of America* (Boston: Little, Brown and Company, 1931). The Merriam-Webster Dictionary defines the American Dream as "an American social ideal that stresses egalitarianism and especially material prosperity," and also as "the prosperity or life that is the realization of this ideal" [https://www.merriamwebster.com/dictionary/American%20dream]. *The Random House Dictionary of the English Language*, Second Edition, 1987, gives a similar definition: "1. The ideals of freedom, equality, and opportunity traditionally held to be available to every American. 2. A life of personal happiness and material comfort as traditionally sought by individuals in the United States." See also Jim Cullen, *The American Dream: A Short History of an Idea that Shaped a Nation* (Oxford-New York: Oxford University Press, 2003).

[4] *Noticia*, no. 1 (5 December 1984), 1.

[5] See the following essential references: Leo Pap, *The Portuguese-Americans* (New York: Twayne Publishers-A Division of G. K. Hall & Co. Boston, 1981); Kimberly DaCosta Holton & Andrea Klimt, eds., *Community, Culture and the Making of Identity: Portuguese-Americans along the Eastern Seaboard* (North Dartmouth: Tagus Press, Center for Portuguese Studies and Culture-University of Massachusetts Dartmouth, 2009); Christian Bannick, *Portuguese Immigration to the United Status: its Distribution and Status* (San Francisco: R&E Research Associates. 1971).

[6] The following can be cited as examples of the cities that had formed communities of Portuguese immigrants, grouped by states. In California: Artesia, Chino, Gustine, Handford, San Leandro, Oakland, Hayward, Hollister, Los Banos, Long Beach, Shasta Lake, Redondo Beach, Riverside, Sacramento, San Diego, San Francisco, San Jose, San Pedro, Sonora, Tulare, and Visalia. In Connecticut: Bridgeport, Danbury, Hartford, and Waterbury. In Florida: Clearwater, Miami, Orlando, and Pompano Beach. In Massachusetts: Boston, Cambridge, Somerville, Dartmouth, Hudson, Fall River, New Bedford, Taunton, Ludlow, Lowell, Framingham, and Mildford. In Nevada: Las Vegas and Reno. In New Jersey: Elizabeth, Hillside, and Newark. In New York: New York City and Mineola (Long Island). In Pennsylvania: Erie and Bethlehem. In Rhode Island: Bristol, Cranston, East Providence, Providence, and Newport.

[7] J. P. Danky, and W. A. Wiegand, *Print Culture in a Diverse America. History of Communication* (Urbana, IL: University of Illinois Press, 1998).

[8] The historic study of the media is a discipline that has been developing both in Europe and in America since the last century, with a bibliography that has become more extensive and rigorous over time, and with journals and academic associations of its own. Scholarly journals in this field include *Journalism History*, *Media History*, *Historical Journal of Film, Radio and Television*, and *Revista Internacional de Historia de la Comunicación*. Some of the professional associations include the Journalism Historians Association, the Association for Education in Journalim and Mass Communication, the International Association for Media & History, the Asociación de Historiadores de la Comunicación, and the Associação Brasileira de Pesquisadores de História da Mídia. For basic references that provide an understanding of the diachronic development of the history of the press on a global level and in the Portuguese context, see Alejandro Pizarroso Quintero, ed., *Historia de la Prensa* (Madrid: Fundación Ramón Areces, 1994). Regarding the specific case of the Portuguese press, see José Tengarrinha, *História da Imprensa Periódica Portuguesa* (Lisbon: Caminho, 2nd edition revised and expanded, 1989); Alberto Pena Rodríguez, and Nuno Rocha, "História do Jornalismo Português," in *História da Imprensa*, Pizarroso Quintero, A., et al (Lisbon: Planeta, 1996), 351-397; José Marques de Melo, et al., *Jornalismo, História, Teoría e Metodologia da Pesquisa. Perspectivas Luso-Brasileiras* (Porto: Universidade Fernando Pessoa, 2008); José Manuel Motta De Sousa, and Lúcia Maria Mariano Veloso, *História da Imprensa Periódica Portuguesa. Subsídios para uma bibliografia* (Coimbra: Imprensa da Universidade, 1987). The most recent general study of media and communication in the Lusophone world was the one edited by Jorge Pedro Sousa, Helena Lima, António Hohlfeldt, and Marialva Barbosa, eds., *A History of the Press in the Portuguese-Speaking Countries* (Porto: Media XXI Publishing, 2014).

[9] For key works with an international scope, see Mário Mesquita, *O Quarto Equívoco. O Poder dos Media na Sociedade Contemporânea* (Coimbra: Minerva Coimbra, 2006).

[10] Gaye Tuchman, *Making News. A Study in the Construction of Reality* (New York: The Free Press, 1980).

[11] For a critical approach, see Dennis McQuail, Peter Golding and Els de Bens, eds., *Communication. Theory & Research. An European Journal of Communication Anthology* (London-California-New Delhi: Sage Publications, 2005).

[12] See, among others, Richard M. Perloff, *Political Communication: Politics, Press and Public in America* (Mahwah, NJ: Lawrence Erlbaum Associates Editors, 1998).

[13] In order to reach a better understanding of this issue, see Jason Phillips, ed., *Storytelling, History and the Postmodern South* (Baton Rouge, LA: Louisiana State University Press, Southern Literary Studies, 2013).

[14] For the history of Portuguese journalistic thought and its historical influence in Portugal, see Jorge Pedro Sousa, ed., *Achegas à Construção do Pensamento Jornalístico Português* (Covilhã: Livros LabCom-Universidade da Beira Interior, 2011); and Jorge Pedro Sousa, et al., *O Pensamento Jornalístico Português: das origens a Abril de 1974*, 2 vols. (Covilhã: Livros LabCom-Universidade da Beira Interior, 2010).

[15] For a general overview of European minorities in the United States, see Dennis Laurence Cuddy, ed., *Contemporary American Immigration. Interpretative Essays (European)* (New York: Twayne Publications, n.d.).

[16] Regarding the Portuguese community in Massachusetts, see Clyde W. Barrow, ed., *Portuguese Americans and Contemporary Civil Culture in Massachusetts* (North Dartmouth: Tagus Press-Center for Portuguese Studies and Culture-UMass Dartmouth, 2002); Donald R. Taft, *Two Portuguese Communities in New England* (New York: Arno Press and the New York Times, 1969). For the Portuguese in California, see, among others: Eduardo Mayone Dias, *A Presença Portuguesa na Califórnia* (Los Angeles: Peregrinação Publications, 2002); Dias, *The Portuguese Presence in California* (San Jose: Portuguese Heritage Publications, 2009); August Mark Vaz, *The Portuguese in California* (Oakland: IDES Supreme Council, 1965); Lionel Holmes, and Joseph D'Alessandro, *Portuguese Pioneers of the Sacramento Area* (Sacramento: Portuguese Historical and Cultural Society, 1990).

[17] Reading in groups occurred frequently during this period. For more on the history of illiteracy see, for example, the work of Attilio Bartoli Langeli, "Historia del analfabetismo y método cuantitativo," *Signo. Revista de Historia de la Cultura Escrita* 3 (1996): 87-106.

[18] See António Luís Vicente, *Os Portugueses nos Estados Unidos da América. Política de Comunidades e Comunidade Política* (Lisbon: Fundação Luso-Americana para o Desenvolvimento, 1998).

[19] For a seminal essay on the Portuguese-American diaspora see Francis Rodgers, "Portuguese," in *Harvard Encyclopedia of American Ethnic Groups*, Stephen Therstrom, Ann Orlov, Oscar Handlin, eds. (Cambridge: Harvard University Press, 1981). For a more recent discussion see George Monteiro, *Caldo Verde is not Stone Soup: Persons, Names, Words and Proverbs in Portuguese America* (New York-Oxford-Berne: Peter Lang, 2017).

[20] There are very few academic references regarding the history of the media in the Portuguese diaspora. Among those that do exist, see João Pedro Rosa Ferreira, *O Jornalismo na Emigração. Ideologia e Política no Correio Braziliense (1808-1822)* (Lisbon: Instituto Nacional de Investigação Científica-Centro de História da Cultura da Universidade Nova de Lisboa, 1992). Regarding Salazar's advertising campaigns in America, see Heloisa Paulo, *Aqui Também é Portugal. A Colónia Portuguesa do Brasil e o Salazarismo* (Coimbra: Quarteto, 2000).

[21] In addition to the works already cited, for information about Portuguese immigration to the United States, see, among others, the following: Alberto Pena, Mário Mesquita, and Paula Vicente, eds., *Emigración e exilio nos Estados Unidos de América: experiencias de Galicia e Azores* (Santiago de Compostela: Consello da Cultura Galega, 2015); Alberto Pena, Mário Mesquita, and Paula Vicente, eds., *Galiza e Açores. A Rota Americana* (Lisbon:

Almedina, 2012); Maria Ioannis Beis Baganha, *Portuguese Emigration to the United States 1820-1930* (New York: Garland Publishers, 1990); Donald Warrin, and Geoffrey L. Gomes, *Land as Far as the Eye Can See. Portuguese in the Old West* (Washington: The Arthur H. Clark Company, 2001); Manuel Mira, *The Portuguese in the Making of América. The Melungeous and Other Groups* (New Bedford: The Portuguese American Historical Foudation, Inc., 1998). Also see, among others, the following scholarly articles: M. L. Marinho Antunes, "Vinte anos de emigração portuguesa: alguns dados e comentários," *Análise Social* XVIII, no. 30-31 (1970): 299-385; Jorge Arroteia, "Portugueses em diáspora: identidade e cidadania," *População e Sociedade* 18 (2010): 145-159; Isaias Gomes dos Santos, "Os Portugueses na América do Norte," *Boletim da Sociedade de Geografia* 117, no. 1-12 (1999): 45-62.

[22] See Donald Warrin, *So Ends This Day. The Portuguese in American Whaling, 1765-1927* (North Dartmouth: Tagus Press, Center for Portuguese Studies and Culture-UMass Dartmouth, 2010).

[23] Edgar C. Knowlton, "The Portuguese Language Press in Hawaii," *Social Process in Hawaii* 24 (1960): 89-99.

[24] Geoffrey L. Gomes, "The Portuguese Language Press in California: The Response to American Politics, 1880-1928," *Gávea-Brown. A Bilingual Journal of Portuguese American Letters and Studies* XV-XVI (Jan. 1994-Dec.1995): 5-90.

[25] Leo Pap, "The Portuguese Press," in *The Ethnic Press in the United States. A Historical Analysis and Handbook*, ed. Sally M. Miller (Westport, CT: Greenwood Press, 1897), 291-302.

[26] Rui Antunes Correia, "Salazar in New Bedford: Political Readings of *Diário de Notícias*, the only Portuguese daily newspaper in the United States," in Holton, and Klimt, 227-247. The author also wishes to thank Rui Antunes Correia for providing a copy of his master thesis on this subject titled "Salazar em New Bedford. Leituras Luso-Americanas do Estado Novo nos anos 30" (Lisbon: Universidade Aberta, 2004).

[27] See Lusa Ponte, "Percursos Identitários na Diáspora Açoriana: O Jornal *Açores-América* (1903)," *Interdisciplinary Journal of Portuguese Diaspora Studies* 3, no. 1 (2014): 221-46; Alberto Pena-Rodríguez, "Noticias del Diálogo Transatlántico. Una mirada sobre la Presencia Ibérica en Estados Unidos a través de la Prensa Inmigrante Portuguesa," *Transatlantic Studies Network. Revista de Estudios Internacionales* 1 (Jan.-Jun. 2016): 75-87; Alberto Pena-Rodríguez, "*For the good of the colony*. El Nacimiento y Expansión de la Prensa Portuguesa en los Estados Unidos de América (1877-1909)," in *Los Medios en Lengua Extranjera: Diversidad Cultural e Integración*, edited by Laura López Romero y Juan Antonio García Galindo, 119-127. Granada: Editorial Comares, 2018; and Alberto Pena-Rodríguez, "El Periodismo Portugués en California. Notas Históricas sobre el *Jornal Português* de Oakland (1932-1997," *Estudios sobre el Mensaje Periodístico* 25, no. 1 (2019): 443-457.

[28] Eduardo de Carvalho, *Os Portugueses na Nova Inglaterra* (Rio de Janeiro: A Leitura Colonial, 1931), 107-149. See also: August Mark Vaz, 139-149; Laurinda C. Andrade, *The Open Door* (New Bedford, MA: Published by Reynolds-De Walt, 1968), 157-227; Manuel da Silveira Cardozo, *The Portuguese in America (590 b.C-1974)* (Dobbs Ferry, New York: Oceana Publications, 1976); Maria Helena Carvalho dos Santos, "Emigração e níveis de

cultura: a União Portuguesa do Estado da Califórnia (1880-1980)," *Análise Social* XIX, no. 77-78-79 (1983): 961-986; Vasco Sousa Jardim, "Retalhos das memórias brancas," *Luso-Americano*, October-November, 1989. Memoires published by in successive numbers of this newspaper. Special 50th Anniversary; Eurico Mendes, "Jornais Portugueses nos EUA. Memórias que desta lida se consentem," *Portuguese Times* (18 November, 1989), 21-22; Lionel Holmes and Joseph D'Alessandro, 158-164; Eduardo Mayone Dias, *A Presença Portuguesa na Califórnia*, 69-79; Duarte Miguel Barcelos Mendonça, *Da Madeira a New Bedford. Um capítulo da emigração portuguesa nos Estados Unidos da América* (Funchal: DRAC, 2007), 328-336; Manuel Adelino Ferreira, "The Impact of the Post-Capelinhos Immigration Wave on the Portuguese Media in the United States: The Portuguese-Language Media on the East Coast" in *Capelinhos. A Volcano of Synergies: Azorean Emigration to America,* Tony Goulart, ed., (San José: Furtado Imports, n. d.), 186-190; Fernando M. Soares Silva, "Os meios de comunicação em língua Portuguesa," *A Tribuna Portuguesa* (15 and 30 March; 1 and 15 April 2012); and Tony Goulart, "Pelo mar, em baleeiras à demanda de El Dorado. Os portugueses/açorianos na costa do Pacífico dos Estados Unidos," in *O Mar na História, na Estratégia e na Ciência*, eds. Mário Mesquita, and Paula Vicente, (eds. Lisbon: Fundação Luso-Americana, 2013), 127-128.

[29] Sally M. Miller, ed.,*The Ethnic Press in the United States* (Westport, CT: Greenwood Press, 1987).

[30] For methodologies on the study of American ethnic cultures, see Jason McDonald, *American Ethnic History. Themes and Perspectives* (News Brunswick, NJ: Rutgers University Press, 2007).

[31] William Leonard Joyce, *Editors and Ethnicity. A History of the Irish-American Press, 1848-1883* (New York: Arno Press, 1976).

[32] Jan Kowalick, *The Polish Press in America* (San Francisco: R&E Research Associate, 1978).

[33] Lauren Kessler, *The Dissident Press: Alternative Journalism in America The Ethnic Press in the United States. A Historical Analysis and Handbook History* (Beverly Hills: Sage Publications, 1984).

[34] H. M. Lai, *The Ethnic Press in the United States: A Historical Analysis and Handbook* (Westport, CT: Greenwood Press, 1987).

[35] Sandra L. Jones Ireland, *Ethnic Periodicals in Contemporary America: An Annotated Guide* (New York: Greenwood Press, 1990).

[36] Melissa A. Johnson, "How Ethnic Are U.S. Ethnic Media: The Case of Latina Magazines," *Mass Communication & Society*, no. 3 (2000) (2-3): 229-248.

[37] K. Vismanath and Pamela Arora, "Ethnic Media in the United States: An Essay on Their Role in Integration, Assimilation, and Social Control," *Mass Communication & Society*, no. 3 (2000) (1): 39-56.

[38] Leara D. Rhodes, *The Ethnic Press. Shaping the American Dream* (New York Washington-Oxford: Peter Lang, 2010).

[39] Most of the sources used in this work come from the Freitas Library of California and the Ferreira-Mendes Portuguese-American Archives, where several collections of Portuguese-American newspapers are held. In some cases only a few issues of a particular newspaper title are preserved.

⁴⁰ In fact, during the course of fieldwork in different archives, numerous indirect clues about Portuguese-American newspapers that were published sometime somewhere were collected, but not all references have led to sufficiently reliable findings. In cases where the data for a certain newspaper was incomplete or could not be verified, the title was not included in the final list. For example, it is believed that a newspaper called *A Voz Caboverdeana* was published in Boston in 1934. However, since this cannot be confirmed, it was not included. There are also indications of newspapers published in New Bedford earlier in the century that were not included because their existence could not be reliably verified. Among these were *A Luz, A Vanguarda,* and *A Liberdade.* It is also believed that in the 1970s there was a newspaper founded and directed by Rev. José Silva, entitled *Família Luso-Americana* (Hartford, Connecticut), which was associated with the church of Nossa Senhora de Fátima. There are even authors who mention titles that cannot be found anywhere else, as is the case of *Correio Português* that, according to Vasco Jardim, was founded in August 1883 by members of the Azorean community of Erie, PA, and belonged to the Sociedade Santíssima Trindade, created May 31, 1883 (See: Jardim, *Luso-Americano,* October 25, 1989, 39). Similarly, the records of the Miguel Corte-Real collection (Ferreira-Mendes Portuguese-American Archives, UMass Dartmouth) contain references to titles whose existence has not been conclusively confirmed by other means, not even through journalistic sources or through searches in the digital media files from various research centers. Among them are *O Notícias* (1923?), *Luz e Vida* (1980-1981?), *O Chacota* (1920s, edited again 1932?), *Cabo Verde* and *Vai ou Racha.* Despite the valuable contribution made by Miguel Corte-Real, who put together a list of Portuguese-American newspapers from New England, his methodology was imprecise and some of the data was confusing or inaccurate. Among the most recent publications not included in the list because of insufficient data are *O Infante,* an ephemeral publication from 1995 founded by Carlos Rodrigues, and *Estádio,* a newspaper founded in the 1980s by Afonso Costa and aimed at soccer fans. Apparently, *Estádio* acquired a large following when the Luso-American Soccer Association (LASA) organized its famous Amateur League.

Chapter 1 Immigration and the Ethnic Press in the United States

¹ Robert E. Park, *The Immigrant Press and Its Control* (New York: Harper and Brothers Publishers, 1922).

² *N. W. Ayer and Son's American Newspaper Annual and Directory* (Pennsylvania: N. W. Ayer and Son, 1880-1909).

³ Ulf Jonas Bjork, "Ethnic Press. Newspapers for non-English speakers have long history," in Margaret A. Blanchard, ed. (Commissioning editor Carol J. Burwash), *History of the Mass Media in the United States. An Encyclopedia* (Chicago-London: Fitzroy Dearbon Publishers), 207.

⁴ Leara D. Rhodes, *The Ethnic Press. Shaping the American Dream* (New York-Washington-Oxford: Peter Lang, 2010), 5-6.

⁵ Ulf Jonas Bjork, 207.

⁶ Sally M. Miller, 13 (data cited were extracted from various works). Also see works cited by Leara D. Rhodes, 5-6.

[7] Leara D. Rhodes, 42-43. See also C. F. Wittke, *The German Language Press in America* (Lexington: University of Kentucky Press, 1957).

[8] Leara D. Rhodes, 43.

[9] Leara D. Rhodes, 43.

[10] Ulf Jonas Bjork, 208.

[11] Jerzy Zubrzycki, "The Role of the Foreign-Language Press in Migrant Integration," *Population Studies* 12, no. 1 (1958): 76.

[12] Benjamin Lee Whorf, *Language, Thought, and Reality* (Cambridge, MA: MIT Press, 1956).

[13] Regarding the cultural traditions of the Luso-American community through their popular celebrations, see, among others: Tony Goulart, *The Holy Ghost Festas: A Historic Perspective of the Portuguese in California* (San Jose, CA: Portuguese Heritage Publications of California, 2002).

[14] Teun A. Van Dijk, *Ideology: A Multi-disciplinary Approach* (London: Sage Publications, 1998). From the same author: *Discourse and Social Interaction* (London: Sage Publications, 1997).

[15] Leara D. Rhodes, 49.

[16] See, for example: C. A. Madison, *Jewish publishing in America. The impact of Jewish Writing on American Culture* (New York: Sanhedrin Press, 1976).

[17] Original: "Para os educar no sentido americano, esses filhos de portugueses ou de qualquer outra colónia, não há mister americanizar as páginas destes jornais. Sobram os americanos." "O americanismo na imprensa colonial," *Diario de Noticias*, no. 1792 (25 November 1932), 2.

[18] Original: "Não temos a menor dúvida em afirmar, em princípio, a nossa discordância com esta prática. Ou há uma necessidade de imprensa colonial ou não. Se há, se é ela que pugna e defende a cultura da língua, como instrumento de coesão rácica, o bilinguismo inutiliza esse instrumento. . . . Nem por espírito sentimental nem por ordem positiva o sistema misto de linguagem é defensável na imprensa colonial. . . . Não combatemos em absoluto a introdução de secções americanas, com destino ao cultivo das novas gerações que ignoram a nossa língua." *Diario de Noticias*, no. 1792 (25 November 1932), 2.

[19] Leara D. Rhodes, 54-55.

[20] Robert E. Park.

[21] Regarding the Catholic press in the United States during the period of largest migratory affluence, see: A. W. Baumgarter, *Catholic Journalism. A Study of its Development, 1789-1930* (New York. Columbia University Press, 1931). See also: D. A. Liptack, *Immigrants and Their Church, Makers of the Catholic Community* (New York-London: McMillan, 1989).

[22] Regarding the expansion of the Catholic faith in the Portuguese-American community, see Joe Machado, et al., *Power of the Spirit. A Portuguese Journey of Building Faith and Churches in California* (San Jose, CA: Portuguese Heritage Publications of California, 2012).

[23] According to Luso-American journalist Vasco de Sousa Jardim, Eduardo de Carvalho was a member of the Movimento da Formiga Branca, which was a semi-clandestine organization that functioned as a type of political espionage service connected to the Portuguese Republican Party. The organization was created in 1913, during the government of Afonso Costa.

[24] Original: "Se cada padre saísse da torre granítica do seu exclusivismo e pusesse a excecional influência de que ainda goza ao magno serviço da Pátria, apagando os rancores e os ódios, . . . seria, na realidade, uma prolongação de Portugal na Nova Inglaterra e não, como é hoje, um estado de transição – cada vez mais curto e mais precário – entre Portugal e a América. Deste modo, a imprensa católica, longe de ajudar a obra comum, é o maior obstáculo para a sua realização – com prejuizo para a própria Igreja." Eduardo de Carvalho, 117.

[25] Original: "Quanto à Imprensa, Nova York tem visto aparecer e desaparecer vários semanários, pelo menos cinco em sete anos, nunca tendo obtido nenhum o desafogo económico para poder subsistir. Todos os diretores têm sido indivíduos de muito boa vontade, mas sem a complexa preparação técnica que o cargo exige." "Inquérito Consular sobre a colónia portuguesa sob a jurisdição do Consulado de Portugal em Nova York" (Historic Diplomatic Archive of Lisbon, AHD. Embassy of Portugal in Washington, Box 36, file "Relações com a colónia portuguesa, 1933-1936," August 20, 1935). Sent to the embassy by Consul General, Verdades de Faria, and addressed to the ambassador.

[26] Leara D. Rhodes, 127.

[27] Bernal Díaz del Castillo, one of the officials of the Spanish conquistador Hernán Cortés, mentioned in his writings the participation of the Portuguese in the service of the Spanish crown during the conquest of Mexico. Perhaps the best known Portuguese figure involved in oceanic exploration and conquest of new territories in the service of Castille was Fernão de Magalhães. After having his navigation proposal to find new sea routes to the East rejected twice by the King of Portugal, Manuel I, Magalhães gave up his Portuguese nationality to gain Spanish financing and, between 1519 and 1522, became the commander of the first expedition to circumnavigate the planet. Regarding this and other aspects related to the history of the circumnavigation, see Joyce Chaplin, *Round About the Earth. Circumnavigation from Magellan to Orbit* (New York-Toronto-Sydney-New Delhi: Simon & Shuster, 2012), 5-35. About Magalhães' travels, see the magnificent work of Laurence Bergreen, *Over the Edge of the World* (New York: HarperCollins Publishers, 2003).

[28] Eduardo Mayone Dias, 9-10.

[29] The composition and organizational chart of the Grand Council Cabrillo Civic Clubs was as follows: Grand President: Manuel F. Sylva (San Francisco); Honorary Grand President: João Antonio de Bianchi, Minister of Portugal in Washington; Grand Treasurer: Alfred A. Baptist; Grand First Vice-president: John D. Pires; Grand Second Vice-president: Alberto A. Almada (Sacramento); Grand Secretary, J. R. de Faria (San Francisco); Grand Historian: Joaquim R. S. Leite (San Leandro); Grand Marshall: Edward Lewis (San Francisco); Grand Directors: J. N. Oliveira (San Francisco), Joseph W. Mento (Sacramento), J. L. Convente (Sacramento), George Mathews (Martinez), Marie Marshall (San Francisco), Joseph C. Light Jr. (Martinez), Peter J. Rose (San Francisco); Deputy Grand Presidents: Law T. Freitas (Stockton), Frank V. Seans (San Francisco), and Carlos R. Freitas (San Rafael).

[30] *Jornal Português*, no. 518 (3 July 1942). Special Edition of 50 pages.

[31] Original: "A Califórnia é linda, a Califórnia é bela!/ Da América do Norte, a mais donosa estrela,/ Terra da Promissão, Terrestre Paraíso,/ Sonho da Natureza, Angélico Sorriso!/ Por séculos esteve envolta na neblina,/ À espera que uma luz, celestial, divina,/ Às suas praias

guiando o Capitão Cabrilho,/ Sobre ela derramasse um deslumbrante brilho!" Guilherme Silveira da Glória, "A Califórnia é linda, a Califórnia é bela" *A União Portuguesa, 1887-1937.* Commemorative collection for the 50th anniversary (28 March 1937), 6.

[32] Original: "dificilmente se encontrará na História outro nome que em si contenha tantas afirmações das mais belas qualidades da raça lusa." Joaquim Rodrigues da Silva Leite, *A União Portuguesa, 1887-1937.* Commemorative collection for the 50th anniversary (28 March 1937), 23.

[33] See, for example, the extensive report by Edmund Delabarre, "Está gravado na pedra de Dighton o nome dum navegador portuguez?" *A Alvorada,* no. 2239 (3 September 1926), 3.

[34] During an inspection of the rock carried out in 1918, Brown University professor Edmund Delabarre believed he found the inscription "1511" and forms that could be crosses and the coat of arms of Portugal. The discovery fueled the flames of Portuguese nationalism both inside and outside the colony, to the point that in 1926 the Estado Novo government decorated the American professor for his work. Although subsequent studies, did not support Delabarre's theory, later on, Manuel Luciano da Silva, a physician and amateur researcher whose work was frequently published by the Portuguese-American press, carried on an intense campaign in favor of Delabarre's theory, which had large media coverage. Regarding Delabarre's theory, see, for example, Louis O. Mazzaneta, "New England's Little Portugal," *National Geographic* (January 1975), 98.

[35] See George Monteiro, "The Unhistorical uses of Peter Francisco," *Southern Folklore Quarterly* 27 (June 1963): 139-159, and George Monteiro, "Peter Francisco, Revolutionary War Hero," in *The Parade of Heroes: Legendary Figures in American Lore,* eds. Tristram Potter Coffin and Hennig Cohen (Garden City, NY: Anchor Press/Doubleday, 1978), 194-197.

[36] See Sherry Norfolk and Bobby Norfolk, *The true story of Peter Francisco* (Charleston: The History Press, 2014).

[37] See "Early Years," *Society of the Descendants of Peter Francisco,* https://peterfrancisco. org/?s=freedom&searchsubmit= (2014).

[38] Harry M. Ward, *For Virginia and for Independence: Twenty-Eight Revolutionary War Soldiers from the Old Dominion* (North Carolina: McFarland & Company Inc., Publishers Jefferson, 2011).

[39] See the web portal: http://www.peterfrancisco.org/

[40] See, for example, the special issue "Aos portugueses na Guerra de Independência americana," *Jornal Português,* no. 939 (22 September 1950).

[41] "Capítulo 21," *Luso-Americano* (18 November 1989), 33.

[42] "Capítulo 21," 33.

[43] *Diario de Noticias,* no. 10.640 (12 March 1954), 2.

[44] According to the figures from the Department of Homeland Security, *Yearbook of Immigration Statistics: 2012* (Washington, D.C.: U.S. Department of Homeland Security, Office of Immigration Statistics, 2013).

[45] Jerry R. Williams, *In Pursuit of their Dreams. A History of Azorean Immigration to the United States* (North Dartmouth: Tagus Press-Center for Portuguese Studies & Culture-University of Massachusetts Dartmouth, 2007).

⁴⁶ *Observatório da Emigração*, http://www.observatorioemigracao.secomunidades.pt/ (2009).

⁴⁷ This chart was graciously provided by Dr. Maria Glória de Sá, Faculty Director of the Ferreira Mendes Portuguese-American Archives at the University of Massachusetts Dartmouth.

⁴⁸ Nancy Gomes, "Os Portugueses nas Américas: Venezuela, Canadá e EUA," *Janus* (2001): 144-145.

⁴⁹ Marcelo J. Borges, *Chains of Gold: Portuguese Migration to Argentina in Transatlantic Perspective* (Leiden: Koninklijke, 2009), 11-12.

⁵⁰ Regarding the Galician emigration to the United States compared with that of the Portuguese, see: Alberto Pena, Mario Mesquita and Paula Vicente, eds., *Galiza e Açores. A Rota Americana* (Lisbon: Almedina, 2012) and *Emigración e exilio nos Estados Unidos. Experiencia de Galicia e Azores* (Santiago de Compostela: Consello da Cultura Galega, 2015).

⁵¹ In order to compare the Portuguese and Spanish emigration to Argentina, consult the excellent work by Jose C. Moya, *Cousins and Strangers: Spanish Immigrants in Buenos Aires* (Berkeley-Los Angeles-London: University of California Press, 1998).

⁵² *Observatório da Emigração Portuguesa.*

⁵³ According to the U.S. Census Bureau, American Community Bureau, the population distribution of the Portuguese colony in the U.S. was the following in 2010: California: 356,704 (25.4% of the total); Massachusetts: 314,978 (22.4%); Rhode Island: 100,811 (7.2%); Florida: 77,303 (5.5%); New Jersey: 84,386 (6%); New York: 51,076 (3.6%); Connecticut: 50,113 (3.6%); Others: 26.4%. Cited by Sonia Pacheco, et al.

⁵⁴ For a more extensive understanding, with precise quantative data, of the evolution of Portuguese emigration, see António Luis Vicente.

⁵⁵ Leo Pap, *The Portuguese-Americans.*

⁵⁶ Donald Warrin, *So Ends This Day. The Portuguese in American Whaling, 1765-1927* (North Dartmouth: Center for Portuguese Studies and Culture, University of Massachusetts Dartmouth, 2010).

⁵⁷ David Bertão, *The Portuguese Shore Whalers of California, 1854-1904* (San Jose, CA: Portuguese Heritage Publications of California, 2006).

⁵⁸ Jerry R. Williams, 29-45.

⁵⁹ See the works of the following authors: Gilberta Pavão Nunes Rocha, *Dinâmica Populacional dos Açores no Século XX: Unidade. Permanência. Diversidade* (Ponta Delgada: Universidade dos Açores, 1991); Rocha, "O impacto das migrações na população dos Açores na segunda metade do século XX" in *História das Ilhas Atlânticas. Actas do IV Colóquio Internacional da História do Atlântico* ll (Funchal: Centro de Estudos de História do Atlântico/Secretaria Regional de Turismo e Cultura, Governo Regional da Madeira, 1997): 449-467. See also Fausto Avendaño, "Portuguese Immigration into the United States," in Dennis Laurence Cuddy, ed. *Contemporary American Immigration. Interpretative Essays (European)* (New York: Twayne Publications, n. d.), 155-171.

⁶⁰ See, for example, Gustavo Luca de Tena, *Noticias de América* (Vigo: Nigra, 1993).

[61] Jerry R. Williams, 33.

[62] Initially, the Portuguese population was found mostly in San Francisco and the San Francisco Bay Area, including Oakland and the Santa Clara Valley. Eventually, in the late nineteenth century and early twentieth century, it spread to the San Joaquin Valley, which explains the publication of *O Lavrador Português* in Tulare. Only later, in the 1920s and 1930s did San Diego attract a significant number of Portuguese, who played an important role in the tuna fish industry.

[63] See the extensive work of Alvin Ray Graves, *The Portuguese Californians: Immigrants in Agriculture* (San Jose, CA: Portuguese Heritage Publications of California, 2004). And also Eduardo Mayone Dias, *A Prenseça Portuguesa na California*; August Mark Vaz, *The Portuguese in California*.

[64] W. Pease Zelph, and George A. Hough, *New Bedford, Massachusetts; Its History, Industries, Institutions and Attractions* (New Bedford: Saguan Press, 1889).

[65] See: Genevieve B. Correa, and Edgar W. Knowlton Jr., "The Portuguese in Hawaii," *Ethnic Sources in Hawai'i. A Special Issue for The University of Hawai'i's Seventy-Fifth Year* 29 (Honolulu: The United Press of Hawaii, 1982): 70-77; Maria Azevedo Coutinho de Vasconcelos e Sousa, and Edgar W. Knowlton Jr., "The Voyage of the *S. Gabriel*, Portuguese Naval Vessel, to Hawai'i in 1910," by Maria Azevedo Coutinho de Vasconcelos e Sousa. Postscript by Edgar C. Knowlton Jr.," *The Hawaiian Journal of History* 21 (1987): 77-97.

[66] See the web portal: "Provisional Convention between Portugal and the Hawaiian Islands." *The Hawaiian Kingdom*, http://hawaiiankingdom.org/treaty_portugal.shtml. My discussion of these aspects is indebted to Sonia Pacheco, librarian of the Ferreira-Mendes Portuguese-American Archives at UMass Dartmouth.

[67] See the following references: John Henry Felix, and Peter F. Senecal, *The Portuguese in Hawaii* (Honolulu: Centennial Edition: copyrighted by the authors, obtainable through the Liberty House, Honolulu, 1978); Maria Azevedo Coutinho de Vasconcelos e Sousa, and Edgar W. Knowlton Jr., 77-97; Genevieve B. Correa, and Edgar W. Knowlton Jr., 70-77. For more on the subject, see the following bibliographical catalogue: Proserfina A. Strone, ed., *Portuguese in Hawaii: A bibliography* (Honolulu: Hawaii State Public Library, 1988).

[68] Edgar C. Knowlton, "The Portuguese Language Press in Hawai," *Social Process in Hawaii* 24 (1960): 89-99.

[69] A quota system created in 1921 dramatically reduced the entrance of immigrants from Eastern and Southern Europe. The entrance of Portuguese was reduced to 440 visas per year. The Great Depression of 1929 worsened these conditions. The economic recovery from the Second World War did not change conditions much either. See Fausto Avendaño, 159.

[70] João de Deus Ramos, Document sent by the secretary of the embassy to the Minister of Foreign Affairs (AHD, Embassy of Portugal in Washington, box 18, no. 117, process 9/34, s.d. [1934]).

[71] "Inquérito Consular segundo o disposto na circular de 20 de Junho de 1934, processo 524/34, da 2ª Repartição da Direcção geral dos Negócios Estrangeiros," prepared by the Consul of Portugal in San Francisco, 2 October 1934 (AHD, Portuguese Embassy in Washington, box 36).

[72] Luis da Câmara Pina, *Dever de Portugal para com as Comunidades Lusíadas da América do Norte (com uma carta-prefácio de Sua Eminência o Senhor Cardeal Patriarca de Lisboa)* (Lisbon: Atelieres Gráficos Bertrand, 1945).

[73] Luís da Câmara Pina, 12.

[74] See Luís Reis Torgal, *Estados Novos, Estado Novo* (Coimbra: Imprensa da Universidade de Coimbra, 2009).

[75] Original: "A vida associativa dos portugueses na América é intensa e proveitosa." Pina, 12.

[76] Pina, 17.

[77] Pina, 18-19.

[78] Original: "É um bloco, é um conjunto que avança, isto é, que melhora. Não se trata de situações individuais brilhantes, de um ou outro triunfando em cheio no cenário americano: trata-se da vida honesta e regrada de meio milhão de portugueses que não se escravizaram ao dinheiro, que, talvez sem o saber, dão um exemplo magnífico de dignidade humana. . . . Exercem com proveito as mais variadas profissões; desempenham cargos na administração, nos serviços públicos, até na política; fazem comércio; impulsionam industrias; detêm, em suma, uma parcela de prosperidade que lhes confere segura e despreocupada mediania." Pina, 18.

[79] João de Deus Ramos, Document sent by the secretary of the embassy to the Minister of Foreign Affairs (AHD, Portuguese Embassy in Washington, box 18, no. 117, process 9/34, s.d. [1934]).

[80] "Relações com a colónia portuguesa," document 54 from the Consul of Portugal in New Bedford to the Consul of Portugal in Boston, José de Sacramento Xara Brazil Rodrigues, 9 August 1934 (AHD, Portuguese Embassy in Washington, box 36).

[81] António Ferro (1895-1957) had a unique intellectual trajectory. From a very young age, he displayed a gift for literature and a penchant for journalism. He joined the Portuguese Modernist Movement and became editor of the magazine *Orpheu* (1915). After a stay in Angola as a non-commissioned officer, Ferro returned to Portugal, where he became immersed in political life. In 1921, he became director of the magazine *Ilustração Portuguesa*, where his cultural nationalism became evident. In 1922, Ferro moved to Brasil, where he worked as a theater critic for the *Diário de Lisboa* and wrote the play *Mar Alto*. Upon his return, in 1924, he conducted interviews with dictators, military leaders, and European nationalist intellectuals for *O Século* and the *Diário de Notícias* of Lisbon. Some of these, including those with Benito Mussolinni, Miguel Primo de Rivera, Marshal Philippe, Gabriel d'Annunzio, and Georges Clemenceau, were later published in his book *Viagem à volta das Ditaduras*. In *Prefácio da República Espanhola* (1933) he provides a snapshot of Spanish public life by describing some of its major figures, such as Marcelino Domingo, José Ortega y Gasset, Indalecio Prieto, and Miguel de Unamuno. Ferro identified with the Salazarista project and in 1932 published a series of interviews with António de Oliveira Salazar in *Diário de Notícias*. These were collected in a volume entitled *Salazar: O Homem e a sua obra* (1933), which was translated into several languages. In 1933, Ferro directed the Secretariado de Propaganda Nacional (SPN), putting into practice his interventionist project for Portuguese art and culture, creating the Cinema Popular Ambulante in 1935 and, shortly after, the Teatro do Povo. He was the director of the SPN until 1945, and of the Secretariado Nacional de Informação until

1950. See also Heloisa Paulo, "Ferro, António Gabriel Quadros" in *Dicionário de História do Estado Novo*, vol. I, eds. Fernando Rosas, and J. M. Brandão de Brito (Lisbon: Bertrand Editora, 1996), 355-357. More information on the biography of António Ferro can be found in: Ernesto Castro Leal, *António Ferro. Espaço Político e Imaginário Social (1918-1932)* (Lisbon: Edições Cosmos, 1994); Raquel Pereira Henriques, *António Ferro. Estudo e Antologia* (Lisbon: Alfa, Testemunhos Contemporâneos, 1990); Fernanda de Castro, *Ao Fim da Memória (1906-1897)*, 2 vols (Lisbon: Verbo, 1988); César Oliveira, *A Preparação do 28 de Maio. António Ferro e a Propaganda do Fascismo 1920-1926* (Lisbon: Moraes Editores, Pistas Passado/Presente, 1980); Jorge Ramos de Ó, *Os Anos de Ferro. O dispositivo cultural durante a política do espírito, 1933-1949* (Lisbon: Editorial Estampa, 1999); and Margarida Acciaiuoli, *Antonio Ferro. A Vertigem na Palavra. Retórica, Política e Propaganda no Estado Novo* (Lisbon: Bizâncio, 2013).

[82] Original: "Os portugueses da Nova Inglaterra não desanimam, nem se deixam vencer pela crise. Uns abalam para a Califórnia, outros para Newark, outros escolhem novo modo de vida, empregam-se nas fábricas de aparelhos de T.S.F., nas fábricas de automóveis, nas fábricas de calçado de Boston. Na América há remédio para todas as crises. Mas a pior crise é a crise da própria colónia, a lei da imigração, que reduziu, espantosamente, a nossa quota . . . A colónia portuguesa, todas as cólonias, as latinas, sobretudo, estão condenadas a desaparecer. Resta verificar se os Estados Unidos não sofrerão, também, no seu futuro, com essa injusta condenação."António Ferro, in *A Colonia Portuguesa* (16 December 1927), 12.

[83] "Os Portugueses em New Bedford," *Diario de Noticias*, no. 4851 (24 April 1935), 1.

[84] *Diario de Noticias*, no. 3225 (9 December 1929), 1.

[85] Original: "Estando a maior parte da colónia ocupada na agricultura, a sua vida, portanto, é a vida simples e abundante dos campos. Na agricultura o português tem-se destacado na Califórnia pela sua perícia no amanho das terras, pelo seu aturado trabalho e pela sua frugalidade. Ele consegue tirar três colheitas donde o americano só tira uma. Não desperdiça, mas também não se priva do necessário à vida. Aproveita as vantagens que o meio lhe oferece e vive com a higiene e conforto de qualquer lavrador americano. Além disto, as suas reconhecidas qualidades de adaptabilidade e brio próprio fazem com que os seus 'standards' de vida não sejam inferiores aos das outras raças." "Relações com a colónia portuguesa"; "Inquérito Consular segundo o disposto na circular de 20 de Junho de 1934, processo 524/34, da 2ª repartição da direcção geral dos Negócios Estrangeiros," from the Consul of Portugal in San Francisco, October 2, 1934 (AHD, Portuguese Embassy in Washington, box no 36).

[86] Original: "As condições higiénicas são boas. Com respeito a vestuário tanto homens como mulheres vestem regularmente; fatos e vestidos têm o mesmo corte e aparência que os das classes mais abastadas sendo a única diferença na qualidade de tecido." "Relações com a colónia portuguesa."

[87] Original quote by Rodrigues: "em conformidade com a sua limitada cultura." "Inquérito Consular sobre a situação das colónias portuguesas no estrangeiro." Response by the consul in Boston, 12 September 1934. (AHD, Portuguese Embassy in Washington, box no 36).

[88] "Inquérito Consular sobre a situação das colónias portuguesas no estrangeiro."

[89] Original: "No que se refere às suas condições de vida e indumentária, poderíamos repetir o que afirmamos no nosso relatório de 1929, isto é, que no que diz respeito às colónias latinas e outras a variante não é grande, havendo exemplos de casas de portugueses limpas, arejadas e com confortos desconhecidos a muita gente de classes mais elevadas em Portugal. É sobretudo entre os portugueses com família nos dois Estados de que tratamos mais desenvolvidamente, e entre os luso-americanos, que tal facto se apresenta, devendo com tudo não deixar de salientar o fenómeno contrário entre muitos outros indivíduos que vivem em condições menos vantajosas, já pelo espírito da economia forçada que os leva a amealhar o que podem e o que não podem para regressar à Pátria, já por falta de hábitos de conforto e higiene. Nao é raro ver-se um grupo de três ou quatro indivíduos compartilhando um mesmo quarto, vivendo numa aglomeração anti-higiénica de promiscuidade desnecessária. No que se refere à indumentária, o português apresenta-se sempre decentemente vestido e calçado. Quanto à alimentação, a não ser por falta de trabalho, quantas Pensões (Casas de Bordo, como lhe chamam por deturpação do inglês 'boarding-house') lhes fiam!, o colono alimenta-se bem. Não existem na área mais próxima do Consulado Geral indústrias portuguesas. Há alguns estabelecimentos dirigidos já por portugueses, já por luso-americanos, especialmente Casas de Pasto, Casas de Hóspedes, Mercearias, Salsicharias, Lojas de Carvão, Floristas, Leitarias e Casas de Peixe." Verdades de Faria, document 21 (proc. 37-34) from the Consul General in New York to the ambassador of Portugal, 20 February 1934 (AHD, Portuguese Embassy in Washington, box 18).

[90] Original: "Congregar os cidadãos portugueses e os da sua origem, tornando-os uma classe forte, respeitada e prestigiada usando como língua oficial a Portuguesa e respeitando os poderes constituídos na Nossa Querida Pátria e os do País em que vivemos." "Propaganda de Portugal," report sent by d'Oliveira, president of Club Social Português de Yorkers, to the Consul of Portugal in New York, 10 January, 1934 (AHD, Portuguese Embassy in Washington, box 18, proc. no 9).

[91] Original: "O facto de a colónia ter deixado de crescer por falta de sangue novo vindo da Pátria que a venha vigorar." *Diario de Noticias*, no. 5274 (16 September 1936), 1.

[92] Leo Pap, *The Portuguese-Americans*, 35-65.

[93] For a sociological, demographic and economic analysis of the Portuguese community in Massachusetts in the early twentieth century, see: Donald R. Taft.

[94] Verdades de Faria, document 21 (proc. 37-34) of the Consul General of New York to the ambassador of Portugal, 20 February 1934 (AHD, Portuguese Embassy in Washington, box 18). Regarding the press, the Consul said the following in his report: "Referring to the Portuguese language press, I think that I only need to inform your Excellency that the owner of the 'tribune' (referring to *A Tribuna Portuguesa*), is an Italian who, in addition to publishing other newspapers in the Italian language newspapers, is also involved in the travel agency business, and that the director-owner of 'Portugal,' which is published sporadically, is also not a Portuguese citizen, adding that both papers are experiencing difficulties." Original: "No que se refere à Imprensa que se publica em língua portuguesa, só julgo necessitar informar V. Excia. de que o proprietário da 'tribuna' [*A Tribuna Portuguesa*] é um italiano que explora, juntamente com a publicação de outras folhas em língua italiana, o ramo de agência de passagens, e que o diretor-proprietário do 'Portugal,' que se publica espasmodicamente, também não é cidadão português, vivendo ambas as folhas com dificuldades."

[95] Document 4 from the Consul of Portugal in San Francisco to the ambassador of Portugal, 8 January 1934 (AHD, Portuguese Embassy in Washington, box 18). Attached: "Relação das agremiações portuguesas e imprensa no Estado de Califórnia e Honolulu, Hawai." The list of associations is the following. In California: Associação Portuguesa Protectora Beneficiente, Irmandade do Divino Espirito Santo, União Portuguesa do Estado de Califórnia, Associação Protectora União Madeirense, União Portuguesa Continental, Real Associação Beneficiente Autonómica Incorporada (sucursal de MA), Fraternidade Portuguesa (sucursal de MA), Sociedade do Espírito Santo, Irmandade de Santa Maria Madalena, Sociedade Portuguesa Rainha Santa Isabel, União Portuguesa do Estado da California; clubs: Clube Lusitânia, Portuguese-American Civic Club, Clube Recreativo Português, Clube Natercia, Sociedade Luso-Americana, and Clube Lusitano. In Honolulu: Santo António Beneficiente de Hawaii, Sociedade Lusitana Beneficiente de Hawaii, and Sociedade de São Martinho Beneficiente de Hawaii.

[96] Fausto Avendaño, 159.

[97] Leo Pap, *The Portuguese-Americans*, 94-102.

[98] Hyon B. Shin with Rosalind Brun, "Language Use and English-Speaking Ability: 2000" https://www.census.gov/prod/2003pubs/c2kbr-29.pdf. [Consulted December 2018]

[99] See Attilio Bartoli Langeli, 87-106.

[100] In 1930, the illiteracy rate in Portugal affected 70% of women and 55% of men. See: Maria Cândida Proença, "Analfabetismo," in *Dicionário de História do Estado Novo*. vol. I, eds. Fernando Rosas, and J. M. Brandão de Brito (Lisbon: Bertrand Editora, 1996). See also Maria Filomena Mónica, "'Deve-se ensinar o povo a ler?': a questão do analfabetismo (1926-39)," *Análise Social*, XIII-50 (1977-2°): 321-353.

[101] Leo Pap, "The Portuguese Press," in *The Ethnic Press in the United States. A Historical Analysis and Handbook*, ed. Sally M. Miller, (New York-Westport-Connecticut-London: Greenwood Press, 1987), 293.

[102] Leo Pap, *Portuguese-American Speech* (New York: King's Crown Press [Columbia University], 1949).

[103] See George Monteiro, *Caldo Verde is not Stone Soup: Persons, Names, Words and Proverbs in Portuguese America* (New York-Oxford-Berne: Peter Lang, 2017).

[104] *O Lavrador Português*, no. 118, (third year, 4 September 1915), 1.

[105] Eduardo Mayone Dias, 74. Editor's Note: Fighter planes are called *aviões caça* (literally, chase planes) in Portuguese. Omitting the cedilla changes the meaning of the word from chase to feces.

[106] Original: "Se a imprensa portuguesa da América do Norte houvesse de ser o único e exclusivo padrão por onde aquilatar o valor da Colónia, seríamos obrigados a confessar, com dolorosa sinceridade, ser ela a mais decadente e atrasada entre todas as que contribuem para a grandeza e progresso deste poderoso povo. Com tão raras como louváveis exceções, os jornais portugueses são feitos de retalhos mal traduzidos e péssimamente cerzidos, numa linguagem que logo se vê ter sido escrita por mãos que a Providência mais fadara para apontar brochas e pôr tombas do que para manejar uma pena. A bela linguagem de Camões e de Vieira sofre tratos de pôle nesses calvários, onde ela nos aparece mais repugnantemente afistulada do que o Leproso de Aosta." Eduardo de

Carvalho, *Os Portugueses na Nova Inglaterra*, 131. The work, based on an official report for the Portuguese government, is a valuable document that contains, among other content, the full list of the existing literature in institutions of higher education and in major U.S. libraries.

[107] Original: "termos ingleses e americanismos, aplicados a coisas e objetos que o imigrante desconhecia em Portugal; termos portugueses empregados numa aceção diferente; frases inglesas e modismos americanos traduzidos à letra para português; uso da sintaxe inglesa." Eduardo de Carvalho, *A Língua Portuguesa nos Estados Unidos* (Boston: Editora Empresa de Propaganda Patriótica, 1925), 67. Extracted from the consular report from Boston, 9 April 1924.

[108] The term "portinglês" was coined by Adalino Cabral in his doctoral dissertation "Portinglês. The Language of Portuguese-Speaking People in Selected English-Speaking Communities" (Ann Arbor: University of Michigan, 1986).

[109] Eduardo de Carvalho, *A Língua Portuguesa nos Estados Unidos*, 68-81.

[110] *Diario de Noticias*, no. 2648 (16 January 1928), 2.

[111] Original: "Porque não devemos esquecer, uma parte também importante no afervoramento desse culto cabe iniludivelmente aos nossos sacerdotes. Se não fosse o jornal e o púlpito quase teria desaparecido o uso da língua portuguesa em território americano. E todavia torna-se necessário, para que o mal não alastre mais ainda, que todos reforcem a propaganda, que todos ponham neste assunto o seu maior interesse e empenho." *A Alvorada* (6 December 1926), 2.

[112] Original: "Em toda a parte um cônsul deve ser justo, imparcial e tolerante. Na América deve ser tudo isto e mais *Enérgico, Eficiente e Expedito*. Quando um português precisa de qualquer serviço numa repartição pública da América, está acostumado a ser servido naquele momento. Venha logo ou venha amanhã são frases que ele já não está acostumado a ouvir." *Alvorada Diária*, no. 728 (26 August 1921), 2.

[113] Original: "Somos tantos mil açoreanos e não temos um cônsul açoreano? É justo que cada grupo colonial tenha o seu representante! Estamos fartos de ser mandados e explorados por meninos do Continente." Eduardo de Carvalho, *Os Portugueses na Nova Inglaterra*, 123.

[114] Original: "sempre que há um jornal feito para dar lucro e não para semear ideias, facilmente o vemos cair, em determinado momento, num inventor ou explorador de escândalos." Eduardo de Carvalho, 120-121.

[115] See: Geoffrey Gomes, "The Portuguese Language Press in California: The Response to American Politics, 1880-1928."

[116] Eduardo Mayone Dias, 70.

[117] "Jornais portugueses querelados." *Jornal Português*, no. 680 (Special Issue of 1945, N.P).

[118] *Diario de Noticias*, no. 3226 (10 December 1929), 1.

[119] Original: "Não nos surpreendeu a notícia por quanto a notícia daquele funcionário desde há muito tempo tinha tornado necessária a sua exoneração, apesar da importância balôfa do seu apregoado patriotismo com que, em várias ocasiões pretendeu conquistar as boas graças dos pobres de espírito." *Diario de Noticias*, no. 3218 (November 1929), 1.

[120] Original: "A colónia, sem dúvida, deve ainda recordar o que a imprensa colonial relatou acerca dos 'rasgos' de má fé e petulância que Abílio O. Águas praticou para conseguir a nomeação de cônsul de Portugal em Providence." *Diario de Noticias*, no. 3218 (November 1929), 1.

[121] "Águas vêm... Águas vão..." *Diario de Noticias, no.* 3230 (14 December 1929), 6.

[122] "A Exoneração de A. Oliveira Águas – As notas fornecidas à imprensa, especialmente aos jornais de Providence, de que a colónia protesta contra a medida do governo português, não passa de 'bluff.' 'Essa colónia' não passa de um 'bando' composto de meia duzia de indivíduos de carácter duvidoso." *Diario de Noticias*, no. 3218 (30 November 1929), 1.

[123] *Diario de Noticias*, no. 3218 (30 November 1929), 1.

[124] The series of articles by João R. Rocha were titled "A situação política de Massachusetts e Rhode Island." Some of them can be read in the following excerpts from the *Diario de Noticias*, no 3495 (29 October 1929), 1; no 3497 (31 October 1929), 1; and no 3499 (3 November 1929), 1.

[125] *Diario de Noticias*, no. 3495 (29 October 1930), 1.

[126] Original: "Com insistência o seu jornal me tem alvejado de maneira que me dispenso de apreciar. Bem ou mal escolhi a atitude de me manter em silêncio, facilitando-lhes o poderem demostrar nos tribunais as agressões que me dirigem e deixando ao meio, aonde somos todos conhecidos, o julgamento que lhes merecermos. Neste mutismo, próprio de quem tem a consciência tranquila, me conservaria se, para me atingirem, não principiassem V. Sres., agora a visar terceiras pessoas . . . pertencentes à sociedade Americana, perante a que me esforcei sempre para que os portugueses aparecessem prestigiados e merecedores de respeito. Vejo-me por isso obrigado a enviar-lhes os meus protestos contra os ataques que dirigem ao antigo Senador Federal Peter Goelet Gerry, só por este senhor me distinguir com a sua amizade." *Diario de Noticias*, no. 3499 (3 November 1930), 1.

[127] See: William Leonard Joyce, *Editors and Ethnicity. A History of the Irish-American Press, 1848-1883* (New York: Arno Press, 1976).

[128] Leara D. Rhodes, 125.

[129] Original: "Mas as vítimas, em sua maioria, preferem levar a contribuir para que os estrangeiros saibam como são alguns portugueses, ou alguns dos que se proclamam portugueses. Dir-se-ia uma desordem dentro de uma casa fechada. Não se chama a polícia. Em nome dos interesses da Pátria, dos interesses da Colónia e dos interesses da Justiça, o articulista arremete contra o Governo e contra os cônsules, contra uma Associação, uma iniciativa, uma tentativa, um colega que teve uma boa encomenda ou um anúncio de meia página, um cidadão que cometeu o erro de fazer fortuna, de conquistar a simpatia de bairro ou de por algo se distinguir. Nunca nos períodos em que a violenta imprensa portuguesa foi mais violenta, se chegou aos extremos a que chegam os foliculários da Colónia, que às vezes parecem atacados dum delírio soez, do sadismo do impropério." Eduardo de Carvalho, *Os Portugueses na Nova Inglaterra*, 121-122.

[130] Original: "Sem estímulo, muito têm feito os portugueses aqui. Precisam de quem os oriente e não os disperse. Necessitam de uma obra de coesão, que os faça sentir todo o poder duma alma nacional, capaz de todos os prodígios. É esse sentimento que realiza

os milagres, tantas vezes apontados, da iniciativa portuguesa fóra da Pátria. Em número temos portugueses que chegam para tudo. Para todas as instituições, para todas as iniciativas. Não as apouquemos. Salientemos, pelo contrário, a sua importância moral ou material, para que elas sejam as instituições de todos os portugueses. Chamem-se todos os nossos à efetividade de serviço na campanha pelo nosso próprio desenvolvimento e prestígio. Não nos degladiemos uns aos outros. Há campo de sobra para que todas as iniciativas frutifiquem. Discutam-se os problemas à luz do dia. Ninguém quer nem mistérios, nem sobas. Nem se compreendem uns, nem se toleram outros. Reconheçamos as boas intenções de toda a gente, o que não quer dizer que aceitemos de olhos fechados tudo o que se apresenta como dogma." editorial "Críticas à Colónia," *Diario de Noticias*, no. 2435 (4 May 1927), 2.

[131] Eduardo de Carvalho, "Pátria Portuguesa," in *Pregar no Deserto* (Rio de Janeiro: Teixeira & C. Ltda. 1929), 12-14.

[132] Original: "Estas cartas constituem uma obra de propaganda, e uma obra de propaganda nunca foi uma obra de rigorosa exactidão e crítica. A propaganda sincera não sai da Verdade, mas tem de sair, necessariamente, das proporções justas a que os factos e os homens se condicionam. O que são, o que valem, o que fazem e o que podem fazer os nossos compatriotas do antigo Consulado em Boston, a excelência das instituições que criaram, o aperfeiçoamento que atingiram, a função que exercem em relação a Portugal e em relação a Estados Unidos, eis o tema de um estudo profundo e meditado, que não tenho competência para escrever." Eduardo de Carvalho, "Pátria Portuguesa," 12.

Chapter 2 The Dimensions of the Portuguese Press in the United States

[1] Figure taken from António Luís Vicente, 61.

[2] Alexandre Alberto Sousa Pinto was the Minister of Public Education in Portugal between July 24, 1933 and October 23, 1934.

[3] The report was published under the title: "A Imprensa Portuguesa nos Estados Unidos de América do Norte," *Diario de Noticias* no. 4333 (4 August 1933), 1 and 8; and no. 4338 (10 August 1933), 4-5 (edited version). (The second version can be found in the study by Rui Antunes Correia, "Salazar em New Bedford. Leituras Luso-Americanas do Estado Novo nos Anos Trinta" (Master's thesis, Centro de Estudos Anglísticos da Universidade de Lisboa, 2004).

[4] Rui Antunes Correia.

[5] Original: "É uma soberba, uma heróica teimosia. Tudo conspira para o seu aniquilamento: a falta de quaisquer estímulos, vindos da Pátria distante, a encorajar essas iniciativas; a hostilidade do ambiente em que se desenvolve, cioso sempre na sua faina de assimilação dos povos; as camadas iletradas, que, em grande parte formam o organismo colonial." *Diario de Noticias* no. 4338 (10 August 1933), 4.

[6] Original: "Vai, nesta hora, a colónia luso-americana ultrapassando o Cabo das Tormentas da crise medonha, que avassalou este país, e que fez acrescentar mais uma página dolorosa à negra tragédia da atividade jornalística dos portugueses. O caso especial

da crise, no entanto, apenas agravou uma situação que foi sempre precária, que foi sempre tempestuosa, quadro em que se inscrevem sempre encalhes, desmantelamentos, naufrágios. Nenhuma empresa jornalística desde que se constituiu aqui uma colónia portuguesa, obteve, em si mesma, recursos para poder singrar através dos tempos. A sua estabilidade, a sua persistência medem-se pelo sacríficio pessoal de quem as tenta, de quem as põe em ação. Por isso desaparecem na voragem, desde os quotidianos às publicações de menor vulto, não dispondo de apetrechamentos tipográficos, sendo redigidos por amadores e 'dillettanti' que não representam sobrecarga no orçamento de despesa. Nestas condições vive a maioria dos jornais coloniais." *Diario de Noticias*, no. 4338 (10 August 1933), 4.

[7] According to the data provided by António Luís Vicente, the number of Portuguese-Americans in the state of Pennsylvania in 1998 was 9,209. Vicente, 61.

[8] *Alvorada*, no. 1005 (15 August 1922), 1.

[9] *A Colonia Portuguesa*, no. 383 (16 December 1927), 1.

[10] *A Colonia Portuguesa*, no. 383 (16 December 1927), 1.

[11] H. W. Kastor & Sons, *Newpaper and Magazine Directory* (Chicago-St. Louis-Kansas City: H.W. Kastor & Sons Advertising Co., 1906), 167.

[12] H. W. Kastor & Sons, 167.

[13] *O Progresso Californiense*, no. 94 (year 3, 1 January 1887), 2.

[14] *A União Portuguesa*, no. 205 (25 August 1892), 3.

[15] Nelson Chesman & Co's Rates Book, *Newspaper Rate Book 1899. Including a Catalogue of Newspapers and Periodicals in the United States and Canada.* St. Louis-Chicago-New York: Nelson Chesman & Co. Publishers, 1899), 234.

[16] See: *Jornal Português*, no. 191 (14 February 1936), 1.

[17] *Alvorada Diária*, no. 864 (year 4, 8 February 1922), 2.

[18] "Artigos e Editorais sobre Política Portuguesa," no. 1182 (AHD, document 335, proc. 3.25). From the ambassador of Portugal in Washington, João de Bianchi, to the Minister of Foreign Affairs, 29 September 1967.

[19] See: www.lusoamericano.com. [Consulted June 2019]

[20] It is necessary to be cautious of some of these figures, since the lack of original newspaper sources to check each figure can lead to inaccuracies.

[21] See Daniel Georgianna (with Roberta Hazen Aaronson), *The Strike of '28*, (New Bedford, MA: Spinner Publications, 2019).

[22] Original: "Ao trazermos de novo às fileiras jornalísticas o antigo Luso-Americano, justo é que, obedecendo às praxes estabelecidas, digamos aos nossos assinantes e leitores quais são as nossas intenções ou, por outras palavras, qual é o programa que pretendemos seguir. Desempenharemo-nos dessa missão duma maneira muito simples e breve declarando que esse programa consiste e consistirá em dedicarmos os nossos esforços ao desenvolvimento e progresso da nossa colónia, a que daremos sempre um lugar de honra nas colunas deste periódico. Isto quer dizer que não faremos política de campanário, assim como não venderemos as nossas penas a pessoas desonestas ou a interesses obscuros por mais que, mercê da boa fé de uns ou da mal justificada complacência e

vergonhosa proteção de outros, constumem medrar entre nós. A BEM DA COLÓNIA, será a nossa divisa e a ela se dedicará o Luso-Americano. Eis o programa que preparamos e para cuja execução pedimos a valiosa cooperação de todos os nosso conterrâneos. A Redação." *Luso-Americano*, no. 1 (7 December 1939), 1. See also: *Luso-Americano* (6 December 1989, Special 50th Anniversary Edition), 2.

[23] "Inquérito Consular sobre a situação das colónias portuguesas no estrangeiro" (AHD, Portuguese Embassy in Washington, document 36). Response from the Consul in Boston, 12 September 1934.

[24] *Luso-Americano* (25 October 1989), 39.

[25] *Luso-Americano* (25 November 1989), 34.

[26] Vamberto A. Freitas, "Algumas considerações sobre a Imprensa Portuguesa nos Estados Unidos," *Portugal/USA* (7 January 1987). Cited by Eduardo Mayone Dias, 75.

[27] August Mark Vaz, *The Portuguese in California* (Oakland, CA: IDES Supreme Council, 1965), 139.

[28] The article appears cited by "Notas do editor", *A Revista Portuguesa*, no. 2 (February 1915). 12.

[29] *A California Alegre* (21 November 1937), 4.

[30] Original: "mercê de uma política reles e escandalosa que se fazia então em Portugal." *Diario de Noticias*, no. 11982 (26 March 1959), 1. Article cited by Rui A. Correia, 34.

[31] Original: "Dá-se até o caso curioso de ser o povo inculto que mais fala o português, facto que revela a ridicula 'inferiority complex' que ataca a maioria das pessoas cultas ou com cursos superiores." *Diario de Noticias*, no 6446 (31 July 1940), 2.

[32] August Mark Vaz, 139-141.

[33] Original: "A Imprensa em geral da Califórnia a par dos muitos serviços que tem prestado a varias gerações de Portugueses é um repositório da gloriosa história do quinhão que coube ao povo Português no deslumbrante desenvolvimento deste próspero Estado e traspondo essas mesmas barreiras como contemporânea que foi dos primeiros passos de tão vertiginoso progresso, encerra a crónica de toda a vida da Califórnia. Saúdo a imprensa Portuguesa, que bem merece da Pátria Portuguesa e do Portugal da Califórnia, pelo passado que a dignifica, e ao desejar-lhe um futuro cheio de prosperidade, confio que continuará a manter a sua valorosa obra a bem do Povo e da Nação Portuguesa." *A Liberdade*, no 3300 (year 35, 7 September 1935), 1.

[34] Original: "Até hoje os governantes de Portugal têm desprezado absolutamente a imprensa portuguesa na América. Têm abandonado, com ingratidão imperdoável, essa poderosa fonte de reclamo e esse elo indispensável para continuar vivo o amor pátrio nos corações portugueses. Esta imprensa, apesar de pobre, muito tem concorrido para que a colónia esteja ainda agregada num todo . . . O que tem feito Portugal no respeitante aos portugueses que emigraram para aqui? Absolutamente nada de concreto. Nunca é tarde para remediar uma falta." *Diario de Noticias*, no. 5930 (16 November 1938), 2.

[35] Rui Antunes Correia, 36.

[36] Original: "A maior culpa deve ser atribuída aos nossos Ministros da Instrução em Portugal que nos votaram ao esquecimento, nunca compensando, pelo menos com

palavras de encorajamento, os esforços dos portugueses neste país que muito têm contribuído para a propaganda da Pátria, tanto por meio dos jornais como escolas particulares." *Diario de Noticias*, no. 6152 (11 August 1939), 1.

[37] Original: "Dependendo duma colónia relativamente pobre e muito dispersa tem além disso que lutar contra dois poderosos obstáculos, a saber: os jornais do país, colossos de informação que abrangem todas as atividades do mundo inteiro; e o que é pior, a indiferença duma grande parte dos colonos que lhe negam o apoio devido." *Diario de Noticias*, no. 5142 (7 April 1936), 4.

[38] *A California Alegre* (January 1 and 15, 1939), 4.

[39] Original: "A imprensa portuguesa é a alma da colónia! É ela que anuncia as nossas festas, defende os interesses dos nosso compatriotas, faz propaganda das coletividades, publica notícias da nossa Pátria, aviva o patriotismo, ventila questões locais e leva através dos núcleos portugueses as notícias tristes dos que exalaram neste país o último sopro de vida, longe da nossa terra que lhes serviu de berço. É ainda a imprensa que no seu dever sagrado para com o público, desmascara os poltrões que vêm para aqui vigarizar a colónia. É a imprensa, que sempre ao serviço dos nossos compatriotas, franqueia as suas colunas para socorrer os necessitados, os doentes e aqueles a quem a crueldade do destino fere profundamente! São os nossos jornais que vão de porta em porta pedir auxílio para os desafortunados, abrindo subscrições e cooperando de braço dado com a Caridade! Não pedimos honras nem proveitos exagerados pelo importante papel que desenmpenhamos na vida colonial, mas pedimos Justiça, Consideração – e COOPERAÇÃO! Chegamos a uma época em que a Colónia Portuguesa DEVE assumir a responsabilidade que lhe cabe para com a Imprensa. Fugir a essa reponsabilidade é uma ação anti-patriótica, anti-portuguesa e desmoralizadora das qualidades cultas de os representantes de um povo no estrangeiro. Investiguem a existência de todos os jornais portugueses neste país, e encontrarão que a sua publicação é uma epopeia de sacrifícios, de desgostos e de desilusões, imolados no altar da Pátria e da Língua Portuguesa. E ainda há imbecis que escarnecem dos nossos jornais, que os lêem de 'borla' e ufanam-se de jamais ter pago uma assinatura: essa insignificante quantia que anualmente não faz falta aos que a desembolsam." *A Luta*, no. 10 (year 2, 2 February 1938), 1.

[40] Original: "mártires do dever e do amor ao país onde nasceram."

[41] Original: "Que vão trabalhar se querem comer, diz a pequenina mentalidade de alguns, como se eles, esses pobres trabalhadores da imprensa, levassem vida ociosa, extravagante e regalada."

[42] Original: "A nossa imprensa deve merecer-nos mais carinho e mais consideração para que os povos civilizados não nos tomem por selvagens. Temos bons jornais portugueses na Califórnia e devemos assiná-los e auxiliá-los para verdadeiro prestígio da nossa colónia e bom nome do povo português deste Estado." *A California Alegre*, no. 1 (series IV, 23 May 1936), 4.

[43] Original: "A profissão de jornalista é muito ingrata, porque o nosso povo ainda não compreendeu a sua missão; vê nele, e algumas vezes com razão, o explorador que vive da tesoura, e que quer impingir esse trabalho ao leitor e trocá-lo pelo suor do rosto de um trabalhador. Mas não, nao há missão mais sublime do que a de alimentar o espírito do nosso povo com leitura sã, que depois de digirida alguma coisa de proveito deixe.

O jornal, com as suas diversas secções, deve ser uma escola onde o povo possa beber a água pura dos conhecimentos humanos, reunidos e coligidos por homens que tenham estudado ou adquirido esses conhecimentos. Infelizmente, dizem, não há jornais na Califórnia que possam atingir esse desideratum. É facto, e a razão é que não tendo o apoio do povo o jornal nao pode progredir por não poder manter pessoal competente." *A Colonia Portuguesa*, no 171 (year 11, 3 November 1925), 4.

44 Original: "O assinante que recebe o jornal e que ao fim do seu dia de trabalho se senta confortavelmente numa cadeira lendo o jornal, não calcula, não imagina, não faz uma pequenina ideia do esforço, das arrelias, e das canseiras do pobre jornalista português na América do Norte. Não avalia o quanto sofrimento e de lutas estão aí representadas nestas páginas que os seus olhos percorrem. Isto, meus caros patrícios, desde a angariação de anúncios, à feitura das gravuras, desde a composição dos artigos, leitura da revisão das provas à paginação do jornal vai uma avalanche de vontade, uma montanha de sacrifícios de trabalho arduo, de trabalho 'duro e forte' no dizer pitoresco da nossa gente. E ainda há pessoas (oh! Santa ignorância!) que dizem que se os jornalistas querem comer que vão trabalhar!" "O Esforço na Confeção do 'Jornal Português'," *Jornal Português* (special issue of 1946).

45 See: Kimberly DaCosta Holton, and Andrea Klimt, eds., *Community, Culture and the Makings of Identity: Portuguese-Americans along the Eastern Seaboard* (North Dartmouht: Tagus Press, Center for Portuguese Studies and Culture-University of Massachusetts Dartmouth, 2009).

46 August Mark Vaz, 140.

47 "Saber ler Português," *Jornal Português* (special issue of 1953).

48 Original: "o mais belo poema de amor à Pátria Portuguesa nos Estados Unidos." Article by Josefina do Canto e Castro, "Da Nossa Imprensa," *Diario de Noticias* (special 50th anniversary issue, 12 May 1969).

49 *Diario de Noticias* (31 December 1935), 2.

50 Original: "Interessa-nos, consequentemente, a existência deste jornal – o *Diário de Notícias* – para quem trabalho e de quem vivo no presente – porque à sua vida e à sua expansão está ligado o nome da Colónia Portuguesa dos Estados Unidos da América. É que, sendo o único diário no Leste a advogar os nossos interesses coletivos e a defender os nossos direitos, o seu desaparecimento, que é uma questão de anos, muitos ou poucos, não importa quando, equivalerá, quando vier, ao princípio do fim da extinção da raça portuguesa nos Estados Unidos o que nós, por todas as razões e motivos devemos protelar, retardar e combater ininterruptamente até não mais poder." *Diario de Noticias*, no 928 (20 January 1928), 1.

51 Original: "Desde o momento que pode travar com o patrão, o camarada ou vizinho estabelece o seguinte diálogo: 'Are you a citizen?' 'I am a citizen,' o neófito passa do receio da deportação ao sentimento de ser candidato a Mayor de New York ou até a Presidente dos Estados Unidos – se não para si, pelo menos para os seus filhos –, que sabe terão uma educação garantida e um 'even chance' com os outros milhões de criaturas que o cercam e que começam a vida pouco mais ou menos da mesma maneira e atingem grandes situações por formas sem paralelo noutros países. Se é esta a revolução que se opera no seu coração, há mutações na vida prática que são imediatas embora menos

pomposas. O evitar que lhe digam que havendo tantos americanos desempregados não podem empregar um estrangeiro; o vencer a barreira do desnível entre os trabalhadores americanos e estrangeiros e até a possibilidade de exercer certas profissões ou negócios por conta própria sem o recurso a subterfúgios ou participação de americanos, além de muitas outras garantias e facilidades." Confidential Letter 47 from ambassador, João de Bianchi, to the Minister of Foreign Affairs (AHD, Portuguese Embassy in Washington, document 36, 19 June 1934, proc. 30/34).

[52] "Relações com a colónia portuguesa" (AHD, Portuguese Embassy in Washington. Document 36, 20 August 1935), 2. Inquérito consular sobre a colónia portuguesa sob a jurisdicção do Consulado Geral de Portugal em Nova York, signed by the General Consul, Verdades de Faria.

[53] Original: "Não se dá geralmente com facilidade não só devido ao amor à Pátria, como também à resistência atávica em adquirir uma nova língua, hábitos e costumes." Idem, 3.

[54] Original: "Americanos verdadeiros só são os indianos."

[55] Original: "A palavra 'naturalizado' ou o ato de se naturalizar cidadão dos Estados Unidos, não tem a interpretação 'negra e feia' ou 'aterradora' que o português lhe dá ou interpreta em Portugal. Um português que se nacionaliza protege os seus direitos civis e ao mesmo tempo torna-se útil nos afazeres e destinos da sua comunidade, na Administração do seu Estado e na deste grande país em geral. Os Estados Unidos é uma nação nova, com menos de duzentos anos e foi fundada por gente de diversas raças e credos, ansiosa por liberdade; e se hoje é a maior democracia e a mais rica do mundo, é porque a amálgama que forma o seu povo. . . . Isto é o que se chama democracia. Pobre ou rico os seus direitos civis são iguais." "Explicações necessárias," *Jornal Português* (special Issue of 1949).

[56] Original: "São dez horas e o jornal está a ir para o prelo. Uma das páginas está incompleta. Falta o editorial. Perdido, gasto o tempo em diversas tecnicalidades, o editorial é sempre a última caldeirada e, muitas vezes, o editor vê-se num labirinto sem saída, à procura de assunto. Escrever. Mas escrever o quê, em dez ou quinze minutos? Oh! Que entaladelas apanha o pobre editor! Mas alguma coisa tem de ser feita, visto que é muito feio o jornal sair sem levar um 'artigo da casa,' como vulgarmente se diz. Pego nalgum jornal americano em busca de alguma coisa de sensação. Crimes, divórcios, suicídios. Assuntos bons, não há dúvida, mas de que nos repugna já falar, por ser o maior prato que todos os dias lemos nos jornais. . . Mas que diabo vou escrever?"

[57] Guilherme Silveira da Glória, *Poesias de Guilherme S. Glória* (Oakland, CA: Tipographia de "A Liberdade," 1935).

[58] Original: "Nas POESIAS de Guilherme Glória não há apenas sentimento, impulsos abstratos, resíduos imperecíveis duma raça; na forma admirável do trovador perpassam os factos, as pessoas, toda a vida da grei portuguesa nestas paragens. Ninguém prodigalizou tanto a inspiração, para retratar a alma portuguesa, em carmes de entusiasmo e de veneração." "Poesias," *Diario de Noticias* (23 February 1935), 2.

[59] Rui Antunes Correia, 49.

[60] Original: "Não sabemos a que atribuir este mau gosto em alguns portugueses de New York e New Jersey. Que compatriotas se naturalizavam americanos por razões várias que se justificam, já nós sabíamos, mas que também os havia com desejo de ser espanhol, isso brada aos céus senhores!! . . . Não aceitamos desculpas que são contrasensos, nem

justificações que nada justificam. É um facto de todos conhecido que os jornais da colónia são pequenos e falhos num sem-número de particularidades. Falta-lhes muito, muito mesmo. Deixam muito, muito a desejar – segundo os críticos alegam. Mas eles, os nossos jornais, são o reflexo de uma colónia pequena e enfezada de múltiplos e vários contratempos. O jornal moderno é o espelho do meio em que a sua ação se faz sentir. Tanto reflete o progresso e o avanço de um povo, como foca o seu estado estagnado ou em descomposição. Como, pois, exigir mais deste jornal, que apenas tem representado um encargo, um dispêndio, digamos mesmo um prejuízo para aqueles que teimam em publicá-lo? . . . Malgrado esse pequeno grupo de "portugueses espanholados," que prefere a mesa espiritual mais atraente do vizinho velhaco à mesa pobre mas acarinhadora da mãe amantiva, a grande maioria, a grande totalidade, quase todos os que formam a Colónia Portuguesa dos estados de Leste apoiam a Imprensa Portuguesa, compreendem a necessidade que há de manter os seus órgãos de publicidade e se mais não fazem é porque isso lhes é impossível, é porque lhes falta os recursos ou o meio e as condições lhes não permitem ir para além na sua coadjuvação." *Diario de Noticias*, no. 928 (20 January 1930), 1. Part of the quotation is collected in the thesis by Rui A. Correia, 50-51.

[61] Original: "A caça ao anúncio não chega para satisfazer as necessidades e os apetites. Os anunciantes, notando que o jornal tem uma circulação reduzida, deixam de lhe dar dinheiro. O leitor desinteressa-se. . . . Não há outro remédio senão abrir uma campanha, atrair as atenções com artigos sensacionais, agitar a opinião." Eduardo de Carvalho, *Os Portugueses na Nova Inglaterra*, 121.

[62] Original: "Um jornal morre todos os dias. Mal se acaba de fazer e já há que pensar na confeção do número seguinte. O leitor percorre os milhões de caracteres nele contidos, dá-lhes uns momentos da manhã ou da tarde, e logo os abandona e os esquece. O jornal viveu a sua efémera existência, cumpriu o seu destino e foi sorvido pela voragem das horas e dos acontecimentos. Tem sido escrito em sua sina: é um rei de vinte e quatro horas." Guilherme Pereira da Rosa, *Estados Unidos* (Lisbon: Editorial Século, 1953), 14-15.

[63] It should be taken into account that some of the editors founded multiple newspapers. In these statistics, each one of them is considered independently. Therefore, if the same editor from Pico was the founder of five newspapers, each one of them is computed as if there are five editors from the same place of origin.

[64] The Italian editor was Joseph Merola, the typographer that published *A Tribuna* for the Portuguese community in New Jersey. In the case of Brazil, the only recorded editor was Manoel Stone, owner of *A Voz Portugueza* from San Francisco and *A Pátria* from Oakland, published at the end of the nineteenth century. Eugénio Tavares was the Cabo Verdean editor and founder of *A Alvorada* of New Bedford.

[65] Original: "Ordinariamente, os jornais têm sido fundados por tipógrafos, que, chegados à América, acham doloroso trabalhar nas fábricas ou por algum indivíduo com jeito para escrever qualquer coisa, mas sem preparação especial. Aliados os dois poderiam realizar um trabalho bastante satisfatório. Mas um sócio representa uma divisão de lucros. Por isso, muitas vezes o tipógrafo trabalha sozinho. Não sabendo escrever todo o seu afã consiste em arranjar anúncios. O texto – que deixa de o ser para se transformar . . . num pretexto – é constituído por transcrições, feitas ao acaso, do primeiro jornal do Continente ou das ilhas que lhe cai nas mãos, e por cartas e artigos de quem quiser mandar-lhos. Não é muito raro que um tipógrafo ambicioso, para fazer desanimar

o diretor, estrague propositadamente o aspeto da publicação, provoque dificuldades administrativas, até o outro se ir embora, passando-lhe a empresa por uma ninharia. O tipógrafo, que era chefe da tipografia, e agente de anúncios, passa a propietário, diretor, administrador, chefe indiscutível de tudo quanto forma a companhia editora (na América, tudo assume aspeto de companhia ou de corporação, tudo é Co. ou Inc.)." Eduardo de Carvalho, *A Lingua Portuguesa nos Estados Unidos*, 119.

[66] Original: "Numa época e num país em que o espaço e o tempo se valorizam dumá forma incrível, a imprensa portuguesa da Nova Inglaterra deu uma prova de senso prático e abriu horizontes vastíssimos à exploração industrial da folha impressa."

[67] Original: "Assim como famílias diversas, crenças opostas, interesses descontrolados, se acolhem sob o mesmo teto, nas casas de muitas moradias ou de muitos escritórios; assim como na mesma parede ou na mesma taipa, há lugar para os anúncios mais contraditórios e para as proclamações políticas mais antagónicas; assim como um campo se divide em talhões, num dos quais se baila, noutro dos quais se joga, noutro dos quais se edifica, noutro dos quais se cantam orações e noutro dos quais há um circo de cavalinhos; assim como a vida moderna, sob tantos aspetos, é a variedade na uniformidade e a fraternidade na rivalidade, a redução ao armazém único geral, onde tudo se encontra, desde a agulha do gramofone às teorias bergsonianas; assim temos o jornal concentrado, o jornal panorâmico, encicplopédico e eclético, o jornal-hospedaria, o jornal-caleidoscópico, o jornal-omnibus, o pan-jornal, com folhas para todos os estilos e para todas as propagandas. Neste ponto os jornalistas da Nova Inglaterra deram uma lição aos jornalistas de Lisboa. Porque não há-de ele ser independente na primeira página, republicano-democrático na segunda, presidencialista na terceira, nacionalista na quarta, monárquico constitucional na quinta, integralista na sexta, comunista na sétima, católico a um canto, protestante a outro, espiritista antes da secção dos teatros, judaico ao pé da secção financeira, ateu aqui, mação ali, pé-leve acolá, mais além pé-de-boi? Ficaria assim o jornal – de todos os portugueses para todos os portugueses." Eduardo de Carvalho, *A Lingua Portuguesa nos Estados Unidos*,113-114.

[68] See the interesting reflection on "periodismo colonial" by Rui Antunes Correia, 51-62.

[69] Original: A exposição pública que qualifica a actividade jornalística impõe a este profissional um código de conduta irrepreensível. Entendese que a figura do jornalista integra um conjunto de distintivos pessoais, particularmente características morais, que devem situarse acima do cidadão comum. Este facto não deve desligarse de um outro pelo qual é possível verificar que, nos seus primórdios, a actividade jornalística na Nova Inglaterra em língua portuguesa muito deve ao labor das comunidades eclesiásticas e ao esforço pessoal de clérigos que encontraram nos jornais uma forma diligente de espalhar a mensagem cristã. Rui Antunes Correia, 51.

[70] For more information on the biography and literary work of Monteiro, see the following articles by George Monteiro: "Manuel Garcia Monteiro, Boston's Portuguese Poet," *Boletim do Núcleo Cultural da Horta* 21 (2012): 285-301, and "Manuel Garcia Monteiro, M.D.," *Gávea-Brown* 32-33 (2010-2011): 36-38.

[71] Original: "um açoriano dos mais vivos, e um dos mais delicados espíritos que temos conhecido." Enrique das Neves, *Traços Caraterísticos. Episódios e Anedotas Autênticas de Indivíduos que se Evidenciaram* (Lisbon: Parceria António Maria Pereira, 1910), 60.

[72] See: Manuel Garcia Monteiro, *A Trança* (Horta: Centro de Estudos e Cultura da Câmara Municipal da Horta, 1989), which contains a compilation of articles from various writers regarding the life and work of M. Garcia Monteiro, among them some from the popular writer, Fialho de Almeida.

[73] Enrique das Neves, 63.

[74] Original: "Ainda que se veja morrer de fome, há-de sustentá-lo sempre, porque ele é o seu regalo, a sua alegria, o seu sonho." Enrique das Neves, 63.

[75] Original: "É verdade, comprei o jornal porque o tal Xavier é um pobre diabo sem atividade e eu não estava disposto para ele só. Tenho lutado com dificuldades, porque o jornal, pela irregularidade da distribuição e pela colaboração insípida, pouco noticiosa, não tinha assinantes que dessem para o custeio. O *Luso-Americano* caiu num grande descrédito e para o lenvantar no espírito desta gente, geralmente ignorante e tapada, levarei algum tempo; mas tenho a esperança de tirar bom resultado." Enrique das Neves, 64.

[76] Original: "é necessário dar-lhes em pequenas doses as ideias modernas." Enrique das Neves, 64.

[77] Monteiro was able to attend college while he worked more than ten hours per day as an assistant typographer for the *Boston Herald*. When he graduated in September of 1890, he wrote a letter to a friend that stated: "I finally won the battle I got myself into. I achieved my medical degree, and I hope to enjoy the lifestyle that it will allow me, after not just a lot of hard work, but also the long suffering caused by deprivation. I survived many days on bread and water alone. But here I am, and my triumph does not make me proud. I am the same Monteiro – as simple as I was when I wore a work shirt at the Guttenberg press." Enrique das Neves, 79.

[78] *Luso-Americano* (25 October 1989), 39. Regarding Manuel Garcia Monteiro in Boston, read Enrique das Neves's work; part of M. Garcia Monteiro's epistolary correspondence is found in this work.

[79] Original: "Aquela fortuna por meio do jornal foi antes uma ruína. Esperava encontrar a felicidade neste país e tenho tido uma vida tristíssima, amargurada, como nunca tive. E não porque eu não me tenha esforçado, não tenha feito o maior empenho, para realizar o que tanto ambicionava e ambiciono. . . . O jornal acabou, porque não pude absolutamente sustentá-lo. Fiz sacrifícios, ao ponto de me alimentar mal, para empregar todo o dinheiro de que podia dispor nas despesas mais urgentes, que eram: composição, impressão e papel; mas nem assim foi possível aguentá-lo. Experimentei todas as formas possíveis de redação. Inclusivamente reduzi o preço de assinatura a metade, e o número de assinantes nunca deu para pagar sequer ao tipógrafo! . . . Se você visse o modo que trabalhei, o modo como vivi, para bem desta colónia de hipopótamos, você admirar-se-ia de quanto aquele boémio se sacrificou."

[80] See documentation about Manuel das Neves Xavier in the Miguel Corte-Real Collection of the Ferreira-Mendes Portuguese-American Archives at UMass Dartmouth.

[81] João Francisco Escobar, *The New Method to Learn the Portuguese Language Without Teacher with Figurated Pronunciation of The Tones and Sounds* (New Bedford: Guilherme M. Luiz & Co., Inc., n.d.).

[82] *Luso-Americano* (25 October 1989), 39.

[83] *O Lavrador Português*, nº 64, 11 de abril de 1914, p. 4.

[84] "Os Portugueses de California, 1888-1938," *Jornal Português* (special dedicated issue, 1938), 9.

[85] "Manuel F. M. Trigueiro e a sua obra," *A União Portuguesa, 1887-1937*, 50th anniversary commemorative issue (28 March 1937), 2.

[86] Original: "Durante esse longo prazo fui cortês e amavelmente tratado pelo proprietário da 'União Portuguesa' e não teria deixado o seu serviço se não fosse o desejo, que desde há muito me açorava, de publicar, por minha conta, um jornal em língua portuguesa." "Manuel F. M. Trigueiro e a sua Obra," *A União Portuguesa, 1887-1937*, 50th anniversary commemorative issue (28 March 1937), 2.

[87] *A União Portuguesa, 1887-1937*, 50th anniversary commemorative issue (28 March 1937), 5.

[88] For more on the history of the UPEC, see: Maria Helena Carvalho dos Santos.

[89] *A Chrónica*, no 7 (year 1, 20 December 1895), 1-7.

[90] "A frequência com que aparecem ultimamente em certos jornais desta cidade afrontosas referências a Portugal e a portugueses, impõe-me o dever sacrossanto de vir hoje ante a população de Califórnia responder aos ataques de inaudita brutalidade uns tantos jornalistas sanfranciscanos têm desacatado a minha gloriosa nacionalidade. Na Europa, porque são outros os processos impostos e seguidos na liquidação das contas desta espécie, já eu teria enfreado alguns dos jumentos que para aí desembestaram por sobre as páginas brilhantíssimas da História que tão prodigamente iluminou com os feitos estupendos e o heroísmo assombroso do seu povo, maravilhando o Mundo; aqui, onde tais processos recebem o *veto* da lei, é força aceitarmos o único recurso capaz de destruir as gratuitas e insolentes diatribes com que alguns pigmeus da imprensa de San Francisco buscam deprimir as velhas glórias da minha pátria, o valor e as virtudes do povo português. Este recurso é o campo da imprensa, de onde dirijo hoje à população da Califórnia este protesto singelíssimo na forma mas soleníssimo no fundo. Desde muito que eu cogitava descobrir o manancial dimanador de tão insólitas agressões, sem resultado, quando o acaso veio providencialmente favorecer-me com o mais pleno *desideratum*. No dia 14 do mês findo, deparei na secção editorial do 'San Francisco Chronicle,' edição daquele dia, com o seguinte: 'Não está nos hábitos dos portugueses alcançar vitórias pela força das armas em África. Eles têm obtido os seus territorios coloniais por meio de artifícios, tomando uma légua quando lhe dão um milha. Por esta forma têm sido vastas as suas aquisições de território, mas a Inglaterra tem-lhes roubado considerável parte desta terra mal-adquirida. Lemos porém agora que os portugueses derrotaram realmente os indígenas do Leste de África em batalha campal. Deve ser uma satisfacção para alguns dos seus soldados trocar missangas por balas.' . . . Desta pintura deprimente de Portugal e de portugueses infere-se desde logo o grau de ignorância do redator do 'Chronicle.' Ora, que se desconheça o passado dum país e do seu povo cuja história não respiga para além do limite das suas fronteiras, compreende-se e tolera-se, mesmo a respeito dum jornalista, se ele oculta a sua ignorância; mas que alguém elementarmente instruído, que um jornalista desconheça o passado de Portugal e dos feitos assombrosos do seu povo, é realmente de embasbacar." *A Chronica*, no. 7 (year 1, 1 February 1896), 1-7.

[91] *A Chrónica*, no. 10 (year 1, May 1896), 1.

[92] Original: "O artigo que anteontem publicámos e no qual transcrevíamos parte da resposta altiva e digna, que serviu de protesto contra as insinuações feitas ao nome português, por dois jornais da Califórnia, emocionou vivamente o público. A homenagem que prestámos àquele nosso colega de imprensa dos Estados Unidos, ecoou no espírito do povo português . . . Patrocinamos a ideia que é de todo o ponto justa, cônscios de que todos os patriotas corresponderão ao nosso apelo, prestando assim o seu tributo a quem tão longe da pátria, soube honrá-la, defendendo-a com a maior altivez. A quantia a subscrever não pode ser superior a 100 réis." *A Chrónica*, no. 10 (year 1, May 1896), 1.

[93] For more on Mário Bettencourt da Câmara, see the following references: Carlos Almeida, *Portuguese Immigrants (The Centennial Story of the Portuguese Union of the State of California)* (San Leandro, CA: Supreme Council of U.P.E.C., 1992), 244-45. As well as: *Jornal Português*, no. 191 (14 February 1936), 1.

[94] For biographical information, see "Ignorância e Maldade," *Jornal Português*, special issue (1949).

[95] *O Independente*, no. 1993 (14 January 1937), 1.

[96] *A Colonia Portuguesa*, no. 171 (year 11, 3 November 1925), 1.

[97] *O Portugal na California*, n° 37 (vol. 1, 24 June 1936) 2.

[98] Geoffrey L. Gomes, "Manuel B. Quaresma, Pioneer Newspaperman," *O Progresso* (*A publication of the Portuguese Historical and Cultural Society*) (Sacramento, December 2002), 3.

[99] *A União Portuguesa*, no. 1823 (year 37, 3 September 1923), 1.

[100] *A União Portuguesa*, no. 1823, (year 37, 3 September 1923), 1.

[101] Original: "Quém há, na Colónia Portuguesa, que não conheça o doutor Alberto Moura, com banca de advogado no edifício do Bank of America, na 12th e Broadway Street? Alberto Moura tem tomado uma parte muito ativa nas nossas sociedades, nas nossas festas, nas nossas empresas, no nosso desenvolvimento; e a colónia deve-lhe alguma coisa de valor, de prestígio para todos nós. Alberto Moura tem sabido granjear simpatias gerais que muito honram o seu aturado trabalho, colocando-o hoje em posição saliente e distinta entre os portugueses da Califórnia. Procurai, pois, ouvi-lo, quando os vossos negócios precisarem um advogado." *A União Portuguesa, 1887-1937*, 50th anniversary commemorative issue (28 March 1937), 23.

[102] See João José Vieira, Jr., *Eu Falo por Mim Mesmo. Autobiografia* (Porto: Tipografia da Livraria Progredior, 1963), 91-114.

[103] João José Vieira, Jr., *A Voz da História* (Oakland: Printed by the author, 1941).

[104] João José Vieira, Jr., *Eu Falo por Mim Mesmo. Autobiografia*.

[105] João José Vieira, Jr., *Aventuras no Eldorado. Novela Idealista* (Porto: Tipografia da Livraria Progredior, 1966).

[106] Carlos Almeida, 255-256.

[107] Idem, p. 256.

[108] "Os Portugueses de California, 1888-1938," *Jornal Português*, special issue (1938), 9. (Also see: Carlos Almeida, 255-56.)

[109] Guilherme Silveira da Glória, *Poesias*. From the same author, *Harpejos* (Oakland, CA: Tipografia do "Jornal Português," 1940).

[110] Original: "Portugal é o nosso caminho adorado; dele partimos, mas por mais longe que nos afastemos em distância, ele está sempre connosco no nosso coração."

[111] Guilherme Silveira da Glória, *Poesias*, I.

[112] Monsignor Joseph Cacella, *Jungle Call* (New York: Francis Cardinal Spellman-Archbishop of New York, 1956).

[113] *Portugal Today*, 2 (I) (January 1960), 16-17.

[114] Ibidem. Biographical note of the flap of the book.

[115] *Portugal Today*, 2 (I) (January 1960), 16-17.

[116] *Portugal Today*, 2 (3) (March 1960), 8.

[117] *Portuguese Times* (16 November 1989), 22.

[118] Ibidem.

[119] Original: "Comprei-lhe roupa dos pés a cabeça, arranjei-lhe casa, mas morreu ao fim de se tirar uma edição do 'Luso.' Faleceu repentinamente depois de ter subido as escadas duma casa na rua Elm, onde vivia. . . . O Padre Greaves alimentava-se de sanduiches e comprimidos. Sofria dos intestinos. Tinha somente 69 anos quando faleceu. Dia em que não bebesse um galão de vinho não era dia para ele." *Portuguese Times* (16 November 1989), 22.

[120] *Portuguese Times* (16 November 1989), 22.

[121] Laurinda C. Andrade, *The Open Door*.

[122] Laurinda C. Andrade, 162.

[123] Laurinda C. Andrade, 162-63.

[124] Laurinda C. Andrade, 164-65.

[125] Laurinda C. Andrade, 168.

[126] Laurinda C. Andrade, 165.

[127] Laurinda C. Andrade, 168.

[128] Laurinda C. Andrade, 167.

[129] Alexander Lawton Mckall, *Portugal for Two* (New York: Dood, Mead & Company, 1931).

[130] Laurinda C. Andrade, 215-24. Also see the article: "A Língua Portuguesa nas Escolas Americanas," *Diario de Noticias*, no. 6924 (23 February 1942), I-2.

[131] Laurinda C. Andrade, 215.

[132] *Jornal Português*, no. 630 (25 August 1944). Special issue: "Número Dedicado aos Nossos Jovens no Serviço Militar dos Estados Unidos", [no page number].

[133] Original: "Muito trabalho e dissabores se sofreram com o ajuste de assinaturas. A escrita sofreu grande transformação: nomes iguais apareciam, alguns em duplicado e outros em triplicado. No ficheiro o mesmo acontecia. . . Muitas horas, muita paciência e grande vontade da administradora, conseguiu-se a normalização e confiança dum serviço quase perfeito." Alberto Corrêa, "Vinte e Oito Anos no Jornalismo," *Jornal Português*, no. 630 (25 August 1944). Special issue: "Número Dedicado aos Nossos Jovens no Serviço Militar dos Estados Unidos", [no page number].

[134] *Jornal Português*, special issue dedicated to "Os Portugueses de Califórnia, 1888-1938" (1938), 10.

[135] "O Palácio da Restauração da Independencia. A nossa Subscrição," *Jornal Português*, no. 192 (21 September 1936), 8. And also: "O Inesperado Falecimento de Dna. Maria Nunes Silveira," *Jornal Português*, no. 142, (year 28, 2nd series, 13 May 1960), 1.

[136] "A Colónia Portuguesa e as Nossas Autoridades Consulares Homenageiam a Nossa Diretora, Senhora Dona Maria Nunes Silveira," *Jornal Português*, no. 1177 (27 May 1955).

[137] See "O Inesperado Falecimento de Dona. Maria Nunes Silveira," *Jornal Português*, no. 142, (year 28, 2nd series, 13 May 1960), 1.

[138] Original: "Ainda penso sonho ter sido/ De ter ouvido a notícia triste/ De a mãe dos pobres já falecido/ A nossa amiga que já não existe!// A Dona Maria Nunes Silveira/ Era a primeira aos pobres dar/ Com seu sorriso tão cativante/ Sempre avante a auxiliar// Que Deus a tenha lá no Céu gozando/ Por nós espr'ando p'ra também gozar/ Todos alegres, todos juntinhos/ Como os Anjinhos e a Deus amar." *Jornal Português*, no. 142 (year 25, 2nd series, 13 May 1960), 1.

Chapter 3 The Birth of the Portuguese-American Press, 1877-1929

[1] Geoffrey Gomes, "The Portuguese-Language Press in California: The Response to American Politics 1880-1928," 17-28.

[2] Ibid., 84.

[3] Leo Pap, "The Portuguese Press," 294.

[4] Leo Pap, *The Portuguese-Americans*, 35-53.

[5] Original: "Esta tipografia encarrega-se da impressão de quaisquer obras: editais, cartas de convite e de enterro, estatutos, documentos relativos a irmandades, juntas e associações. Garante-se boa impressão e os preços são os mais módicos. Os nossos patrícios nestes Estados quando desejarem um obra impressa em Português (e são poucos ou nenhumas as tipografias do país em idiomas de que não têm conhecimento), lembrem-se que há aqui quem o faz do melhor modo possível, e por preços realmente baratíssimos. O JORNAL DE NOTICIAS tem um sortimento de material, e os tipos são todos novos. Enviem-nos suas obras, que serão executadas com esmero e promtidão. Quando desejarem a impressão de uma obra qualquer, consultem primeiramente com nós." *O Jornal de Noticias*, no. 173 (year 4, 12 February 1881), 6.

[6] Geo P. Rowell & Co., *American Newspaper Directory* (New York: Geo P. Rowell & Co. Publishers, 1878), 265.

[7] *O Jornal de Noticias*, no. 144 (year 3, 24 July 1880), 4.

[8] *O Jornal de Noticias*, no. 173 (year 4, 12 February 1881), 1.

[9] Original: "Quando algum dos nossos leitores tiver conhecimento de um ocorrido qualquer entre os nossos patrícios: um casamento, óbito, desastre, o que quer que seja, rogamos que nos dê notícias do mesmo o mais breve possível, pelo que será muito agradecido. O que exigimos é só os factos e data, e cá arranjaremos um artigo sobre o

mesmo. Não receiem de escrever o que souberem." *Jornal de Noticias*, no. 173 (year 4, 12 February 1881), 6.

[10] See, for example, these two bibliographic references: Lionel Holmes, and Joseph D'Alessandro, *Portuguese Pioneers of the Sacramento Area*, 158; and August Mark Vaz, *The Portuguese in California*, 142.

[11] Original: "que sejam escritos em linguagem moderada e decente."

[12] Original: "escritos sobre assuntos de interesse pessoal serão admissíveis mediante o pagamento de 10 cts. por linha, isto é se a sua linguagem for própria e admissível. Quando não emitirmos a nossa opinião, comentando escritos alheios, não se deve atribuir nosso silêncio a um tácito apoio. Reservamos sempre a nossa opinião." See any of the conserved covers of *A Voz Portugueza* in the Freitas Library of California or the Library of Congress.

[13] Original: "Depois de mil investigações e aturados estudos, já afugentando o caruncho dos seus alfarrábios e consultando-os, já corrigindo mais de vinte vezes outras tantas "provas" das suas 'escreveduras' que para esse fim lhe foram enviadas, tomando mil precauções, incluindo a de 'molhar as mãos do tipógrafo,' para este passar a 'revisão final,' inserindo um 'l' aqui, omitindo um 'p' ali, mudando uma virgula para acolá, etc., e estando ciente de que nem Camilo Castelo Branco o podia apanhar numa letra que fosse, enfim, ao cabo de cinco semanas, o homem desembuchou!! Sim senhor, o homem vomitou o pouco que sabia . . . e o muito que não sabia!! Sim senhor o homem vomitou o muito que não sabia! Porque logo na décima-quinta linha do primeiro parágrafo divide a palavra 'producções' desta maneira: 'produc-ções.' Regra: Quando concorrem dois 'cç,' sendo o segundo cedilhado, pertencem ambos à vogal seguinte: fa-cção, pro-du-cção, etc. Ai Jesus! Esta agora é de cabo de esquadra. Vejam o que ele diz: 'Respondemos ao crítico (e ainda lhe dispensamos essa fineza) que a palavra 'subjecto' de etimologia latina, se encontra em muitos dicionários em lugar de sujeito, assim como subjecção em vez de sujeição.' Ora bem, agora também respondemos ao Zig-Zag que 'subjecto' não é palavra portuguesa, nem se encontra em dicionário nenhum da nossa língua, logo por conseguinte Zig-Zag falta à verdade e vomita uma asneira!" *A Voz Portugueza*, no. 13 (29 June 1887), 1.

[14] Original: "É realmente maçada e bem grande, a de aturar o tal colega da *Voz*, estamos na verdade aborrecidos de lhe ministrar cataplasmas mas infelizmente para nós, tem produzido pouco efeito o que prova a consistência real do grande *orador, ditador e escritor Stone*, no entretanto o nosso laboratório abunda em preparados químicos por consequências perseverança, e avante, procuremos outro *calmante*, que prove ser mais ativo e consequentemente mais eficaz. O colega por quem é, visite as escolas noturnas, aceite o nosso conselho de amigo e verá que dele obterá grandes, inúmeros resultados, demais o colega há de necessariamente confessar que muito precisa do nosso conselho, pelas faltas as mais frisantes da gramática; a local *um intrigante* bem demonstra a incompatibilidade jornalística do sr. *Stone*, o colega esforça-se mas nada consegue, quer empregar temor empolado e engasga-se, quer figuras de retórica, qual história, entala-se." *A Civilização*, no. 114 (year 3, 5 April 1884), 1.

[15] Original: "O sr. Governador civil substituto do distrito nomeou uma comissão para colher donativos a fim de acudir as desgraças sucedidas na ilha de S. Miguel com os violentos abalos de terra. O carnaval passou naquela cidade sem ocorrência desagradável. A Sociedade da União Ginástica deu duas soirées, e a Assembleia Angrense três bailes,

havendo em todas estas reuniões muita concorrência. . . . Partiu para Santa Maria o sr. José de Bettencourt da Silveira, despachado juiz de direito para aquela comarca." *A Civilização*, no. 3 (year 1, 7 May 1881), 3.

[16] Original: "Devem-se acostumar cedo a submeter os seus caprichos à razão dos outros para que um dia possam escutar a sua própria razão e obedecer aos ditames dela. O hábito tudo faz; os meninos a quem no berço se deixaram fazer todas as vontades tornam-se altivos, coléricos e teimosos. Querem, mas já tarde, vencer as suas paixões, e então já sujeitos como escravos ao império dele, choram a sua fraqueza, e não podem mais ser senhores de si." *A Civilização*, no. 2 (year 1, 23 April 1881), 4.

[17] Original: "O nosso patriotismo estende-se de pólo a pólo; interessa-nos o bem estar de todo o português; e pela nossa missão especial não podemos deixar de tomar a sério, e muito, o facto do mau tratamento dado aos nossos patrícios, que para vergonha nossa e para deslustre da nossa nacionalidade estão sendo obrigados a emigrar para as longínquas ilhas de Sandwich a fim de fugirem ao negro espetro da fome, motivado pela indiferença e corrupção do governo, que não obstante ser composto de homens inteligentes, é deleitoso e insuportável. E ninguém deve culpar senão ao governo; e a ele exigir responsabilidade. Temos imensas e riquíssimas possessões na África, na Ásia e até na Oceania, para onde se poderiam mandar os braços úteis que vão enriquecer as ilhas inóspitas de Sandwich, cujos indígenas só tarde poderão ter alguma consideração nos países civilizados." *A Civilização*, no. 118 (year 3, 3 May 1884), 1.

[18] *O Progresso Californiense*, no. 94 (year 3, 1 January 1887), 2.

[19] Original: "Era a sombra dum gigante/ Corpulento posto em pé!/ Que inda ostenta que possante/ Fora outrora se o não é!/ Das grandezas do passado/ Só lhe resta o seu mau fado/ Duro peito retalhado/ Pela pátria e pela fé." *O Progresso Californiense*, no. 95 (year 3, 8 January 1887), 1.

[20] Original: "As brumas e os ventos das últimas semanas de junho derrotaram completamente as batatas inglesas semeadas em maio. O prejuízo porém, não influi sensivelmente na subsistência pública porque a cultura daquela batata feita na época referida é insignificante."

[21] Original: "Na lomba de Santo António do Nordeste, faleceu repentinamente no mato, onde fora cortar lenha um pobre homem chefe de numerosa família. Encontraram o cadáver junto de uma porção de lenha." *A União Portuguesa*, (issue number not visible, 1 September 1888), 2.

[22] *A União Portuguesa*, no. 2452 (year 49, 23 September 1935), multiple pages.

[23] Original: "bem conhecido e estimado por todos os portugueses." *A União Portuguesa*, no. 330 (year 8, 17 January 1895), 4.

[24] *A União Portuguesa*, no. 2803 (8 June 1942), 1.

[25] Original: "pontualidade de um cronómetro."

[26] Original: "No vasto campo do jornalismo mais uma pedra tumular se levanta a indicar em duas palavras, três sílabas apenas – AQUI JAZ – uma longa biografia, se quisermos volver ao passado e seguir horas de suprema amargura e horas de íntima alegria, que as houve, nesse mais de meio século existência da 'União Portuguesa.' Ontem foi um jornal de Crockett, pouco antes um de Pinole, nesta vizinhança; e mais além no tempo e no espaço, com mais de 100 anos, um dos principais diários desta República, o 'Boston

Evening Transript,' e muitos outros. Porquê? Porque todo o trabalho do homem tem limite. Durante cerca de 55 anos tem a 'União Portuguesa,' o mais antigo jornal da nossa colónia, visitado semanalmente os seus assinantes, excetuando a semana do terramoto de 1906, quando a cidade de San Francisco foi totalmente arruinada. Desde então, como dantes, tem sido publicada com a pontualidade de um cronómetro, mas em Oakland, durante estes 36 anos da sua existência. À tenacidade do seu propietário e administrador, auxiliado pelo seu dedicado e genial irmão Félix Trigueiro, se deve a longa vida deste bem conhecido semanário que ora desaparece." *A União Portuguesa*, no. 2808 (year 55, 13 July 1942).

[27] According to Leo Pap, Father Fernandes had worked in mining and sheep raising in California until 1877, when he decided to move to the Azores to enter the seminary. Upon returning to California, he was ordained a priest in Santa Barbara and began missionary work in Hawaii and Macao before becoming pastor of a church in Oakland in 1892. Leo Pap, "The Portuguese Press," 294.

[28] Original: "*O Arauto* é o jornal de maior circulação entre os 100,000 Portugueses dos Estados Unidos, por ser o mais noticioso e por ser o único que oferece valiosos prémios aos seus assinantes. *O Arauto* publica romances de muito interesse, traduzidos expressamente para as suas colunas." *O Arauto*, no. 13 (year IX, 4 September 1909).

[29] Original: "Pior: Têm-se agravado os padecimentos do senhor José C. B. de Carvalho, que se acha no hospital português desta cidade." *O Arauto*, no. 13 (year IX, 4 September 1909).

[30] See: Cristiana Bastos, "Portuguese in the Cane: the Racialization of Labor in Hawaiian Plantations", in Sofia Aboim, Paulo Granjo e Alice Ramos, eds., *Changing Societies: Legacies and Challenges.* Vol. 1: *Ambigous Inclusions: Inside Out, Inside In* (Lisboa: Imprensa de Ciências Sociais, 2018), 65-96; J. H. Galloway, *The Sugar Cane Industry: A Historical Geography from its Origins to 1914* (Cambridge: Cambridge University Press, 1989).

[31] Augustus Marques, "Potugese immigration to the Hawaiian islands", in Thomas G., Thrum, ed., *Hawaiian Almanaque and Annual for 1887-A Handbook of Information* (Honolulu: Press Publishing Company, 1886), 74-78.

[32] Katherine Coman, *The history of contract labor in the Hawaiian islands* (New York: American Economic Association, 1903), 27-32.

[33] United States Department of Commerce (Bureau of the Census), "Statistics for Hawaii", *Thirteenth census of the United States taken in the year 1910* (Washington, DC: Government Printing Office, 1913, v. 2), p. 10.

[34] See "Hawai'i Historical Census", in University of Hawai at Manoa Lbrary. URL: https://guides.library.manoa.hawaii.edu/c.php?g=105181&p=684171

[35] Edgar C. Knowlton, "The Portuguese Language Press in Hawaii," 89-90.

[36] See Jerry Williams, *In Pursuit of their Dreams: A History of Azorean Immigration to the United States* (North Dartmouth: University of Massachusetts Dartmouth: Center for Portuguese Studies and Culture, 2007), 99-104.

[37] Knowlton, 90.

[38] Knowlton, 89.

[39] See Joaquim Francisco Freitas, *Portuguese-Hawaiian Memories* (Honolulu: edition of the author, 1930), cited by the following URL: https://www.ancestry.com/boards/surnames.osorio/13.1/mb.ashx. [Consulted July 2019]

[40] Ibid.

[41] George F. Nellist, ed., *Men of Hawaii. (vol. V). Territory of Hawaii* (Honolulu: The Honolulu Star-Bulletin, Ltd., 1935), 342.

[42] Elvira Osorio Roll is the author of *Background, a novel of Hawaii.* (Honolulu: Exposition Press, 1964).

[43] George F. Nellist, ed., 342. See also: Joaquim Francisco Freitas, *Portuguese-Hawaiian Memories* (Honolulu: edition of the author, 1930).

[44] See: *Hawaiian Historical Society*, www.hawaiianhistory.org. [Consulted in 2013]

[45] Translation: "Litterary, liberal, business and educational newspaper dedicated to the Portuguese community in the Sandwich Islands."

[46] Knowlton, 89.

[47] See: *Hawaiian Historical Society* [URL: https://www.hawaiianhistory.org/]

[48] Translation: "Independent Weekly Dedicated Strictly to the Political, Moral and Material Interests of the Portuguese Colony on the Sandwich Islands."

[49] Knowlton, 90.

[50] Translation: "Political and Literary Newspaper Specially Dedicated to the General Interests of the Portuguese Community in Hawaii."

[51] Knowlton, 90.

[52] Knowlton, 90.

[53] According to the data in Edgar C. Knowlton, 89. See also Manuel da Silveira Cardozo, *The Portuguese in America (590 b.C-1974)*, 46.

[54] According to the data cited by Edgar C. Knowlton. See also Manuel da Silveira Cardozo, 46.

[55] Knowlton, 90.

[56] Knowlton, 90.

[57] L. C. Newton, ed., *Who's Who of the Island of Hawaii 1938. A Biographical and Statistical Record of Men and Women on the Island of Hawaii, Territory of Hawaii, U.S.A. vol I* (Hilo: Published by John A, Lee, 1939), 55-56. Also: George F. Nellist, 152-53.

[58] L. C. Newton, 55.

[59] Ibid.

[60] L. C. Newton, 55-56; George F. Nellist, 152-53. Also refer to Augusto Souza Costa: Manoel da Silveira Cardozo dates his arrival in Hawaii as 1898 (81). According to Cardozo, in Hawaii A. Souza Costa was also "county supervisor" between 1903 and 1908.

[61] Knowlton, 90.

[62] Manuel da Silveira Cardozo, 49.

[63] Knowlton, 90-91.

[64] Knowlton, 90-91.

[65] Knowlton, 90.

[66] Manuel da Silveira Cardozo, 79.

[67] Knowlton, 90.

[68] Knowlton, 91.

[69] Knowlton, 91.

[70] Knowlton, 91.

[71] Knowlton, 91.

[72] Knowlton, 91.

[73] Knowlton, 91.

[74] Knowlton, 91.

[75] Knowlton, 91

[76] Knowlton, 91.

[77] Knowlton, 91.

[78] Knowlton, 91.

[79] Knowlton, 91.

[80] Knowlton, 91.

[81] Knowlton, 91.

[82] Knowlton, 91.

[83] Geoffrey Gomes, "The Portuguese-Language Press in California: The Response to American Politics 1880-1928," 17-44.

[84] *A Chrónica*, no. 1 (6 July 1895), 1 and 2.

[85] Original: "Tribunal Íntimo da Consciência Pública – Eu e o Padre Glória"

[86] Original: "Carta Aberta ao Ilustríssimo, Excelentíssimo, Reverendíssimo Senhor Arcebispo P. W. Riordan, Muito Preclaro Prelado da Diocese Católica de San Francisco da Califórnia."

[87] Original: "Há mais de dois anos preclaríssimo Prelado, que o padre Guilherme Gloria, redator-chefe dum semanário pseudo-advogado dos interesses da Igreja Católica, cospe sobre mim as injúrias mais vis, em linguagem não menos abjeta, chegando ao ponto de lançar sobre mim tamanho descrédito que me forçou à publicação deste periódico para me defender perante os meus compatriotas que não nos conheçam, a fim de poderem julgar entre os escritores *sacro* e *profano*, entre o *clérigo* e o *leigo*." *A Chrónica*, no. 1 (6 July 1895), 3.

[88] Original: "porque lendo-se no alto da primera página daquele semanário a declaração seguinte 'Este jornal é aprovado e recomendado pelo Exmo. Revmo. Prelado desta Arquidiocese, P. W. RIORDAN, Arcebispo de San Francisco' está bem claro que, ou vós sois solidário com o padre Glória nos ultrajes que aquele semanário me tem desferido, ou que fostes e estais sendo iludido, e assim ignorais o que nele se tem escrito e qual a sua verdadeira missão." *A Chrónica*, no. 2 (20 July 1895), 10.

[89] *A Chrónica*, no. 2 (20 July 1895), 1 and 10.

[90] Original: "Não foi, pois, o *zelo religioso* interessado em destruir o erro e a heresia que forçou o padre Glória a atacar-nos porque até então teve a religião catholica – bem como os seus ministros – melhor e maior apoio da *União Portuguesa* que no *Amigo dos Católicos*. O que foi então? That is the question! Remontemos aos primeiros escritos do

padre Glória, a nosso respeito. É claro que se entende como a minha pessoa quando se referia à redação da 'União' desde que nos cometeram o honroso encargo de lhe imprimir feição mais consoante os interesses da Pátria em geral e da colónia em particular. Talvez possamos no encadeamento de tais escritos e na exposição de alguns factos e documentos que com eles se relacionam, descobrir algo de iluminante na escura questão." *A Chrónica*, no. 3 (10 August 1895), 19.

[91] *A Chrónica* no. 3 (10 August 1895), 20.

[92] Original: "Tal qual nos classificou esse asno de forma humana, esse pescador de águas turvas, esse cão esfomeado que se lançou ao primeiro osso que lhe atiraram." *A Chrónica*, no. 10 (May 1896), 74.

[93] Original: "No dia 10 de julho de 1893 foi lançada na caixa de redação da minha mesa de trabalho, no escritório da *União Portuguesa*, pelo seu proprietário, um artigo de colaboração, original do sr. Joaquim de Menezes, tendo por título 'O S. João de Boston e o S. João dos Açores.' Li a prosa, e o verso – também tinha verso – e repeti a leitura por duas ou três vezes. Quando me voltava para inquirir do autor do escritor [*sic*] vi duas caras a sorrir desenhando nas feições esta interrogação:
– Que tal? – Era o proprietário da *União* e o inditoso Ferreira d'Avila, ao tempo naquela folha.
– Quem é este literato, inquiri?
– É um mestre de escola lá da aldeia que está agora no Leste, para onde veio mercê de ter tido lá os seus dares e tomares por motivos políticos.
– Ah!... Para mestre de escola... está bom, isto; para articulista que merece as honras de perseguição política, salvo a dalgum pobre regedor da aldeia, deixa algo que desejar. Tornei a fazer nova leitura, desta vez em voz alta, acentuando algumas incorreções, sem valor se não se tratasse de um trabalho com pretensões literárias. E meti o São João na caixa de reserva." *A Chrónica*, no. 10 (May 1896), 75.

[94] Original: "Então o Sr. Cônsul classifica de ataques e insultos violentos às Majestades o havermos dito que a rainha Amélia está empenhada em transformar aquele país em antro de malandros das diversas sub-secções e de ambos os sexos do jesuitismo, como desventuradamente se prova com a sua colaboração activa na inundação daquela pobre terra de quanta vagabunda e de quanto masmarro excede a lotação dos coios franceses da seita negra? Então isto não é verdade? Onde, pois o insulto à rainha? Não executa ela todos os atos dessa política reacionária semi-oficialmente com a passiva tolerância do rei?" *A Chrónica*, no. 5 (1 October 1895), 1.

[95] See Maria Helena Carvalho dos Santos, "Emigração e níveis de cultura: a União Portuguesa do Estado da Califórnia (1880-1980)", *Análise Social*, vol XIX (77-78-79) (1983): 961-986.

[96] Its headquarters changed over time. It was founded in San Francisco, and later moved to San Leandro (on 1124 E 14th Street). In the 1930s and 1940s, the publication was edited in Atwater. In September of 1950, it moved to Oakland (735 Chestnut Street), only to return to San Leandro later on.

[97] The Portuguese Society of America was created on January 1, 2010 as the result of the merger of four societies: Conselho Supremo da Irmandade Do Divino Espírito Santo do Estado da Califórnia, Conselho Supremo da Sociedade do Espírito Santo do Estado da Califórnia, Conselho Supremo da União Portuguesa do Estado da Califórnia, Conselho

Supremo da União Portuguesa Protectora do Estado da Califória. See URL: https://www.mypfsa.org/about-us/#/. [Consulted in 2019]

[98] See the *Jornal Português*, no. 191 (14 February 1936), 1.

[99] The *Boletim da UPEC* experimented with various changes in its size, number of pages and design. Its standard format, however, was always small and illustrated, after the 1930s. After January of 1968, under the coordination of Carlos Almeida (who became its editor), the *Boletim* modernized its typographic design, adding color and better quality paper. See: *Boletim da UPEC*, no. 1 (vol. LXVII).

[100] *Boletim da UPEC*, no. 10 (vol. XLII).

[101] Treasurer Carlos Almeida wrote an article about the travels of the presidents of the institution to different centers within the community: *Boletim da UPEC*, no. 4 (vol. LX), 2. An illustrated report also appeared in this same issue entitled "Costumes Açorianos," penned by Manuel Dionisio, among others (3 and 13).

[102] This and other data were amicably facilitated by Mr. Carlos Almeida, who provided fundamental help the archival research on the Portuguese-American press in California.

[103] The J. A. Freitas Library is a private library operated by the Portuguese Fraternal Society of America, founded by Carlos Almeida in 1964. The library houses more than 12,000 books on issues related to Portuguese culture, as well as a collection of several newspapers and magazines published by the Portuguese immigrant community in California, as well as videos, microfilms and other materials of special symbolic value for the history of the Portuguese community in the United States. See URL: https://www.mypfsa.org/library/#/

[104] The author wishes to thank Mr. Timothy Borges, director of the Portuguese Fraternal Society of America, for the cordiality and the resources of the Freitas Library of San Leandro (CA).

[105] Geoffrey Gomes, "The Portuguese-Language Press in California. The Response to American Politics, 1880-1928", 12.

[106] *A Liberdade*, no. 3274 (year 34, 29 December 1934).

[107] Original: "Nenhum rei da Nação Portuguesa, nem antes nem depois, viveu tanto com o povo e para o povo, como o rei D. Dinis, e foi tal a popularidade de que ele gozou, que repercutindo-se de um século em século ainda hoje ecoa suavemente na memória do povo. O agrícola, ao vê-lo interessar-se pelo sucesso do seu labor, chamava-lhe ufano, 'o rei lavrador,' e os homens das classes populares, ao vê-lo arcar com as classes priviligiadas da nobreza e do clero, rebatendo as suas desregradas ambições e fazendo-os entrar na senda da justiça e do dever em prol dos homens do arado e da enxada, exclamavam anchos de si mesmos: 'El-rei D. Dinis fez tudo quanto quiz'." *A Liberdade*, no. 3257 (year 34, 7 July 1934), 2.

[108] *A Liberdade*, no. 3333, (year 37, 23 January 1937), 1.

[109] Original: "Esta venda torna-se necessária, devido à minha idade avançada, e principalmente pelo meu estado de depressão ocasionado pela irreparável falta da minha esposa, que era a alma deste negócio, e pela perda dolorosa do meu filho, única esperança que me restava na amarga e escabrosa senda da vida." *A Liberdade*, no. 3344, (year 37, 3 July 1937), 4.

[110] Francisco Caetano Borges da Silva, native of São Miguel (Azores), edited the newspaper for some time. Its contents were related to the Baptist church in New Bedford, or which

he was a member. When the weekly *O Progresso* was sold to José Escobar, son of João Francisco Escobar, it became a daily for several months.

[111] *A Revista Portuguesa* was founded in New Bedford on August 15, 1895. Joaquim de Menezes, originally from the island of Terceira (Azores), quickly abandoned this project to move to California, where he directed *O Amigo dos Cathólicos*. He succeeded the Azorean, Eugénio Escobar (son João Francisco Escobar), publishing just a few more issues afterwards.

[112] The *Jornal das Senhoras* was published in New Bedford and was directed towards women. It had short existence.

[113] There is a collection of this magazine in the Regional Library and Archives of Ponta Delgada (Azores). The author thanks the director of the magazine *Mundo Açoriano*, Lusa Ponte, for some of the information data here presented about *Açores-América*. See: Lusa Ponte, "Percursos Identitários na Diáspora Açoriana: O Jornal *Açores-América* (1903)."

[114] H. W. Kastor & Sons, 167.

[115] Original: "Ainda hoje muita gente pensa que matar é unicamente tirar a vida do outro com um punhal ou um revólver; que roubar é só arrebatar o que outrem possui. Nada mais errado. Mata-se outrem quando se lhe impede o meio de alcançar a sua subsistência, ou quando o obrigam a trabalhar superior às suas forças, ou quando lhe limitam a alimentação, vestuário ou habitação a termos antihigiénicos; ou quando com calúnias se mancha a sua reputação. . . . Enfim todo o interesse pessoal que se possa adquirir à custa de outrem, ou seja no comércio ou na indústria, é sempre furto, quando não é morte também. Pela mesma lei do instinto da conservação da espécie, sempre que beneficiamos outrem sentimos satisfação íntima e essa satisfação é tanto mais intensa quanto maior é o número de remediados e mais duradoiro o remédio, sendo a satisfação máxima o remediar perpetuamente a espécie inteira." *O Correio Português*, no. 21 (year 1, 4 January 1896), 1.

[116] *O Independente* had headquarters at 157-A Acushnet Avenue, New Bedford, MA.

[117] Vasco de Sousa Jardim mentions in his memoirs that it was founded by João Francisco Escobar. See the *Luso-Americano* (25 October 1989), 39.

[118] Miguel F. Policarpo was born on 1873 in Ribeira Grande, on the island of São Miguel, Azores, and moved to New Bedford in 1890 to join his four brothers, Luciano, Maria Estrela da Costa, David, and Joaquim Furtado Policarpo. He married Rosa Emilia de Mello's in 1895 and had four children. According to Rui Antunes Correia, he was the director of the *Jornal do Povo* and owner of *O Popular* (in partnership with Frederico A. Costa, editor of *O Colonial*), which would later be passed to António C. Vieira. Miguel F. Policarpo died in January of 1944. See Rui Antunes Correia, "Salazar em New Bedford," 53.

[119] *Diario de Noticias*, no. 6922 (20 February 1942), 6.

[120] Alípio Coelho Bartholo was born in Figueiró dos Vinhos, on the island of Flores (Azores), and died in New Bedford on March 24, 1929. He emigrated first to California and later to New England, where he worked as a carpenter, in Providence. There he married Maria L. Souza. Despite being from humble origins, he immersed himself in the study of Portuguese language and literature. After tiring of the journalistic world, Alípio C. Bartholo sold his share of *O Independente* to his partner, António Claudio Vieira.

He was the first editor of *A Alvorada*, founded in 1919. He abandoned journalism for medical reasons, as a result of diabetes. From then on, he dedicated himself solely to his profession as a notary public. Correia, "Salazar em New Bedford," 41.

[121] Correia, "Salazar em New Bedford," 53; see the footnote on page 79.

[122] *Luso-Americano* (25 October 1989), 39.

[123] *O Independente*, no. 1967 (18 June 1936), 1.

[124] *O Independente*, no. 1993 (14 January 1937), 1.

[125] Original: "Oliveira Salazar, Presidente do Ministério, responsável pelos últimos atos internacionais do Governo Português e que, pela sua grande e trascendente importância, no dizer de muitos – will make or break Portugal!" *O Independente*, no. 1993 (14 January 1937), 1.

[126] *O Independente*, no. 2152 (8 February 1940), 1.

[127] Correia, "Salazar em New Bedford," 52.

[128] Correia, "Salazar em New Bedford," 52-59.

[129] Original: "O 'Independente,' um cabeçalho de jornal que o seu proprietário António Fernandes Fortes, em hora de liquidação atirou para o barril do lixo, por não haver ninguém que, mesmo de graça, o quizesse para continuar, na sua retirada da América, a publicação de um semanário que, em suas mãos só teve um mérito, o de ser limpo e honrado; esse título, cabeçalho ou tabuleta foi apanhado do lugar das coisas inúteis, do monturo de imundícies pelas mãos sujas de um J. R. Rocha, o 'rochinha' para si e para o bando de intrujões que formaram a quadrilha do olho-vivo em assalto permanente a esta pobre colónia. . . . Toda a escória, tudo o que há de baixo, reles e infame ali foi encontrar esconderijo. . . . A mariolagem começou logo a fazer das suas. O 'Independente' tornou-se, como era lógico, o esterqueiro da colónia. . . . Vem, porém, o caso do assalto à casa da batota, mantida pelo mais estrondeante paladino da firma dos 'independentes' da moral. Miguel Policarpo, o 'casto' Miguel Policarpo, o 'moralista,' Miguel Policarpo o cérebro daquele coito de piratas fora apanhado pela polícia em flagrante." *Diario de Noticias*, no. 4494 (16 February 1934), 1. Cited by Correia, "Salazar em New Bedford," 54-55.

[130] Correia, "Salazar em New Bedford," 54-55.

[131] Confidential letter from João R. Rocha to António Ferro (Arquivos Nacionais Torre do Tombo [ANTT], Arquivo Oliveira Salazar [AOS], CO/PC-12D, Box 661, 18 February 1939).

[132] Confidential letter from João R. Rocha to António Ferro.

[133] Original: "Durante duas semanas fui alvo – e indiretamente também se pretendia atingir de morte o Cônsul Agostinho de Oliveira – do ataque mais vil que se pode conceber. Mas eu conhecia os homens do 'Diário de Notícias,' e na defesa esmagámos e reduzimos a cinzas todas as calúnias e mentiras que sobre nós atiravam. Publicámos, pouco depois, um número especial dedicado ao Ministro de Portugal em Washington, no qual vieram em nosso apoio mais de 400 figuras de destaque da colónia, membros do clero, etc."

[134] Confidential letter from João R. Rocha to António Ferro.

[135] An unidentified contributor to *O Independente*, who said he worked for the Portuguese government (possibly a diplomat), criticized Rocha's change of political orientation in a letter that stated: "From 1929 until 1936 you fiercely defended the Portuguese political

situation. How can you now, with any degree of coherence, if that means anything to you, publish in one column Policarpo's articles and in another articles like the one I've been referring to?" The author of the letter, realizing that Rocha had changed because he had not gotten what he expected from the Estado Novo, writes the following in reference to himself: "You are aware that I tried to improve my situation within the structure of the public service organization where I carry out my modest functions and my request was turned down. Did I change my political position because of that? no. I stand where where I stood ten years ago and even more at ease to talk to you as am doing now." Private letter sent by an unidentified person to João R. Rocha (AHD, Embassy of Portugal in Washington, box 37, document 15, 15 March 1937).

[136] Manuel da Silveira Cardozo, 53.

[137] See *Luso-Americano* (28 October 1989), 31.

[138] Miguel Barcelos Duarte Mendonça, 332.

[139] Original: "Quando entre nós havemos de fazer o mesmo? Temos falta de padres que continuem a grande obra religiosa e patriótica, que nossos antepassados ergueram, com seus sacrifícios, nestas paragens. O venerando Bispo desta diocese não se tem cansado de, por uma e muitas vezes, manifestar a necessidade urgente que a Igreja tem de vocações religiosas, neste meio, para atender as nosas paróquias." *Novidades*, (issue number not visible, 29 February 1940), 1.

[140] See the web portal: *Biografia e Obra – Eugénio Tavares.org*, URL: http://www.eugeniotavares.org/docs/pt/biografia/index_biografia.html. [Consulted in 2019]

[141] Eugénio Tavares (1867-1930), was born on October 18, 1867, on Ilha Brava (Cabo Verde). He was a politician, writer, poet, journalist, and defender of the independence of Cabo Verde. He started to publish texts in 1899, in the *Revista de Cabo Verde*, in Lisbon. In June, fleeing the colonial authorities, he went into exile in the United States, where he began publishing *Alvorada*. When the Republic was established in 1910, Eugénio Tavares returned to Cabo Verde, where he worked with various local newspapers: *Manduco, O Futuro de Cabo Verde, Progresso,* and *Mindelensede São Vicente*. In 1911, he founded *A Voz de Cabo Verde* and in 1912, he started working with *O Correio Portuguez* of New Bedford. In 1913, he also published in the Cabo Verdean newspaper *A Tribuna*. In 1914, he composed a song dedicated to the Republic. In 1915, he published *Cartas Caboverdeanas* in Praia, and in 1916 *Amor que Salva (Santificação do Beijo)* and *Mal de Amor: Coroa de Espinhos*. See the URL http://www.eugeniotavares.org/docs/pt/biografia/index_biografia.html [Consulted in 2019]

[142] António G. Faria was the manager of the paper. Carlos Alberto Supico started his career as a journalist working at *O Independente* between February 23, 1925, and November of 1926. Afterwards, he went to New York, where he worked in a store. Years later he returned to New Bedford to work as an editor at the *Diario de Noticias*, starting October 7, 1935. He also wrote for the satirical *O Pé de Vento* and the *Eco do Funchal*, in Madeira. Cf.: Duarte Miguel Barcelos Mendonça, 334.

[143] *A Pátria* was a weekly with a broadsheet type format, illustrated with photographs, with four pages of average size, and an editorial line that favored the Estado Novo. In an editorial published on April 14, 1936, about the financial situation of the Banco de Portugal, the paper commends its last economic report: "The annual reports of the issuing bank constitute the best proof of the sound financial policy of the State.

Revealing a clear understanding of the obligations involved in handling this delicate economic instrument that is the currency, it not only honors the administration of the same establishment, but also reflects the benefits of a national order that seemed to have disappeared from our country forever. . . The remarkable management report of 1935, which we examine, clearly exposes the framework of the economic phenomena that took place last year. It is a succinct and clear-sighted analysis of the difficulties and the political and economic upheavals that occurred everywhere this year. Banco de Portugal provided a precious service to this policy of rebirth of the Portuguese currency and the careful regulation of credit and interest rates. [Original: "Os relatórios anuais do banco emissor constituem nos últimos anos o documento mais expressivo da sã política financeira do Estado. Revelando uma nítida compreensão dos deveres que incumbem ao manejo desse delicado instrumento económico que é a moeda, não só honram a administração do mesmo estabelecimento, mas refletem os benefícios de uma ordem nacional que parecia para sempre arredada do nosso país. O notável relatório da gerência de 1935, que examinámos, expõe com lúcida clareza o quadro dos fenómenos económicos desenvolvidos no ano que passou. É uma análise sucinta e clarividente das dificuldades e dos sobressaltos de natureza política e económica em que o ano decorreu por toda a parte. . . Serviu o Banco de Portugal de precioso auxiliar desta política de renascimento da moeda portuguesa e regulando criteriosamente o crédito e as taxas de juros."] See: *A Pátria*, no. 10 (year 1, April 14, 1936), 2.

[144] *A União Portuguesa*, no. 1823 (year 37, 3 September 1923), 1.

[145] Joaquim dos Santos Oliveira worked at the *Jornal do Povo* between October of 1921 and June of 1922, and Francisco Santos also worked for the paper, writing for the humor page. See: Duarte Mendonça, 328.

[146] Original: "muito bem redigido e sem ideas políticas e religiosas." *O Lavrador Português*, no. 64 (11 April 1914), 4.

[147] *O Popular* was first located in New Bedford (MA) on 143 Acushnet Avenue. In East Providence (RI), the address was 144 Freeborn Avenue.

[148] Eduardo de Carvalho, *Os Portugueses na Nova Inglaterra*, 112-113.

[149] Original: "Brevemente vai aparecer uma revista nesta cidade intitulada – 'Jornal das Damas' – dedicada às Senhoras portuguesas. Conterá lindos contos, romances e explêndidas gravuras em papel fino. Esta revista será publicada sob a direção de um comité de senhoras, à frente das quais se acha Mrs. Virginia C. Escobar. Todas as pessoas que desejarem obter o primeiro nº desta revista, gratuitamente, queiram ter a bondade de encher e enviar, o mais breve possível, o seguinte coupon para a direção abaixo mencionada." *Alvorada Diária* no.131 (2 July 1919), 1.

[150] Testimony of Vasco Jardim, *Luso-Americano* (28 October 1989), 31.

[151] Its headquarters in Cambridge was located at 73 Highland Avenue. *Aurora* continued publication until 1934. It included some articles in English and published a wide variety of notices, especially on the last page, about churches and religious publications. The directorial team was formed by the following people in 1934: President: Rev. João F. de Oliveira; Editor: Rev. João Gomes Loja; Assistant Editor: Rev. J. Mendes dos Reis; Treasurer: António Vaz da Costa. Data extracted from the last issue, consulted in July-August of 1934, Freitas Library of California.

[152] "O Vigilante," *Diario de Noticias*, no. 737 (7 September 1921), 1.

[153] Domingos J. F. Spinney (Spínola) was born in Terceira (Azores) on January 18, 1878, son of Esteves Spínola and Maria Júlia Ferreira. He died in New Bedford on April 24, 1942. He married Augustina Maria da Trindade and had ten children. Data taken from the portal: www.ancestry.com. [Consulted in 2018]

[154] According to R. Antunes Correia's calculation from the number of issues registered for the weekly in 1919. See: Correia, "Salazar em New Bedford," 24. Detailed explanation in the footnote on page 26.

[155] According to data from the *New Bedford and Fairhaven Directory*, cited by Duarte Mendonça, 330.

[156] In the first issue, the newspaper notes that the launching of the first Portuguese daily was celebrated by the Portuguese community, resulting in many requests for subscriptions. *Alvorada*, no. 1 (25 January 1919), 2.

[157] Original: "o presente título 'ALVORADA DIÁRIA' foi-nos sugerido pelas autoridades postais, em vista do outro título – 'ALVORADA' – se assemelhar muito ao do semanário – 'A ALVORADA' – e causar confusão naquele departamento." "Aumento de formato do nosso diário," *Alvorada Diária*, no. 33 (6 March 1919), 3.

[158] *Alvorada*'s caption changed often during its six years of existence, between January 25, 1919 and December 31, 1926: "Jornal Diário"; "Portuguese Daily Newspaper"; "Jornal Imparcial e Noticioso"; and "Jornal Diário Imparcial e Noticioso."

[159] "Querer é poder," *Alvorada Diária*, no. 1071 (year IV, 8 December 1922), 1.

[160] Original: "A direção da Alvorada Publishing Company, Inc., reunida em assembleia, resolveu, a partir do dia 3 de janeiro de 1927, publicar este diário sob o novo nome de *Diario de Noticias* por ser este o mais apropriado em virtude do papel que esta publicação desempenha no meio da Colónia Portuguesa, levando, todos os dias úteis, ao lar de quase todas as famílias que a compõem, as últimas notícias do que se passa pelo mundo, sendo também o único meio pelo qual, dia-a-dia, os comerciantes, tanto nacionais como portugueses, podem dar conhecimento aos seus numerosos leitores e aos portugueses em geral do que têm para vender. Esta Empresa está convencida de que o Público Português receberá o 'Diario de Noticias' com a mesma boa vontade com que tem recebido a 'Alvorada' até agora, visto que a orientação a seguir com o novo nome será exatamente idêntica àquela seguida pela 'Alvorada,' procurando a empresa, além disso, introduzir todos os melhoramentos que estiverem ao seu alcance. O 'Diario de Noticias' será, como tem sido até agora o 'Alvorada,' incontestavelmente, o primeiro jornal português da América do Norte, tanto na sua tiragem que excede em New Bedford e Fall River a de todas as outras publicações portuguesas juntas, como na qualidade de órgão informador." *A Alvorada*, no. 2337 (31 December 1926), 1.

[161] See the information in the catalog at the Library of Congress. The registration form of this newspaper collected this data, based on a copy from no 521, (year 11, 18 September 1919), in which Guilherme Machado Luiz appears as "Publisher."

[162] António Vieira de Freitas Jr. was a native of Gaula, in Santa Cruz (Madeira). He had worked as an editor from 1914 at the *Alvorada* of Francisco Caetano Borges da Silva. In 1917, he married Guilherme M. Luiz's daughter. See: Duarte Mendonça, 333-34.

[163] *A Alvorada*, River Section (20 August 1924), 1.

[164] *Alvorada*, no. 1 (year 1, 25 January 1919), 4.

[165] *Diario de Noticias* no. 3474 (5 October 1930)

[166] Leo Pap, *Portuguese-Americans*, 79-85.

[167] See: Filipe Ribeiro de Menezes, org., *Paiva Couceiro. Diários, Correspondência e Escritos Dispersos* (Lisbon: D. Quixote, 2011).

[168] Eduardo de Carvalho, *Os Portugueses na Nova Inglaterra*, 107-11.

[169] *A Restauração* had headquarters located at 503 North Front Street (New Bedford).

[170] According to the data extracted from an article published by Manuel Moutinho, *Diario de Noticias*, no. 5655 (16 December 1937), 1. El Ateneu de Estudos Sociais was integrated in October of 1933 in the Aliança Liberal Portuguesa. See: *Diario de Noticias* no. 4397 (20 October 1933), 2.

[171] *A Alvorada*, no. 2179 (24 June, 1926).

[172] Original: "O Pe. Ferrraz, que era um orador de nome e de cultura invulgar, aspirava a um jornal bem feito e bem escrito. Fê-lo. Por má sorte não agradou aos seus colegas. Ferraz e Capeto aumentaram a tipografia. Compram dois linotipos, um 'Ludlow,' o nome da máquina que em Portugal era conhecida por 'tituleira' e ainda de uma rotativa. Capeto tinha bom gosto pelas artes gráficas. Porém, o jornal nunca deu para as despesas. Todos gostavam do 'Era Nova' mas ninguém, a não ser os trabalhadores das fábricas, pagava por ele." "Capítulo 8," *Luso-Americano* (28 October 1989), 31.

[173] See the *Diario de Noticias*, no. 14167 (14 December 1963), 6.

[174] In New Bedford, *A Imprensa*'s headquarters was located on 629 First Street.

[175] *A Alvorada*, no. 2088 (8 March 1926), 1.

[176] *A Crítica* was founded on November 5, 1921, and had 4 pages. Its motto was "Laugh and the world will laugh with you." Its headquarters was located on 157-A Acushmet Ave. New Bedford, MA.

[177] *Alvorada Diária*, no. 789 (8 November 1921), 1.

[178] See the biographical profile written by Vasco S. Jardim for the *Luso-Americano* (29 November 1989), 49.

[179] Original: "O célebre Francisco Santos tentou há semanas embarcar clandestinamente para aí no vapor 'Vulcania,' porém, duas horas depois de o vapor ter levantado ferro foi descoberta a sua fuga, tendo sido entregue às autoridades de Ponta Delgada, vindo depois para Lisboa sob prisão e entregue à política internacional que o conduziu novamente à prisão em que ainda se encontra detido para ser julgado; o patife desde que se encontra em Portugal já tem cometido várias proezas, intrujando e vigarizando todos aqueles que se aproximam dele. Há tempos foi vítima um irmão do falecido Padre Carmo de Fall River com uma máquina de escrever, etc. etc." See the news about his detainment in the *Diario de Noticias*, no. 6013 (25 February 1939), 2.

[180] *O Colonial*'s headquarters were located at 122 Walnut Street, Fairhaven.

[181] A sample of *O Colonial*'s advertisers included: Dr. Joseph Goulart – Dentist; Frates Funeral Home; Ster Optical Compan; Silva Bros. Creamery; North End Provision

Company; Dr. A. J. Taveira; Massachusetts Ass. P. de Socorros Mútuos; Professor José da Costa – Solfejo, Armonia e Piano; Frederico A. Costa – Notário Público; Joseph Sylvia – Seguros; Dr. A. Brunelle – Especialista dos olhos, ouvidos, nariz e garganta, etc. The price for these ads was 45 cents per inch (except for the first page), with special prices for permanent ads. See: *O Colonial* no. 459 (28 January 1938), 2.

[182] See, for instance: "Mais Um Crime Abominável. Nas Horríveis Prissões do Estado Novo os Presos são Bárbara e Cruelmente Assassinados", *O Colonial*, no. 406 (9 July 1936), 1.

[183] Affonso Gil Mendes Ferreira was a popular radio journalist who founded the program "A Voz de Portugal" on July 23, 1933. The program was broadcast initially from WNBH New Bedford and aired for over half a century. See Affonso Mendes Ferreira Papers. FM-PAA-UMD. MC 92/PAA.

[184] *Pé de Vento* was founded as a biweekly and became weekly after its fifth issue.

[185] Its headquarters was located on 193 Coggeshall Street, New Bedford.

[186] Duarte Mendonça, 328.

[187] Located at two different addresses: 1348 Cambridge Street, and 159 Hampshire Street.

[188] A general idea of the types of contentes published by *Revista Portugal-América Portuguesa*, can be gleaned from the titles of some of the articles in the March issue of 1928 (the only one found in the archives), such as: "Aviação nos Açores," by J. Carlos Pinto; "O Crime," by De Santa Cruz; "Alguma Coisa sobre as Relações Luso-Norte-Americanas," by Fidelino de Figueiredo; "Música, Arte e Teatro," by Frederico Rosa; or "Uma Mulher Sedutora," novel, by M. Delly.

[189] Geoffrey L. Gomes cites the founding of *O Mundo* in 1916.

[190] Address in Hanford was 529 W. 8th Street (Kings County). In Tulare: Box 473. And in Oakland: 1011 Franklin Street (Alameda County).

[191] Original: "A maior parte dos nossos lavradores já são amigos de ler, são estudiosos, e sempre prontos a tirar proveito de qualquer ideia nova que se lhes apresente. Por isso ao publicarmos o nosso jornalzinho no San Joaquin Valley onde noventa por cento dos portugueses são lavradores, dedicámo-lo a eles, O Lavrador Português. O nosso jornal não tem fumos de jornal literário, não, é simplesmente uma folha noticiosa que dará aos portugueses do vale de San Joaquin notícias das suas terras dos Estados Unidos e de todo o mundo." *O Lavrador Português*, no. 1 (vol. 1, 3 December 1912), 4.

[192] On January 9, 1915 the following companies published ads in the newspaper: The First National Bank of Riverdale, Armona Fish Market, Tulare Cooperative Creamery, Lester C. Kurtz – Ferreiro, New Lisbon Bakery, J. Grabow – Abridor de poços, Macedo Brown & Co., Eureka Market, Great Horse Harness Shop, James & Duncan – Reloajeiros e papeleiros, etc. *O Lavrador Português*, no. 92 (year 2, 9 January 1915).

[193] The following journalists were among the correspondents: Arthur B. Barcelos, Joe George, João Martias Soares, D. S. Pereira, João Baptista Serralheiro, Frank S. Soares, M. S. Bezerra, Mrs. Isabel Rodrigues Duarte Mrs. Emília Fernandes, John G. Loureiro, John Dutra, Maria de Jesus Cardoso, Miss Mamie Trigueiro, Mrs. Mary Oliveira, John Mendosa, Miss M. Maurizio, Aurélio Pessoa, Tony Smith, José A. Sousa, Maria Rita Silveira, Maria B. Dias, João Dias, João A. Espínola, Mrs. Fanny B. Relvas, M. M. Barros, Frank V. Bettencourt, Isaac A. Fontes, J. C. Bettencourt and A. S. Domingos. *O Lavrador Português*

also had numerous contributors, such as J. J. Baptista Jr., F. B. Machado, Teotónio Martins, Anthony B. Patrício, João Roldão, António S. Brazil, J. R. Cruz, F. G. Mattos, J. S. George, M. H. Gama, E. A. Melo, Maregrafo, Maduro Costa, J. Carraca, J. Vidal, Pompeu Maia, and A. Mendes.

[194] Its address in Oakland was 1926 East 14th Street.

[195] Original: "Isto significa que *A Colonia Portuguesa* deixou de pertencer a meia dúzia de indivíduos para poder ser propriedade de todos os seus assinantes."

[196] Original: "*A Colonia Portuguesa* é do povo português. Para o servir, para o recrear e para lhe dar nome. A maior parte dos atuais sócios não estão à espera de viver dos lucros desta empresa. São homens que à custa do seu trabalho honesto e enérgica inteligência, conseguiram acumular razóaveis meios de fortuna e possuem posições de destaque entre a nossa gente." *A Colonia Portuguesa*, no. 171 (year II, 3 November 1925), I.

[197] Its headquarters were located at 1927 East 14th Street (Oakland). *A Colonia Portuguesa*, no. 383 (16 December 1927), I.

[198] Original: "para pugnar pelos interesses do Povo Português deste Estado e estreitar, quanto possível, as relações políticas e comerciais entre Portugal e os Estados Unidos."

[199] The following are among the advertisements: Agência Carvalho, Rosa's Bakery, Dr. J. de Glória – Óculos, Yokohama Laundry, Hadley Funeral Parlors, Knudsen Creamary Company, Anderson & Scranton – Fazendas, Omata's Meat Market, Gallaher's Market – Carnes frescas e curadas, Dodge Brother's – Carros a motor, etc. *A Colonia Portuguesa*, no. 581 (5 January 1930).

[200] *A Colonia Portuguesa*, no. 383 (6 December 1927), 6.

[201] Headquarters in Sacramento was on 1811 X Street (1913-1930); in Alameda: 736 Lincoln Avenue (1930-1932). In October of 1930, Oakland and Chico also appeared on its front page. Its advertising agents had headquarters in San Francisco: Advertising Representatives "All Languages Advertising" (1705 Russ Bldg.).

[202] Original: "Deveis comprar das casas que anunciam neste jornal e dizerdes que vistes o anúncio no Imparcial. Sem vos custar, fazeis-nos um favor que muito nos auxiliará." The following commercial companies are found among the advertisements: California National Bank, Joseph W. Mento – Advogado, Eastmont Sanatorium, The Gardiner Company – Mercadorias Gerais, Kuroko – Photo Studio, American Cleaning & Dyeing Co., American Trust Co., Lusitania Corporation Limited, Dr. Chas J. Dean – Clínica do Recto e Colon, Grove Auto Camp, Miller & Jackson – Mercadorias Gerais, Bank of Italy, Dr. Almeida Rego, etc.

[203] Original: "No dia 1 de outubro, de tarde, foi encontrado morto num quarto do Hotel Elmer, de San Leandro, o seu proprietário José V. Mendonça, que à esquina da avenida Callan e rua East 14th, daquela localidade, dirigiu durante muitos anos negócio de restaurante. Uma grinalda de luto na porta daquele estabelecimento, fechado no dia 2, e um cartão explicando a causa pela morte repentina de J. V. Mendonça, de conjunto com uma pequena notícia nos diários locais, dando conta, ligeiramente, de tentativas de assassinato – cinco na última semana – foi o que se soube publicamente da tragédia, que é o epílogo provável de diligências domésticas. O senhor J. V. Mendonça era de um carácter em extremo decidido e de um génio inquebrantável, e ao que parece formou tenção de pôr fim à existência, e fê-lo." *O Imparcial*, no. 840 (year XVII, 11 October 1930), 6.

[204] *Jornal de Notícias*, no. 658 (year XIII, 16 August 1929).

[205] Original: "Em um orfanato de Angra do Heroísmo albergam-se quarenta crianças de quatro a dez anos de idade, pobres órfãozinhos que a sorte adversa, depois de lhes roubar o seio carinhoso da mãe e o braço potente de um pai para os guiar no trilho da existência, agora, mais uma vez os ameaça, expondo-os ao risco de perderem aquele beiral de caridade onde recebem o pão do corpo e do espírito. O velho edifício, onde estes infelizes se albergam, está desmantelado, arruinado, precisando de grandes reparos para se tornar habitável. Além disto a carestia da vida assumiu tais proporções, que se torna impossível, sem mais rendimentos, manter por mais tempo aquele instituto em tais circunstâncias. . . . Portugueses da vasta e rica Califórnia, socorrei com o vosso óvulo aqueles nossos irmãozinhos que de longe nos estendem as frágeis mãozinhas a pedir uma esmola! Portugueses, lembrai-vos que o Grande Cristo chamou a si os pequeninos, e se quiserdes ser dignos da Sua sublime doutrina, deixar vir a vós as criancinhas que por meio deste jornal hoje vos imploram proteção. Atendei às suas súplicas! Aqui fica pois aberta a subscrição para auxiliar o orfanato da Angra do Heroísmo e os pobres órfãozinhos que ali se albergam." *Jornal de Notícias*, no. 241 (year V, 16 September 1921), 1.

[206] In Oakland, its headquarters was located on 237 E. 14th Street.

[207] Original: "Rija e tesa bordoada/ Tesa e rija, para doer/ Havemos dar a valer/ Pancadaria danada/ Em toda a cavalgadura;/ Pois nos ensinou o rifão/ Que tudo o que arde cura/ Mazelas de patifão./ Vamos a rir, pois; o riso é um castigo, o riso é uma filosofia, muitas vezes o riso é uma salvação."

[208] *A California Alegre*, no. 97 (year III, 1 and 15 November 1940).

[209] Original: "No dia 17 de setembro andava o nosso filhinho, depois da hora da escola, brincando com outras crianças, quando teve a infelicidade de meter um prego no pé direito, prego que lhe atravessou a sola do sapato e espetou na carne um bom bocado. Depois de, ele próprio, ter arrancado o dito prego, voltou para casa, dizendo à mãe o que havia sucedido. A mãe, aflita, aplicou-lhe os remédios caseiros que lhe aconselharam algumas pessoas presentes. O caso passou e José voltou a brincar, continuando a ir, nos dias que se seguiram, para a escola, não voltando a queixar-se. Na noite de sábado, 25 de setembro, para o domingo, 26, o pequenino principiou a queixar-se com dores no pescoço e nas costas. Ao romper da manhã do domingo, chamámos um médico, o ilustre cirurgião, sr. Dr. Abílio Reis, que, mal entrou no quarto do enfermo, nos aconselhou a conduzi-lo sem perda de tempo ao hospital. O pobre José estorcia-se com dores, e os seus gritos cortavam-nos o coração. Era o terrível tétano." *A California Alegre*, no. 49 (series IV, 14 October 1937), 1.

[210] Original poem: "Quando o íris da bonança/ Meigamente lhe sorria,/ Quando em flor a meiga esp'rança/ O arroubava de alegria,/ Quando, além de cada monte,/ Divisava um horizonte,/ Da mais deslumbrante cor –/ Mal pensava – em tenra idade –/ Que os umbrais da eternidade/ Em breve iria transpor!/ 'Num pé, um prego! Isso é nada'/ Diziam. 'Um incidente!'/ Mas a f'rida, mal pensada,/ Mais e mais se fez dolente,/ Até que por derradeiro,/ O tétano traiçoeiro/ O levou ao hospital,/ Lá, a parca inexorável,/ Porque o mal era incurável/ Vibrou-lhe o golpe fatal!/ Pobre Joe tão novo ainda" *A California Alegre*, no. 49 (series IV, 14 October 1937), 1.

[211] Headquarters in Hayward was located on 1304 B Street.

[212] J. C. Valim was also a music composer. He co-authored a hymn to the Portuguese Pavillion at the Panama-Pacific International Exposition of 1915, held in San Francisco (CA). See the hymn in *A Revista Portuguesa*, no. 2 (February 1915), 4-5.

[213] Original: "A nossa REVISTA é simples, mas ao mesmo tempo atrativa a correta, o que decerto a tornará distinta entre os outros jornais portugueses em circulação, pela NOVIDADE e VARIEDADE de leitura. Isto de per (sic) é suficiente para, desde já contarmos como o vosso alto e valioso patrocínio. Não pouparemos trabalho e sacrifícios para bem servir o público e tentaremos melhorar a REVISTA o melhor possível. Assinai A REVISTA PORTUGUESA e tereis muito que ler nas compridas noites de inverno." *A Revista Portuguesa*, no. 2 (backcover, February 1915).

[214] In the first issue of *A Revista Portuguesa*, from January 1915, the following articles appear: "A Cidade de Hayward" by J. S. Melo Jr., "Os Portugueses na Agricultura – Germano Silva" by C. de Serpa, "Os Portugueses no Comércio – J. F. Prioste" by J. S. Melo Jr., "Portugal e Açores," "Administração de J. S. Costa na I.D.E.S.," "Guerra na Europa" by J. S. Melo Jr., "Exposição Panamá-Pacífico" by C. de Serpa, "A Nossa Revista – Editor e Redatores," "Secção Literária – Primeiro de Dezembro de 1640" by J. C. Valim, "O Homem Misterioso – Conto Histórico" by C. de Serpa, "As Modas" and "Benita – Romance Histórico" by H. Rider Haggard. *A Revista Portuguesa. Agrícola, Comercial e Literária*, no. 1 (year 1, January 1915).

[215] Original: "Ao darmos à nossa publicação mensal o nome de 'Revista,' não foi intuito nosso que os leitores encontrassem, nos seus primeiros números, tudo o que se possa presumir do título. Para se publicar uma 'Revista' portuguesa de igual formato, constando de iguais secções às de Portugal e Brasil, ou – numa palavra – que abrangesse os 'oito mandamentos' do nosso dedicado amigo Valim, seria necessário que tivéssemos um capital fabuloso às nossas disposições. Capital para se adquirir um maquinismo de expediente necessário; capital para se conservar os tipógrafos mais aptos na arte; capital para angariar bons escritores e depender das suas 'promessas'; – Capital, três vezes capital! Mas como as graças daquele 'deus terrestre' nunca caíssem sobre nós, tivemos de valer-nos das nossas poucas abilitações e experiência da arte tipográfica, conjuntamente dos nossos estimáveis amigos, Valim e Serpa, para podermos pôr em prática a ideia que eu e este último já de há muito alimentávamos. Tivemos de planear a maneira mais económica por que se podesse dar aos portugueses da nossa colónia uma publicação mensal que lhes prendesse a atenção; que lhes despertasse a indiferença pela leitura; que lhes mostrasse o bom que são e o melhor que poderiam ser; que lhes inspirasse amor a tudo o que é português; e, depois de noites de insónia, de dias dum constante labutar, a 'Revista,' que aqui apresentamos é um bom que podemos fazer, mas não o melhor que desejávamos. Assim como Roma não se fez num dia, assim também levará meses, e talvez anos, antes que a nossa 'Revista' seja tal qual o que se possa esperar duma publicação desta índole." *A Revista Portuguesa. Agrícola, Comercial e Literária*, no. 1 (year 1, January 1915), 12.

[216] Cited in the report composed by Guilherme M. Luiz in 1933 for the Ministério de Instrução Pública de Portugal, published under the title, "A Imprensa Portuguesa nos Estados Unidos de América do Norte." *Diario de Noticias*, no. 4333 (4 August 1933), 1 and 8; and no. 4338 (10 August 1933), 4-5 (edited version). The newspaper is also mentioned by Geoffrey L. Gomes.

[217] Newspaper referred to in a report written by Guilherme M. Luiz in 1933. Also cited by Geoffrey L. Gomes and by Fernando M. Soares Silva, who situates its existence in 1933: *A Tribuna Portuguesa* (15 and 30 of March; 1 and 15 April 2012), 19.

[218] Data taken from a single copy held at the New Bedford Whaling Museum (Kendall Institute Research Institute: Portuguese Immigration Records, 1864-1976).

[219] Printing, writing and administration took place at 432 East 135th Street, New York.

[220] Original: "Assinai *O Portugal*. É dever do bom Português auxiliar a imprensa Portuguesa que semanalmente aviva o sagrado idioma da nossa língua Pátria, e nos aviva a memória do nosso torrão natal, da nossa história, e dos nossos costumes. O patriotismo ou amor à Pátria mostra-se só com obras." Data extracted from *O Portugal*, no. 78 (year III, vol. 3, 14 July 1932), the only copy kept at the Freitas Library of San Leandro.

[221] Leo Pap, *The Portuguese-Americans* (New York: Twayne Publishers-A Division of G. K. Hall & Co. Boston, 1981), 88.

[222] Headquarters in Providence is located on 301 Wickenden Street.

[223] Data extracted from the Ferreira Mendes Portuguese-American Archives (Miguel Corte-Real Collection) at UMass Dartmouth Library.

Chapter 4 New Challenges: Portuguese-American Newspapers, 1930-2015

[1] See Leo Pap, *The Portuguese-Americans* (New York: Twayne Publishers-A Division of G. K. Hall & Co. Boston, 1981).

[2] Jerry Williams, *In Pursuit of their Dreams: A History of Azorean Immigration to the United States* (North Dartmouth: University of Massachusetts Dartmouth: Center for Portuguese Studies and Culture, 2007), 100-102.

[3] Information extracted from the report carried out by Guilherme M. Luiz in 1933 for the Ministério de Instrução Pública de Portugal, "A Imprensa Portuguesa nos Estados Unidos da América do Norte." *Diario de Noticias*, no. 4333 (4 August 1933), 1 and 8; and no. 4338 (10 August 1933), 4-5 (updated version).

[4] Original: "Dizei sempre a verdade e a verdade te fará livre."

[5] Original: "Trabalhadores de todo o mundo, uni-vos."

[6] Original: "Vívida, como um sulco profundo e indelével de bisturi monstruoso numa página brônzea da História, existe ainda gravada no coração e no espírito da humanidade, essa bacanal macabra e hedionda conhecida pela Grande Guerra! Concebida e posta em prática por velhos capitalistas, cruéis e devassos, para mais facilmente satisfazerem os seus depravados e orgíacos vícios, não hesitaram sacrificar milhões de vidas inocentes, porque assim o mandava a sua ilimitada ambição, o seu egoísmo feroz. A guerra, com todos os seus atributos, representada nos quatro simbólicos ginetes do Apocalipse, por toda a parte deixava a marca inapagável da sua passagem: a FOME, a peste, a destruição, a morte!" *A Emancipação* (May 1934), 1. Copy located in the Ferreira-Mendes Portuguese-American Archives (FM-PAA) at the UMass Dartmouth Library (Miguel Corte-Real Collection).

[7] Data extracted from the only copy found: *O Teatro*, no. 9 (year I, 30 June 1936, AHD, Portuguese Embassy in Washington). Discontinued copy. Tabloid format, 4 pages. Annual subscription cost $.75. Headquarters in New Bedford was located on 153 County Street. The following advertisements were in this issue: Bettencourt Furniture, Gonsalves

Studio, Dr. Albert J. Clement, Silvia Bros. Creamary, Livraria e Papelaria Portuguesa, Atlantic Market-Manuel Franco, Martins Clothes Shop, Santos Bakery, among others.

[8] Data from the copies of the original preserved in the Ferreira Mendes Portuguese-American Archives (Miguel Corte-Real Collection): *O Mensageiro*, no. 1 (24 December 1936), 1. It is believed to be the only extant edition.

[9] Vasco S. Jardim, "Chapter 9: De Volta aos Jornais Portugueses de Newark," in "Retalhos das Memórias Brancas," *Luso-Americano* (1 November 1989), 37.

[10] See: *Diario de Noticias*, no. 5244 (30 January 1937), 7.

[11] The majority of the data on Luiz Antunes was taken from the *Diario de Noticias*. UMass Dartmouth Professor Ron Fortier provided us with the records in which the paper of New Bedford mentions Luiz Antunes: *Diario de Noticias* (12 August 1930), 2; (23 May 1932), 2; (15 October 1932), 2; and (30 January 1937), 7. Also see, *Luso-Americano* (1 November 1989), 37.

[12] A.C. Benavides was the representative for the paper in Hamilton, Bermuda.

[13] Among the advertisers in *O Evangelista* were Dr. A. J. T. Lima – Dentist, Daniel Jordão – Funeral director, Monte-Pio Operário, Joseph M. Ferreira – Watchmaker, Ramos Service Station Manuel J. Barboza – Sapataria, Silva Funeral, North End Provision Company, Travis & Aguiar – Refrigerators, Joaquim Cunha – Florista, A. F. Pimentel – Notary Public, and Sebastião & Freitas – Meats, groceries and vegetables. Data taken from *O Evangelista*, no. 17 (year ll, February 1936). All data about this newspaper is based on this issue, found in the Freitas Library of San Leandro (CA).

[14] *O Portugal*'s team consisted of M. S. Teles, Cândido Vaz, António Santo and António S. Frade, as correspondent in Newark. Editorial secretary and representatives were A. F. Cruz, A. B. Cordeiro and José Machado. Data based on a copy found in the Freitas Library: *O Portugal*, (Oakland), unnumbered copy (7 September 1935). Headquarters was located in Oakland (1552, 34th Street, Alameda County). Printing was done at the print shop of *O Colonial*, Colonial Printing Co. (1927 East 14th Street).

[15] Advertisements included those from Dariglen – Creamaries Ltd., Superior Supply Company, Fábrica de Linguiça Portuguesa de M. Moniz, Ecos do Ar – Desafios radiofónicos, Morton Hospital – Dr. Carlos Fernandes, Manuel Vieira – Loja de géneros alimentícios, Rosa Baking Co, António Barroca – Duas Mercearias, Lisbon Restaurant, J. A. Mendes – Artista em pintura e empapelador,Valey Creamery, Dr. Abílio Reis – Médico e cirurgião, Dr. J. C. Lopes – Dentista Português, The American Pharmacy Inc, Charles E. Pine – Automobile Service, and António Fernandes – Comerciante Português.

[16] Manoel da Silveira Cardozo notes that the newspaper served as a mouthpiece for the immigrants from Ílhavo. See: *The Portuguese in America (590 b.C-1974)*, 68.

[17] Original: "Lindas crianças, belas, formosas/ Que graça infinda que Deus vos deu!/ Meigas estrelas, fulgentes rosas,/ Semelhais anjos vindos do céu/ . . . / Lindas crianças da Pátria o templo/ Defendei sempre com todo o afã/ Heróis da Pátria dai-vos o exemplo.../ Eles são de hoje, vós de amanhã./ A descoberta das vastas plagas/ Da Califórnia, singrado as vagas/ Quem foi que a fez?/ Um nobre filho da vossa raça/ Que aqui se passa.../ De Deus na graça.../ Um português!/ Foi João Rodrigues – um tal Cabrilho –/ Nauta, perito, distinto filho/ De Portugal.../ Servindo embora vaidosa Espanha/ como tal façanha." *O Portugal*, (Oakland, 7 September 1935), 2.

[18] According to data from Frederick G. Bohme, "The Portuguese in California," *California Historical Society Quarterly* 35, no. 3 (September 1956): 233-52.

[19] Headquarters in Sacramento was first located on 1411 21st Street and afterwards on 5217 V Street. Printing location: 1820 Y Street, Sacramento.

[20] The management team of the Lusitania Club in 1936 was comprised of James Ormond, Alberto Correia, J. N. Almeida, Dr. J. C. Lopes, and A. A. Rogers.

[21] The headquarters for *The Lusitanian* was located on 1146 Jefferson Street, Oakland. Its format was quarter-sheet size. It used color on its front page and the printing and paper were of high quality. Initially, the total number of pages was 10, but reaching up to 20 in some issues. It also included advertisements. A complete collection of the magazine can be found in the Ferreira Mendes Portuguese-American Archives (Miguel Corte-Real Collection) at UMass Dartmouth.

[22] Its headquarters was in the following locations: San Francisco (948 Market Street) in 1937; and San Leandro in 1938. Information about this magazine comes from the only copy found (non-catalogued), and refers to the first issue, April 1937 (AHD, historical documentation from the embassy of Portugal).

[23] "Why this Magazine," *Cabrillo Commentator. Discoverer of California*, no. 1 (April 1937), 3.

[24] Original: "E Conhecereis a Verdade e a Verdade vos Libertará." Location of headquarters in Oakland: 2412 E. 15th Street. Several copies of *O Heraldo* are held in the Freitas Library.

[25] Original: "No Heraldo de Setembro p.p. saiu um artigozinho sobre a guerra civil em Espanha que deu no goto do Sr. Redator do 'Portugal da Califórnia.' Ora o artigo em questão acusava a Igreja Católica de ser a instigadora da terrível guerra civil que tanta miséria está causando àquela nação, baseando-se este facto nas declarações dum padre socialista espanhol, o Rev. João Garcia Morales. Realmente isto deu no goto do Sr. Redator do 'Portugal da Califórnia' que, dum modo atrabiliário, vem a público no seu jornal, acusando-nos de termos forjado a notícia que dissemos nos ter sido fornecida pelo Associated Press. ... Não inventámos mas apenas publicámos factos, e contra factos não há argumentos. A ignorância, Sr. Redator, é muito atrevida. Que a lição lhe sirva para o futuro." Editorial entitled: "A Ignorância É Muito Atravida," *O Heraldo*, no. 11, (year I, November 1936), I.

[26] See the advertisement for the agency in "Página de New Jersey-New York," *Diario de Noticias*, issue without number (18 October 1945).

[27] Its headquarters was located on 443 de la E. 135 Street.

[28] Leo Pap notes that *A Luta* survived until 1970: "The Portuguese Press," 302.

[29] In the May 26, 1937 issue, for example, one can read the following news and articles: "Inauguração da Casa em Elisabeth," "Portuguese-American Club Inc. – A sua Nova Sede," "Portugal na Imprensa Estrangeira," "O 48º Aniversário de *O Independente*," "Federação Associativa," "Anti-Marx" (article), "Jornais há Muitos – Comentários sobre as Proezas de um Correspondente," "Vida Colonial," "A Família" (editorial), "Estrangeirismos," "Ecos da Pátria," and the series, "A Capela de Rosas," by Ana de Castro Osório. *A Luta*, no. 26 (year I, 26 May 1937).

[30] Document 432 (proc. 37) from the ambassador of Portugal in Washington, Pedro T. Pereira, to Oliveira Salazar (25 June 1949, AHD. 2º P, A59, M251).

[31] Headquarters was located on 81 de Ferry Street, Newark. Several out of print issues can be found in the Arquivo Histórico Diplomático de Lisboa, in the documentation from the Embassy of Portugal.

[32] In the issue from March 15, 1934, *A Tribuna* published the following sections: "Boaventura Fala sobre Portugal," "Comércio, Indústria, Finanças," "Os Mercados Portugueses," "Notícias de Todo o Mundo," "Mais uma Carta sobre as Missões," "Os Autómatos da Finança," "A Festa Comemorativa do Portuguese-American Club no Claridge Hotel na Cidade de New York," "Ecos daqui e d'além Mar," "Propaganda Portuguesa" (editorial), "Perfis da Colónia," "Notas da Semana," "Divagações Oportunas," "As Aventuras de um Bebé," "Folhetim: Cidade Eterna," by Hal Caine; and "Desportos." *A Tribuna*, no. 140 (year III, 15 March 1934).

[33] Headquarters moved to 15 Monroe Street, New York.

[34] Original: "nem o dinheiro do Bianchi (o embaixador), nem do Verdades (cônsul geral em N. York), nem de um Ford era suficiente." *Luso-Americano* (1 November 1989), 37.

[35] Original: "O parlamento francês acaba de aprovar a quantia de dois milhões, cento e sessenta e sete mil e quatrocentos e quarenta dólares para serem gastos em propaganda francesa na América do Norte e do Sul. Essa fabulosa soma que a França vai gastar em reclamo, é uma demonstração de bom senso e esperteza, que voltará multiplicada muitas vezes, aos cofres franceses do governo e dos industriais que por meio do reclamo venderão para o estrangeiro os seus produtos. . . . Estes factos bastante significativos deveriam 'abrir os olhos' a Portugal e aos nossos comodistas comerciantes-exportadores para que fizessem mais alguma coisa do que as crónicas reuniões, com conferências e mais conferências, e afinal, nada se vê de concreto, de ação portuguesa – NÃO POR INTERMÉDIO DE FIRMAS INGLESAS – neste vastíssimo e rico mercado americano! Em tempos que já lá vão esteve 'quase' a fechar-se um contrato entre o nosso país e uma companhia de propaganda comercial de New York, o qual montava a quantia de cento e vinte cinco mil dólares (salvo erro), para propaganda de produtos portugueses. Não chegou a ter vida o contrato por em Portugal acharem ser a soma FABULOSA! Não se lembraram que hoje em dia, comercialmente. sem reclamo nada se vende, e que essa quantia gasta em propaganda de produtos nossos poderia fazer ao comércio e indústria de Portugal MUITÍSSIMAS vezes mais a importância gasta." *A Tribuna*, no. 140 (year III, 15 March 1934), 6.

[36] Headquarters was located on 79 Ferry Street, Newark.

[37] *Luso-Americano* (1 November 1989), 37.

[38] Manuel Nascimento died at age 56 in his home on 105 Ferry Street. He came to the U.S. when he was 31. He first lived in Pawtucket, RI, and, in 1921, moved to Newark, where he founded the Iberic Press and *A Pátria Portuguesa*. Nascimento left a widow, 2 sons (Alberto and Ernesto) and 4 daughters. See: *Diario de Noticias*, New Jersey and New York edition (7 April 1933), 7.

[39] Original: "O Manuel Nascimento era um homem sério e muito competente. Conhecia as leis portuguesas e americanas. Fora tradutor em New York. A mulher e filhos viviam em Pawtucket. Foi nessa altura que se mudaram para Newark. Houve um homem, o Francisco Ribeiro, que se ofereceu para salvar a derrotada família Nascimento. Como? Atualizando os pagamentos do seguro de vida do sr. Nascimento nas condições de ele ser

nomeado o beneficiário do seguro. Morreu o Nascimento e o Ribeiro paga todas as dívidas do casal e entrega o restante à viúva e filhos. Francisco Ribeiro, que era um gigante de homem, foi ainda maior gigante na sua ação filantrópica. Com mais de 52 anos aprendeu a ler e escrever." "Capítulo 9," *Luso-Americano* (1 November 1989), 37.

[40] The report was published as "A Imprensa Portuguesa nos Estados Unidos da América do Norte," *Diario de Noticias*, no. 4333 (4 August 1933), 1 and 8; and no 4338 (10 August 1933), 4-5 (edited version).

[41] *Diario de Noticias*, nº 6295 (1 February 1940), 3. See also: Duarte Mendonça, "José Rodrigues Miguéis na Imprensa Lusa de New Bedford: Uma Presença Assídua," *Gávea-Brown* 32-33 (2010-2011): 55.

[42] Original: "Recebemos hoje o número 3 de 'O Trabalho,' que se publica na cidade de Danbury, estado de Connecticut, sob a direção do nosso prezado colaborador sr. Joaquim de Oliveira, seu redator. O número 3 deste bem redigido jornal, traz na sua página da frente uma bela fotogravura do grande vulto micaelense Dr. Teófilo Braga, de saudosa memória, que foi o primeiro presidente da República Portuguesa (governo provisório). Número comemorativo da data histórica de 31 de Janeiro de 1891, tendo colaboração dos bem conhecidos Drs. João Camoesas e José Rodrigues Miguéis. Agradecendo a visita de 'O Trabalho' fazemos votos pelas suas prosperidades bem como do seu diretor e editor para quem vão os nossos sinceros cumprimentos." Taken from the article by Duarte Mendonça, "José Rodrigues Miguéis na Imprensa Lusa de New Bedford: Uma Presença Assídua," *Gávea-Brown* 32-33 (2010-2011): 55.

[43] See *A Voz da Colónia*, no. 37 (year 1, 12 November 1942).

[44] Data taken from *A Voz da Colónia*, no. 163 (year IV, 17 May 1945).

[45] Its headquarters had the following address: New York City: Writing and Administration at 89-23-143rd Street, Jamaica 2, L. I.; and administrative offices on 15 Moore Street.

[46] According to the magazine, distribution and sales were in N. Bedford, Fall River, Cambridge, Taunton and Newport (Massachusetts); Providence and East Providence (Rhode Island); New York City, Brooklyn, Jamaica, Yorkers (New York), and Newark (New Jersey).

[47] See: *O Mundo Lusíada*, no. 1 (September 1949).

[48] Editor's note: Reference to the last verse of the second stanza of *The Lusiads*, "Se a tanto me ajudar o engenho e arte."

[49] Original: "Esta revista propõe-se, se para isso nos ajudar o 'engenho da arte': Primeiro, pugnar pela cultura Lusa, e pela Luso-Brasileira. Segundo, intensificar o problema da propagação do ensino da língua portuguesa nas escolas públicas deste país bem como desenvolver na mocidade académica Americana, o gosto pelas letras portuguesas e cultura luso-brasileira. Terceiro, homenagear os espíritos mais esclarecidos e cultos da grande Família Lusíada, dando publicidade às suas melhores páginas, das obras da literatura, filosofia e ciência, música e arte. Corrigir toda ou quaisquer injúria feita na Imprensa contra a nossa prole, quer ela viva aqui, na Europa, na África, na Ásia, ou na Oceania. E, finalmente, publicitar os méritos ou deméritos dos filhos da lusitanidade, porque julgamos que as boas como as más ações dos cidadãos devem ser tornadas públicas: as primeiras para que se galardoem e as segundas para que se reprimam." *O Mundo Lusíada*, no. 1 (September 1949), 1.

[50] Its headquarters in New York City had two addresses: 40 East 54th Street, and 501 Madison Avenue. It was also available from offices in San Francisco and Lisbon.

[51] *Portugal Today* was comprised of the following team. Executive editor: George Roosen. Editors: P. Kenneth Macker, Evelyn J. Heyward, William D. Forrester, Ruy Leitão; Assistant editor: Hilda Wickerhausser; Editors of photography: Eduardo Gonzales y Jaime Cruz; Director of art: Douglas S. Kent; Production Liaison: Gloria L. Pistilli; Correspondents: Rodrigo L. Rodrigues (S. Paulo), José A. Carpio (Manila), Sara Sevel (Milán), Daisy Brown (Tokyo).

[52] *Portugal Today*, no. 1 (October 1959), 1.

[53] The content of *Voz de Portugal* related to the Luso-American community and issues regarding the Lusophone world in general. In its first issue, the following titles appear on the cover: "Nova Aurora!" (editorial), "Mensagens de Saudação da Sua Exa. o Embaixador de Portugal nos E.U.A, Sr. Luis Esteves Fernandes," and "O Primeiro Número." In the center of the first page, in bold letters, one can read the following message: "Voz de Portugal é um jornal feito por portugueses para servir as causas lusitanas dos portugueses da Califórnia" (*Voz de Portugal* is a newspaper made by Portuguese to serve the needs of the Portuguese of California). See *A Voz de Portugal*, no. 1 (year 1, 1 September 1960), 1.

[54] Original: "Aparece, à luz da publicidade neste prodigioso Estado da Califórnia, um novo jornal na maviosa Língua de Camões. ... Não nos consta que qualquer proprietário ou editor de jornal no nosso idioma, neste Estado, haja feito fortuna, ou sequer vivido desafogadamente, com os lucros de qualquer empresa jornalística do género. Pelo contrário, as perspetivas nunca foram as melhores, pois, duma maneira geral, quase todos acabaram por se dedicar a outras atividades que melhor pudessem satisfazer o seu ganha-pão quotidiano e aqueles que, melhor ou pior, têm conseguido levar até junto da Comunidade, a voz portuguesa, podem considerar-se como Heróis e Patriotas. Sabemos isto perfeitamente, mas também sabemos que a Colónia Portuguesa da Califórnia tem a necessidade premente de ser servida por uma Imprensa que vá ao encontro das suas justas aspirações. Dois jornais, no nosso entender, não são o suficiente para servir os quinhentos mil portugueses radicados no Estado mais rico e progressivo da União Americana. A reduzida tiragem do único jornal em idioma português, nestas paragens, para servir tão vasta Colónia como é a nossa, traduz bem o marasmo em que caiu nestes últimos anos a Imprensa portuguesa na Califórnia. Creio, pois, ser um passo útil, não só para a Comunidade Portuguesa da Califórnia, como também para a própria Imprensa que, deixando de ser única passará a ser melhor e, por conseguinte, a despertar o interesse geral." *Voz de Portugal*, no. 1 (year 1, 1 September 1960), 1.

[55] The first issue of *O Companheiro da Alegria* had the following sections: "Postais de Portugal," "Só Alegria," "Coisas do Arco da Velha," "Bom Humor," "Miscelânea," "Castanhas Piladas," "Passatempo," "Poesia," "Contos para os Nossos Filhos: As felicidades de Bonifácio," "Cozinha Portuguesa," "Quadras Soltas," "Cantoria de Manuel Pavão com uma Ceguinha," and "Tempos Modernos."

[56] Headquarters was located at 253 Lafayette Street, Newark, NJ.

[57] For a sample, read the titles from the cover of *Novos Rumos Estados Unidos*, no. 148 (year VII, June 15, 1967): "A Colónia Portuguesa de N. J. Saúda o Ilustre Comandante e Guarnição do Navio-Escola Sagres na sua Visita ao Porto de Newark"; "Festejos de Santo

António"; "Bolsas de Estudo"; "Rifa," and "Picnic." It was a tabloid of 12 pages, with many advertisements. The cited issue included the following advertisers: Sport Club Português; Sport Club Murtoense; Olshins Farmacy; Iberia; Agência Central de Viagens; TAP; Buyus Funeral Home; Santoro Lumber Co.; Ourivesaria Moraes; and Dads & Grads – radios.

[58] Location in New Bedford of *A Chama* was on 355 Coggeshall Street.

[59] Original: "Revista semanal e independente de quaisquer filiações partidárias, fundada em 1968."

[60] In 1978, *A Chama* was comprised of the following team: Chief of Publicity, June Dias Medeiros; International Section Director, Carlos Matos; Community, John M. Raposo; Sports from Portugal, John Lourenço; and Women's Section, Maria Luisa Carreiro. It also had the following correspondents: in Boston, Jorge Correia; in Stoughton, José Martins and Vitorino América; in Providence, Albert Silva; in Ponta Delgada, Nuno da Câmara; in Lisbon, Eduardo Camilo; and in Funchal, José Cabrita.

[61] The *Oportunidades* team was comprised of the following people: General Director (Associate): José da Silva; Publicity: Fernando Pais; Mechanography: Octávia Marinho; Collaborator in Connecticut: Manuel Gaspar; Collaborator in Bethelu: José Viçoso; Collaborator in Massachusetts: Miguel de Figueiredo Corte Real. Correspondents: in Porto, Octávio Marinho; in Minho, Manuel A. Moreira. Delegates: in Massachusetts, Franklin Duarte; in Philadelphia, Urgel Santos. Public Relations: Maria Fernanda Rocha.

[62] In August of 2012, the following people were responsible for other areas of *O Jornal*: Marketing, Maria V. Vieira; Advertising designer, Karen Pearson; News, Manuel F. Estrela, and Melissa Costa; Foreign correspondent: Lusa Ponte, *Açoriano Oriental*.

[63] *O Jornal*, https://www.heraldnews.com/ojornal/about

[64] The address in San José was 1617-B East Santa Clara Street.

[65] In the first issue, the following people formed part of the management team of *The Portuguese Tribune*. Director: João P. Brum; publisher: Duarte Santos; editors: Carlos Ramos, Padre José Ribeiro and S. J. Heraldo da Silva; correspondents: José Teixeira (Açores); Necas Madruga (Artesia) and Leonel Medeiros (San Leandro). Collaborators: João Afonso, Vamberto Freitas, Maria Amélia Neves, Onésimo T. Almeida, Álamo de Oliveira, Manuel Duarte, Coelho de Sousa, Maduro Dias, Goretti Silveira, Jaime Baptista, Pedro de Merelim, Helder S. Lima, Fernando Pereira, Reis Leite, Jose Mattos, James Guill, Maria Vitorino, Hilse Barbosa, Velma Santos and M. Ávila Simas.

[66] In 2011, the management team of *A Tribuna Portuguesa* was comprised of the following: Publisher and editor: José Ávila; English section and assistant editor: Miguel Ávila; Sports editor: Armando Antunes; Art director: Roberto Ávila. Correspondents: Fernando Dutra (Artesia), Filomena Rocha (San José) and David Borges (Tulare). In its list of collaborators were (Issue 1102, February 2011): Eduardo Mayone Dias, Ferreira Moreno, Onésimo T. Almeida, Adalino Cabral, José Brites, Diniz Borges, Luciano Cardoso, José Raposo, Margarida Silva, Josefina Canto e Castro, Mercês Coelho, Edmundo Macedo, João Luis de Medeiros, Malhão Pereira, Caetano Valadão Serpa, Manuel Calado, Maria das Dores Beirão, Henrique Dedalo, António Vallacorda, Egídio Almeida, Fernando M. Soares Silva, José Duarte da Silveira, Dimas Alves, Goretti Silveira, Rufino Vargas, Elen de Moraes, Paul Mello and Ana Cristina Sousa.

[67] Website for digital edition: http://www.tribunaportuguesa.com. [Consulted in 2019]

[68] The Comité Açoriano 75 – Non Profit Corp. received correspondence at: P.O. Box 9264 Providence; P.O. Box 358 Bristol; and P.O. Box 351 Somerset, Massachusetts.

[69] The management team for *The Azorean Times* included: Director: Albert Silva; publicity: Edgar Rebelo, José Cabral, Cristina Maria Silva, António Matos and Manuel António Oliveira; Photography: António Goulart; Administration: Luís Machado.

[70] According to José A. Tavares dos Anjos' book *Cape Verdean-American WWII Veterans of New Bedford* (New Bedford: Lulu.com, 2nd edition, 2010), p. 158, Manuel T. Neves was a World War II Army veteran who served from 1941 to 1946.

[71] See *Diario de Noticias*, n°15.587 (20 August 1969), 2.

[72] According to the figures from the *Yearbook of Immigration Statistics 2012*.

[73] Headquarters in New Bedford of *Novo Mundo em Revista* was on 1515 Acushnet Avenue. Editor-in-Chief: Manuel Maria Duarte. Collaborators: Dr. Manuel Luciano da Silva, Prof. Luís Aguiar, António Cabral, António Silva, Miguel Corte-Real, Padre José Maria de Sousa, A. Dionisio da Costa, Dr. Caetano Valadão Costa, Manuel Calado and Joaquim F. Gaio.

[74] Headquarters in San José was located on 1629-B E Santa Clara Street. And its subtitle was: "Semanário Português – Portuguese Weekly." Among its collaborators (in the first issue): António Silveira, José Mendes, João M. Rubens, Henrique Dinis, Artur Ramos, Joaquim Ávila, Heldera Santos, João da Maia, Eurico Mendes, Francisco Cota, Adulcino Silva, Alfredo Cunha, Maria J. Brantuas, Manuel Faria, Joel Silva, A. Sousa Vieira, Velma Santos, Bernardete Vieira, Euclides Álvares, Fátima Contente, Ana M. Frederico, Zeta Cruz, José Silva, Leonesa Silva, Nélia Sousa, Luís Leonel and Luís Cordeiro. "Typesetters": Judy Ávila and Eduarda Brasil. Composition and Photography: São Bettencourt. *Noticia*'s format was of reduced proportions (large sheet), with more than 20 pages on average for each issue. After the April 2, 1986 issue, it would adopt a tabloid format, with a more business feel, incorporating ads of different sizes and creative styles. This is exactly the format that its successor, *Portugal-USA*, would adopt. There is a collection of both newspapers in the Bancroft Library (UC Berkeley) and the Freitas Library of California.

[75] Original: "Foi um parto difícil. Nem toda a gente gostou de que eu estava para nascer. Houve um pouco de tudo para impedir o meu aparecimento. Choros e lágrimas. Lamentações e gritos. Ameaças de suicídio. Reuniões e pactos. Experimentaram a pílula, sugeriram o aborto e até foram à bruxa. Tem sido um movimento desusado. Por minha causa, alguns inimigos, que não se podiam ver, andam agora aos beijinhos. Outros, que se sentiam desesperados, ganharam um ânimo novo. E tudo porquê? Por um simples jornal. Um negócio que ninguém quer. Pelo menos em mãos alheias. Se este mérito não merecesse este puto, o facto de ter fomentado tanto interesse por jornais, nesta comunidade, seria mais que suficiente para justificar e agradecer o seu nascimento. Até aqui fazer jornais era negócio de poetas, de idealistas, de tesos sem poderem com um a gata pelo rabo. Agora, por amor e ódio a esta criança, os ricos entraram na corrida. Mas para quê mais um jornal? – perguntam uns. Para quê? – perguntamos nós – 3 restaurantes, 3 agências de viagens, 3 casas de roupa de homem, 3 ourivesarias, só no centro comercial português? Para quê tantas filarmónicas, tantas fraternais, tantas irmandades e tantos clubes? O Eurico Mendes, do Portuguese Times, disse-me numa carta: com certeza que já lhe disseram que não vai haver espaço para mais um jornal na Califórnia. Talvez goste de

saber o que, em relação a uma situação idêntica, um amigo meu afirmou: 'O espaço somos nós que o criamos.' Gostamos da frase e estamos determinados a criar o nosso próprio espaço. Não vamos mendigar assinaturas, nem atirar à comunidade as culpas da nossa incapacidade e incompetência." *Notícia*, no. 1 (5 December 1984), 1.

[76] It had a tabloid format with abundant photographs, and between 20 and 30 pages. In its first issue, the editorial board was composed of João Brum, Manuel Duarte and Tito Rebelo. The sections were organized in the following manner: Religion (Rev. Leonel Noia and Rev. Padre Carlos); Sports (Tito Rebelo, Gregório Araújo); Correspondents: David Melo (Chino, Ontario, Corona); Jesuíno Reis and Humberto Peixoto (Turlock); Frank Dias (Sacramento); José Batista (San Diego); Hélio Sousa (Artesia); Margarida da Silva (Novato); and António Brasil (Handford); Composition: Judy Ávila and Madalena Sousa; Photography and Assembly: São Bettencourt; Design and Graphics: Manuel Duarte; Publicity: Tito Rebelo; Information: Carlos Alonso and David Vieira; Collaborators (on the first issue): Onésimo T. Almeida, Inácio Antunes, José A. Batista, José Brites, Miguel Canto e Castro, Josefina Canto e Castro, Francisco Cota, Eduardo Mayone Dias, Ramiro Dutra, João José Encarnação, Vamberto A. Freitas, João da Maia, Ferreira Moreno, Urbino San-Payo, and Tony Silveira.

[77] Cited by Geoffrey L. Gomes, "The Portuguese Language Press in California, 1880-1928" (Master's Thesis, California State University, 1983).

[78] Original: "o único jornal diário da comunidade."

[79] Headquarters for *Luso-Americano California* in Hayward was located on 2378 Mission Boulevard. Its subtitle was "Portuguese-American Newspaper." Executive Editor: António Matinho (native of continental Portugal); Associate Editor: Manuel Ávila Simas (who acted as Director); Office Manager: Rui Silva; Advertising Director: Fátima Ferreira. Team of correspondents: Los Angeles, Arnaldo Baptista; San Diego, Manuel Coelho; Tulare, Dinis Borges. Its content was related to the Portuguese-American community and Portugal, with a special preference for news about the Azores. In the first issue, the following articles were published: "Banco Comercial dos Açores Abre Escritórios na Cidade de S. José," "Tony Coelho Poderá Decidir Regressar à Política depois das Eleições de Novembro," "Netos de Terceirenses Produzem na Califórnia Vinhos Premiados e também Réplicas de Vinhos Portugueses," "90 Associações, 10 Filarmónicas e Muitos Milhares de Pessoas nas Tradicionais Festas de Gustine," and "Franceses Vão Abandonar Base das Flores." Colaborators (in the first issue): Fernando A. dos Santos, Maria do Carmo Pereira, Joaquim Martins, António Oliveira, Ilídio Martins, Maria de Lurdes Meco Alves, Franklin Cruz, José Martins, and João Carlos Tavares. It was in tabloid format, with many photos, comprising between 20 and 40 pages. There is a complete collection in the Freitas Library de San Leandro (CA).

[80] Headquarters for the newspaper in Tracy was located on 711 Central Avenue. It was of tabloid format, between 20 and 40 pages, with color print on the cover and abundant advertisements. The newspaper's team from the first issue was comprised of the following: director/editor-in-chief, João P. Brum; graphic arts/copy editor, Pamela S. Williams; copy editor/accounting, Magda C. Bettencourt; marketing promotion, Frank I. Silva. Editors: Dianne Costa, English Section; Padre José Carlos, Religion; Rev. Leonel Noia, "Five Wounds;" Gregório Araújo, Sports; Dores Beirão, "Mulher Hoje;" Manuel Dias, "Valley's View;" Joaquim Ávila, Bullfighting. Correspondents: Osvaldo Palhinha and Fernando Dutra (Artesia/Chino/Cerritos); Paulo Goulart (San Diego); Helder Martins

(Tulare); Carlos Diniz (Lemoore, Handford), Jose João Encarnação (Los Baños); Artur Tomás (Gustine/Newman); Lonnie Correia (Hilmar); Francisco de Sousa (Turlock); Fernando Silva (Tracy/Manteca/Stockton); Mario Vargas (San Jose/Santa Clara); João Leite (San Leandro/Hayward); Nelo Bettencourt (Benicia/Vallejo/Concord); João de Melo (San Ramon/Dublin/Pleasanton/Castro Valley); Manuel Dias, Manuel Cristiano and João Freitas (Photographers). Publisher: Portuguese-American Publications, Inc. Chairman of the Board, Frank I. Silva; President, Manuel Rosário; secretary/treasurer, Rodriguez L. Alvernaz; directors, José Mendes, John de Melo, Guilherme Mendonça, Manuel Minhoto, Fernando Morais and João Brum; Collaborators: Onésimo Almeida, Vamberto Freitas, E. Mayone Dias, Ramiro Dutra, Emanuell Félix, Álamo Oliveira, Rod Alvernaz, Manuel Duarte, Ferreira Moreno, Margarida Silva, António Borba, Elmano Costa. Miguel do Canto e Castro, Teresinha Tomás, Carlos Almeida, Tony Silveira, Frei Bartolomeu, and Maria Carvalhal, among others. The first issue contains the following content: editorials; articles from Vamberto Freitas and from Onésimo Almeida; sections about Madeira and the Azores, international news, sports, the community and the diaspora, etc. There is a collection of the newspaper in the Freitas Library de San Leandro (CA).

[81] Headquarters for the *Portuguese Heritage Journal* in Coral Gables was located on 6851 Yumuri Street, Suite 9. The newspaper's team was comprised of the following people: Circulation Manager, Maria-Adelaide Cavaco; Collaborators: Tina-Maria Cavaco (Miami, Florida); Art Coelho (Big Timber, Montana); Luis Fagundes Duarte (Lisboa); Edgar C. Knowlton Jr. (Honolulu); Gisela Medek (Providence, Rhode Island); Eugénio Matos Meneses (Lisboa); Ferreira Moreno (San Leandro, California); Manuel L. Ponte (St. Louis, Missouri), and Robert Salgueiro (Cranford, New Jersey). Data taken from the first issue.

[82] It is believed that the publishing of the *Portuguese Heritage Journal* did not extend past 1994. There are issues of the newspaper in the Freitas Library in San Leandro (CA).

[83] In the first issue, on November 4, 1991, the titles on the cover were the following: "State Department Reviews Visa Policy on Portugal," "Growing Up Portuguese American – Educator Reflects on His Life in Newark," "Pope's Visit Gives Temporary Lift Brazilians Beset by Problems." In the interior pages: "Portugal Boom," "The Cardoso Affair," "Andrade Surges in Golf," and various sections dedicated to Portugal, the U.S.A., Brazil, the world, sports, business, lifestyle, and opinion.

[84] *Portuguese Heritage Journal*, no. 1 (4 November 1991), 22.

[85] See the newspaper's website: https://24horasnewspaper.com/

[86] Content from *Luzonet Magazine* ranged from a section "Para rir," to biographies of famous people, such as "Malcom X," to the reproduction of brief theoretical essays about Portuguese writers. Contributors include Onésimo T. Almeida, José Barreto, S. Kostoff, Mike Kostoff, Rui Martins, Bary Traxler and Avadora. Art and Culture: Albano Garcia. See: *Luzonet Magazine*, no. 13 (March 2004).

[87] According to the figure published by the newspaper itself. See: *Lusitânia News*, no. 1 (7 April 2006).

[88] *Lusitânia News* was subtitled "A Portuguese-American Newspaper." Its headquarters was located on 793 S. Tracy Boulevard, San Joaquin Valley, California. The majority of the content was dedicated to informing the public on activities and celebrations of different institutions within the community. See: *Lusitânia News*, no. 1 (7 April 2006).

[89] *ComunidadesUSA* had its headquarters in Manassas (9255 Center Street), but also had offices in New York and collaborators in several North American states, in Portugal, and Canada. Its subtitle was "The Portuguese-American Magazine in the USA." According to the editorial posted on its digital platform, the project intended to "be a link between all the portuguese communities scattered throughout the United States, as well as a way to keep them connected to the Portuguese culture, language, and traditions" (Original: "ser um elo de união entre todas as comunidades portuguesas espalhadas pelos Estados Unidos e também uma forma de as manter ligadas à cultura, língua e tradições portuguesas"). The cover of the first issue contained the following news: "Conselho das Comunidades dos EUA e Bermuda. Eleitos Democraticamente pelos Emigrantes dos Estados Unidos para Aconselharem o Governo Português, Dizem-se Ignorados por Lisboa." This issue also highlights the fact that the name of a Portuguese-American hero of the Vietnam War, Joe do Padre, was used to baptize a crater on Mars by the American space agency, NASA. *ComunidadesUSA* was published in color, in reduced size and distributed by subscription in New York, Connecticut, New Jersey, Massachusetts, Rhode Island, and Massachusetts.

Chapter 5 Four Newspapers that Made History

[1] Rui Antunes Correia, "Salazar em New Bedford. Leituras Luso-Americanas do Estado Novo" (2004).

[2] Original: "Se é português e sente a necessidade de que o 'Diário de Notícias' viva, indique-nos novos assinantes," *Diario de Noticias*, no. 14,690 (3 January 1966), 2.

[3] Torre do Tombo National Archives. Oliveira Salazar Archive (ANTT/AOS): SGPCM-GPM, box no. 5, PC-156, 3, no. 4. Official Letter no. 1273 of the Deputy Director of the Secretariat of National Propaganda, António Eça de Queiroz, to the President of the Minister of Ministers, September 19, 1938, informing about the pressures exerted on several Portuguese-American newspapers.

[4] Rui Antunes Correia transcribed António Santos's testimony in his M.A. thesis, relating that the political police had incarcerated a man for having read *Diario de Noticias*. "Pela Nossa terra – Na Ilha de X É-se Preso por Ler o 'Diário de Notícias'," *Diario de Noticias*, no. 5790 (27 May 1938), 5. Quoted by Correia in "Salazar in New Bedford," 157-158.

[5] In 1933, the *Fabre Line* advertised in the *Diario de Noticias* routes between New York and Portugal in the ships S.S. *Sinaia* and S.S. *Rochambeau*. In 1933, the S.S. *Sinaia* went from New York to Lisbon, with stops in Providence and Horta. From there, the company transfered passengers from other islands in the "vapor de carreira" on the day of arrival of the ship. See: *Diario de Noticias*, no. 4338 (10 August 1933), 4.

[6] *Diario de Noticias*, no. 14663 (23 November 1965), 1-2.

[7] According to Rui Antunes Correia, Luiz married Maria Trigueiro, a native of Oporto, who died during the epidemic of 1919. He then married Maria Mercês Maciel Luiz, who was the sister of Manuel and Joaquim Maciel, both employees at *Diario de Noticias*. He lived until he was 96 years old and died in 1982.

[8] Original: "o problema dos câmbios para uma população maioritariamente iletrada ou mesmo analfabeta, suscitava inúmeras possibilidades de fraude, pelo que se sentia

necessidade de constituição de uma sociedade de portugueses de confiança, que servisse de intermediária, tanto na questão dos valores cambiais, como na vinda de outros membros das suas famílias." Correia, "Salazar em New Bedford," 28.

[9] *A Alvorada*, no. 2337 (31 December 1926), 1.

[10] Original: "Para Guilherme Luiz pouco lhe interessava que o nome do seu quotidiano fosse este ou aquele. O seu maior desejo era que o jornal entrasse em muitas casas, fosse um órgão noticioso para os milhares de leitores espalhados por todas as parcelas do território americano. E não se enganou este homem de reduzidos conhecimentos literários. Se o fosse o diário teria tido uma vida mais ampla e proveitosa para o seu esforço e persistência. Mesmo assim, o diário foi o jornal de mais anos de existência em New Bedford." *Luso-Americano* (28 October 1989), 31.

[11] See the epigraph from the thesis of Correia, "Salazar em New Bedford": "Os 'Olhos da Cara' – a aventura dispendiosa do 'Diário de Notícias'," 32-34.

[12] Original: "Foi uma aventura dispendiosa que me tem custado os olhos da cara." *Diario de Noticias*, no. 6152 (11 August 1939), 1.

[13] Original: "que tem dispendido dezenas de milhar de dólares para que esta fonte de informação mundial na maviosa língua de Camões não desaparecesse deste meio americano." *Diario de Noticias*, no. 5930 (16 November 1938), 2, cited by Correia, "Salazar em New Bedford," 33.

[14] See the editorial from the *Diario de Noticias*, no. 6402 (8 June 1940), 1.

[15] Original: "O único diário, e por isso o mais importante periódico, é o 'Diário de Notícias' de New Bedford, que pertence ao Sr. Guilherme M. Luiz, o banqueiro por excelência das tranferências dos emigrados portugueses; agente das passagens para e de Portugal e Ilhas; negociante noutros ramos, o que tudo lhe angariou, nos bons tempos, uma boa fortuna, hoje muito dizimada até pelos processos que procurou utilizar para enriquecer, alguns dos quais foram levados ao conhecimento desse Ministério." Letter of the ambassador, João de Bianchi, to the minister of Foreign Affairs, 20 October 1938 (AHD, Ambassador of Portugal in Washington, box 36).

[16] Original: "Quantos portugueses foram para Portugal e vieram de lá por intermédio da sua casa; e quais as somas de dinheiro remetidas? / – Não sei o número exato, mas contam-se aos milhares. Quanto às somas de dinheiro remetidas pelo nosso (sic) compatriotas por intermédio desta Casa Bancária, tanto para o continente como para as Ilhas Adjacentes, sobem a milhões de dólares! . . . Note que a pesar das dezenas, senão centenas de milhar de remessas que têm sido mandadas por intermédio desta Casa, algumas delas de quantias bastante elevadas, nunca português algum teve jamais motivo de se arrepender por confiar em mim. . . ./ Decerto que nas três décadas passadas tem ajudado muitos compatriotas nossos.../ – Não gosto de alardear o que tenho feito a favor do nosso povo, porque considero um dever de nós todos ajudarmo-nos uns aos outros.../ Apreciámos a sua modéstia, mas insistimos./ – Pois bem. Sim, tenho auxiliado muitas pessoas, tanto aqui como nas nossas terras. Nas minhas viagens a Portugal e às Ilhas, tratei da papelada legal de centenas de compatriotas que desejavam emigrar para a América e adiantei a muitos somas de dinheiro que necessitavam para a passagem e outras formalidades indispensáveis que lhes permitissem entrar neste país. Não lhes exigi qualquer fiança por este dinheiro. Eram portugueses, isso bastava. Aqui, tenho regularizado a situação de muitos que entraram

ilegalmente no país, e tenho ajudado muitos outros como fiador, que nem sempre corresponderam à confiança que neles depositava." "O 30º Aniversário da Casa Bancária Guilherme M. Luiz," *Diario de Noticias*, no. 6152 (11 August 1939), 1. This interview is also cited by Correia, "Salazar em New Bedford," 29-30.

[17] Original: "Se nos Estados Unidos se mantém, há vinte e dois anos um jornal diário publicado em língua portuguesa, deve-se-o, sem dúvida, à admirável perseverança e à admirável tenacidade do sr. Guilherme M. Luiz. Nunca é demais repetir que foi com sacrifícios de toda a sorte que ele, como nenhum outro português, soube manter sempre aceso o amor da terra que lhe foi mãe, comunicando, através da letra redonda, aos seus compatriotas essa elevada e nobre virtude. Para com ele e, de resto, para com todos aqueles que assim procedem, Portugal tem a saldar uma dívida de gratidão." "À Colónia Portuguesa e, em Particular aos Amigos e Leitores do 'Diário de Notícias'," *Diario de Noticias*, no. 6402 (8 June 1940), 1.

[18] Correia, "Salazar em New Bedford," 36 (footnote).

[19] Correia, "Salazar em New Bedford," 30. Correia relates some of the anecdotes reported to him by relatives of Luiz he interviewed, which show the kindness of heis character. One of them tells the story of a Portuguese man imprisoned in Philadelphia who wrote to him asking for help. Luiz visited him, paid his bail, and freed him. On another occasion, he started a protest against the *Fabre Line* because in the company's ships that connected the Azores with the U.S., the doctor on board did not speak Portuguese, when that was the language of 95% of the passengers, which obligated the company to place Portuguese doctors on its lines. He also pressured the Portuguese authorities for the opening of consulates in New Bedford and Fall River.

[20] Correia, "Salazar em New Bedford," 30-31.

[21] Original: "É possível que sem a sua 'audácia,' sem o seu 'temperamento,' não teria sido lançado o alicerce que serviu de base ao 'Diário de Notícias.' E apenas por isto, mesmo que nada mais tivesse feito em toda a sua vida, e descontadas as suas limitações humanas, a Comunidade Portuguesa da América tem para com Guilherme Machado Luiz uma grande dívida de gratidão. E todos nós, seus continuadores, assim o sentimos na sua partida." *Diario de Noticias*, no. 14663 (26 November 1965), 1.

[22] "Medalhas por Atacado," *Diario de Noticias*, no. 7684 (14 August 1944), 1. Cited by Correia, "Salazar em New Bedford," 31.

[23] Original: "Sucessivos anos já passaram, afinal,/ Que revelas novidades, sem malícias;/ Por isso mereces as nossas carícias,/ Digno propagador da voz de Portugal!// Não há na América, nenhum outro jornal,/ Que na leitura nos dê, tantas delícias;/ Como tu, belo, 'Diário de Notícias,'/ Arauto da nossa língua, sem teres rival!// Que tua voz se prolongasse por muitos anos,/ Foi esforço, que o teu impulsionador quis;/ Fazendo sacrifícios mais que humanos.// Felicitamos pois, não haja mais enganos,/ O benemérito, Guilherme Machado Luiz;/ Que entre a Colónia, honra os Lusitanos!" *Diario de Noticias*, no. 6294 (31 January 1940), 4.

[24] *Portuguese Times* (16 November 1989), 22.

[25] Ferreira Mendes Portuguese-American Archives at Umass Dartmouth (FM-PAA/UMD), MC 100/PAA. "João Rocha papers". "Biographical note". Read also to Vasco Jardim in the *Luso-Americano*, 28 de octubre de 1989, p. 31. "Capítulo 7".

[26] Vasco Jardim in the *Luso-Americano*, 28 de octubre de 1989, p. 31. "Capítulo 7".

[27] "Biographical note," "João Rocha Papers," Ferreira Mendes Portuguese-American Archives at Umass Dartmouth (FM-PAA/UMD, MC 100/PAA).

[28] Original: "João R. Rocha foi a surpresa do jornalismo português no estrangeiro."

[29] Original: "De empregado de balcão a jornalista vai uma grande distância. Despois de ter falhado com a revista e 'vivido' com 'O Independente,' Rocha despe o casaco, enrola as mangas da camisa e às seis horas da manhã começa a luta na Redação do jornal. . . . João Rocha, mesmo sem saber nada de artes gráficas, conquistou uma posição frutuosa. Antes de suspender a publicação do diário, pagou todas as contas e enviou a todos os assinantes alguns milhares de dólares das assinaturas pagas adiantadamente. Ninguém se gabou de lhe comprar a empresa enquanto ele estava nos últimos dias da sua vida." "Capítulo 7," *Luso-Americano* (28 October 1989), 31.

[30] "O Dr. Oliveira Salazar Manifestou Vivo Interesse pelos Portugueses da América," *Diario de Noticias*, no. 11,749 (2 May 1958) 1 and 6.

[31] Letter from Richard Nixon to João R. Rocha, "João Rocha Papers," 2 December 1968 (FM-PAA/UMD. MC 100/PAA).

[32] Letter from Gerard J. Gagne, "Acquisitions Librarian," to João R. Rocha, "João Rocha Papers," 7 November 1973 (FM-PAA/UMD. MC 100/PAA).

[33] Letter from Donald E. Walker, President of Sotheastern Massachusetts University to João R. Rocha, "João Rocha Papers," 27 October 1975 (FM-PAA/UMD. MC 100/PAA).

[34] Letter from Gerald T. Tache, "president and Publisher" of *The Standard Times* to Mrs. Mary Mello Rocha, "João Rocha papers," 8 March 1977 (FM-PAA/UMD. MC 100/PAA).

[35] The *Diario de Noticias* had offices in other places: In Fall River (MA): 10 Bedford Street; and in Newark (NJ): 78 Jefferson Street.

[36] "O 'Diário de Notícias' em Fall River," *Diario de Noticias*, no. 1 (3 January 1927), 1.

[37] Original: "Várias razões existem para que os anunciantes do 'Diário de Notícias' mereçam o patrocínio da colónia Portuguesa. Uma delas, e a principal, é porque para levarem ao conhecimento dos portugueses que desejam o seu patrocínio, eles usam as colunas do diário que é publicado na nossa língua para anunciarem os artigos dos seus comércios, auxiliando assim uma empresa portuguesa, cuja existência eleva o nosso prestígio nestas paragens. Na certeza de que todos os nossos anunciantes são comerciantes de integridade e pessoas que se prezam em tratar com gente da nossa raça, não hesitamos em pedir aos nossos leitores que se habituem a ler os anúncios que são pubicados neste jornal, e que encontrando neles o artigo de que carecem e que estão prestes a comprar, o façam nas casas que anunciam connosco e que mostram assim serem amigos nossos." "Aos Leitores," *Diario de Noticias*, no. 3461 (24 April 1931), 1.

[38] Regarding this aspect, read: Rui Antunes Correia, "Salazar em New Bedford," 45 on.

[39] For more on this campaign, see "A Nossa Campanha de Expansão," *Diario de Noticias*, no. 928 (20 January 1930), 1.

[40] "A Nossa Campanha de Expansão," *Diario de Noticias*, no. 928 (20 January 1930), 1.

[41] Confidential letter form João R. Rocha to António Ferro, 18 February 1939, Arquivos Nacionais Torre do Tombo (ANTT, Arquivo Oliveira Salazar [AOS], CO/PC-12-D, Box 661).

[42] In his story on January 20, 1930 ("A nossa Campanha de Expansão"), he describes the enormous difficulties of his work: "É uma tarefa árdua, que nem todos aceitariam e bem poucos se encontrariam com disposição de levar a cabo. Depende, embora muitos pensem que não, de muita coragem, muita paciência, de uma grande dose de persistência, ambição e de feitio agressivo. Sem estas qualidades tão essenciais ao caixeiro de praça na hora que passa, tudo é desalento, tudo é dobrar a finados, é a morte certa que chega. E essa missão foi por nós aceite, não porque nos sentíssemos senhor[es] de todos esses indispensáveis predicados, mas porque contávamos com a ajuda de 62 correspondentes, que são também 62 amigos, dispostos a auxiliar e evangelizar a língua portuguesa por essa América em fora." ("It is an arduous task, that not everyone would accept and even fewer would be willing to carry out. It depends, although many think otherwise, on a lot of courage, a lot of patience, a large dose of persistence, ambition, and an aggressive personality. Without these qualities so essential to the salesman these days, everything is gloomy, everything is a death knell, the coming of certain death. And we picked that mission, not because we felt ourselves masters of all these indispensable qualities, but because we have the help of 62 correspondents, who are also 62 friends, available to help and to preach the Portuguese language throughout America"). Article also cited by Correia.

[43] Original: "Na sua passagem por estes núcleos teve ele a oportunidade de visitar todos os grémios e clubes, nos quais apresentou o 'Diário de Notícias,' o jornal português de mais larga informação e de mais circulação em todos os Estados Unidos da América do Norte. Mas não foi somente os clubes que João Rocha visitou; os domicílios dos nossos compatriotas foram também por ele visitados, angariando novos assinantes que vieram aumentar a nossa lista, João Rocha não descansa e aí o vemos partir novamente para outras cidades e vilas, que ainda não teve tempo de visitar, na nobre missão de que foi incumbido." "João R. Rocha," *Diario de Noticias*, no. 3202 (9 November 1929), 2.

[44] The states of vending were Massachusetts, Rhode island, Pennsylvania, New Jersey, Connecticut, New York and Illinois. Correia, "Salazar em New Bedford," 47-48.

[45] Correia, "Salazar em New Bedford," 43.

[46] *Diario de Noticias*, no. 9610 (27 December 1950), 6.

[47] Among the typographers were: Alfredo Mascarenhas, António Pereira, António Santinho, Luciano R. Mota, António Pereira, and Jacinto A. Almeida. See: Correira, "Salazar em New Bedford," 41.

[48] *Diario de Noticias*, no. 4939 (8 August 1935), 1.

[49] "O Diário de Notícias Está de Luto. Faleceu o Brilhante Jornalista Ferreira Martins, Redator Principal deste Jornal, que Foi um Ornamento do Jornalismo Português," *Diario de Noticias*, no. 4940 (8 August 1935), 1 and 8. After a heart attack that left him an invalid, Ferreira Martins died three months after, on August 7, 1935. After his death, in the article cited, the *Diario de Noticias* described him in the following manner: "Domingos Ferreira Martins foi um astro que brilhou no jornalismo colonial português dos Estados Unidos e a sua morte foi uma perda irreparável, não só para nós e para o Diário de Notícias, como também para a colónia inteira. Erudito como poucos, possuidor duma memória privilegiada, pode dizer-se que era um enciclopédico. Feito na imprensa lisbonense, ele pertencia à classe dos grandes jornalistas. Durante doze anos ele, juntamente com Jorge d'Abreu e Avelino d'Almeida, brilharam no 'Século' como sendo os três principais

jornalistas do seu tempo. Ferreira Martins foi, na imprensa da capital portuguesa, um grande propagandista da participação de Portugal na Grande Guerra. . . . Era republicano leal, intransigente, e bem que não estivesse filiado em qualquer partido político, ele foi uma vítima da política. Em 1925, o governo português nomeou-o Cônsul de Portugal para a cidade de Valladolid, Espanha. Conhecidas as suas ideias liberais em Espanha, e o facto de ser amigo íntimo de Blasco Ibañez, levantou-se ali contra ele uma oposição que fez com que nunca fosse tomar posse desse lugar. Quis então o destino trazê-lo para os Estados Unidos."/ "Domingos Ferreira Martins was a star of Portuguese-American journalism in the United States and his death was an irreparable loss, not only for us and for the *Diario de Noticias,* but also for the whole community. More erudite than most, possessed of a privileged memory, he was truly encyclopedic in his knowlede. Having cut his teeth in the Lisbon press, he belonged to the class of great journalists. For twelve years he, along with Jorge d'Abreu and Avelino d'Almeida, shined in the *Século* as the three major journalists of their time. While in the Lisbon press, Ferreira Martins was a great apologist of Portugal's participation in Great War. . . . He was a loyal, uncompromising Republican and while he was not affiliated with any political party, he was a victim of politics. In 1925, the Portuguese government named him the Consul of Portugal to the city of Valladolid, Spain. Since his liberal ideas were known in Spain, and he was a close friends of Blasco Ibañez, there was such opposition against his nomination that he was never able to occupy the post. Fate would then bring him to the United States." According to the biographical profile from the newspaper, Domingos Ferreira Martins was born in Lisbon on July 20, 1879, son of Vicente Ferreira Martins and Angélica Martins. He was married in 1911 to Aida Paes Martins. (This source is also cited by Correia).

[50] Others who contributed to the paper include Laertes de Figueiredo, Quirino de Sousa, Father Alves Correia, Martha de Mesquista da Câmara, Frank Torres, Josefina do Canto e Castro, Antero de Alburquerque, Manuel P. Melo, Raul Alves Loureiro, João M. Tavares, Francisco Rebelo, António Maria Freitas, Augusto Gil, Leal Furtado, and Paes de Aguiar. In addition, there were pieces by the pseudonyms Onix, Argus, Lanceta, and Ignotus, which was the pen name of the editor of A União Portuguesa in California, José Trindade Salgueiro.

[51] Original: "As ditaduras são, em regra, governos que não exprimem a vontade do povo, mas sim a de um grupo ou partido que salta sobre todos os direitos constitucionais para impor a sua autoridade. . . . É de crer que em todos os governos e partidos haja pessoas bem intencionadas que não receiem os seus atos sejam comentados e esclarecidos pela opinião pública. Se os dirigentes de um país gostam de pôr a claro as suas intenções para que o povo acredite nelas, se fazem estendal das suas conquistas e põem em relevo uma obra de reconstrução económica, não devem recear a crítica justa do seu trabalho. Antes, pelo contrário, devem apreciá-la como recompensa merecida aos seus propósitos de bem servir a Nação. A censura é sempre uma mordaça odiosa e absurda que a autoridade põe na boca ou na pena daqueles que podem apreciar os factos serenamente. É uma opressão exagerada e vexatória sobre a inteligência." "Liberdade de Imprensa," *Diario de Noticias,* no. 5092 (7 February 1936), 2 and 4.

[52] Editorial "Imprensa!," *Diario de Noticias,* no. 4773 (21 January 1935), 2.

[53] Original: "Com o pedido de publicação, temos, há tempos a esta parte, recebido alguns artigos, aliás ponderosos, doutrinários e oportunos. Muito constrangidamente

recusamo-nos a satisfazer esse pedido, por esses artigos virem, uns assinados com pseudónimos e outros com iniciais, sem que os seus autores, como seria do seu dever e manda a praxe jornalística, nos revelem a sua identidade. Posto isto, para que aos artigos em questão se possa dar a publicidade que merecem, torna-se absolutamente necessário que nos sejam fornecidos os nomes e endereços dos seus autores, a quem garantimos completo sigilo sobre a sua identidade." "Publicação de Artigos no 'Diário de Notícias'," *Diario de Noticias*, no. 5643 (2 December 1937), 1.

[54] "John B. Nunes, um Político Português da Velha Guarda," *Diario de Noticias*, no. 12,102 (11 September 1959), 1

[55] "Equilíbrio nas Contas e nos Espíritos," *Diario de Noticias* no. 3820 (New Jersey Section, 25 November 1931).

[56] "Camisas e Mais Camisas," *Diario de Noticias* no. 4298 (23 June 1933), 2.

[57] "Espírito Latino," *Diario de Noticias* no. 3135 (21 August 1929), 2.

[58] "Coisas Práticas," *Diario de Noticias* no. 3170 (28 May 1931), 2.

[59] "Fraternidade," *Diario de Noticias* no. 3370 (2 June 1930), 2.

[60] "As Eleições de 13 de Fevereiro," *Diario de Noticias*, no. 9038 (4 February 1949), 1-2; "Os Emolumentos Consulares," *Diario de Noticias* no. 4819 (16 March 1935), 2.

[61] "Portugal e o Problema Ibérico," *Diario de Noticias*, no. 8160 (27 March 1946), 1 and 6.

[62] "O Dia de Colombo," *Diario de Noticias* no. 3170 (11 October 1929), 2.

[63] "Aspetos da Emigração," *Diario de Noticias* no. 4172 (24 January 1933), 2.

[64] "Uma Indústria Muito Explorada," *Diario de Noticias* no. 3181 (16 October 1929), 2.

[65] "Os 'Leadres' e as Escolas na Colónia," *Diario de Noticias* no. 3765 (19 September 1931), 2.

[66] "O Problema Bancário e o Valor da Nota," *Diario de Noticias* no. 4125 (16 March 1933), 2.

[67] "Solidariedade Colonial," *Diario de Noticias* no. 4338 (10 August 1933), 1.

[68] "Um Homenzinho," *Diario de Noticias* no. 2980 (17 February 1929), 2.

[69] "John Filipe de Sousa," *Diario de Noticias* no. 3905 (8 March 1932), 2.

[70] "A 'Paz' no Mundo," *Diario de Noticias* no. 4203 (2 March 1933), 2.

[71] "Os Portugueses Fora da Casa," *Diario de Noticias* no. 3464 (22 September 1930), 2.

[72] Original: "Porque as pessoas estejam altamente colocadas, não adquirem imunidade com a altura, em relação aos órgãos da opinião pública. E, precisamente porque o acaso as colocou fora do âmbito vulgar, onde vegetam os outros concidadãos, e muito acima deles, em categoria social, não é isso circunstância para serem poupadas da crítica e, ao invés, os seus atos mais facilmente caem no domínio da censura. Os representantes duma nação, junto doutra, têm deveres a cumprir. Não residem nas capitais de Estado exclusivamente para salamaleques oficiais. Os interesses do país que representam e os cidadãos filhos desse país devem merecer-lhes desvelada atenção. Quem cumpre como deve esse papel não levanta atritos nem na colónia nem na imprensa. Todos lhes manifestam respeito. Há quem não cumpra esses deveres não deve estranhar as recriminações." "A Missão dos Diplomatas na América," *Diario de Noticias* (22 March 1929), 2.

[73] The addresses for the headquarters of *Jornal Português* were in Oakland (1927 East 14th Street and 3240 E. 14th St.), 1932-1978; and San Pablo (1912 Church Lane), 1978-1997.

It was published weekly, except in the first week of January and the last of December, between 1980 and 1997, when it was published daily.

74 In order to enhance its prestige, the *Jornal Português* claimed 1888 as the year of its creation, when Frs. Manuel Francisco Fernandes and João Francisco Tavares founded *O Amigo dos Católicos*, the precedecesor *O Arauto*, and Pedro L. C. da Silveira's *Jornal de Notícias.*

75 Original: "SEMPRE INTERESSANTE EM TODAS AS SUAS SECÇÕES – Este jornal esforça-se por informar os seus leitores dos acontecimentos mais interessantes neste país e no estrangeiro, e muito especialmente em Portugal e suas possessões. A nossa colónia merece sempre menção especial."

76 Original: "[Era] um moço bem parecido, bem apessoado, bem vestido e de modos atrativos e corteses. Falava bem o português e dava provas de saber alguma coisa de arte tipográfica. . . Principiou, desde logo, a manifestar a sua inteligência e atividade, fazendo o seu trabalho tipográfico com presteza e perfeição e, nas horas vagas, escrevendo para o jornal algumas notícias e traduções, com admirável correção. Por vezes, na minha ausência em serviço financeiro do jornal, e a meu pedido, escreveu alguns artiguinhos editoriais, que lhe mereceram a minha aprovação e elogio, e que tiveram bom acolhimento dos numerosos leitores. . . Tudo corria bem. Pedro respeitava-me e obedecia-me como um pai, e eu tratava-o com o afeto e carinho com que se trata a um irmão ou a um filho. . . Qual foi o meu espanto, quando um belo dia, o nosso bom Pedro – não me lembro em que mês do ano 1902 – todo cabisbaixo e meio pálido, me veio dizer que procurasse outro homem para o seu lugar." *Jornal Português*, special issue dedicated to "Os Portugueses de Califórnia, 1888-1938" (1938), 7.

77 Other members of the initial team wree: Heike D. Lemos, Ed Phillips, John Neves, Rodrigo Cunha Velho, Carlos Costa, Maria C. Leal, Rosa P. Vilão, and Fátima Ferreira. In the seventies, Alberto Lemos appears as "Publisher-Editor" and Elvin Goulart as "Public Relations & Advertising." In the eighties, Heike D. Lemos was in charge of publicity and advertising, and Ed Phillips and John Neves are listed as section leaders. Sports correspondents were Rodrigo Cunha Velho and Carlos Costa. In the nineties, Maria C. Leal was named editor-in-chief; secretary, Rosa P. Vilão; and Fátima Ferreira, advertising.

78 Serialized novels.

79 His obituary can be read on: http://www.legacy.com/obituaries/contracostatimes/ obituary.aspx?n=Alberto-emos&pid=152500896#fbLoggedOut. See also the biographical sketch by his daughter, Mónica Lemos: http://corisco-california.blogspot.com/2011/07/ alberto-s-lemos-1921-2011-by-monica.html. [Consulted in 2019]

80 Original: "Eu, além de pequeno editor, redator, fotógrafo, varredor, carregador de sacos, promotor de vendas, angariador de assinaturas, etc., também tenho de ser gerente, administrador e um dos mais cuidadosos." Cited by Eduardo Mayone Dias, from an interview conducted by Hélder Pinho. See: Eduardo Mayone Dias, *A Prenseça Portuguesa na California*, 72.

81 Read biographical sketch by Fernando M. Soares Silva, *A Tribuna Portuguesa* (15 July 2011), 9.

82 Magda C. Bettencourt assumed the duties of secretary in this new phase.

[83] The following titles provide a sample of the type of editorials from the thirties and forties: "Um Portugal Independente" (25 September 1936), 8; "A Nova Diplomacia" (5 February 1937), 5; "Um Jesuíta Caluniador" (23 April 1937), 8; "A Representação de Portugal na Exposição" (21 May 1940), 8; "Uma Interessante Sessão Cinematográfica" (18 April 1941), 8; "Irmandade do Divino Espírito Santo" (5 September 1941), 8; "Vamos Ter um Milagre" (17 October 1941), 8; "Na Irmandade de Santo Cristo" (23 February 1945), 8; etc.

[84] See, for example, the following articles: "Brilhante Discurso do Presidente do Conselho de Ministros de Portugal, Dr. Oliveira Salazar," *Jornal Português*, no. 1212 (3 February 1956), 1; J. Marques Jardim, "O Magistral Discurso do Grande Estadista Doutor António de Oliveira Salazar foi Uma Oração a Portugal," *Jornal Português*, no. 1124 (7 May 1954), 1; "Uma Espontânea Manifestação de Reconhecimento do Governo de Portugal e de Simpatia ao Seu Vice-Cônsul, Sr. G. A. de Amaral," *Jornal Português*, no. 995 (26 October 1951), 1.

[85] On January 29, 1937, the *Jornal Português* published an official note from the ambassador of Portugal, João de Bianchi, in which he rejected the rumors regarding the future of the Portuguese colonies in Africa. In the context of the Spanish Civil War, some international intelligence agencies had spread an alleged secret agreement to cede some Portuguese territories to Hitler's Germany.

[86] Original: "[Q]uem odeia Portugal não pode ser um verdadeiro amigo da América." Phrase taken from the article "Portugal," *Jornal Português*, no. 786 (26 September 1947).

[87] Original: "Nesta rica Califórnia,/ Da pátria longe a viver!/ As glórias de Portugal/ Orgulhoso a escrever./ . . . / Portugueses de todo mundo/ Vieram à nossa Capital!/ De homenagem a Salazar,/ Um herói filho de Portugal/ . . . / Orgulha-te ó Portugal,/ Do teu filho a brilhar!/ Que te salvou do abismo,/ Do coração sem falhar/ . . . / Meio século se passou/ Do seu coração, Salazar!/ Do seu brilhante governo/ O império todo a festejar!/ . . . / Do maior heroísmo/ Abrilhantou a nação!/ A nossa terra lusitana/ De amor no coração/ . . . / Salazar, no palácio/ Recebeu a multidão!/ De vivas a Salazar/ De imortal recordação." *Jornal Português* (29 January 1954), 5.

[88] See particularly the documentation with the following reference: Arquivo Histórico Diplomático de Lisboa (AHD), file 335, which contains letters and documents from the director of the *Jornal Português* and from the ambassador of Portugal in Washington between the years of 1966 and 1970.

[89] Original: "grandiosa obra civilizadora ultramarina de Portugal."

[90] Letter from the director of the *Jornal Português*, Alberto Lemos, to the ambassador of Portugal in Washington, Vasco Vieira Garin, 7 March 1966 (AHD, file 335, record entry: 17 March, no. 217, proc. 3.25).

[91] Lemos took advantage of his contacts with the ambassador of Portugal to promote one of his businesses, the LuzitaniaTravel Agency, founded with his brother and another partner in 1948 (AHD, file 335).

[92] "Mensagem do Presidente dos Estados Unidos aos Portugueses da California," *Jornal Português*, "Número Especial: Os Portugueses da California (1988-1938)," 3.

[93] Original: "Não há divergências em reconhecer aos Portugueses o seu temor a Deus; o seu amor à família; o seu ardor pelo trabalho; a sua parcimónia e sobriedade de hábitos;

o seu espírito de sacrifício; o seu procedimento ordeiro; o seu voto consciencioso. Muitas contribuições espirituais e materiais têm dado para esta grande civilização americana no campo da administração pública, da administração da justiça, na música, na indústria, na pesca, na lavoura de tantas outras actividades e os Portugueses estão ainda longe de ter realizado toda a extensão do seu destino nos Estados Unidos." *Jornal Português*, "Número Especial: Os Portugueses da California (1988-1938)," 5.

[94] Among its many other contributors, at different historical periods, were J. Marques Jardim, Armando de Aguiar, João Amaral Moniz, John R. Vieira, John J. Valim, Joaquim R. S. Leite, F. de Carvalho, Maria da Ascensão Carvalho, Alberto P. Wellington, João C. de Lacerda, Simões Teles, Ávila Simas, Joaquim Esteves, António C. Teixeira, Zé do Vale, Manuel da Cruz, Ramiro C. Dutra, Rev. João J. Vieira Jr., and Diniz da Luz.

[95] Original: "Fiquei desgostoso de não ter tido a sorte de me acotovelar com belas espanholas e serranas. Comia na primeira classe e dormia, quando dormia, num divã à entrada da sala de jantar. O navio abalançava como uma besta. Dava vómitos ir até aos porões e aí ver como os emigrantes eram engarrafados em cima uns dos outros, nas armações metálicas. A podridão mais nojenta que vimos na vida. Eram passados apenas dois anos do fim da guerra. Os navios antiquados e a França arruinada pelas dívidas. À noite, a vida era mais atrativa, mais fulgurante e até mais poética. Quando o vento era brando e o mar brilhava no oceano, os homens tocavam viola, bandolim e outros instrumentos. Os portugueses, com as suas concertinas e guitarras, faziam serão no convés. As raparigas das Beiras rivalizavam com as andaluzas e italianas. Ninguém pensava em divertimentos. Todos vinham com a ideia de arranjar em pouco tempo um pecúnio para a família. No entanto, a música trazia a inspiração e as saias o perfume da sedução humana. Cá da ponte, só tínhamos liberdade de assistir ao espectáculo que acabava quase sempre em pancadaria." "Capítulo 9," *Luso-Americano* (18 October 1989), 39.

[96] *Portuguese Times* (16 November 1989), 22.

[97] Ibid.

[98] *A Alvorada*, no. 1809 (4 April 1925), 3.

[99] See the following issues of *A Alvorada*, no. 1811 (7 April 1925), 5; and no. 1815 (11 April 1925).

[100] Original: "Fundou o semanário de quatro páginas, que ele compunha sem qualquer original diante de si, imprimia uma página de cada vez, dobrava-o à mão e ia ele próprio espalhá-lo pela cidade. Não eram as quatro igrejas portuguesas que se construíam em Fall River que interessavam ao Botelho. Eram as mulheres, pois estas o que queriam era mexericos e má língua. O jornal era procurado e comentado. O Manuel Botelho, com três caixas de tipo de tamanho 8, 10 e 12, fazia a composição e imprimia o periódico numa pequena loja na South Main Street, quase em frente à sede do Monte Pio, embora o Ramos nada quisesse com ele. Tinha medo da má língua, segundo confessava o próprio Ramos, o terror dos presidentes das sociedades. Um dia quase por brincadeira comprei-lhe o jornal e o equipamento na mesma ocasião em que comprei ao Leonidio Cabral. . . Depressa verifiquei que o Botelho tirava apenas 300 cópias por semana do seu jornal. Juntei as duas tipografias e estabeleci-me no segundo andar de um casebre do D. Casey. Pensei em dar vida ao 'Vigilante' com um formato maior, novo título, algumas fotogravuras e o Botelho a trabalhar com um ordenado certo de $22 por semana. Eu,

o Botelho, o Cabral e um jovem irlandês, aprendiz de tipógrafo, levámos três semanas a preparar a primeira edição. Paguei ao Anibal Branco $6 por dois artigos de humor. No fim meti toda a edição de 12 páginas num fogão. O jornal não estava de maneira nenhuma como eu queria que aparecesse. No terceiro número do jornal publiquei um editorial na primeira página avisando que o 'Vigilante' suspendia a sua publicação por constatar que apenas tinha 82 assinaturas pagas e outros motivos que agora não interessam. Não estava disposto a sofrer as dissipações de um Botelho e perder os encargos que havia assumido no 'Fall River Globe' e 'Diário de Notícias.' Devolvi $37 aos assinantes, aprendi e diverti-me." *Luso-Americano*, special 50th anniversary edition (28 October 1989), 31.

[101] According to Vasco Jardim's report, John Enos, son of Azorean immigrants in Massachusetts, arrived in Newark in 1926. He earned degrees from Brown University and Harvard University, and married an Irish citizen. His office was located on 86 Jefferson Street, later moved to Clinton Avenue. He was a specialist in diabetes and smoking. He never charged for his appointments and treatments for athletes from the Sport Club Português teams. See: *Luso-Americano* (1 November 1989), 37; *Luso-Americano* (29 November 1989), 48; and *Portuguese Times* (16 November 1989), 22. Guilherme M. Luiz, 'publisher' of the *Diario de Noticias*, also notes that José Paulo Lobo had been a senator of the República Portuguesa and the civil governor of Portalegre (Alentejo). See: *Diario de Noticias*, no. 4338 (10 August 1933), 5.

[102] "Capítulo 9," *Luso-Americano* (1 November 1989), 37.

[103] See the website: www.lusoamericano.com.

[104] Jerry R. Williams, 134.

[105] There is some indication that Manuel Carvalho may have acquired the paper on June 15, 1942, and owned it for some time. *Luso-Americano* (6 December 1989), 3.

[106] With Vasco S. Jardim as "Publisher Emeritus (1939-1979)," in 2012 the newspaper team was comprised of the following people: Publisher: António Matinho; Director of operations: Paul Matinho; News editor: Luis Pires; Associate news editor: Maria do Carmo Pereira; Sports editor: Ilídio Martins; Editor at large: Ricardo Durães; Art director: Gina Vilar; Office manager: Maria Glória Afonso; Circulation department: Teresa Ferreira; Classified advertising: Paula Ribau; Customer relations: Cibelle Nuno, Joana Pato, and Lúcia de Jesús. There were correspondents in New Jersey (Elisabeth and Long Branch), New York, Connecticut, Pennsylvania, Florida, and California.

[107] *Luso-Americano*, special 50th anniversary edition (14 October 1989), 31.

[108] See, for instance, *Luso-Americano*, special 50th anniversary issue (6 December 1989), 3.

[109] See: Clémence Jouët-Pastré and Leticia J. Braga (eds.). *Becoming Bazuca. Brazilian Immigration to the United States* (Cambridge: David Rockefeller Center Series os Latin American Studies, Harvard University Press, 2008).

[110] See the website: www.lusoamericano.com.

[111] Adelino Ferreira, "The Impact of the Post-Capelinhos Immigration Wave on the Portuguese Media in the United States. The Portuguese-Language Media on the East Coast," in *Capelinhos. A Volcano of Synergies. Azorean Emigration to America*, ed. Tony Goulart (San Jose, CA: Presidência do Governo Regional dos Açores, 2007), 187.

[112] Its first headquarters was at 61 W. Rodney French Boulevard, before moving to 1501 Acushnet Avenue.

[113] Adelino Ferreira, 187.

[114] The other members of the *Potuguese Times* team were the following: administrator, Eduardo Sousa Lima; accounting, Olinda M. Lima; advertising, Augusto Pessoa; sports, Afonso Costa; and secretary, Maria Novo. The complete team of the newspaper in 1975 included the following. Editors: Manuel Adelino Ferreira, Eurico José Mendes, and Manuel M. Duarte; advertising: John Lima; accounting: Gary Emken; costumer service: Luis Rodrigues; composition: Donzília Sousa and Natalia Carreiro; photography: Carlos A. Costa, Antonio J. Cordeiro; lithography: António F. Almeida; "dispatchers": Paul Martins and Luis Pereira. Ferreira Matos was responsible for the Newark branch.

[115] The network of correspondents in 2012 included the following: in Connecticut, António G. Ferreira; in Massachusetts, Arlindo do Val; in New York, Jorge Dias; in New Jersey, Maria Helena Luis; in Rhode Island, Agostinho P. de Mattos; and in Pennsylvania, Nelson V. Baptista.

[116] Among many others, contributors included the following: Diniz Borges, José Brites, Manuel Calado, José Teixeira Dias, Manuel S. M. Leal, Caetano Valadão Serpa, João Luis de Medeiros, Délia DeMello, Ferreira Moreno, Lélia Pereira da Silva Nunes, Eduardo Bettencourt Pinto, Gonçalo Rego, José Serpa, Osvaldo Cabral, António Silva and João Gago da Câmara, Henrique B. Medeiros, António Cirurgião, Joaquim Lopes Morgato, Helena R. Costa, Ruy Nunes, José Rebelo Mota, and Amadeu Casanova Fernandes.

[117] For example, the issue of May 2, 2012, prints the questions from the exam with the answers: "O que celebramos no dia 4 de julho?" (What do we celebrate on the 4th of July); "Quem foi o primeiro presidente dos EUA?" (Who was the first president of the United States?); "O que é a constituição?" (What is the constitution?); "Como se chamam as 10 primeiras emendas da Constituição?" (What do we call the first 10 amendments to the Constitution?); "Quem elege os congressistas?" (Who elects the members of congress?). Some of the data were provided by Manuel Adelino Ferreira. *Portuguese Times*, no. 2132 (2 May 2012).

[118] See: Mário Mesquita and José Rebelo, eds., *O 25 de Abril nos Media Internacionais* (Porto: Afrontamento, 1994).

[119] "Campanha 20,000 Assinantes," *Portuguese Times* (10 April 1975), 8.

[120] Original: "não podemos conceber que haja um único português (ou descendente) espalhado pelo mundo, que não se preocupe com a situação de Portugal." António Alberto Costa, "A Maior Riqueza Humana," *Portuguese Times* (10 April 1975), 8.

[121] Original: "até porque profissionalmente, comercialmente e socialmente sempre temos estado ligados à Comunidade de Língua Portuguesa dos Estados Unidos." Costa, "A Maior Riqueza Humana," 8.

[122] Original: "Aquilo que somos hoje não é mais do que uma mistura do que aprendemos ao longo da nossa vida. E os ensinamentos adquiridos nos nossos 19 anos, foram todos do Portugal de então. A América do Norte deu-nos a oportunidade de compreender com maior visão e sentido de justiça o bem e o mal. Foi aqui, nesta nação, que concede a todos os mesmos direitos e oportunidades, que principiámos a compreender todo o significado de Democracia, Liberdade e Justiça." Costa, "A Maior Riqueza Humana," 8.

[123] "Eleições no Dia 12 de Abril," *Portuguese Times*, no. 207 (year IV, 13 February 1975), 1.

[124] "Entrevista com Ted Kennedy," *Portuguese Times*, no. 208 (year IV, 20 February 1975), 1.

[125] Original: "Indica o poder ilimitado de um governo ditatorial ou de um partido único. Um governo é arbitrário quando decide, arbitrária e abusivamente, sobre toda a vida (e a morte!) dos cidadãos." "Totalitário," *Portuguese Times*, no. 208 (year IV, 20 February 1975), 1.

[126] The result of the votes was as follows: António de Spínola, 328 votes; Sá Carneiro, 192; Marcelo Caetano, 54; Costa Gomes, 46; Mário Soares, 14; Álvaro Cunhal, 8; Palma Carlos, 6; Saraiva de Carvalho, 4; Vasco Gonçalves, 2; Melo Antunes, 2, and Américo Tomás, 2. The paper highlights the high voting turnout, considering that each voter should send their ballot by mail. "O Inquérito do 'Portuguese Times.' Spínola o Mais Votado," *Portuguese Times*, no. 217 (year IV, 13 February 1975), 1.

[127] Original: "Os acontecimentos de Portugal, como os interpretamos, convencem-nos de que chegou a hora de tomarmos uma ação consciente e ativa. Antes de que seja tarde demais – se já não o é. Mais do que qualquer outra consideração de momento, interessa-nos que Portugal se vire para uma autêntica Democracia, que se oponha a extremismos da esquerda e da direita, preservando os Direitos sagrados do indivíduo. Convencidos de que muito pode fazer o governo norte-americano para evitar que Portugal chegue a ponto de não retorno, acreditamos que compete a cada um de nós – aos que acreditam na verdadeira Democracia política – agir imediatamente a fim de pressionar os líderes dos Estados Unidos da América do Norte a utilizarem toda a sua influência junto do atual governo provisório de Portugal, para que não se continue a violar o direito de associação, a liberdade de imprensa e o direito de votar livremente (sem coesões [*sic*] de espécie alguma). O 'Portuguese Times' tomou a iniciativa de endereçar aos senadores Kennedy, Brooke, Pastore, Pell e Buckley o seguinte telegrama que traduzimos em português para benefício dos nossos leitores: 'Urgimos forte oposição ao Comunismo em Portugal. Sabemos que jornalistas que criticam a política do governo são multados e detidos. Publicações anti-comunistas estão a ser suspensas. E.U. têm de se pronunciar abertamente.' Sugerimos hoje que todos os nossos leitores que o possam fazer dirijam aos senadores e congressitas que representam o povo das áreas onde estão radicados, telegramas de teor idêntico, a fim de os conscencializar dos receios que estão patentes em todos os bons portugueses e luso-americanos, independentemente das suas fações políticas. Parece-nos, também, que seria útil organizar uma demostração em massa à Embaixada de Portugal, em Washington e à Casa Branca. A sugestão aqui fica, com a melhor das intenções. Tudo dependerá da forma como a ideia, com a melhor das intenções for acolhida por aqueles que nos lêem." *Portuguese Times*, no. 213 (year IV, 27 March 1975), 1.

[128] Original: "Se está preocupado com a possibilidade de uma ditadura em Portugal, participe."

[129] Original: "o maior inimigo da Democracia é o regime Comunista totalitário." "Se Está Preocupado com a Possibilidade de uma Ditadura em Portugal, Participe," *Portuguese Times*, no. 214 (year IV, 3 April 1975), 20.

[130] Original: "não é mais do que o reflexo de um estado de espírito de que é culpado inteiramente o egoísmo dos homens déspotas que benfeitorizaram durante cinco décadas

de uma situação que os beneficiava a ponto de escândalo. . . . Os comunistas mais não fizeram do que tirar partido (embora desonestamente) do descontentamento geral e da falta de preocupação do povo português." António Alberto Costa, "A 'Ingenuidade' do Povo Português," *Portuguese Times*, no. 214 (year IV, 3 April 1975), 1.

[131] Original: "As decisões arbitrárias do governo provisório de Portugal são tanto mais condenáveis, quanto é certo que se trata apenas dum governo provisório que não pode, por muito que o tente, justificar-se representante da vontade do povo que ainda não teve oportunidade de se pronunciar por voto secreto e livre." "Editorial," *Portuguese Times*, no. 214 (year IV, 3 April 1975), 1.

[132] Original: "pequeno em número, mas muito ativo. Muito dedicado à causa, à conspiração internacional marxista." António Alberto Costa, "Os Comunistas da Comunidade," *Portuguese Times*, no. 207 (year IV, 13 February 1975), 9.

[133] António Alberto Costa, "Os Comunistas da Comunidade," *Portuguese Times*, no. 207 (year IV, 13 February 1975), 9.

[134] In 1975, José de Almeida became de the leader of the Azores Liberation Front (FLA), a right-wing separatist organization whose main goal was to achieve the independence of the Azores. It was said that the leaders of FLA approached the United States government about getting support to separate from Portugal.

[135] "Dr. José de Almeida ao PT: 'O M.A.P.A. é a Dignificação do Povo Açoriano'," *Portuguese Times*, no. 214 (year IV, 3 April 1975), 1.

[136] Original: "por natureza auxílios económicos vantajosos provenientes doutros países, nomeadamente dos Estados Unidos e da França, já lá instalados." "Queremos liberdade" ("Fala o Leitor"), *Portuguese Times*, no. 215 (year IV, 10 April 1975), 8.

[137] Motto of the Coast of Arms of the Azores.

[138] Original: "ANTES MORRER LIVRES QUE EM PAZ SUJEITOS. Sete palavras que neste momento de perigo para as nossas ilhas não encontram melhor ocasião para voltar a reclamar a nossa liberdade. Mas liberdade em toda a sua extensão. Sete palavras, que há longos anos exprimiram a vontade do Povo Açoriano. Desse Povo, que ignorado e explorado sempre tem vivido isolado da verdadeira civilização. Desse Povo que cada vez mais pobre tornava os ricos mais ricos. Desse povo que tem sofrido sempre a sua desdita em silêncio. Desse povo que anseia a liberdade desde o passado, no presente e para o futuro. Desse Povo, que sem governantes que o protegesse se tem acolhido nesta nação amiga e livre. Desse povo desprotegido e abandonado eu saí. Por esse povo abandonado eu lanço o grito de alarme e de luta. Lutemos para que nossos irmãos isolados do Atlântico tenham a liberdade a que têm direito." "Queremos liberdade" ("Fala o Leitor"), *Portuguese Times*, no. 215 (year IV, 10 April 1975), 8.

[139] Original: "no entanto, desde o dia da sua descoberta até hoje, as ilhas dos Açores têm sido pura e simplesmente escravizadas pelos mouriscos de Lisboa." "A República Açoriana" ("Fala o Leitor"), *Portuguese Times*, no. 217 (year IV, 24 April 1975), 8.

[140] "Pouco senso" ("Fala o Leitor"), *Portuguese Times*, no. 215 (year IV, 10 April 1975), 9.

[141] Original: "possibilidade de uma tomada de Portugal por fações esquerdistas." "O Vereador John Medeiros Interessa-se pela Situação em Portugal," *Portuguese Times*, no. 215 (year IV, 10 April 1975), 1.

[142] "Cerca de 3 Mil Portugueses Manifestaram-se em Favor de uma Democracia, junto à ONU," *Portuguese Times*, no. 215 (year IV, 10 April 1975), 1.

[143] Original: "Portugueses residentes Costa Leste Estados Unidos da America do Norte manifestaram hoje dia 5 de abril de 1975 junto Nações Unidas em Nova Iorque, desejo cumprimento promessa programa Movimento Forças Armadas em relação dar povo português eleições livres 25 de Abril para estabelecimento Democracia nosso querido Portugal e repúdio por regimes ditatoriais sejam quais forem as suas ideologias." *Portuguese Times*, no. 215 (year IV, 10 April 1975), 1.

[144] Original: "prever um futuro brilhante para Portugal e uma vida digna para os portugueses."

[145] Original: "Foi de tal forma profundamente adulterado que, quando o comparamos com o programa de hoje, verificamos que são dois programas totalmente distintos, senão opostos." *Portuguese Times*, no. 215 (year IV, 10 April 1975), 1.

[146] Original: "Assim, encontramo-nos aqui em Washington para expressarmos publicamente a nossa grande ansiedade pelo futuro de Portugal e também para nos declararmos contra. Contra qualquer forma de censura. Contra as eleições que não sejam completamente livres ou que não respeitem a vontade expressa pelo povo. Contra a prisão sem culpa provada. . . . Somos contra a instalação em Portugal de qualquer partido único, venha ele das direitas ou das esquerdas. Portugueses, nós viemos a Washington porque amamos a terra onde nascemos. Queremos que Portugal seja uma nação livre num mundo livre e que todos os portugueses possam viver em tranquila liberdade. Viva Portugal!" *Portuguese Times*, no. 215 (year IV, 10 April 1975), 1.

[147] Original: "O que nós e todos os bons democratas querem saber é: O que é feito dos 10 jornalistas portugueses de Angola que foram detidos e enviados para Lisboa? Com que direito se suspendeu a revista 'Notícia' e o jornal 'Liberdade'? Como se justificam as prisões arbitrárias sem culpa formulada de indivíduos que se encontram nas masmorras, sem tão pouco terem o direito de receber a visita dos seus advogados de defesa? Estas são apenas três preguntas que merecem esclarecimento da parte do 'Expresso' ou do governo provisório que se pretende tornar permanente a 'bem do povo'." António Alberto Costa, "O Expresso e o P. T.," *Portuguese Times*, no. 217 (year IV, 24 April 1975), 8.

[148] For the role of Portuguese press during the Carnation Revolution and its coverage in the international media, see, among others: Rezola, Maria Inácia, e Pedro Marques Gomes, coord. *A Revolução nos Media* (Lisbon: Edições Tinta da China, 2014) and Mesquita, Mário and José Rebelo, *O 25 de Abril nos media inernacionais* (Porto: Edições Afrontamento, 1994).

[149] "Acção antidemocrática de orgãos de informação portugueses na América" ("Fala o Leitor"), *Portuguese Times*, no. 217 (year IV, 24 April 1975), 8.

[150] Original: "Senhores reacionários: deixai o Povo Português; o povo que vive em Portugal; o povo que no dia-a-dia sofre e sente; o povo que não necessitou de nós para fazer o 25 de abril, escolher o que melhor lhe convém." "Alerta Portugueses" ("Fala o Leitor"), *Portuguese Times*, no. 215 (year IV, 10 April 1975), 8.

[151] Original: "Pela maneira como V. Exa. se refere a Portugal e aos atuais membros do Governo, dá-me a certeza de que V. Exa. está envolvido numa tarefa, que visa estabelecer dentro da Colónia Portuguesa, um clima de descrédito, a tudo o que os governantes portugueses fazem, a favor do povo português. Não satisfeito com todas estas afrontas, V. Exa. arquitetou a mensagem ao Presidente Ford. Pede pura e simplesmente a

INGERÊNCIA NOS ASSUNTOS INTERNOS PORTUGUESES, a uma potência estrangeira: os Estados Unidos. Claro que não posso chamar-lhe Traidor, porque V. Exa. é cidadão americano, mas sei qual é a definição que se dá aos indivíduos da sua natureza. Por tudo o que me é dado observar, protesto; e protesto ainda contra o facto de V. Exa. usar o seu jornal, como meio para influenciar os portugueses a tomarem atitudes anti-patriotas, utilizando para o efeito os mesmos 'slogans,' usados em Portugal no tempo do fascismo."

[152] Original: "Por ti sinto um não sei quê/ Que embacia os olhos meus.../ Quem te viu e quem te vê?/ Que mal fizeste a Deus?// Se sempre soubeste amar,/ A VIRGEM que em ti desceu/ Porque te há de esmagar,/ Um comunismo ateu?// Ó minha Pátria adorada,/ De tanta beleza infinita./ És agora profanada/ Por uma *corja* maldita.// E o "Castro" com denodo,/ Carrega no retrocesso,/ E chama-te um Portugal novo/ Ao virar-te do avesso." "Portugal," *Portuguese Times*, no. 217, (year IV, 24 April 1975), 9.

[153] Original: "SER SOCIALISTA é acreditar no poder revolucionário da liberdade; é acreditar no poder criador e progressista do nosso Povo através da liberdade de pensamento, liberdade de expressão e liberdade de associação. . . . É admitir que todos e cada um de nós possamos escrever e dizer publicamente o que pensamos sobre a vida política e social, sem sermos por isso perseguidos ou diminuídos nos nossos direitos e deveres." "Como uma socialista vê as eleições" (Fala o leitor"), *Portuguese Times*, no. 215 (year IV, 10 April 1975), 9.

Bibliography

1. General History of the Portuguese Press

Alves, José Augusto dos Santos. *A Imprensa de Língua Portuguesa no Oriente. De O Português na China (1839-1843) a O Investigador Português em Bombaim (1835-1837)*. Lisbon: Biblioteca Nacional de Portugal, 2017.

Cabrera, Ana. *Marcello Caetano: Poder e Imprensa*. Lisbon: Livros Horizonte, 2006.

Cavaco, Suzana. *Mercado Media em Portugal no Periodo Marcelista. Os Media no Cruzamento de Interesses Políticos e Negócios Privados*. Lisbon: Colibrí, 2012.

———. "Imprensa portuguesa em busca de um mercado luso-brasileiro (1825-1914)." *Revista Portuguesa de História da Comunicação* 0, (2017): 154-172.

Correia, Fernando and Carla Baptista. *Jornalistas: Do Ofício à Profissão. Mudanças no Jornalismo Português 1956-1968*. Lisbon: Caminho, 2007.

Cunha, Alfredo da. *Elementos para a História da Imprensa Periódica Portuguesa (1641-1821)*. Lisbon: Academia das Ciências de Lisboa, 1941.

Cunha, António Maria da. *A evolução do jornalismo na India Portuguesa*. Nova Goa: Imprensa Nacional 1923.

De Luca, Tania Regina. *A Ilustração (1884-1892)*. São Paulo: Unesp, 2019.

De Sousa, José Manuel Motta, and Lúcia Maria Mariano Veloso. *História da Imprensa Periódica Portuguesa. Subsídios para uma Bibliografia*. Coimbra: Imprensa da Universidade, 1987.

Garcia, Jose Luis, Tânia Alves, and Yves Léonard, coords. *Salazar, o Estado Novo e os Media*. Lisbon: Almedina, 2017.

Ferreira, João Pedro Rosa. *O Jornalismo na Emigração. Ideologia e Política no Correio Braziliense (1808-1822)*. Lisbon: Instituto Nacional de Investigação Científica – Centro de História da Cultura da Universidade Nova de Lisboa, 1992.

Hohlfeldt, António et al. "Os médias e o império português dos séculos XIX e XX." *Revista Portuguesa de História da Comunicação* 0, (2017): 61-80.

———. "Imprensa das colónias de expressão portuguesa. Visão de conjunto." *Interin* 12, no. 2 (2011): 1-15.

Lemos, Mário Matos e. *Jornais Diários Portugueses do Século XX. Um Dicionário*. Coimbra: Ariadne Editora, 2006.

Lima, Helena. *A imprensa portuense e os desafios da modernização*. Lisbon: Livros Horizonte, 2012.

———. "Oporto newspapers and the city readers. The construction of editorial and audiences identities." *Revista internacional de Historia de la Comunicación* 1, no. 1 (2013): 74-91.

Martins, Rocha. *Pequena História da Imprensa Portuguesa*. Lisbon: Inquérito, 1941.

Mesquita, Mário. *O Quarto Equívoco. O Poder dos Media na Sociedade Contemporânea*. Coimbra: Minerva, 2006.

———. *O Jornalismo em Análise. A Coluna do Provedor dos Leitores*. Coimbra: Minerva, 1998.

———, and José Rebelo, orgs. *O 25 de Abril nos Media Internacionais*. Porto: Afrontamento, 1994.

Neves, João Alves da. *História breve da imprensa de língua portuguesa no mundo*. Lisbon: Direcção-geral da Comunicação Social, 1989.

Pena, Alberto. *Salazar, a Imprensa e a Guerra Civil de Espanha*. Coimbra, MinervaCoimbra, 2007.

———, and Nuno Rocha. "História do Jornalismo Português." In *História da Imprensa*, edited by A. Pizarroso Quintero, 351-97. Lisbon: Planeta Editora, 1996.

Pires, Daniel. *Dicionário da Imprensa Periódica Literária Portuguesa do Século XX (1900-11940)*. Lisbon: Grifo, 1996.

Pizarroso Quintero, Alejandro (coord.). *Historia de la Prensa*. Madrid: Fundación Ramón Areces, 1994.

Rafael, Gina Guedes, and Manuela Santos. *Jornais e Revistas Portugueses do Século XIX*. Vol. I (1998) and II (2002). Lisbon: Biblioteca Nacional.

Rêgo, Ana Regina et al. (orgs.). *Os desafios da pesquisa em História da Comunicação: entre a historicidade e as lacunas da historiografia*. Porto Alegre: ediPUCRS, 2019.

Rezola, Maria Inácia, e Pedro Marques Gomes, eds. *A Revolução nos Media*. Lisbon: Edições Tinta da China, 2014.

Sobreira, Rosa Maria. *Os Jornalistas Portugueses 1933-1974*. Lisbon: Livros Horizonte, 2003.

Sousa, Fernando de. *Jornal de Notícias: a memória de um século (1888-1988)*. Porto: Empresa do Jornal de Notícias.

Sousa, Jorge Pedro. *Elementos de Teoria e Pesquisa da Comunicação e dos Media*. Porto: Edições Universidade Fernando Pessoa, 2003.

———, ed. *Notícias em Portugal. Estudos sobre a Imprensa Informativa (Séculos XVI-XX)*. Lisbon: Instituto de Comunicação da Nova-ICNOVA, 2018.

———. "Uma História do Jornalismo em Portugal até ao 25 de Abril de 1974." In *Jornalismo, História, Teoria e Metodologia da Pesquisa. Perspetivas Luso-Brasileiras*, edited by Sousa et al., 93-129. Porto: Edições Universidade Fernando Pessoa, 2008.

———, et al. *O Pensamento Jornalístico Português: Das Origens a Abril de 1974*. Covilhã: Livros LabCom – Universidade da Beira Interior, 2010.

———, Helena Lima, António Hohlfeldt, and Marialva Barbosa, orgs. *A History of the Press in the Portuguese-Speaking Countries*. Porto: Media XXI Publishing, 2014.

Tengarrinha, José. *História da Imprensa Periódica Portuguesa*, 2nd ed. Lisbon: Caminho, 1989.

———. *Imprensa e opinião pública em Portugal*. Coimbra: MinervaCoimbra, 2006.

Valente, Jose Carlos. *Elementos para a História do Sindicalismo dos Jornalistas Portugueses. Parte I: (1834-1934)*. Lisbon: Sindicato dos Jornalistas, 1998.

Vargues, Isabel Nobre. *A Aprendizagem da Cidadania em Portugal (1820- 1823)*. Coimbra: Minerva, 1997.

Veloso, Lúcia Maria Mariano, e José Manuel Motta de Sousa. *História da Imprensa Periódica Portuguesa. Subsídios para uma Bibliografia*. Coimbra: Biblioteca Geral da Universidade de Coimbra, 1987.

Veríssimo, Helena Ângelo. *Os Jornalistas nos Anos 30/40. Elite do Estado Novo*. Coimbra: Minerva, 2003.

2. Portuguese Emigration to North America

Anido, Náyade, and Rubens Freire. "A Existência de Ciclos Emigratórios na Emigração Portuguesa." *Análise Social* XII, no. 45 (1973): 179-186.

Antunes, M. L. Marinho. "Vinte Anos de Emigração Portuguesa: Alguns Dados e Comentários." *Análise Social* XVIII, no. 30-31 (1970): 299-385.

Avendaño, Fausto. "Portuguese Immigration into the United States." In *Contemporary American Immigration. Interpretative Essays (European)*, edited by Dennis Laurence Cuddy, 155-71. New York: Twayne Publications, 1982.

Baganha, Maria Ioannis Beis. *Portuguese Emigration to the United States 1820-1930*. New York: Garland Publishers, 1990.

———. "The Lusophone Migratory System: Patterns and Trends." *International Migration* 47, no. 3 (2009): 5-20.

Bannick, Christian. *Portuguese Immigration to the United Status: Its Distribution and Status*. San Francisco: R&E Research Associates, 1971.

Bohme, Frederick G. "The Portuguese in California." *California Historical Society Quarterly* 35, no. 3 (September 1956): 233-52.

Cuddy, Dennis Laurence, ed. *Contemporary American Immigration. Interpretative Essays (European)*. New York: Twayne Publications, 1982.

Cullen, Jim. *The American Dream: A Short History of an Idea that Shaped a Nation*. Oxford- New York: Oxford University Press, 2003.

Davie, Maurice R. et al. *Refugees in America: Report of the Committee for the Study of Recent Immigration from Europe*. New York: Harper, 1947.

De Carvalho, Serafim Alves. *Emigrar, Emigrar. As Contas do Meu Rosário! Autobriografia*. New York: Rocha Artes Gráficas, 1985.

De Vasconcelos e Sousa, Maria Azevedo Coutinho (introduction), and Edgar W. Knowlton Jr. (postscript). "The Voyage of the S. Gabriel, Portuguese Naval Vessel, to Hawai'i in 1910." *The Hawaiian Journal of History* 21 (1987): 77-97.

Dos Santos, Isaias Gomes. "Os Portugueses na América do Norte." *Boletim da Sociedade de Geografia* 117, no. 1-12 (1999): 45-62.

Gomes, Nancy. "Os Portugueses nas Américas: Venezuela, Canadá e EUA." *Janus* (2001): 144-45.

Marques, Augustus. "Portuguese immigration to the Hawaiian islands." In Thomas G., Thrum, ed., 74-78. *Hawaiian Almanaque and Annual for 1887-A Handbook of Information*. Honolulu: Press Publishing Company, 1886.

Pena, Alberto, Mário Mesquita, and Paula Vicente, coords. *Emigración e Exilio nos Estados Unidos. Experiencias de Galicia e Azores*. Santiago de Compostela: Consello da Cultura Galega and Fundação Luso-Americana, 2015.

———. *Galiza e os Açores. A Rota Americana*. Lisbon: Almedina, Fundação Luso-Americana, and Consello da Cultura Galega, 2012.

Rocha, Gilberta Pavão Nunes. *Dinâmica Populacional dos Açores no Século XX: Unidade. Permanência. Diversidade*. Ponta Delgada: Universidade dos Açores, 1991.

———. "O Impacto das Migrações na População dos Açores na Segunda Metade do século XX." In *História das Ilhas Atlânticas. Atas do IV Colóquio Internacional da História do Atlântico* II, 449-467. Funchal: Centro de Estudos de História do Atlântico/Secretaria Regional de Turismo e Cultura, Governo Regional da Madeira, 1997.

Serrão, Joel. "Notas sobre a Migração e Mudança Social no Portugal Contemporâneo." *Análise Social* XXI, no. 87-88-89 (1985): 995-1004.

———. "Conspecto Histórico da Emigração Portuguesa." *Análise Social* XVIII, no. 32 (1970): 597-617.

Teixeira, Carlos, and Victor M. P. da Rosa, eds. *The Portuguese in Canada*. Toronto: University of Toronto Press, 2000.

United States Department of Commerce (Bureau of the Census). *Statistics for Hawaii. Thirteenth Census of the United States Taken in the Year 1910*. Washington: Government Printing Office, 1913.

3. Press and Ethnic Culture in the United States

Archdeacon, Thomas J. *Becoming American: An Ethnic History*. New York: Free Press, 1983.

Bataille, Gretchen M., Miguel A. Carranza, and Laurie Lisa. *Ethnic Studies in the United States. A Guide to Research*. New York-London: Garland Publishing, 1996.

Bean, Frank, and Gillian Stevens. *America's Newcomers and the Dynamics of Diversity*. New York: Russel Sage Foundation): 2003.

Blanchard, Margaret A., ed. *History of the Mass Media in the United States. An Encyclopedia.* Chicago-London: Fitzroy Dearborn Publishers, 1998.

Brye, David L., ed. *European Immigration and Ethnicity in the United States and Canada: A Historical Bibliography.* Santa Barbara: ABC-Clio Information Services, 1983.

Danky, James P., and Wayne A. Wiegand. *Print Culture in a Diverse America. History of Communication.* Urbana: University of Illinois Press, 1998.

Dinnerstein, Leonard, Roger L. Nichols, and David M. Reimers. *Natives and Strangers: Ethnic Groups in the Building of America.* New York: Oxford University Press, 1979.

Gregory, Winifred, ed. *American Newspapers, 1821-1936: A Union List of Files Available in the United States and Canada.* New York: The H. W. Wilson Company, 1937.

Hoerder, Dirk, and Christiane Harzig, eds. *The Immigrant Labor Press in North America, 1840s-1970s. Vol. 1: Migrants from Northern Europe. Vol. 2: Migrants from Eastern and Southeastern Europe.* New York-Westport-Connecticut-London: Greenwood Press, 1987.

Ireland, Sandra L. Jones. *Ethnic Periodicals in Contemporary America: An Annotated Guide.* New York: Greenwood Press, 1990.

Johnson, Melissa A. (2000). "How Ethnic Are U.S. Ethnic Media: The Case of Latina Magazines." *Mass Communication & Society,* no. 3 (2-3): 229-248.

Joyce, William Leonard. *Editors and Ethnicity. A History of the Irish-American Press, 1848-1883.* New York: Arno Press, 1976.

Kessler, Lauren. *The Dissident Press: Alternative Journalism in America. The Ethnic Press in the United States. A Historical Analysis and Handbook History.* Beverly Hills: Sage Publications, 1984.

Kowalick, Jan. *The Polish Press in America.* San Francisco: R&E Research Associate, 1978.

Lai, H. M. *The Ethnic Press in the United States: A Historical Analysis and Handbook.* Westport: Greenwood Press, 1987.

Lieberson, Stanley, and Mary C. Waters. *From Many Strands. Ethnic and Racial Groups in Contemporary America.* New York: Russell Sage Foundation, 1988.

Liptack, Dolores. A. *Immigrants and Their Church, Makers of the Catholic Community.* New York-London: McMillan, 1989.

Madison, C. A. *Jewish Publishing in America. The impact of Jewish Writing on American Culture.* New York: Sanhedrin Press, 1976.

McDonald, Jason. *American Ethnic History. Themes and Perspectives.* News Brunswick: Rutgers University Press, 2007.

McKee, Jesse O., ed. *Ethnicity in Contemporary America. A Geographical Appraisal,* 2nd ed. Lanham-Boulder-New York-Oxford: Rowman & Littlefield Publishers, 2000.

Meléndez, Anthony Gabriel. *So All Is Not Lost: The Poetics of Print in Nuevomexicano Communities.* Albuquerque: University of New Mexico, 1997.

Miller, Sally M., ed. *The Ethnic Press in the United States.* New York-Westport-Connecticut-London: Greenwood Press, 1987.

Minnesota University: Immigration History Research Center. *The Newspaper and Serial Holdings of the Immigration History Research Center, University of Minnesota.* Bremen: Labor Newspaper Preservations Project, University of Bremen, 1985.

Muller, Thomas. *Immigrants and the American City.* New York: New York University Press, 1993.

N. W. *Ayer and Son's American Newspaper Annual and Directory.* Pennsylvania: N. W. Ayer and Son, 1880-1909.

Park, Robert E. *The Immigrant Press and Its Control.* New York: Harper and Brothers Publishers, 1922.

Pozzetta, George, ed. *American Immigration & Ethnicity: Immigrant Institutions: The Organization of Immigrant Life,* vol. 5. New York: Garland, 1991.

Reimers, David M. *Unwelcome Strangers. American identity and the Turn against Immigration.* New York: Columbia University Press, 1992.

Rhodes, Leara D. *The Ethnic Press. Shaping the American Dream.* New York-Washington-Oxford: Peter Lang, 2010.

Rodríguez, América. *Making Latino News: Race, Language, Class.* Thousand Oaks: Sage Publications, 1999.

Shah, Hermant, and Michael C. Thomton. *Newspaper Coverage of Interethnic Conflict: Competing Visions of America.* Thousand Oaks: Sage Publications, 2003.

Thernstrom, Stephan. *Harvard Encyclopedia of American Ethnic Groups.* Boston: Belknap Press, 1980.

Vismanath, K. and Pamela Arora (2000). "Ethnic Media in the United States: An Essay on Their Role in Integration, Assimilation, and Social Control." *Mass Communication & Society,* no. 3 (1): 39-56.

Waters, Mary. *Ethnic Options. Choosing Identities in America.* Berkeley: University of California Press, 1990.

Wittke, Carl Frederick. *The German Language Press in America.* Lexington: University of Kentucky Press, 1957.

Wymar, Lubomyr Roman. *Encyclopedic Directory of Ethnic Newspapers and Periodicals in the United States.* Littleton: Libraries Unlimited, 1972.

Zubrzycki, Jerzy. "The Role of the Foreign-Language Press in Migrant Integration." *Population Studies* 12, no. 1 (1958): 73-82.

4. Portuguese Immigration, Culture, and Identity

Aguiar, Maria Manuela. "O Conselho das Comunidades Portuguesas e a Representação dos Emigrantes." *Revista Migrações* 5 (2009): 257-62.

Almeida, Carlos, ed. *Portuguese Immigrants (The Centennial Story of the Portuguese Union of the State of California)*. San Leandro: Supreme Council of UPEC, 1992.

———. *Centenial Album. 1880-1890: UPEC Centenial (União Portuguesa do Estado da Califórnia)*. San Leandro: UPEC Centennial Committee, 1980.

Almeida, Onésimo T. *O Peso do Hífen. Ensaios sobre a Experiência Luso-Americana*. Lisbon: Imprensa de Ciências Sociais, 2010.

———. *L(USA)LÂNDIA, a Décima Ilha*. Angra do Heroísmo: Direção dos Serviços de Emigração, 1987.

———. *Da Vida Quotidiana na LUSALÂNDIA*. Coimbra: Atlântida Editora, 1975.

Alves-Calhoun, Donna. *Portuguese Community of San Diego*. Charlesston: Arcadia Publishing, 2009.

Arroteia, Jorge. "Portugueses em Diáspora: Identidade e Cidadania." *População e Sociedade* 18 (2010):145-59.

Barrow, Clyde W., ed. *Portuguese Americans and Contemporary Civil Culture in Massachusetts*. North Dartmouth: Tagus Press – Center for Portuguese Studies and Culture – UMass Dartmouth, 2002.

Bastos, Cristiana. "Portuguese in the cane: the racialization of labour in Hawaiian plantations". In Aboim, Sofia, Paulo Granjo and Alice Ramos, eds., 65-96. *Changing Societies: Legacies and Challenges. Vol. 1. Ambiguous Inclusions: Inside Out, Inside In*. Lisboa: Imprensa de Ciências Sociais, 2018.

Bertão, David. *The Portuguese Shore Whalers of California, 1854-1904*. San Jose: Portuguese Heritage Publications of California, 2006.

Cabral, Adalino. "Portinglês. The Language of Portuguese-Speaking People in Selected English-Speaking Communities." Doctoral dissertation. Ann Arbor: University of Michigan, 1986.

Cardozo, Manuel da Silveira. *The Portuguese in America (590 b.C-1974)*. Dobbs Ferry: Oceana Publications, 1976.

Correa, Genevieve B., and Edgar W. Knowlton Jr. "The Portuguese in Hawaii." *Ethnic Sources in Hawai'i. A Special Issue for The University of Hawai'i's Seventy-Fifth Year* 29. Honolulu: The United Press of Hawaii, 1982, 70-77.

Cortés, Carlos E., ed. *Portuguese Americans and Spanish Americans*. New York: Arno Press (A New York Times Company), 1980.

Dias, Eduardo Mayone. *The Portuguese Presence in California*. San Jose: Portuguese Heritage Publications, 2009.

———. *A Presença Portuguesa na Califórnia*. Los Angeles: Peregrinação Publications, 2002.

———. *Açorianos na Califórnia*. Angra do Heroísmo: Coleção da Diáspora, 1982.

Dos Santos, Maria Helena Carvalho. "Emigração e Níveis de Cultura: A União Portuguesa do Estado da Califórnia (1880-1980)." *Análise Social* XIX, no. 77-78-79 (1983): 961-86.

Felix, John Henry, and Peter F. Senecal. *The Portuguese in Hawaii*. Honolulu: Centennial Edition (copyrighted by the authors, obtainable through the Liberty House, Honolulu), 1978.

Fernandes, Ferreira. *Os Primos da América*. Lisbon: Relógio d'Água Editores, 1991.

Freitas, Joaquim Francisco. *Portuguese-Hawaiian Memories*. Honolulu: edition of the author, 1930.

Freitas, Vamberto. *Para Cada Amanhã. Jornal de Emigrante*. Lisbon: Salamandra, 1993.

——. *Pátria ao Longe. Jornal da Emigração II*. Ponta Delgada: Marinho Mato Eurosigno Publicações, 1992.

——. *Jornal da Emigração. A L(USA)lândia Reinventada*. Angra do Heroísmo: Gabinete de Emigração e Apoio às Comunidades Açorianas, 1990.

Georgianna, Daniel (with Roberta Hazen Aaronson): *The Strike of 28*. New Bedford: Spinner Publications, 2019.

Graves, Alvin Ray. *The Portuguese Californians: Immigrants in Agriculture*. San Jose: Portuguese Heritage Publications of California, 2004.

Goulart, Tony, ed. *Capelinhos. A Volcano of Synergies: Azorean Emigration to America*. San José: Furtado Imports, 2007.

——. *The Holy Ghost Festas: A Historic Perspective of the Portuguese in California*. San Jose: Portuguese Heritage Publications of California, 2002.

Hawaiian Historical Society. www.hawaiianhistory.org, 2013.

Holmes, Lionel, and Joseph D'Alessandro. *Portuguese Pioneers of the Sacramento Area*. Sacramento: Portuguese Historical and Cultural Society, 1990.

Holton, Kimberly DaCosta, and Andrea Klimt, eds. *Community, Culture and the Making of Identity: Portuguese-Americans along the Eastern Seaboard*. North Dartmouth: Tagus Press – Center for Portuguese Studies and Culture – University of Massachusetts Dartmouth, 2009.

Leal, João. *Açores, EUA, Brasil. Imigração e Etnicidade*. Horta: Direção Regional das Comunidades, 2007.

Machado, Joe, et al. *Power of the Spirit. A Portuguese Journey of Building Faith and Churches in California*. San Jose: Portuguese Heritage Publications of California, 2012.

Mazzaneta, Louis O. "New England's Little Portugal." *National Geographic* (January 1975): 98.

McCabe, Marsha L., and Joseph D. Thomas. *Portuguese Spinner: An American Story. Stories of History, Culture and Life from Portuguese Americans in Southeastern New England*. New Bedford: Spinner Publications, 1998.

Mendes, Ana Paulo Coutinho. "The Turn and the Voice of the Diaspora Daughters: Memory(ies) and Literary Creation." *Gávea Brown. A Bilingual Journal of Portuguese-American Letters and Studies* XVIII-XXIX (2007-2008): 45-56.

Mendonça, Duarte Miguel Barcelos. *Da Madeira a New Bedford. Um Capítulo da Emigração Portuguesa nos Estados Unidos da América.* Funchal: DRAC, 2007.

Mesquita, Mário, and Paula Vicente, coords. *O Mar na História, na Estratégia e na Ciência.* Lisbon: Fundação Luso-Americana, 2013.

Mira, Manuel. *The Portuguese in the Making of América. The Melungeous and Other Groups.* New Bedford: The Portuguese American Historical Foudation, Inc., 1998.

Moniz, Rita. "The Portuguese of New Bedford, Massachusetts and Providence, Rhode Island: A Comparative Micro-Analysis of Political Attitudes and Behaviour." PhD diss. Providence: Brown University, 1979.

Monteiro, George. *Caldo Verde is not Stone Soup: Persons, Names, Words and Proverbs In Portuguese America.* New York-Oxford-Berne: Peter Lang, 2017.

———. "Manuel Garcia Monteiro, Boston's Portuguese Poet." *Boletim do Núcleo Cultural da Horta* 21 (2012): 285-301.

———. "Manuel Garcia Monteiro, M.D." *Gávea-Brown* 32-33 (2010-2011): 36-38.

———. "Peter Francisco, Revolutionary War Hero." In *The Parade of Heroes: Legendary Figures in American Lore,* edited by Tristram Potter Coffin and Hennig Cohen, 194-197. Garden City, NY: Anchor Press/Doubleday, 1978.

———. "The Unhistorical uses of Peter Francisco." *Southern Folklore Quarterly* 27 (June 1963): 139-159.

Observatório da Emigração. http://www.observatorioemigracao.secomunidades.pt/, 2009.

Olivier, Lawrence. *Never Backward. The Autobiography of Lawrence Olivier, a Portuguese-American,* edited by Rita Larkin Wolin. San Diego: Neyenesch Printers, 1972.

Pap, Leo. *The Portuguese Americans.* Boston: Portuguese Continental Union of USA, 1992.

———. *The Portuguese-Americans.* New York-Boston: Twayne Publishers-A Division of G. K. Hall & Co., 1981.

———. *The Portuguese in the United States: A Bibliography.* New York: Center for Migration Studies – Bibliographies and Documents, 1976.

———. *Portuguese-American Speech. An Outline of Speech Conditions among Portuguese Immigrants in New England and Elsewhere in the United States.* New York: King's Crown Press (Columbia University), 1949.

"Provisional Convention between Portugal and the Hawaiian Islands." *The Hawaiian Kingdom,* URL: http://hawaiiankingdom.org/treaty_portugal.shtml.

Pina, Luis da Câmara. *Dever de Portugal para com as Comunidades Lusíadas da América do Norte (com uma Carta-Prefácio de Sua Eminência o Senhor Cardeal Patriarca de Lisboa).* Lisbon: Ateliers Gráficos Bertrand (Irmãos), 1945.

Pires, Rui Pena. *Portugal. Atlas das Migrações Internacionais.* Lisbon: Tinta da China, 2010.

Rodgers, Francis. "Portuguese." In *Harvard Encyclopedia of American Ethnic Groups,* Stephen Therstrom, Ann Orlov, and Oscar Handlin, eds., 813-820. Cambridge: Harvard University Press, 1981.

Strone, Proserfina A., ed. *Portuguese in Hawaii: A Bibliography*. Honolulu: Hawaii State
    Public Library, 1988.

San Payo, Urbino. *Os Portugueses na Califórnia*. Lisbon: Fundo Documental da Emigração
    e das Comunidades Portuguesas – Comunidades Portuguesas – Secretaria de
    Estado da Emigração, 1985.

Santos, Fernando. *Os Portugueses no Hawai*. Newark: Luso American Newspaper, 1996.

Silva, Reinaldo. *Representations of the Portuguese in American Literature*. North Dartmouth:
    Tagus Press – Center for Portuguese Studies and Culture – University of
    Massachusetts Dartmouth, 2008.

Smith, M. Estellie. "Portuguese Enclaves: The Invisible Minority." In *Social and Cultural
    Identity: Problems of Persistence and Change*, edited by Thomas Fitzgerald, 81-91.
    Athens: Southern Anthropological Society, University of Georgia Press, 1974.

Taft, Donald R. *Two Portuguese Communities in New England*. New York: Arno Press and
    the New York Times, 1969.

Vaz, August Mark. *The Portuguese in California*. Oakland: IDES Supreme Council, 1965.

Vicente, António Luís. *Os Portugueses nos Estados Unidos da América. Política de
    Comunidades e Comunidade Política*. Lisbon: Fundação Luso-Americana para
    o Desenvolvimento, 1998.

Warrin, Donald. *So Ends This Day. The Portuguese in American Whaling, 1765-1927*. North
    Dartmouth: Tagus Press – Center for Portuguese Studies and Culture – UMass
    Dartmouth, 2010.

——, and Geoffrey L. Gomes. *Land as Far as the Eye Can See. Portuguese in the Old West*.
    Washington: The Arthur H. Clark Company, 2001.

Williams, Jerry R. *In Pursuit of their Dreams. A History of Azorean Immigration to the
    United States*. North Dartmouth: Tagus Press – Center for Portuguese Studies &
    Culture – University of Massachusetts Dartmouth, 2007.

5. Press, Language, and Communication in the Portuguese-American Diaspora

Biblioteca Pública e Arquivo de Ponta Delgada. *Jornais Açorianos: Catálogo*. Ponta
    Delgada: Câmara Municipal, 1995.

Carvalho, Eduardo de. *Os Portugueses na Nova Inglaterra*. Rio de Janeiro: A Leitura
    Colonial, 1931.

——. *Pregar no Deserto*. Rio de Janeiro: Teixeira & C. Ltda., 1929.

——. *A Língua Portuguesa nos Estados Unidos*. Boston: Editora Empresa de Propaganda
    Patriótica, 1925.

Correia, Rui Antunes. "Salazar em New Bedford. Leituras Luso-Americanas do Estado Novo nos Anos Trinta." MA Thesis, Centro de Estudos Anglísticos da Universidade de Lisboa, 2004.

Da Rosa, Guilherme Pereira. *Estados Unidos*. Lisbon: Editorial Século, 1953.

De Sá, M. Glória, Sonia Pacheco, and Judy Farrar. "Preserving and Promoting Ethnic Heritage, Identity and Representation in the U.S.: The Ferreira-Mendes Portuguese-American Archives." Http://conference.ifla.org/ifla77 (World Library and Information Congress: 77th IFLA), 2009.

Faria, Dutra. *S. Francisco e o Problema da Paz*. Lisbon: Pro Domo, 1945.

Ferreira, Adelino. "The Impact of the Post-Capelinhos Immigration Wave on the Portuguese Media in the United States. The Portuguese-Language Media on the East Coast." In *Capelinhos. A Volcano of Synergies. Azorean Emigration to America*, edited by Tony Goulart. San Jose: Presidência do Governo Regional dos Açores, 2007.

Gomes, Geoffrey L. "The Portuguese Language Press in California, 1880-1928." MA Thesis, Hayward: History Department, California State University, 1983.

———. "The Portuguese Language Press in California: The Response to American Politics, 1880-1928." *Gávea-Brown. A Bilingual Journal of Portuguese American Letters and Studies* XV-XVI (Jan. 1994-Dec.1995): 5-90.

———. "Manuel B. Quaresma, Pioneer Newspaperman." In *O Progresso* (Portuguese Historical and Cultural Society). Sacramento, December 2002.

Knowlton, Edgar C. "The Portuguese Language Press in Hawaii." *Social Process in Hawaii* 24 (1960): 89-99.

Mendonça, Duarte Miguel Barcelos. "José Rodrigues Miguéis na Imprensa Lusa de New Bedford: Uma Presença Assídua." *Gávea Brown. A Bilingual Journal of Portuguese-American Letters and Studies* 32-33 (2010-2011): 39-43.

Pacheco, Sonia, Judy Farrar, and M. Glória de Sá. "The Portuguese American Digital Newspaper Collection at the University of Massachusetts." Http://conference.ifla.org/ifla78. (World Library and Information Congress: 78th IFLA), 2012.

Pap, Leo. "The Portuguese Press." In *The Ethnic Press in the United States. A Historical Analysis and Handbook*, edited by Sally M. Miller, 291-302. New York-Westport-Connecticut-London: Greenwood Press, 1987.

Pena-Rodríguez, Alberto. "El Periodismo Portugués en California. Notas Históricas sobre el *Jornal Português* de Oakland (1932-1997)." *Estudios sobre el Mensaje Periodístico* 25, no. 1 (2019): 443-457.

———. "Noticias de América. Reflexiones sobre el Valor de la Prensa Inmigrante como Fuente Histórica: El Caso de la Comunidad Portuguesa en Estados Unidos." In *Os Desafios da Pesquisa em História da Comunicação: entre a Historicidade e as Lacunas da Historiografia*, edited by Ana Regina Rêgo et al., 331-354. Porto Alegre: ediPUCRS, 2019.

———. "*For the good of the colony.* El Nacimiento y Expansión de la Prensa Portuguesa en los Estados Unidos de América (1877-1909)." In *Los Medios en Lengua Extranjera: Diversidad Cultural e Integración*, edited by Laura López Romero y Juan Antonio García Galindo, 119-127. Granada: Editorial Comares, 2018.

———. "Noticias del Diálogo Transatlántico. Una mirada sobre la Presencia Ibérica en Estados Unidos a través de la Prensa Inmigrante Portuguesa." *Transatlantic Studies Network. Revista de Estudios Internacionales* 1 (Jan.-Jun. 2016): 75-87.

Pinho, Helder. *Portugueses na Califórnia. A História e o Quotidiano de uma das Mais Vivas Comunidades Lusas no Mundo.* Lisbon: Editorial de Notícias, 1978.

Ponte, Lusa. "Percursos Identitários na Diáspora Açoriana: O Jornal *Açores-América* (1903)." *Interdisciplinary Journal of Portuguese Diaspora Studies* 3, no. 1 (2014): 221-46.

Silva, Fernando M. Soares. "Os meios de comunicação em língua Portuguesa." Modesto: *A Tribuna Portuguesa* (15 and 30 March; 1 and 15 April), 2012.

Soares, Celestino. *California and the Portuguese. How the Portuguese Helped to Build Up California: A Monograph Written for the Golden Gate International Exposition on San Francisco Bay 1939.* Lisbon: SPN, 1939.

Whorf, Benjamin Lee. *Language, Thought, and Reality.* Cambridge: MIT Press, 1956.

6. Works by (or about) Portuguese Editors and Journalists in the United States

Andrade, Laurinda C. *The Open Door.* New Bedford: Published by Reynolds-De Walt, 1968.

Ávila, Arthur Vieira. *Desafio Radiofónico.* Oakland: Oficinas Gráficas Ramos Afonso & Moita (Lisbon), 1961.

———. *Rimas de Um Imigrante (Versos para a Rádio).* Oakland: Oficinas Gráficas Ramos Afonso & Moita (Lisbon), 1961.

———. *Écos do Ar. Desafios pelo Rádio entre Arthur Ávila e Manuel Carvalho.* Oakland: Latin-American Broadcasting Co., n.d.

Biografia e Obra – Eugénio Tavares. http://www.eugeniotavares.org/docs/pt/biografia/index_biografia.html, 2004.

Cacella, Monsignor Joseph. *Jungle Call.* New York: Francis Cardinal Spellman-Archbishop of New York, 1956.

———, ed. *The White Doves of Peace.* New York: Francis Cardenal Spellman – Archbishop of New York, 1949.

Das Neves, Enrique. *Traços Caraterísticos. Episódios e Anedotas Autênticas de Indivíduos que se Evidenciaram.* Lisbon: Parceria António Maria Pereira, 1910.

"Early Years." *Society of the Descendants of Peter Francisco*, https://peterfrancisco.org/?s=freedom&searchsubmit=_2014.

Escobar, João Francisco. *The New Method to Learn the Portuguese Language without Teacher with Figurated Pronunciation of the Tones and Sounds*. New Bedford: Guilherme M. Luiz & Co., Inc., n.d.

Gloria, Guilerme S. *Harpejos*. Oakland: Tipografia do "Jornal Português," 1940.

———. *Poesias de Guilherme S. Gloria*. Oakland: Tipografia de "A Liberdade," 1935.

———. *Florence. A Formosa Rapariga da Fábrica Condenada pelos Pecados Doutra. História de Duas Mulheres Parecidas: Um Anjo e um Demónio*. Sacramento: Tipografia de "A Liberdade," 1918.

Jardim, Vasco Sousa. "Retalhos das memórias brancas." Newark: *Luso-Americano*, October-November 1989.

Monteiro, Manuel Garcia. *A Trança*. Horta: Centro de Estudos e Cultura da Câmara Municipal da Horta, 1989.

Nellist, George F., and John William Siddall, eds. *Men of Hawaii. A Biographical Record of Men of Substantial Achievement in the Hawaiian Islands*. Honolulu: The Honolulu Star-Bulletin, Ltd., 1935.

Neves, Mário. *José Rodrigues Miguéis. Vida e Obra*. Lisbon: Editora Caminho, 1990.

Newton, L. C., ed. *Who's Who of the Island of Hawaii 1938. A Biographical and Statistical Record of Men and Women on the Island of Hawaii, Territory of Hawaii, U.S.A. vol I*. Hilo: Published by John A, Lee, 1939.

Oliveira, Joaquim. *Fraternidade Universal*. Newark: Tipografia do "Luso-Americano," n.d.

Vieira Jr., João José. *Aventuras no Eldorado. Novela Idealista*. Porto: Tipografia da Livraria Progredior, 1966.

———. *Eu Falo por Mim Mesmo. Autobiografia*. Porto: Tipografia da Livraria Progredior, 1963.

———. *A Voz da História*. Oakland: Printed by the author, 1941.

7. Other Complementary References

Ata, Ibrahim W., and Colin Ryan. *The Ethnic Press in Australia*. Melbourne: Academia Press and Footprint Publications, 1989.

Barbosa, Rosana. *Immigration and Xenophobia: Portuguese Immigrants in Early 19th Century Rio de Janeiro*. Plymouth: United Press of America, 2009.

Bergreen, Laurence. *Over the Edge of the World*. New York: HarperCollins Publishers, 2003.

Borges, Marcelo J. *Chains of Gold: Portuguese Migration to Argentina in Transatlantic Perspective*. Leiden: Koninklijke, 2009.

Borjas, George. *Heaven's Door. Immigrations Policy and the American Economy*. Princeton: University Press, 1999.

Castro, Fernanda de. *Ao Fim da Memória (1906-1897)*. Lisbon: Verbo, 1988.

Chaplin, Joyce. *Round About the Earth. Circumnavigation from Magellan to Orbit*. New York-Toronto-Sydney-New Delhi: Simon & Shuster, 2012.

Coman, Katherine. *The history of contract labor in the Hawaiian islands.* New York: American Economic Association, 1903.

De la Torre Gómez, Hipólito and Josep Sánchez Cervelló. *Portugal en la Edad Contemporánea (1807-2000).* Madrid: UNED, 2000.

Department of Homeland Security. *Yearbook of Immigration Statistics: 2012.* Washington, DC: U.S. Department of Homeland Security, Office of Immigration Statistics, 2013.

Dos Anjos, José A. Tavares. *Cape Verdean-American WWII Veterans of New Bedford.* New Bedford: Lulu.com, 2010.

Ferro, António. *Dez Anos de Política do Espírito (1933-1943). Discurso Proferido no X Aniversário do SPN.* Lisbon: Edições do SPN, 1943.

———. *Mar Alto.* Lisbon: Livraria Portugália Editora, 1924.

———. *Prefácio da Ditadura Espanhola.* Lisbon: Empresa Nacional de Publicidade, 1933.

———. *Salazar – O Homem e a sua Obra.* Lisbon: Empresa Nacional de Publicidade, 1933.

———. *Viagem à Volta das Ditaduras.* Lisbon: Empresa "Diário de Notícias," 1927.

Foner, Nancy, ed. *New Immigrants in New York.* New York: Columbia University Press, 2001.

Galloway, J. H. *The Sugar Cane Industry: A Historical Geography from its Origins to 1914.* Cambridge: Cambridge University Press, 1989.

Gregory, James N. *The Southern Diaspora. How the Great Migrations of Black and White Southerners Change America.* Chapel Hill: University of North Carolina Press, 2005.

Jouët-Pastré, Clémence and Leticia J. Braga, eds. *Becoming Bazuca. Brazilian Immigration to the United States.* Cambridge: David Rockefeller Center Series os Latin American Studies, Harvard University Press, 2008.

Kastor & Sons, H. W. *Newspaper and Magazine Directory.* Chicago-St. Louis and Kansas City: H.W. Kastor & Sons Advertising Co., 1906.

Langeli, Attilio Bartoli: "Historia del Analfabetismo y Método Cuantitativo." *Signo. Revista de Historia de la Cultura Escrita* 3 (1996): 87-106.

Mackall, Alexander Lawton. *Portugal for Two.* New York: Dood, Mead & Company, 1931.

McQuail, Dennis, Peter Golding, and Els de Bens, eds. *Communication. Theory & Research. An European Journal of Communication Anthology.* London-California-New Delhi: Sage Publications, 2005.

Ming, Pyong Gap. *Mass Migration to the United States: Classical and Contemporary Periods.* Walnut Creek: Altmira Press, 2002.

Mónica, Maria Filomena. "«Deve-se ensinar o povo a ler?»: a questão do analfabetismo (1926-39)." *Análise Social* XIII-50 (1977-2º): 321-353.

Moya, Jose C. *Cousins and Strangers: Spanish Immigrants in Buenos Aires.* Berkeley-Los Angeles-London: University of California Press, 1998.

Nelson Chesman & Co's Newspaper Rate Book 1899. Including a Catalogue of Newspapers and Periodicals in the United States and Canada. St. Louis-Chicago-New York: Nelson Chesman & Co. Publishers, 1899.

Norfolk, Sherry and Bobby Norfolk. *The true story of Peter Francisco*. Charleston: The History Press, 2014.

Nugent, Walter. *Crossings. The Great Transatlantic Migrations, 1870-1914*. Bloomington: Indiana University Press, 1992.

Paulo, Heloisa. *Aqui Também é Portugal. A Colónia Portuguesa do Brasil e o Salazarismo*. Coimbra: Quarteto, 2000.

Perloff, Richard M. *Political Communication: Politics, Press and Public in America*. Mahwah: Lawrence Erlbaum Associates Editors, 1998.

Phillips, Jason, ed. *Storytelling, History and the Postmodern South*. Baton Rouge: Louisiana State University Press (Southern Literary Studies), 2013.

Proença, Maria Cândida: "Analfabetismo." In *Dicionário de História do Estado Novo*, vol. I, edited by Fernando Rosas and J. M. Brandão de Brito. Lisbon: Bertrand Editora, 1996.

Pizarroso Quintero, Alejandro, coord. *Historia de la Prensa*. Madrid: Fundación Ramón Areces, 1994.

Roll, Elvira Osorio. *Background, a novel of Hawaii*. Honolulu: Exposition Press, 1964.

Rowell & Co., Geo P. *American Newspaper Directory*. New York: Geo P. Rowell & Co. Publishers, 1878.

Sardica, José Miguel. *O Século XX Português*. Lisbon: Texto Editores, 2011.

Tena, Gustavo Luca de. *Noticias de América*. Vigo: Nigra, 1993.

Torgal, Luis Reis. *Estados Novos, Estado Novo*. Coimbra: Imprensa da Universidade de Coimbra, 2009.

Truslow Adams, James. *The Epic of America*. Boston: Little, Brown and Company, 1931.

Tuchman, Gaye. *Making News. A Study in the Construction of Reality*. New York: The Free Press, 1980.

Tungate, Mark. *Adland. A Global History of Advertising*, 2nd ed. London: Kogan Page Limited, 2013.

Van Dijk, Teun A. *Discourse and Social Interaction*. London: Sage Publications, 1997.

———. *Ideology: A Multi-disciplinary Approach*. London: Sage Publications, 1998.

Vecoli, Rudolph J., and Suzanne Sinke, eds. *A Century of European Migrations, 1830-930*. Urbana: University of Illinois Press, 1991.

Zelph, W. Pease, and George A. Hough. *New Bedford, Massachusetts. Its History, Industries, Institutions and Attractions*. New Bedford: Saguan Press, 1889.

Index of Names

AARONSON, Roberta Hazen 291, 354.

ABOIM, Sofia 305.

ABREU, Avelino de 138, 253.

ABREU, Jorge de 334.

ADAMS, F. E. 160.

ADAMS, James Truslow 273.

AFFONSO, Godfrey (Godofredo) Ferreira 122, 124.

AFONSO, João 326.

AFONSO, Maria Glória 340.

ÁGUAS, Abílio de Oliveira 40, 41, 289, 308.

AGUIAR, Armando de 339.

AGUIAR, Gilberto Lopes de 177, 262.

AGUIAR, Lourenço da Costa de 178, 244.

AGUIAR, Luís 327.

AGUIAR, Paes de 335.

ALBURQUERQUE, Antero de 335.

ALIGHIERI, Dante 18

ALMEIDA, António Francisco 213.

ALMEIDA, Avelino de 334.

ALMEIDA, Carlos 24, 129, 130, 130,

ALMEIDA, J. N. 322.

ALMEIDA, Jacinto A. 334.

ALMEIDA, José de 223, 343.

ALMEIDA, José M. 133

ALMEIDA, Onésimo Teotónio 218, 326, 328, 329.

ÁLVARES, Euclides 327.

ALVES, João 201.

ALVES, Laura 201.

ALVES, Victor M. 186, 262.

AMARAL, G. A. de 338.

AMÉRICA, Vitorino 326.

ANDRADE, Laurinda C. de 99, 100, 104, 173, 276, 301.

ANTÃO, (Fr.) John S. 179.

ANTUNES, Armando F. 181.

ANTUNES, Helder 181.

ANTUNES, Luiz 81, 176, 215, 244, 250, 251, 262, 321.

ANTUNES, Melo 225, 342.

ANTUNES, M. L. Marinho 276.

ARGUS, pseud. 335.

ARORA, Pamela 9, 277.

ARROTEIA, Jorge 276.

AVENDAÑO, Fausto 282, 283, 287.

ÁVILA, Arthur Vieira 3, 70, 80, 92, 93, 100, 134, 154, 156, 243, 249, 255, 258, 358.

ÁVILA, Joaquim 327, 328.

ÁVILA, José 181, 326.

ÁVILA, Judy 327, 328.

AVILLEZ, Martin 183, 250.

AZEVEDO, Anthony D. 180.

AZEVEDO, Leonel Soares de 93, 255.

BAGANHA, Maria Ioannis B. 276.

BAPTISTA, J. J. (Jr.) 317.

BAPTISTA, Jaime 326.

MACHADO, Luís 327.

MACKER, P. Kenneth 325.

McKALL, Alexander Lawton 102, 301.

McQUAIL, Dennis 274.

MADISON, Charles A. 279.

MADRUGA, Necas 326.

MAGALHÃES, Fernão de 280.

MAIA, João da 327.

MAIA, Pompeu 317.

MANHÃES, Daniel

MANUEL I (King of Portugal) 280.

MARINHO, Octavia 326.

MARINHO, Octavio 326.

MARQUES, Augustus 305.

MARQUES, August Jean Baptiste 122, 123.

MARQUES, J. B. 121.

MARSHALL, Joseph S. 114.

MARTIN, Joseph 24.

MARTINS, Angélica Ferreira 335

MARTINS, António Rebelo 163, 239.

MARTINS, Cândido da Vila 85.

MARTINS, Domingos Ferreira 201, 334, 335.

MARTINS, Ilídio 328.

MARTINS, José 328.

MARTINS, Paul 341.

MARTINS, Rocha 204.

MARTINS, Rui 329.

MARTINS, Teotónio 317.

MARTINS, Theotónio I. 176.

MARTINS, Vicente Ferreira 335.

MARX, Karl 166.

MAURIZIO, M.

MASCARENHAS, Alfredo 334.

MATINHO, António (or Tony) 184, 216, 250, 328, 340.

MATINHO, Paul 340.

MATOS, António 327.

MATOS, Carlos 326.

MATOS, Carolina 100, 186, 256.

MATOS. Eugénio 329.

MATOS, Ferreira 341.

MATOS, José de 176.

MATOS, (General) José Norton de 135.

MATTOS, Agostinho P. de 341.

MATTOS, F. G. 317.

MATTOS, Jose 176, 326.

MAZZANETA, Louis O. 281.

MEDEIROS, Henrique B. 341.

MEDEIROS, João Luis de 341.

MEDEIROS, John 224, 344.

MEDEIROS, June Dias 326.

MEDEIROS, Leonel 326.

MEDEIROS, Manuel 179, 242.

MEDEK, Gisela 329.

MELO, E. A. 317.

MELO, João de Simas (Jr.) 93, 152, 162, 249, 258.

MELO, John de 329.

MELO, José Marques de 274.

MELO, Manuel P. 335.

MELLO, Rosa Emilia de 310.

MENDES, A. 317.

MENDES, Eurico José 341.

MENDES, Filomena Rocha 100, 326.

MENDES, J. A. 321.

MENDES, José 327.

MENDONÇA, Duarte Miguel Barcelos 242, 277, 312, 313, 314, 316, 324.

MENDONÇA, José V. 157, 317.

MENDOSA, John 316.

MENESES, Eugénio Matos 329

MENEZES, Filipe Ribeiro de 315.

MENEZES, Joaquim Borges de 46, 79, 86, 97, 117, 127, 131, 132, 241, 245, 258, 259.

MENTO, Joseph W. 280, 317.

MERELIM, Pedro de 326.

MEROLA, Joseph 99, 101, 102, 134, 167, 172, 173, 260, 296.

SILVA, A. D. 154.
SILVA, Adulcino 327.
SILVA, Albert 241, 326, 327.
SILVA, Alfredo (Alfred) Dias da 81, 154, 162, 170, 239, 257.
SILVA, António 327, 341.
SILVA, (Fr.) António 137.
SILVA, António Martins da 154.
SILVA, Cristina Maria 327.
SILVA, Ernest Gomes da 122, 124.
SILVA, Fernando M. Soares 277, 319, 326, 337.
SILVA, (Rev.) Francisco 146, 147, 247.
SILVA, (Rev.) Francisco Caetano Borges da 79, 86, 90, 96, 132, 138, 140, 193, 140, 267, 291, 309, 314.
SILVA, Frank 129, 257.
SILVA, Frank J. 184, 256.
SILVA, Joel 327.
SILVA, (Rev.) José 278, 357.
SILVA, José da 326.
SILVA, Joseph (Jr.) 162, 251.
SILVA, Leonesa 327.
SILVA, Lúcio Gonçalves da 79, 90, 242, 243.
SILVA, Luiz H. da 108.
SILVA, Lurdes C. da 100.
SILVA, M. C. da 108.
SILVA, M. P. 154, 156.
SILVA, Manuel A. 122, 124.
SILVA, (Dr.) Manuel Luciano da 281, 327.
SILVA, Mary (Maria) Aurora 95, 100.
SILVA, Mary L. 184.
SILVA, S. J. Heraldo da 326.
SILVEIRA, Ana L. 71.
SILVEIRA, António 327.
SILVEIRA, Goretti 326.
SILVEIRA, John Rodrigues da 181.
SILVEIRA, Manoel Cardoso da 217.
SILVEIRA, Maria Rita 316.

SILVEIRA, Mary (Maria) Nunes 100, 103, 104, 206, 302.
SILVEIRA, Pedro Laureano Claudino da 3, 80, 89, 95, 157, 206, 248, 249, 255.
SIMAS, Manuel Ávila 131, 326, 328, 337, 339.
SMITH, Tony 316.
SPINNEY, Domingos J. F. 140, 254, 314.
SPÍNOLA, António de 342.
SOARES, Alberto 181.
SOARES, Frank S. 316.
SOARES, João Martias 316.
SOARES, Mário 342.
SOARES, M. S. 156.
SOUSA, Coelho de 326.
SOUSA, Delfina 134, 273.
SOUSA, Donzília 341.
SOUSA, John Filipe de 336
SOUSA, Jorge Pedro 274, 275.
SOUSA, José A. 316.
SOUSA, (Fr.) José Maria de 327.
SOUSA, Maria Azevedo Coutinho de Vasconcelos e 283.
SOUSA, Nélia 327.
SOUSA, Quirino de 143, 144, 151, 242, 259, 335.
SOUZA, António 122.
SOUZA, António Mariano de 62.
SOUZA, Maria L. 310.
SOUZA, Zósimo S. 170, 250.
STONE, Gil 99, 101, 172, 173, 176, 202, 260, 262.
STONE, Manoel 8, 79, 89, 108, 109, 111, 129, 253, 262, 296, 303.
SUPICO, Carlos Alberto 158, 253, 312.
SYLVA, Manuel F. 170, 242, 280.

TACHE, Gerald T. 333.
TAFT, Donald R. 275, 286.
TAVARES, Eugénio 138, 240, 296, 312.
TAVARES, (Fr.) João Francisco 117, 211, 240, 337.

Index of Newspapers and Magazines

CPSIA information can be obtained
at www.ICGtesting.com
Printed in the USA
BVHW031159110520
578996BV00001B/1